TRAVELS

IN

CENTRAL AMERICA,

PARTICULARLY IN

NICARAGUA:

WITH A DESCRIPTION OF ITS

ABORIGINAL MONUMENTS, SCENERY AND PEOPLE,

THEIR LANGUAGES, INSTITUTIONS, RELIGION, &c.,

ILLUSTRATED BY

NUMEROUS MAPS AND COLOURED ILLUSTRATIONS.

BY

E. G. SQUIER,

LATE CHARGÉ-D'AFFAIRES OF THE UNITED STATES TO THE REPUBLICS OF CENTRAL AMERICA.

IN TWO VOLUMES.

VOL. I.

D. APPLETON & Co., PUBLISHERS,

NEW YORK:

MDCCCLIII.

CONTENTS OF VOLUME I.

INTRODUCTION.

NARRATIVE.

ILLUSTRATIONS.

LITHOGRAPHY BY SARONY AND MAJOR; WOOD ENGRAVINGS BY J. W. ORR: FROM ORIGINAL DRAWINGS, CHIEFLY BY JAMES M'DONOUGH.

ORIGINAL MAPS.

OCTAVO PLATES.

WOOD ENGRAVINGS.

VOLUME II.

PREFACE.

The character in which I visited Nicaragua, of an accredited Representative of the United States, made me the witness of many extraordinary demonstrations of respect and affection for my country, and the recipient of numerous marked attentions, private and popular. It enabled me to see the country under a very favorable aspect, enlivened everywhere by cheerful and enthusiastic assemblages, which the presence of an Envoy of the Great Republic of the North, had inspired with passionate hopes of their own future glory and prosperity. And as it is my object to give a true picture, not only of the country, but of the character, condition, and relations of the people, I have not hesitated to refer to many scenes and occurrences, in which, as a public man, I received singular marks of favor. With the judicious reader I am not afraid to trust myself in these descriptions; I am willing even to risk the imputation of vanity, if I can thereby awaken a true sympathy in the hearts of the American people, for their simple, but unfortunate friends and allies in Central America; or contribute, however slightly, to impress the great truth upon this nation, that the United States is the natural head of the great American family, and that it is a duty which it owes, alike to God and man, to extend its advice, its encouragement, and its support to the oppressed and struggling Republics of Central America.

Yet, with all the latitude which I have ventured to give myself in these respects, there are many things that the unofficial visitor might mention and remark upon without impropriety, to which, for obvious reasons, I cannot refer. Nor can I, in the following pages, make anything more than a very limited use of my journal, which, whatever may be its value hereafter in illustrating the *transition period* of the country in question, is, from necessity, full of references to political transactions and events, upon which it is not my present purpose to speak; and to persons whose names it would not be delicate or proper to introduce into these pages.

I have divided my work into five parts or divisions, as follows:

I. A Geographical and Topographical Account of Nicaragua, and of the other States of Central America, with observations on their climate, agricultural and mineral productions, and general resources.

II. A Narrative of my residence in Nicaragua, containing an account of my explorations of its aboriginal monuments, notices of the people, their habits, customs, and modes of life, descriptions of scenery, etc. This narrative might have been greatly amplified, but it is believed that it contains enough to enable the reader to form a very accurate idea of the great natural beauty of the country, and of the character and condition of its people.

III. An Account of the Geography and Topography of Nicaragua, as connected with the proposed Interoceanic Canal; a Historical Sketch of the various negociations in respect to that enterprize; and also some speculations as to the probable commercial and political results of its construction. In this part, I have written without fear or concealment, and with no design of subserving the interests of any set of men. I regard the proposed work as one of vital importance to our country, which should be kept free from every taint of mere speculation, and be pursued in entire good faith by those who may connect themselves with it. Any delinquency, in this respect, is treachery to the interests alike of Nicaragua and the United States, which it would be the duty of every American to expose to public reprobation. The facts contained in this part may be relied on, as being generally, and in all important respects, entirely accurate. Should there be any errors, it must be remembered that my means of investigation were imperfect, and that nothing more than approximate accuracy can be reached, except by actual and detailed surveys.

IV. Notes on the Aborigines of the country, with such original and accumulated information respecting their geographical distribution and relations, languages, institutions, customs and religion, as shall serve to define their ethnical position, in respect to the other semi-civilized, aboriginal nations of this continent.

V. An Outline of the Political History of Central America since its independence of Spain. Previous to 1839 Nicaragua constituted a part of the Republic of Central America. In that year the Republic was dissolved. But the history of Nicaragua, both before and since that event, has been so involved with that of the country at large as to preclude its separate consideration. I have, therefore, been compelled to trace the outlines of the history of the entire country, in order to show the causes which have reduced the State in question to its present unfortunate condition. Some of the most conspicuous actôrs in the political drama which has been enacted in Central America are still living; but, however much I regret to arraign their policy, or denounce their principles, I regret still more that this severity is demanded by every consideration of truth and impartiality. I have, nevertheless, avoided, as far as possible, any allusion to individuals, living or dead, and confined myself to a general recital of events. It would be a most instructive task to fill up these outlines, and trace, minutely, the operation of the causes which led to the destruction of the Central America Republic—a task which I may consider it proper to undertake, unless it should be performed by abler hands. But if, in this outline, I shall succeed in showing that the distractions of the Spanish American Republics, are not so much to be ascribed to the insensate passions of their people as to foreign intervention, and the unfavorable conditions which surround them, and that there is, in all of them, and particularly in those of Central America, a large body of devoted, patriotic, and liberal men, who are struggling against the popular ignorance and superstition, and the machinations and unscrupulous policy of monarchists and oligarchists, at home and abroad, to vindicate the principles of self-government and free institutions, and who deserve, and should receive, the support and encouragement of the American people and Government,—then I shall have the satisfaction of accomplishing the object which I have in view, in presenting this outline, to the exclusion of other matters of perhaps more general interest.

It was my original purpose to have embodied, in the form of a Supplement, an account of that part of Nicaragua which has acquired notoriety under the denomination of the "Mosquito Shore;" as also of its savage inhabitants, the relations of Great Britain with them; the pretensions which she has set up on their behalf, and the aggressions which she has committed upon a weak and unoffending state, under pretext of supporting them. I had also proposed to present a sketch of the political relations of Nicaragua with the United States for the past three years, with a statement of their present condition. But both these subjects involve matters of a personal and controversial character, and might lead to discussions which I do not care to have started in connection with the present work. Should circumstances, or self-vindication require it, they will find their way before the public in another, and probably more appropriate form.

The Maps, Plans, etc, contained in this work, are from my own hand, while the engravings are chiefly from the original drawings of Mr. Jas. McDonough, who accompanied me to Central America in the capacity of artist. They are faithful copies from nature, in which accuracy has been consulted, rather than artistical effect.

In the chapters on the Aborigines of Nicaragua, I have presented a brief vocabulary, obtained by Mr. Julius Frœbel, in the district of Chontales, which I have named, suggestively, *Chondal.* Since those chapters passed into the hands of the printer, I have obtained information, showing conclusively, that this is the language of the *Woolwa* Indians, who have their seats on the head waters of the Rio Escondido or Blewfields River.

NICARAGUA.

I.—INTRODUCTION; GEOGRAPHY AND TOPOGRAPHY.

II.—PERSONAL NARRATIVE; ANTIQUITIES, ETC.

III.—PROPOSED INTEROCEANIC CANAL

IV.—ABORIGINAL INHABITANTS.

V.—OUTLINE OF POLITICAL HISTORY.

INTRODUCTION.

INTRODUCTION.

CHAPTER I.

CENTRAL AMERICA.—ITS GEOGRAPHY, TOPOGRAPHY, CLIMATE, ETC.

THE conquest of Asia or the acquisition of its commerce has been, from the earliest periods of history to the present hour, the aim of the several generations of men to whom, from their valor or their successful ambition, succeeding ages have accorded the title of heroic. Between the nomadic hordes on the steppes of Tatary, the dwellers in Cashmerian valleys, the daring mountaineers of the Caucasus, the swarthy myriads of Indostan, and the population of that enigmatical Chinese empire (into which the ferocity of the Tatars penetrated further than all the blandishments of civilization), on the one hand, and the more western nations who have laid claim to a higher social order, to more comprehensive faculties of combination, and were possessed of greater greed of rule or aggrandisement, on the other, a perpetual war has existed for more thousands of years, perhaps, than popular, belief has allotted to the duration of history. The might of Assyria exhausted itself in the Tatar and Indian conquests of Nimroud and Semiramis. The Achaian republics sought, in the subjugation of the Persian Empire, to assert their sway over the traditional nursery of mankind. Alexander, son of Ammon, led his armies to the Indus and the very feet of the Himalahs; and not until Rome directed the ambition of the world upon the west of Europe and the shores of Carthage and Egypt, did the tide of conquest ebb from the gorgeous but hapless East. In after times, when the dust of tradition rested on the ruins of the Roman empire, when the fabric of social order and polity, founded upon it, had begun to crack and crumble before the enterprise of schismatic republics and rival empires, the dream of Alexander was revived. The republics of Venice and Genoa struggled in rivalry for the carrying trade in Persian and Indian shawls, and the gems and spices which brighten the earth and sweeten the air from the Caspian to Cape Comorin. And as the sway of empire passed from territory to territory and from race to race over the surface of Europe, to the mightiest amongst them fell ever, by the conquest of her rivals, that unfailing source of wealth and power, "the Eastern Trade."

In fact, the ability of using or abusing the resources of the largest continent of the earth has been, in all modern history, the test of supremacy amongst the nations boastful of civilization. As Venice and Genoa wasted themselves in the strife of faction, Holland and Spain sprang into rivalry on the shores of India. Portugal also mixed in the contest, and fixed her factories and her garrisons on the shores of the southern Asiatic peninsula. The conquest and plunder of the Indian nations seemed the one object of European empires, when the overshadowing power of the papacy had yielded somewhat to Lowland burghers and ambitious France. With the greatness of the latter country, a new rival entered the arena, and the rule of Mazarin, and the overthrow of the feudal noblesse by Louis XIV., found for it an additional field for conquest in Pondicherry and the islands of the Eastern Archipelago. But the designs of Louis le Grand were blasted with his death. France fell into the imbecile hands of his amorous successor, and the conquests of the French arms in India passed to the more vigorous and not more scrupulous hands of the Islanders, who had beaten down in succession the manufacturing monopolies of Holland, had destroyed the maritime ascendancy of Spain, and won in the New World an undying lustre for their arms.

Then sprang into a great and vigorous existence the maritime power of England. Gibraltar, the Cape of Good Hope, ports of protection from storm and foe, and ports of supply and outfit all the way to the great East,—fell successively into her possession; and the flag, which in the days of Ferdinand and Isabella was cooped up within the limits of England, soon flew in triumph from the fortresses of Calcutta and Madras. The rule of smaller or older rivals vanished from the fated East. To a company of London merchants, greedy of gold and profitable dominion, and never encumbered by scruples of justice or dispositions of mercy, were leased out for plunder and servitude the then almost numberless and unconquered peoples of Hindustan. Gradually, but surely, from the factories on the coast spread out the webs of ambition and avarice. Through intrigues and wars, kingdom after kingdom fell under the control of England; and the work commenced by Clive and Hastings, and continued by Wellington, we see completed in our own day, on the banks of the Sutlej, and at the feet of the mighty Himalahs, by the vengeful victories of a Gough and a Napier. But these conquests were not perfected by England without rivalry. When France, having recovered, by the necessary infliction of a revolution, from the state of unnatural weakness and premature decay to which the vices of monarchy had reduced her, assumed once more the attitude of an empire, defiant, haughty, and strong, the great embodiment of her militant republicanism, Napoleon, flung himself upon the shores of Asia, determined, like Alexander, to carry his standards in triumph from the deserts of the Bedouin to the mouth of the Ganges. But on the fortress of Acre his magnificent designs were wrecked; and back on Europe, discomfited, and broken into fragments, rolled the remnants of that ambitious army which essayed once again to change the fortunes of the world by arms. With the fall of the Imperial Soldier passed away the terror of invasion from the English empire of the East. But with his fall arose another and even mightier power in the distant North, which, by the same agency of force, when craft shall fail, aims to assume the sway of all mankind,—whose grim flag is now reflected in the waters of the Mediterranean, and is poised with wavering fortunes on the summit of the Caucasus. Between the two great powers of the Old World, England and Russia, a contest now lies for the dominion of the East; a contest which involves, if not the very existence of the first, at least her predominance among nations.

But the destinies of men are not, nor have they ever been, ruled wholly by arms. For three hundred years agencies have been at work, seen in part only in fantasy by the dreamer, unseen in their grand magnificence until our day, which have so far tended to deprive the Old World and all its empires of the sway of Asia, and bestow its commerce and its wealth upon a younger world, a newer empire, and a more equitable policy. We should lose one great lesson of history, if we failed to attribute the future greatness of the United States, even more than its present position, to that ambition of gain and that commercial enterprise which impelled the Spaniards, the Hollanders, and the English, three centuries ago, into a contest of war and adventurous seamanship, the one to retain, the other to acquire possession of the centres of the Oriental trade. Speed and ease of transport, amongst maritime nations, must ever be the conditions of commercial supremacy; and hence was undertaken the search for that "Passage to the East" which had been the day-dream of the enthusiast, and the ambition of rival empires—

that search which led to the discovery of a New World by Columbus, and to the voyages of Cabot and Vespucius, of Raleigh and Verrazzano, from the river of Hudson southward to the Cape of Storms, and northward to the yet impenetrable fields of Arctic ice. But though these adventurous captains failed in their cherished hope of discovering a passage through the American Continent by water, to the descendants of the upright and daring Republicans who sought in a new world an escape from the injustice and perfidy of the old, an overruling but unseen hand has accorded the success denied to other and older nations. That hand has drawn a line of eternal division between the men and the institutions, the tyrannies and superstitions, which crushed mankind from the fall of Rome to the middle of the sixteenth century, and all succeeding history and time. The judgment seems to have been recorded, that they who should dare to bring to this continent the systems or ideas of the old, should themselves share the doom of the savages which they supplanted, and with them pass away for ever. So, though knights of Spain built castles strong and high upon the shores of both great oceans, though Spain transferred all her force and bigotry to the mountains and plains of Central and South America, though colonial empires north and south were established, though the doctrines of absolutism and systems of feudalism struggled over the entire continent for predominance, all have passed away like the dew before the sun; and to the wise and simple Republicans, made up of all nations, equally opposed to superstition and to tyranny, has fallen the dominion of the New World, will fall the control of the Old.

To us is given, in this modern time, the ability, if we choose to exercise it, of acquiring the rule of the East, of placing at defiance alike the menaces and power of England and Russia, and of transferring into our unarmed hands that passage for which Columbus strove in vain, those eastern conquests for which Alexander was deified, that power in

Asia which won an infamous immortality for Clive and Hastings, that vast and incalculable trade upon which is mainly based the maritime power of England, hitherto the mightiest empire among men. The fortune of war has planted our eagles on the Pacific: across the entire continent from ocean to ocean, for twenty-five degrees of latitude, our Republic is supreme. Our trim-built fairies of the deep dance over either ocean, and in conjunction with those giant steamers which push aside the waves along the shores of half the continent, sweep in the trade of Europe on one hand, and on the other bring to the mouth of the Sacramento the treasures of the Oriental world. To gird the world as with a hoop, to pass a current of American Republicanism, vivifying dead nations and emancipating mankind, over the continents of the earth, it needs but that one small spot should be left free from foreign threats and aggression, to exercise for itself its inherent sovereign rights. The key of the continent, destined to unlock the riches of two hemispheres, and which eager nations even now are aiming to snatch, with felon hand, from its rightful possessors, lies between the States of Mexico and the disrupted Republic of Colombia. It is only by preserving its freedom and its territory inviolate, and enabling and encouraging it to open an inter-oceanic highway, that the Republican world can ever hope to reclaim from tyranny and servitude the myriads of Asia, that Americans can ever hope to reach that commercial and national pre-eminence to which their elastic institutions and their individual superiority amongst races of lesser vitality, invites and enables them to aspire.

That small spot of earth—small as compared with the gigantic continent, great in reference to its geographical position and future destiny—is known as Central America.

From the period of The Discovery, in the fifteenth century, when Balboa, crossing its narrowest isthmus at Darien, rushed, buckler and sword in hand, into the waters of the South Sea, and claimed its almost limitless shores for the crown of Castile and Leon, until the present hour, that country has been regarded with a constantly increasing interest; an interest which the requirements of commerce, and the recent acquisitions and newly-developed resources of our own country on the Pacific, have not only augmented but turned to a practical direction. Columbus, not yet comprehending the importance of his own discoveries, coasted along its eastern shores from the Gulf of Honduras to the Bight of Darien, in anxious hope and vain endeavor to find a passage whereby the treasures of the Indies might be poured into the lap of Spain. The same rich prize, augmented in value by the lapse of time and the force of events, is still offered to the enterprise of the world. Asia, with its vast populations and increasing wants, furnishes a market worthy of the competition of nations. New and progressing States have sprung into existence on the Pacific coast of the American continent, which are destined, in the course of time, to attain a pitch of greatness rivalling that of the proudest nations of Europe. The Australian and Polynesian islands, by the double process of colonization and civilization, have already risen into importance, and now enter largely into the commercial and political calculations of the maritime world. A new empire is laying deep its foundations on the coast of New Holland, and it requires no extraordinary prescience to discover that it will soon take rank amongst independent nations. In short, the great tides of civilization, for three centuries moving majestically eastward to India, and westward to the New World, from the European centre, now meet in the waters of the Pacific; they have encircled the earth; and the "short and easy passage to the Indies" which Columbus sought, from a leading desideratum, has became the great necessity of the age. This alone is wanting to secure for ever American preponderance in the Pacific,—that placid sea where steam navigation is destined to achieve its greatest triumphs, and American enterprise and American Republicanism their most imposing results.

Geographical discovery early demonstrated the fact that to this short and easy "passage to the East," the American continent presents an unbroken barrier, extending from the realms of northern ice to the stormy cape of the south, lashed by the turbulent Antarctic Sea. From that period the daring of man has contemplated the Titanic enterprise of cutting through the continent, and opening an artificial water communication between the two great oceans. Within twenty years after The Discovery, the three routes which by common consent have come to be regarded as the only feasible ones for such communication, had been indicated.[1]

[1] Gomara, one of the earliest writers on America, in common with the best informed men of Spain, judged that the junction of the Atlantic with the Pacific was by no means an impracticable task. A translation of his brief chapter, entitled "The Possibility of a Shorter Passage to the Maluccas," is subjoined. "The voyage from Spain to the Maluccas, (Malay Islands,) by the Straits of Magellan, is so long and hazardous, that having had frequent occasion to discuss the subject with men well acquainted with the Indies, as well as with other persons conversant with history and of an inquiring turn of mind, I have heard of another good though extensive passage, which, if it were made, would be no less honorable than profitable to the maker. The passage would have to be opened across the main land from one sea to the other, by whichever might appear most profitable of these four lines; either by the river Lagartos, which, rising in Chagres, at the distance of four leagues from Panama, over which space of territory they proceed in carts, flows to the sea-coast of Nombre de Dios; or by the channel through which the Lake of Nicaragua empties itself into the sea, up and down which large vessels sail, and the lake is distant only three or four leagues from the sea; by either of these two rivers the passage is already traced and half made. There is likewise another river which flows from Vera Cruz to Tecoantepec, along which the inhabitants of New Spain tow and drag barks from one

All of these are comprehended in what is properly Central America; and that which seems to offer peculiar advantages for this purpose, if indeed it is not the only one which has the merit of practicability, passes through the very centre of this interesting country. Indeed, in respect of geographical position, it almost realizes the ancient idea of the centre of the world. Not only does it connect the two grand divisions of the American continent, the northern and the southern hemispheres, but its ports open to Europe and

sea to the other. The distance from Nombre de Dios to Panama is seventeen leagues, and from the Gulf of Uraba to the Gulf of San Miguel twenty-five, which are the two most difficult lines. There are mountains, it is true, but there are likewise hands; let but the resolve be formed to make the passage, and it can be made. If inclination be not wanting, there will be no want of means: the Indies, to which the passage is to be made, will supply them. To a King of Spain, with the wealth of the Indies at his command, when the object to be attained is the spice trade, that which is possible is, in fact, easy. It appeared an impossibility, and really was one, to unite Brindez to Belona by a causeway over twenty leagues of the sea; yet Pyrrhus and Marcus Varro wished and attempted it, in order to go by land from Italy to Greece. Nicanor began to open a canal of more than a hundred leagues extent by land, without reckoning rivers, for the sake of transporting merchandise from the Caspian to the Pontic or Black Sea; but having been put to death by Ptolemy Ceraunus, his generous and princely design was abandoned. Nitocris, Sesostris, Psammeticus, Darius, Ptolemy, and other kings, projected the junction of the Red Sea with the Nile by means of a canal, in order that perfumes, spices, and medicines might be conveyed straight from the ocean to the Mediterranean; but being apprehensive lest the sea should inundate Egypt by bursting the aqueducts, or an over supply of water, they were deterred from the undertaking; and because the sea might be detrimental to the river, without which Egypt would be nothing. If the passage of which I have been speaking was accomplished, the navigation to the Maluccas would be shortened by one-third of the distance, since ships proceeding thither would always sail by the Canaries under the equator, in a warm latitude, within the dominions of Spain, and without fear of meeting with a foe; nor would our Indies derive less advantage from it, since merchandise would be conveyed to Peru and other provinces in the

Africa on the east, and to Polynesia, Asia, and Australia on the west. Here, too, the continent shrinks to its narrowest limits, and its great mountain barriers subside into low and broken ranges. The adventurous traveller, standing beneath the sky of an eternal summer, with the exuberance of tropical verdure around him, may look down upon the restless Atlantic, the great highway of the commerce of the Old World, on the one hand, and upon the broad Pacific, rolling its unbroken waves over half the globe, on the other. These conditions unerringly point out this country as the theatre of great events, and will give it a prominence in the future

same ships which brought it from Spain, and much expense and trouble be thus saved."—*La Istoria de las Indias*, fol. lviii.

Herrara, Historiographer to the King of Spain, writing of the events of 1527, refers to these routes and the project of inter-oceanic communication, in these words:

"The lake of Nicaragua is remarkable for its extent, the towns and islands in it, for ebbing and flowing, and for that, being three or four leagues from the South Sea, it empties itself into the North Sea. Those who desired to please the Emperor, seeing him intent on finding a way to the Spice Islands, said that since there was no strait in those parts—that is, between the *Gulf of Uraba* and the drain of Nicaragua—a passage might be made by any of four ways which they proposed; the first along the drain of said lake, (the San Juan,) on which large boats go up and down, though there are some dangerous falls, and then making a canal along these four leagues from the lake to the South Sea; and second, along the river de Lagartos, (Chagres,) which rises five or six leagues from Panama, where the way being all plain, as we have said before, a canal might also be cut for the sea and river to meet; the third, by way of Vera Cruz to Tecoantepec, on which, in New Spain, they convey boats from one sea to the other; fourth, the path from Nombre de Dios to Panama, where, they asserted, though there were mountains, it was no difficult matter to make a way. They added, that from the *Gulf of Uraba* to San Miguel, there were only twenty-five leagues; and though it would be a difficult matter, yet nothing was too much for the King of Spain's power, and this would open a much shorter way to the Spice Islands through his own dominions, without any opposition."—*History of America*, vol. iv. p. 14.

history of the world, second to no other equal extent of the earth's surface.

Glancing at the map, we find, at the isthmus of Tehuantepec on the north, the Gulf of Mexico approaching to within two hundred miles of the Western Ocean; the waters of the river Coazacalco, which flows into the former, interlocking with those of the Chicapa, flowing into the latter. This line affords certain facilities of transit which cannot fail to be used by the inhabitants of the great Mississippi Valley, to whom it offers the easiest and speediest mode of communication with the western coast of the continent. They will prove themselves strangely negligent of their present, and blind to their prospective interests, if they do not secure permanently the control of that isthmus. Below this point the continent widens, embracing the high table lands of Guatemala upon the west, and the broad plains of Tobasco, Chiapas, and Yucatan upon the east. The Gulf of Honduras, however, closes around this section upon the south-east, and again narrows the continent to less than two hundred miles. The country intervening between it and the Pacific nevertheless loses its elevated character, and constitutes two great valleys, through which the Motagua finds its way to the Atlantic by the Gulf of Honduras, and the Lempa flows to the Western Ocean. Still lower down, and passing the great transverse basin of Nicaragua, is the well-known narrow isthmus of Panama or Darien, over which the tide of European migration, within a period of three hundred years, has twice poured its floods,—once upon Peru, and once upon the glittering shores of California.

Nor are the topographical features of Central America less remarkable than its geographical. In its physical aspect and configuration, it has very justly been observed, it is an epitome of all other countries and climates of the globe. High mountain ranges, isolated volcanic peaks, elevated table-lands, deep valleys, broad and fertile plains, and extensive alluvions, are here found grouped together, relieved by large and beautiful lakes, and majestic rivers, the whole teeming with animal and vegetable life, and possessing every variety of climate, from torrid heats to the cool and bracing temperature of an eternal spring. The great chain of the Cordilleras here, as in South America, runs close along the Pacific coast, but in places is interrupted, and assumes the form of detached ranges and isolated elevations, of groups or knots of hills, between which the streams from the interior wind their way to either ocean. As a consequence, the principal alluvions border on the Gulf of Mexico and the Caribbean Sea. Here rains fall in greater or less quantities for the entire year; vegetation is rank, and the climate is damp and proportionably insalubrious. The trade winds blow from the north-east; and the moisture with which they are saturated, condensed on the elevated parts of the continent, flows down towards the Atlantic. The Pacific slope is therefore comparatively dry and healthful, as are also the elevated table-lands of the interior.[1]

Topographically, Central America presents three marked centres of elevation, which have, to a certain extent, fixed its political divisions. The first is the great plain in which is situated the city of Guatemala, and which is nearly six thousand feet above the sea. Here the large rivers, Usumasinta and Tobasco, flowing northward through Chiapa and Tobasco, into the Gulf of Mexico, take their rise,—their sources interlocking with those of the Motagua or Gualan, running eastward into the Gulf of Honduras, and with those of the small streams which send their waters westward into the

[1] "Experience," says Mr. Baily, "shows that the places which are most prejudicial to health in Central America lie on the northern coast and the Mosquito shore, where endemic and intermittent fevers are not unfrequent. The Pacific coast is exposed to a temperature equally high, but is much more salubrious, and seldom visited by epidemic or contagious diseases."

Pacific. Another high plain occupies the centre of Honduras, and extends into the northern part of Nicaragua, from which radiate a hundred streams, north and east into the Caribbean Sea, and south and west into the great lakes of Nicaragua and the Southern Ocean. Among these the most remarkable are the Rio Escondido (called by the English "Blewfields river") the river Vanks, Coco, or Segovia, the Roman, Poyais, and Guyapi, upon the eastern slope; the Lempa, La Paz, Nacaome, and Choluteca, upon the western. Intervening between this and the third great centre of elevation in Costa Rica, is the basin of the Nicaraguan lakes, with its verdant slopes and gently undulating plains. The nucleus of the Costa Rican elevation is the volcano of Cartago, which towers in its midst. Here the Cordilleras resume their general character of a great unbroken mountain barrier, but soon subside again into low ridges on the isthmus of Panama.

These peculiarities of configuration will explain the endless variety of climate to which we have alluded, and which is nowhere more remarkable than in Central America. Situated between 8° and 17° north latitude, were it not for these features, the general temperature would be somewhat hotter than that of the West Indies. As it is, the climate of the coast is nearly the same as that of the islands alluded to, and exceedingly uniform; modified somewhat by the shape and position of the shore, and by the proximity of the mountains, as well as by the prevailing winds. The heat on the Pacific coast is not, however, so oppressive as on the Atlantic; less perhaps because of any considerable difference of temperature, than on account of the greater dryness and purity of the atmosphere.[1]

[1] Dunlap, a very good authority when his personal feelings have no opportunity of being exhibited, has the following correct observations upon the respective climates of the Atlantic and Pacific coasts. "On the south-west (Pacific) coast the rains commence regularly in the beginning

In the northern part of the state of Guatemala, and what is called Los Altos, the Highlands, the average temperature is lower than in any other part of the country. Snow sometimes falls in the vicinity of Quezaltenango, the capital of this department, but disappears immediately, as the thermometer rarely, if ever, falls to the freezing point. In the vicinity of Guatemala, the range of the thermometer is from 55° to 80°, averaging about 72° of Fahrenheit. Vera Paz, lying between Guatemala and Yucatan, is nearly ten degrees warmer, and the coast from Belize around the Gulf of Honduras, embracing the ports of Santo Tomas and Izabal, to Omoa and Truxillo, is still hotter, and very unhealthy. The State of San Salvador lies wholly on the Pacific. It is smaller than any of the other states, and better populated. It is less elevated than either Guatemala or Honduras, and its general temperature is probably higher. The heat, however, is

of May; and, with the exception of a short intermission (in some seasons only) of about twenty days, towards the end of July and the beginning of August, continue till the month of October, and in some parts and seasons till the middle of November. During the rest of the year rain is almost unknown, a slight shower, not sufficient to lay the dust, occurring very rarely. On the north-east (Atlantic) coast the rains, on the contrary, continue nearly all the year, with a short and uncertain intermission of three or four months; the dryest period being from June to October, and the wettest from October to May. As may be supposed, the consequence of this is, that while the interior and south-west coast possesses an almost equal temperature during the whole year, the north-east coast is extremely sultry during the summer months; and is also found to be very unhealthy on accunt of the superabundant moisture; while the rest of the republic, with some local exceptions, is perhaps more healthy than any other country within the same degrees of latitude."—*Travels in Central America*, (1846), p. 257.

Mr. Baily observes that "the temperature of Central America may be said to be relatively mild, and, taken altogether, undoubtedly salubrious. The degree of absolute heat from the coasts to the interior differs considerably; but only in a few places on the former is it found unfavorable to general health." Mr. Baily estimates the average heat of the interior at 68° Fah., and of the coast at 82° to 84°.

never oppressive, except at a few points on or near the coast, as for instance, Sonsonate, La Union, and San Miguel. The latter place is very closely shut in by mountains, and is not reached by the prevailing winds, to which circumstance its high temperature and proverbial unhealthiness is mainly to be ascribed. Honduras, as its name implies, (plural of *Hondura*, "depth,") has a very diversified surface. The coasts upon both oceans are low; but, as we have already said, the country in the interior is elevated, and there the climate is really delightful; the average temperature at Tegucigalpa and Comayagua, the principal towns, being about 75°. The department of Segovia, in Nicaragua, borders on Honduras, and has a like surface and temperature. The principal part of Nicaragua, however, is different in all respects, and has a topography and climate peculiarly its own. These will form the subject of a separate chapter. It will be sufficient to observe here, that the lakes of Nicaragua form a great inland basin, with broad and undulating slopes, relieved only by steep volcanic cones, and a few ranges of hills along the shores of the Pacific; and that, although the general surface is low, as compared with the other states of Central America, its climate is so favorably modified by a variety of causes as to be rendered not only agreeable, but quite as salubrious as that of any equal extent of country under the tropics. The population of Costa Rica is concentrated on the western or Pacific slope of the great volcano of Cartago; and, as a consequence, any degree of temperature may be obtained, according to the elevation—from intense heat at the port of Punta Arenas to the constant spring of San Jose, or to the autumnal temperature of the belt above the ancient, earthquake-shattered capitol of Cartago. The eastern slopes of Costa Rica may be said to be uninhabited, and the coast from Chiriqui lagoon northward is low and unhealthy. Indeed, the entire Atlantic coast of Central America, embracing the whole of what is called the

Mosquito shore, is subject to the same remark. But yet there are points which are singularly exempt from disease, and where the inhabitants, for a radius of a few miles, enjoy general good health, while beyond these limits the evidences of insalubrity are unmistakable. This coast has, however, scarcely any inhabitants except a few squalid Indians of the Carib stock, of which the Moscos or Mosquitos, in consequence of certain equivocal relations with Great Britain, are the best known. This "nation," as it is called, is a mongrel breed, crossed between negroes and Indians, in every degree of mixture. They are few in number, and have only a factitious importance; for the mass of the Indians, inhabiting what is geographically known as the "Mosquito Shore," neither recognise them as their masters, nor maintain any relations with them.

I have said that the ports of Central America open to Europe and Africa on the one hand, and to Asia and Polynesia and Australia upon the other. No country could be more favorably situated for commerce. Guatemala has upon the east the ports of Belize, (now occupied by the English, in violation of treaty stipulations,) Santo Tomas, and Izabal; Honduras, Cabo Caballo, Omoa, Coxenhole (island of Roatan,) and Truxillo; Nicaragua, Cape Gracias a Dios, Blewfields, and San Juan; Costa Rica, Matina, and Boca del Toro. Upon the Pacific are Golfo Dulce, Punta Arenas, and Caldera, in Costa Rica; the bays of Culebra, Salinas, San Juan del Sur, Tamarinda, and Realejo, in Nicaragua; Amapala and San Lorenzo, in Honduras; La Union, Jiquilisco, Acajutla, Sonsonate, (or La Libertad,) in San Salvador; and Istapa and Ocus, in Guatemala. Sonsonate, Libertad, and Istapa are roadsteads rather than harbors. Acajutla may perhaps be called a roadstead, but the anchorage is partially protected by a long ledge of rocks called "Punta de los Remedios." The landing is therefore comparatively easy, and at low water entirely so. It should also be mentioned that the

Pacific Ocean is much less turbulent than the Atlantic, so that vessels may load and discharge their cargoes with little difficulty, at all these points, for the greater part of the year.

Besides the rivers of Central America, the principal of which have already been enumerated, there are a number of large and beautiful lakes, viz.: Nicaragua and Managua, in Nicaragua; Guija and Ylopango, in San Salvador; Golfo Dulce, Peten, Atitlan, and Amatitan, in Guatemala; and Yojos, in Honduras. Of these, the lakes of Managua and Nicaragua alone are navigable.

The area of Central America may be estimated, in round numbers, at 150,000 square miles,—very nearly equal to that of the New England and Middle States combined, and considerably greater than that of Peru or Chili, which are estimated to contain, the first, 109,000, and the second, 127,000 square miles.

CHAPTER II.

NICARAGUA; ITS EXTENT, TOPOGRAPHY, CLIMATE, POPULATION, PRODUCTIONS, MINERALS, PORTS, ETC., ETC.

THE ancient Kingdom or Captain-Generalcy of Guatemala embraced the principal provinces or intendencies of Guatemala, Honduras, San Salvador, Nicaragua, and Costa Rica.[1] These threw off their allegiance to Spain in 1821, and following the great example of the British colonies in North America, assumed the rank of sovereign States. They subsequently united in a confederacy, called the "Republic of Central America," which, in consequence of internal dissensions, and the strife of factions, was practically dissolved in 1839, since which time the several States have asserted and exercised their original sovereign powers, as distinct Republics. Three of the number, namely, Nicaragua, Honduras, and San Salvador, have recently taken steps towards a new

[1] I speak now of the principal provinces. For the convenience of government and administration, other minor divisions were made, which were called provinces, and which had different limits at different periods. The large province, now State of Chiapas, and included in the Mexican Republic, belonged to the ancient Kingdom of Guatemala. Subsequently to the Independence, it was appropriated by Mexico, which country, under the brief rule of Iturbide, attempted to annex to itself the whole of Central America. A portion of what is now the district of Veragua, attached to New Granada, (it is also claimed,) belonged to the old kingdom of Guatemala. The country from north-west to south-east was therefore not much less than four hundred leagues, or twelve hundred miles in length.

confederation, have agreed upon certain bases of union, and have called a constituent assembly.[1]

The Republic of Nicaragua, therefore, comprises the territory which pertained to it as a province. Its boundaries are the Caribbean Sea upon the east, extending from the lower or Colorado mouth of the San Juan River, to Cape Gracias a Dios; and upon the west, the Pacific Ocean from the Gulf of Nicoya to that of Fonseca, embracing about one-third of the latter. The northern boundary, separating it from Honduras, follows the river Vanks, or Segovia, from its mouth at Cape Gracias a Dios, for about two-thirds of its length, thence runs in a right line, northwest by north, to the head of the River Roman, and thence, also in a right line, to the point already indicated on the Gulf of Fonseca. The southern boundary, separating it from Costa Rica, runs in a right line from the mouth of the River Salto de Nicoya, or Alvarado, emptying into the head of the Gulf of Nicoya, to the lower mouth of the San Juan river. The State is therefore embraced entirely between 83° 20′ and 87° 30′, (from Greenwich, 6° 20′, and 10° 30′ from Washington,) west longitude, and between 9° 45′ and 15° of north latitude; and has an area of about 59,000 square miles, or about an equal extent of territory with the New England States, exclusive of Connecticut and Rhode Island.

A claim to upwards of half of this territory has been set up by Great Britain, on behalf of the supposititious "King of the Mosquitos." The boundaries of this claim have been extended from time to time, but, as last defined, embrace the whole coast of Central America, from Cape Honduras to the northern limits of New Granada, as will appear in a subsequent chapter. A claim to another large section of Nicaragua, including the entire department of Guanacaste, or

[1] The history of these events is reserved for the Chapters on the Political State of Central America, near the close of this work.

Nicoya, (lying between Lake Nicaragua and the Gulf of Nicoya,) as also to the entire country south of the lake just named and the River San Juan, has recently been asserted by Costa Rica. But neither the pretensions of Great Britain or Costa Rica are well founded, nor are they admitted by Nicaragua, or recognized by civilized nations. These are points which will be elucidated elsewhere.

As we have already intimated, the geographical and topographical features of Nicaragua are equally remarkable and interesting. If an accurate map of Central America existed, it would exhibit in this State a separation of the great chain of the Cordilleras into two divergent ranges, of less general height than the great ridge itself, and having occasional partial interruptions. This divergence takes place in the northern department of Segovia, one branch extending due southeast towards the Atlantic. Its outposts come down to the very shore, and form prominent landmarks upon that coast. The range itself intersects the San Juan River about fifty miles above its mouth. At its northern base, and nearly parallel to it, flows a large and long stream, the Rio Escondido, sometimes indicated in the maps as "Blewfields River." All the streams upon the southern side of the range fall into Lakes Managua and Nicaragua, or into the San Juan River. This range resumes its course upon the southern shore of the San Juan, but now bears nearly due south, connecting with the Pacific range in the elevated regions of Costa Rica.

The Pacific range follows the general direction of the coast, sometimes rising into lofty volcanic cones, but generally sustaining the character of a high ridge, and in places subsiding into low hills and plains. It preserves a nearly uniform distance from the sea of from ten to twenty miles; consequently there are no considerable streams falling into the Pacific for the distance which it continues. It unites, as I have already said, with the eastern range in Costa Rica. Its course seems to have been the principal line of volcanic action, and extinct craters and beds of lava are to be met with at short intervals throughout its length. The lofty cones of the Viejo, Santa Clara, Axusco, Momotombo, Momobacho, Ometepec, Madeira, Orosi, and Abogado, not to mention many others which may be regarded as belonging to this range, are prominent landmarks, and form remarkable features in the landscape.[1]

The two ranges of the Cordilleras here referred to form, with their slopes, a great interior basin, not far from three hundred miles long by one hundred and fifty wide, consisting in great part of broad, beautiful, and fertile plains. The waters of this region fall into the lakes already named, of which the San Juan River is the only outlet. Many of the streams flowing into these lakes, especially from the north, are of considerable size, and furnish a supply of water which could not be sensibly affected by drains for artificial purposes.

The lake Managua approaches, at its nearest point, to within four or five leagues of the Pacific, from which it is separated on the south by the range of hills already described; but between its northern extremity and the sea there are only the broad and magnificent plains of Leon and El Conejo, in the midst of which, with all the regularity of the pyramids, rise the volcanoes of Axusco, Telica, and El Viejo.

Lake Managua is a beautiful sheet of water, of much larger size than has hitherto been represented. It is certainly not far from fifty or sixty miles in greatest length by thirty-five

[1] "In proceeding from Realejo southward and westward, there is, at a few leagues distant from the ocean, a range of hills, nowhere of great height until they approach the confines of Costa Rica, where they are elevated into mountains of from 5,000 to 11,000 feet in height. Between this ridge and the lake the land may be termed moderately level, and is not much broken; the contrary is the case along the borders of Honduras, where the country is intersected by several lofty ridges, running in various directions."—*Baily's Central America*, p. 114.

in width, and ranges from two to ten and fifteen, and even forty fathoms in depth. The scenery which borders it is unsurpassed in beauty and grandeur. Upon the northern and eastern shore, lifting their blue rugged peaks one above the other, are the mountains of Matagalpa, merging into those of Segovia, rich in metallic veins. Upon the south and west are broad and fertile slopes and level plains, covered with luxuriant verdure, and of almost unlimited productiveness. The volcano of Momotombo, like a giant warder, stands out boldly into the lake, its bare and blackened summit, which no man has ever reached, covered with a light wreath of smoke, attesting the continued existence of those internal fires which have seamed its steep sides with burning floods, and which still send forth hot and sulphurous springs at its base. Within the lake itself rises the regular cone of Momotombita, so regular that it seems a work of art, covered with a dense forest, under the shadows and within the deep recesses of which, frayed by the storms of ages, stand the rude and frowning statues of the gods of aboriginal superstition, raised there long before European feet trod the soil of America, and to which the mind of the christianized Indian still reverts with a mysterious reverence.

The town or city of Santiago de Managua, which gives its name to the lake, and which is the place of the meeting of the Legislative Chambers of the State, is situated upon the south-western shore. Some considerable streams flow into the lake from the direction of Segovia, and the level of water undergoes very slight changes with the different seasons. The town of Leon was first built on the shore of the north-western extremity of Lake Managua, at a place now called Moabita, but it was subsequently abandoned for the present site, in the midst of the great plain of Leon. From this circumstance the lake in question is sometimes called Lake Leon.

Lake Nicaragua is nevertheless the great feature of the

country, and is unquestionably, in all respects, one of the finest bodies of water on the continent, needing only to be made easy of access to become as famous a resort of the lovers of the grand and beautiful in nature, as any now known in the Old or New World. In common with Lake Managua, its size has been rather under than over-estimated. Mr. Baily calculated its greatest length at one hundred miles, and its greatest width at forty or forty-five miles. It is probably nearer one hundred and twenty miles in length, by fifty or sixty in breadth. Upon its southern shore, near the head of the lake, is the ancient city of Granada, the most important commercial point in the republic. A few miles below Granada, and projecting boldly into the lake, is the extinct volcano of Momobacho, not far from five thousand feet in height. At its base, in the lake, is a group of innumerable small islands of volcanic origin, rising in the form of cones from twenty to one hundred feet, and covered with verdure. Some of them, upon which the soil has accumulated, are inhabited by Indians, and their thatched cottages, shadowed over by tall palms, and with a dense background of broad-leaved plantains, form the most picturesque objects which can be conceived. Upon the same shore with Granada, but forty miles distant, is the city of Nicaragua, or Rivas, the capital of a very large, fertile, and comparatively well-cultivated district. The remaining section of the southern shore of the lake has scarcely any inhabitants, except a few wild Indians, called "Bravos," who alternate between the mountainous district towards Costa Rica and the shore. The northern shore, called Chontales, is undulating, and well adapted to grazing. Here are a great number of cattle estates, some embracing many thousand head of cattle and mules. There are a number of considerable islands in the lake, the largest of which is Madeira or Ometepec, which is almost wholly inhabited by Indians. It abounds in numerous traces of aboriginal occupation and art, and is distinguished by two immense cones, visible from every point of the lake and from the Pacific. These are called respectively Ometepec and Madeira. The cone of Ometepec is the most regular in outline of any which I have seen, and is, I think, the highest in the country. Its summit is generally enveloped in clouds. The water of the lake, in most places, shoals gradually, but at some points vessels of the largest class may approach close to the shore. The depth, except in the immediate vicinity of its outlet, is for all purposes of navigation ample, ranging from eight to twenty, and even forty fathoms. The prevailing winds are from the north-east (the direction of the summer trades on the coast,) and when the breeze is considerable, the waves of the lake roll with all the regularity and with much of the majesty of those of the sea. At such times, the surf upon the shore at Granada is nearly as high as it is, during a brisk wind, upon the beach at Newport or Cape May.

The sole outlet to this great interior basin, and of the lakes just described, is the River San Juan, debouching into the Atlantic at the now well-known port of the same name. This river is certainly a magnificent stream, but its capabilities have been greatly exaggerated. It flows from the south-eastern extremity of Lake Nicaragua, nearly due east, to the Atlantic. Its length has been variously estimated, from seventy to one hundred and four miles. The first estimate is obviously too little. Mr. Baily calculated it at ninety miles, and he is probably not far from correct.

The body of water which flows through this stream is at all times considerable, but it varies greatly in amount at different seasons of the year. It is greatest during what is termed the "rainy season" in the interior, that is to say, from May to October, at which period the volume of water is nearly doubled. To this circumstance in some degree may be ascribed the wide difference, in the statements of the depths and capacity of the river, made by different individuals.

Several considerable streams enter the San Juan, the principal of which are the San Carlos and the Serapiqui, both rising towards the south in the highlands of Costa Rica. The streams flowing in from the north are comparatively small, indicating that the mountains are not far distant in this direction, and that upon this side the valley is comparatively narrow. The Serapiqui is ascended by boats to a point where the Costa Rica road (trail) commences. This is the route by which Costa Rica keeps up communication with the San Juan; and to the point here named she is now endeavoring to construct a road for mules, starting from San Jose, her capital. The banks of the San Juan, from the fort of San Carlos, at the outlet of the lake, to the Rapides del Toro, a distance of twenty miles, are generally low, and covered with palms, canes, and a species of high, coarse grass called *gamalote.* The river here sometimes overflows its shores, which for a considerable distance back seem to be flat and swampy. From the port of San Juan upwards to the point of the divergence of the Colorado, a distance of eighteen miles, the banks of the river present a corresponding appearance. In fact, the entire country from this point to the sea is flat, as is shown by the divergence of the Colorado, the Juanillo, and Tauro, and by the occurrence of numerous *lagunas.* It is nevertheless fertile, and capable of producing in the utmost luxuriance rice, sugar, and those other articles which require moist and fertile soils. From the Colorado to the Rapides del Toro, a distance of more than fifty miles, the banks of the river vary from six to twenty feet in height, and are densely wooded; the forests coming down to the water's edge, forming an almost impenetrable wall of verdure. The passenger in the boats is so completely shut in by vegetation, that it is impossible to discover what is the character of the back country. At intervals hills and high grounds are to be discerned, and sometimes these come down to the edge of the river. At the mouth of the San Carlos there are hills two thousand feet high, and the river is much contracted. The entrance of the passage between them, from the west, somewhat resembles the opening of the highlands of the Hudson from the north.

The banks of the river are in some places rocky; elsewhere they are far from being as crumbling as those of the Ohio and Mississippi, and other rivers of the Western States of the Union. This is perhaps due, to some extent, to the roots of trees and plants which penetrate and bind the earth in all directions. The bed of the river may be regarded as essentially permanent; it nevertheless abounds in islands, of which there are hundreds. Some of these are low, and covered with *gamalote*, or with canes; but most are as high as the banks of the river, and wooded in like manner.

The width of the river varies from one hundred to four hundred yards, and its depth from two to twenty feet. The average volume of water I should estimate at about that of the Connecticut River, or the Hudson above the reach of the tides.

In respect of climate, little need be added to the remarks made on that subject in the preceding chapter. Upon the Atlantic declivity it is unquestionably warmer than in the interior, or upon the borders of the Pacific—more humid and more subject to rain. The country too, is low along the coast, with numerous lagoons and inlets, and consequently more infested with annoying insects and more subject to fevers. The climate, however, is more salubrious than would be supposed under the circumstances. This is illustrated by the fact that in the months of March and April, 1849, a party of American emigrants, one hundred and thirty in number, spent upward of six months at this point; and notwithstanding the sudden transition from midwinter to tropical heats, not to mention inadequate shelter and indifferent food, not one was seriously affected by illness. The same party, it may also be mentioned, passed up the San Juan under the worst of circumstances, suffering great exposures, and remained in the interior and upon the northern coast until the middle of August, with scarcely any sickness among them, and that little generally the result of carelessness or excesses.

The valley of the San Juan once passed, the climate is unsurpassed in salubrity by any equal extent of territory under the tropics, or perhaps in the world. The year is divided, rather anomalously to the stranger, into two seasons—the wet and the dry—the first of which is called Winter and the latter Summer. The wet season commences in May and lasts until November; during which time, but usually near the commencement or close, rains of some days' duration are of occasional occurrence, and showers are common, but do not often happen except late in the afternoon, (commencing about four o'clock,) or in the night. They are seldom of long continuance; and often days and weeks elapse without a cloud obscuring the sky. From this it will be seen, that the popular idea concerning the "rainy season" is erroneous. Probably but little more than one half the amount of rain which falls in the latitude of New York during the same period falls, during these six months, in Nicaragua. Throughout this season the verdure and the crops, which, during the dry season, become sere and withered, appear in full luxuriance; the temperature is very equable, differing a little in different localities, but preserving great uniformity all over the country, except in the mountainous regions. The range of the thermometer is from 78° to 88°, in rare instances sinking to 70° during the night, and rising to 90° in the afternoon. During the month of June, at Granada, the average height of the thermometer was 82° of Fah.; in Leon, during the months of July, August, and September, 83°. Out of the sun, this weather would prove agreeable to most persons. There is almost constantly a cool and pleasant breeze blowing, for the most part from the north-east. The nights are delicious, and sleep is seldom, if ever, interrupted by heat.

For weeks together the thermometer marked 77° at ten o'clock in the evening, and 76° at sunrise. During the dry season, in January, the temperature is less, the nights positively cool, and occasionally the winds are chilling. The sky is cloudless, and trifling showers fall at rare intervals. The fields become dry, cattle are driven to the hills and forests for pasturage, and the dust in the towns becomes almost insupportable. It penetrates everywhere, permeating even through the tiled roofs in showers, and sweeping in clouds through the unglazed windows. Were it not for this, the dry season would not be pronounced unpleasant. It is esteemed healthier than the wet season.

The effect of the dry season is practically that of our winter, and it no doubt contributes efficiently to the general health of the country. During that period the exuberance of vegetable growth is checked, and the ephemeral vegetation, which, where the rain falls for the entire year, goes on accumulating, forming dense, dank jungles, the home and birthplace of malaria, is entirely dried up. At this period, also, nearly the whole country is burned over. The consequence is, that the forests, for a great part of the year, are nearly as open and penetrable as our own. The favorable influences of these conditions upon the general health can readily be understood.[1]

[1] "The climate of all the state may be said to be good and healthy, but is distinguished, as is that of the other states, by much variety. In the interior, or mountainous parts, the temperature is mild, as compared with the most populous portion of the territory adjacent to the sea-coast, where it is hot, and rather humid, owing to evaporation from the surfaces of two great lakes; which, from the combined effects of a powerful sun, and a fresh breeze from the north-east, blowing over them almost constantly, must be great. Both climate and temperature appear to be extremely favorable to the general health of natives as well as well as foreigners; the exceptions in this important point being very few, and of trifling consequence in the injury which they occasion. The changes of season take place with the same almost undeviating regularity as in other parts of

Nicaragua is divided into six Departments, each of which has several Judicial Districts, as follows:

DEPARTMENTS.	POPULATION.	DISTRICTS.
1. Meridional	20,000	Rivas or Nicaragua.
2. Oriental	95,000	Acoyapa or Chontales, Granada, Masaya, and Managua.
3. Occidental	90,000	Leon and Chinandega
4. Septentrional of Matagalpa	40,000	Matagalpa.
5. Septentrional of Segovia .	12,000	Segovia.
6. Nicoya or Guanacaste . .	7,000	Guanacaste.
Total	264,000	

The population here given is the result arrived at, in round numbers, by a census attempted in 1846. It was only partially successful, as the people supposed it preliminary to some military conscription, or new tax.

The principal towns of the State, with their estimated population, are as follows:—

Leon, (the capital,) including Subtiaba	30,000
Chinandega	11,000
Chinandega Viejo	3,000
Realejo	1,000
Chichigalpa	2,800
Posultega	900
Telica	1,000
Somotillo	2,000
Villa Nueva	1,000
Pueblo Nuevo	2,900
Nagarote	1,800
Souci	2,500
Managua	12,000
Masaya	15,090
Granada	10,000
Nicaragua	8,000
Segovia	8,000
Matagalpa.	2,000
Acoyapa, ...	500

It is a singular fact that the females greatly exceed the males in number. In the Department Occidental, according to the census, the proportions are as three to two. It is difficult to account for this disparity, except by supposing it

Central America; but the rains often continue a month longer here, and the quantity during the season appears to be considerably more copious; also casual showers, out of the periodical limit, are not unfrequent between the lakes, and the lakes and the sea, affording much benefit to vegetation on the cultivated lands."—BAILY.

to be the result of the civil commotions to which the country has been so long subjected.

The civilized Indians of Nicaragua, and those of Spanish and negro stocks crossed with them, constitute the mass of the population. The white individuals of pure European stock are but a small part of the whole, and are nearly equalled in number by those of pure negro blood. The entire population may be divided as follows:

Whites,	25,000
Negroes,	15,000
Indians,	80,000
Mixed,	130,000
Total,	250,000

Most of these live in towns, many of them going two, four, and six miles daily, to labor in the fields, starting before day and returning at night. The plantations, "haciendas," "hattos," "huertas," "ranchos," and "chacras," are scattered pretty equally over the country, and are often reached by paths so obscure as almost wholly to escape the notice of travellers, who, passing through what appears to be a continuous forest from one town to the other, are liable to fall into the error of supposing the country almost wholly uninhabited. Their dwellings are usually of canes, thatched with palm, many of them open at the sides, and with no other floor than the bare earth. These fragile structures, so equable and mild is the climate, are adequate to such protection as the natives are accustomed to consider necessary. Some of them are more pretending, and have the canes plastered over and whitewashed, with tiled roofs and other improvements; and there are a few, belonging to large proprietors, which are exceedingly neat and comfortable, approaching nearer our ideas of habitations for human beings.

A large part of the dwellings in the towns are much of the same character; the residences of the better classes, however, are built of adobes, are of one story, and enclose large courts, which are entered under archways, often constructed with great beauty. The court-yard has generally a great number of shade trees, usually orange, making the corridors, upon which all the rooms open, exceedingly pleasant.

I have already said that the natural resources of Nicaragua are immense, but they have been very imperfectly developed. The portion of lands brought under cultivation is very small, but ample for the support of its population. There is no difficulty in increasing the amount to an indefinite extent, for the forests are easily removed, and genial nature needs no forcing to return rich harvests. There are many cattle estates, particularly in Chontales, Matagalpa, and Segovia, which cover wide tracts of country; some of these have not less than 10,000 or 15,000 head of cattle each. The cattle are generally fine, quite equal to those of the United States.

Among the staples of the State, and which are produced in great perfection, I may mention sugar, cotton, coffee, indigo, tobacco, rice, and maize, or Indian corn.

SUGAR.—The description of sugar-cane grown in Nicaragua is a native of the country, and very different from the Asiatic cane cultivated in the West Indies and the United States. It is said to be equally productive with the foreign species; the canes are softer and more slender, and contain more and stronger juice, in proportion to their size, than the Asiatic variety. Two crops (under favorable circumstances three crops) are taken annually, and the cane does not require replanting but once in twelve or fourteen years. The best kind of sugar produced from the sugar estates is nearly as white as the refined sugar of commerce, the crystals being large and hard. The greater part of the supply for ordinary consumption is what is called "*chancaca*," and is the juice of the cane merely boiled till it crystallizes, without being cleared of the molasses. A quantity of this is exported to Peru, and elsewhere in South America. It is stated that the "chancaca" may be produced, ready for sale, at $1 25 per quintal (101½ lbs. English.) The most profitable part of the sugar establishment is the manufacture of "*aguardiente*," a species of rum. It is impossible to say, in the absence of data, what amount of sugar is manufactured in Nicaragua; it is perhaps enough to know that it may be produced indefinitely. The export has been estimated at 200,000 lbs.

COTTON.—Cotton of a superior quality to that of Brazil may be produced in any quantity in Nicaragua. "As many as 50,000 bales, of 300 pounds each," says Dunlap, "of clean pressed cotton have been exported from this State in a single year; the cultivation is, however, at present (1846) at a very low ebb." Considerable quantities are nevertheless raised, which are manufactured by the natives, but chiefly by the Indians, into hammocks, sail-cloth, and ordinary clothing. The domestic cloth is coarse, but compact, neat, and durable.

Mr. Baily observes of the cotton of Nicaragua, "that it has already a high standard in the Manchester market, and offers a splendid speculation to agriculturists, if a good port of export on the Atlantic shall be established."

COFFEE.—Coffee of an excellent quality, and probably equal to any in the world, may also be produced indefinitely in this republic; but for the reason that hitherto it has been exceedingly difficult to get it to a market, it is not very extensively cultivated. The plantations which I have seen are very flourishing, and the proprietors find them quite as profitable as any other. The limited cultivation is perhaps due to the circumstance that chocolate is the common beverage of the people; and coffee, never having become an article of trade or export, has consequently been neglected. There is no reason why as good coffee may not be produced here as in Costa Rica; and the Costa Rican coffee, when offered in good condition in England, commands as high a price as any other. As, however, it is usually shipped by way of Cape Horn, it often suffers from the protracted voyage. It has, nevertheless, been the almost exclusive source of wealth in Costa Rica. The crop of 1847 amounted to 8,000,000 pounds, which, at $12 50 per cwt., (the average price in the English market,) gives $1,000,000 as the return—a considerable sum for a State of less than 100,000 inhabitants, and where the culture has been introduced but fourteen years. The cost of production, per quintal (101½ pounds,) at the present rate of wages, (twenty-five cents per day) is about $2 50. If the attention of the people of Nicaragua should be seriously directed to the production of coffee, it would prove a source of great profit.

CACAO.—Cacao, only equalled by that of Soconosco, on the coast of Guatemala, (and which was once monopolized for the use of the royal establishment of Spain,) is cultivated in considerable quantities. It is, however, an article of general consumption among the inhabitants; and consequently, commands so high a price that it would not bear exportation, even though it could be obtained in requisite quantities. About all that finds its way abroad goes in the form of presents from one friend to the other. There is no reason why this should not become an article of large trade, and a source of great wealth. The obvious cause why its production is not greater, is, the length of time and great outlay required in getting a cacao plantation into paying operation. Few have now the requisite capital; and these few are in too feverish a state, in consequence of the distracted condition of public affairs, to venture upon any investment. Under a stable condition of things, and by the opening of a short and easy channel to market, the cultivation of cacao will rise to be of the first importance. The trees give two principal crops in the year. It is sold from $15 to $20 the quintal, while the Guayaquil is worth but $5 or $6.

INDIGO.—Indigo was formerly cultivated to a considerable extent, but has of late years much fallen off; and there are a number of fine indigo estates in various parts of the republic which have been quite given up, with all their appurtenances, by their respective proprietors. The plant cultivated for the manufacture of Indigo is the *indigofera*, a triennial plant, supposed to be a native of America. There is also an indigenous triennial plant abounding in many parts of Central America, which produces indigo of a very excellent quality, but gives less than half the weight which is produced by the cultivated species. The indigo of Nicaragua is of very superior quality, and its export once came up to 5,000 bales of 150 lbs. each. It is impossible to say what the export is at present; probably not more than 1,000 or 2,000 bales. Under the government of Spain, the State of San Salvador produced from 8,000 to 10,000 bales annually. A piece of ground equal to two acres generally produces about 100 to 120 pounds, at a cost of not far from $30 to $40, including the cost of clearing the field and all other expenses.

TOBACCO.—A large amount of tobacco is used in Nicaragua, all of which is produced in the country. A considerable quantity was this year (1849) shipped to California. It may be cultivated to any desirable extent, and is of a very superior quality. That of San Salvador and Honduras is said to be equal to the best Havana for cigars.

MAIZE flourishes luxuriantly, and three crops may be raised on the same ground annually. It is essentially the "staff of life" in all Central America, being the material of which the eternal *tortilla* is composed. The green stalks, "sacate," constitute about the only fodder for horses and cattle in the country, and is supplied daily in all the principal towns. The abundance of this grain may be inferred from the fact that a *fanega of Leon* (equivalent to about five bushels of English) of shelled corn, in 1849, commanded in the capital but one dollar.

WHEAT and all other cereal grains, as well as the fruits of temperate climates, flourish in the elevated districts of Segovia, in the northern part of the republic, bordering upon Honduras, where, it is said, except in the absence of snow, little difference is to be observed, in respect to climate, from the southern parts of the United States.

RICE is abundant in Nicaragua, and is extensively used, and, like maize, may be easily cultivated to any extent desirable. It is sold at from $1 50 to $2 per cwt.

In short, nearly all the edibles and fruits of the tropics are produced naturally, or may be cultivated in great perfection. Plantains, bananas, beans, chile, tomatoes, bread-fruit, arrow-root, ocra, citrons, oranges, limes, lemons, pine-apples (the delicious white Guayaquil, as well as the yellow variety), mamays, anonas or chirimoyas, guavas, cocoa-nuts, and a hundred other varieties of plants and fruits. Among the vegetable productions of commerce may be mentioned sarsaparilla, anota, aloes, ipecacuanha, ginger, vanilla, Peruvian bark (quinine), cowhage, copal, gum arabic, copaiva, caoutchouc, dragon's blood, and vanglo, or oil plant. Among the valuable trees: mahogany, log-wood, Brazil-wood, lignum-vitæ, fustic, yellow sanders, pine (on the heights), dragon's blood tree, silk-cotton tree, oak, copal tree, cedar, button-wood, iron-wood, rose-wood, Nicaragua wood, calabash, etc., etc. Of these, Brazil wood, cedar, and mahogany are found in the forests in what may be termed inexhaustible quantities. The cedar is a large tree, like the red cedar of the North in nothing except color and durability, and in solidity and other respects closely resembling the black walnut. Five or six cargoes of Brazil wood are exported from Realejo yearly, and something more from San Juan. A quantity of cedar plank is also exported to South America.

The raising of cattle and the production of cheese is a most important item in the actual resources of Nicaragua. The cheese is for common consumption, and great quantities are used. Large droves of cattle are annually sent to the other

States, where they command very fair prices. About thirty-five or forty thousand hides are also exported annually.

The mineral resources of Nicaragua are also very great. Gold, silver, copper, lead, and iron, may be found in considerable quantities in various parts, but more particularly in Segovia, which district is probably not exceeded in its mineral wealth by any equal portion of the continent. The working of the mines has of course vastly fallen off from the time of the Spaniards; still, their produce is considerable, but it is impossible to obtain any satisfactory statistics concerning it. A portion of the gold and silver finds its way through Izabal to the Balize; other portions pass on through the ports of Truxillo and Omoa, in Honduras; and another but smaller part reaches the ports of Nicaragua.

There is now no mint in Central America, excepting a small one in Costa Rica, which coins from $50,000 to $100,000 annually, principally in dollar pieces of gold. These are short of weight, and are not generally current. Their true value is ninety-three cents. Humboldt, in his statement of the produce of the respective mining districts of America, has put against that of Guatemala, "nothing;" but it is certain from the accounts of Gage and others, as also of the buccaneers, who made a number of profitable expeditions to the mining districts, that the precious metals were early produced in considerable abundance. From a report by the master of the old mint, made in 1825, it appears that, for the fifteen years anterior to 1810, gold and silver had been coined to the amount of $2,193,832, and for the fifteen years posterior to that date, to the amount of $3,810,382. This officer remarks, "that it must not be deduced from hence that this is all our mines have produced in this period, as great quantities of the metal have been manufactured and exported in their native state." He estimates the actual products of the mines at ten times the amount coined; which would give upwards of $50,000,000 for the thirty years preceding 1825. This estimate will probably bear some deduction.[1]

Other minerals are abundant. Sulphur may be obtained

[1] Dunlap, who paid considerable attention to the mines and minerals of Central America, observes:

"Though the vegetable productions of Central America are so valuable, the hidden treasures are scarcely of inferior worth; and in no part of the world are mines so generally found in nearly every district. Many of these were successfully worked after the conquest and during the Spanish dominion. Besides the mines of gold and silver, there are others containing lead in nearly a pure state; the ore yielding 90 per cent. of metal. In some specimens 25 per cent. of silver is said to be mixed with the lead.

"At the village of Patapa, nine leagues from Santa Ana, in the State of San Salvador, are some rich mines of iron, which produce a purer and more malleable metal than any imported from Europe: the ore is close to the surface, and very abundant, and there are extensive forests in the immediate vicinity, which serve for making charcoal. But, notwithstanding, the amount of iron manufactured is only equal to the supply of the State, where it is worth $10 the 100 lbs., or $200 per ton. In the same neighborhood are several silver mines, which were successfully worked in the time of the Spaniards, but are now abandoned for want of capital to carry them on.

"Five leagues north of San Miguel are a number of mines, principally of silver; among them was one called La Carolina, worked by a Spaniard about thirty years ago. He invested his own property, borrowed $100,000, and, after getting the mine in working order, in less than six months was enabled to pay his obligations; and, although he died before the end of the year, left $70,000 in gold and silver, the produce of the mine. After his death, the ownership was disputed, the works fell into ruins, and the mine became filled with water, in which condition it remains. The mines of Tabanco were more celebrated than those in this vicinity, and when worked yielded upward of $1,000,000 annually, although worked in a rude manner, without machinery. The principal of these once yielded $200,000 annual profit to the proprietors.

"Near the town of Tegucigalpa, the capital of Honduras, there are a number of mines which still produce a considerable amount of the precious metals, although not one-tenth of what they formerly yielded. All the hills in the neighborhood abound in gold and silver, generally intermixed; and though none of them have been excavated to any depth, or worked in great quantities, crude and nearly pure, from the volcanoes; and nitre is easily procured, as also sulphate of iron.

by proper machinery, they have formerly yielded more than $2,000,000 per year; and were European capital and science introduced, the produce would be great. From all I have been able to collect, this neighborhood appears to possess natural stores of the precious metals, even exceeding those of the celebrated mines of Potosi, in Bolivia. For a scientific and practical miner, supported by capital, they probably offer the best adventure to be found in Spanish America.

"The ores generally contain from 12 to 15 per cent. of silver, and from one to one and a half per cent. of gold; but the latter metal is often found pure in many places, and the value of some thousands of dollars is annually collected by the Indians in the sands of the rivers, pieces of gold weighing as many as five and six pounds having occasionally been discovered.

"Some rich gold washings exist at Matagalpa, near Segovia, in Nicaragua, which are only worked by the Indians, who annually collect and dispose of a few pounds of very pure gold. Some copper mines have also been discovered here, the ore of which, when shipped to England, yielded 35 per cent. of copper.

"In the district of Nicoya, in the same State, many traces of the precious metals are said to exist, but as the country is almost wholly uninhabited, little is known concerning them.

"In the mountain of Aguacate, in Costa Rica, several profitable gold mines are still worked with fair profits."—*Dunlap's Central America*, 1847, pp. 277, 284.

An English traveller named Byam, who, although destitute of scientific knowledge, seems to have visited Nicaragua for mining purposes, states that the silver mines which he observed "were fine, broad, but rather irregular veins, the ore combined with sulphur and lead. The ore is hard but clean." The copper ores, he informs us, "are almost all uncombined with sulphur, or any other combination which requires calcining to be got rid of. They may all be smelted in a common blast furnace, with the aid of equal quantities of iron-stone, which lies in large quantities on the surface of all the hilly country. They are what the Spanish miners call 'metal de color,' red and blue oxides and green carbonates, with now and then the brown or pigeon-breasted. They cut easily and smoothly with the knife, and yield from twenty-five to sixty per cent. The copper veins are generally vertical, and the larger ones run east and west." This

The modes of mining practised in Central America are exceedingly rude, and render it surprising that profitable

writer has the following references to the gold washings of the country:

"Some adventurers, generally of the very lowest class, both in manners and morals, proceed to the auriferous streams, that run through the south part of the Honduras nearest to Segovia, for two or three months during the dryest part of the year, and when the rains have entirely subsided. Their baggage is very light and easily carried on a donkey or half-starved mule, for they only provide each for himself and his female helpmate a small load of Indian corn, barely enough for the pair, some tobacco, a small stone for grinding the corn, an earthen pan or two, a hatchet, and a small leathern bag to put the gold in *when found*. They also take a few half gourds dried, to wash the earth in, and a grass hammock to sleep in. and away they start, driving their animals before them, each man carrying his machete or short heavy broad sword, and some, bows and arrows, The part of the country is almost uninhabited, and, on their arrival at the different streams, they generally separate, and each pair chooses a spot often miles apart, where they commence operations. The first thing is to build a "Ramada," or hut of branches, as the name signifies; but they always select a place where two good-sized trees are near enough together, to enable them to swing their hammocks between them. With a few poles and branches with the leaf on, a hut is made in two or three hours; the man then makes a pile of dry wood near at hand, and leaves the entire care of the household to the woman, who grinds the corn, and every day makes a few cakes, looking like thin pancakes, which are toasted on a flat earthen pan over the wood ashes. Their drink is a little maize meal and cacao nut ground together, mixed with water and stirred up in a gourd; and thus the pair vegetate for two or three months, supported by the hopes of living well for the remainder of the year. The man is always within sight of the hut, in case assistance be wanted in such a wild spot; and he digs holes into the ground near the stream, and after having piled up a heap of earth close to the water, washes it in the half gourds, when, after repeated changes of water, and the spot chosen having proved a good one, a little fine gold dust is often visible in the gourd. It requires a great deal of nicety to balance the gourd backwards and forwards, up and down, and round about, so as to get rid of the earth; and it is still more difficult, at the last washing, to manage to leave the gold altogether, at the very end of the remaining deposit, which is generally of a black or results should be attained. The silver and gold ores are crushed in a basin of masonry, in which rises a vertical shaft, driven generally by a horizontal water-wheel. This shaft has two arms, to each of which is suspended a large stone or boulder. These are the crushers. After the ore is reduced to sufficient fineness, the metal is separated by amalgam; a long and expensive process, which is now beginning to be much facilitated and cheapened by the introduction of the German or "barrel process." The machines for crushing the ores have, however, as yet, undergone but slight improvement. Some of the mines in San Salvador and Costa Rica have European machinery, and are worked to great advantage.

The most important silver mines in Nicaragua, at present, are those called Dipilta, in the northern part of the republic. These have been worked only for a short period, and under very disadvantageous circumstances. They have, nevertheless, during the last three years, produced upwards of 26,000 marks (17,300 lbs.) of silver. The average yield of the ores is something over one and a half per cent. The better qualities of ore produce nearly two per cent. of pure metal.

Nicaragua has a number of excellent ports, the best known of which are San Juan, on the Atlantic, and Realejo, on the Pacific. These will be specially noticed in another connection. It may, nevertheless, be observed that they are adequate to all the wants of commerce, and are not surpassed in natural advantages by any of the American ports under the tropics. No returns of their commerce have been made public for many years; and there are, in consequence, no

dark gray color. The grains of gold are often large enough to be picked out after one or two washings, and often of a size to be discerned whilst digging, and a man in good luck may find enough gold in a week to keep him comfortably the whole year; but money easily got generally soon goes; and on the return of the lucky pair to their town, it is too often quickly spent in gambling and low debauchery."

means of determining what has been the trade of the country. This information, however, is now of little importance; for recent events have opened entirely new markets,[1] and new

[1] In a report made to the British government in 1837, by Mr. Foster, British Vice-Consul, and one of the principal traders of the country, the character of the imports and exports of the country are exhibited as follows:

"The prices of foreign manufactures have now found their level in these markets, and the consumption of those articles used by the poorer classes has increased in a wonderful degree both in quantity and quality; and the demand for foreign manufactures (of which British cottons of inferior quality have a prominent part) will naturally go on at an increased rate.

"The foreign imports may be classed under the following heads:

"British—consist of calicoes, printed cottons, (domestic or gray,) and power-loom shirtings, linen and cotton mixed, or unions, linens, muslins, hosiery, hard earthenware, iron, steel, lead, powder, etc., etc.

"French—consist of silks, printed cottons, cambrics, wine, spirits, jewelry, and fancy articles.

"United States—consist of domestic cottons, soap, sperm candles, hardware, spirits of inferior quality, and powder.

"Spanish—consist of paper, silk, riband, wine, oil, spirits, etc.

"Germany—consist of osnaburgs, glassware, wax, furniture, hardware, steel, wine, etc.

"Italy—consist of paper, oil, silk, and liquors.

"Colombia—consist of cacao and straw hats.

"Peru—consist of xerga, (a coarse woollen cloth,) tin, spirits, and common sweet wine.

"Chile—consist of sweet wine and pelones.

"The value of British goods imported may be taken at two-thirds of the whole of the imports.

"The consumption of French goods, being principally articles of luxury, is chiefly confined to the cities of Guatemala, San Salvador, Leon, Granada, etc. German linens, shirtings, and glassware are articles of general consumption. In Spanish goods, with the exception of ribands, the imports are trivial. They have given way to those of France and Italy.

"The sickness of this year has had considerable influence on the exports. Cochineal and indigo form the principal; great quantities, particularly of the former, are shipped from the ports on the northern side of Honduras.

avenues of trade, and the past can be no criterion for the future in estimating the present and future commercial importance of the country.

From the ports of the Pacific, 1,500 ceroons have been exported during the year to Europe, and the ports of Peru and Chile. Hides, horns, sarsaparilla, and balsam, for Europe and the United Sates, and mahogany, cedar, and sugar, for Chile and Peru. Those form the principal articles of the export trade, which, in proportion to the imports, is on the increase. Brazil wood, with which this State as well as Costa Rica abounds, formerly afforded employment to a great number of British vessels. The fall of this article in the home markets has for the present caused it to be but little sought for.

"In agriculture, this State is rapidly improving. In addition to indigo, sugar, cacao, wheat, etc., etc., coffee and cotton are now better attended to, but more particularly cotton and indigo. The former, which is much esteemed and known in the European market as 'green suche,' is an annual plant. The staple is short, which defect is overbalanced by its superior texture; and it is particularly adapted to certain manufactures."

NARRATIVE.

NARRATIVE.

CHAPTER I.

THE BRIG FRANCIS—DEPARTURE FROM NEW YORK—SAN DOMINGO—THE COAST OF CENTRAL AMERICA—MONKEY POINT—SHREWD SPECULATIONS—A NAKED PILOT—ALMOST A SHIPWRECK—SAN JUAN DE NICARAGUA—MUSIC OF THE CHAIN CABLE—A POMPOUS OFFICIAL—DELIVERING A LETTER OF INTRODUCTION—TERRA FIRMA AGAIN—"NAGUAS" AND "GUIPILS"—THE TOWN AND ITS LAGUNA—SNAKES AND ALLIGATORS—PRACTICAL EQUALITY—CELT *vs.* NEGRO—A WAN POLICEMAN—THE BRITISH CONSUL GENERAL FOR MOSQUITIA—"OUR HOUSE" IN SAN JUAN—AN EMEUTE—PIGS AND POLICE—A VISCOMTE ON THE STUMP—A SERENADE—MOSQUITO INDIANS—A PICTURE OF PRIMITIVE SIMPLICITY.

THE preceding general observations will serve to give an outline view of Central America and Nicaragua, and prepare the way for more detailed accounts of the country and its inhabitants. In attempting to give these, I shall refer to localities as they fell under my notice in entering and passing through the country, and record incidents very nearly in the order in which they occurred.

The point in Nicaragua most accessible from the United States, and that to which the traveller would most naturally take his course, is the now well-known port of San Juan de Nicaragua, situated upon the shores of the Caribbean Sea, about three hundred miles to the north-west of Chagres. The little brig Francis, of New York, was "up" for this port in the early part of May, in the year of grace 1849; and, for satisfactory reasons, overruling all choice in the premises, berths were engaged in her for myself and companions. She lay at the foot of Roosevelt street, in the *terra incognita* beyond the Bowery,—a pigmy amongst the larger vessels which surrounded her. We reported ourselves on board, in compliance with the special request of the owners, at 9 o'clock on the morning of the 11th, just as the human tide ebbed from the high-water mark of Fourth street and Union Square, and subsided for the day amongst the rugged banks and dangerous shallows of Wall and Pearl streets.

The Francis had received her freight, and her decks were encumbered with pigs and poultry, spars and tarpaulins, to say nothing of water casks and tar barrels, forbidding in advance any peregrinations, by unsteady landsmen, beyond the quarter deck. The quarter deck was so called by courtesy only: it was elevated but a few inches above the waist, and, deducting the room occupied by hen-coops, water-casks, and the man at the helm, afforded but about ten square feet of space, in which the unfortunate passengers might "recreate" themselves. This might have sufficed for men of moderate desires, but then it was far from being "contiguous territory."

In a word, we found ourselves in the midst of a confusion which none but the experienced traveller can coolly contemplate. Our friends, or rather the more daring of them, scrambled over the intervening decks, or hailed us from the rigging of the neighboring vessels. We would have invited them on board, but there was no room to receive them; besides the descent was perilous. All partings are much alike, but ours were made with a prodigious affectation of good spirits. We were to have sailed precisely at ten; but when eleven was chimed, the number which had come "expressly to see us off," was sensibly diminished; and at twelve we were left to our own contemplations.

There was a prodigious pulling of ropes; the same boxes were tumbled from one place to another and back again; trunks disappeared and came to light, and it seemed as if everybody was engaged in a grand search for nobody knew what. At one o'clock the pilot came on board. The delay had become painful, and now we thought the time for sailing had arrived. But the pilot was a fat man, and sat down imperturbably upon a water-cask. "Well, Mr. Pilot, are we off?" He deigned no audible reply, but glanced upwards significantly towards the streamer at the masthead. The wind blew briskly in from the Narrows. So we seated ourselves upon the water-casks also, and watched the men who were painting the next ship, and almost nodded ourselves to sleep, to the monotonous "yo-ho" of the sailors unloading an Indiaman near by. The roar of Broadway fell subdued and distant upon our ears; and the ferry-boats and little steamers in the river seemed to move about in silence, going to and fro apparently without an object, like ants around an ant-hill.

By-and-by a little, black bull-dog of a steamer thrust itself valiantly through the crowd of vessels, made a rope fast to our bows, and dragged us, with a jerk, triumphantly into the stream, past Governor's Island, down to the outer bay, and then left us to take care of ourselves. That night the sun went down cold and filmy, and the Francis tumbled roughly about amidst the dark waves of the Atlantic. * * * A calm under the high capes of San Domingo,—an infinitude of thunder squalls, with the pleasant consciousness of a hundred kegs of gunpowder stowed snugly around the foot of the mainmast,—a "close shave" on the coral reefs below Jamaica,—for twenty-six mortal days this was all which we had of relief from the detestable monotony of shipboard. Blessed be steam! * * * *

It was a dark and rainy morning, when "Land on the lee-bow," was sung out by the man at the helm, and in less time than is occupied in writing it, the occupants of the close little cabin made their way on deck, to look for the first time upon the coast of Central America. The dim outlines of the land were just discernible through the murky atmosphere, and many and profound were the conjectures hazarded as to what precise point was then in view. The result finally arrived at was, that we were off "Monkey Point," about thirty miles to the northward of our destined port. This conclusion was soon confirmed by observing, close under the shadow of the shore, an immense rock, rising with all the regularity of the Pyramids to the height of three hundred feet; a landmark too characteristic to be mistaken.

We were sweeping along with a stiff breeze, and were comforted with the assurance that we should be in port to breakfast, "*if*," as the cautious captain observed, "the wind held." But the perverse wind did not hold, and in half an hour thereafter we were rocking about with a wash-tubby motion, the most disagreeable that can be imagined, and of which we had had three days' experience under the Capes of San Domingo. The haze cleared a little, and with our glasses we could make out a long, low line of shore, covered with the densest verdure, with here and there the feathery palm, which forms so picturesque a feature in all tropical scenery, lifting itself proudly above the rest of the forest, and the whole relieved against a background of high hills, over which the gray mist still hung like a veil.

Some of the party could even make out the huts on the shore; but the old man at the helm smiled incredulously, and said there were no huts there, and that the unbroken and untenanted forest extended far back to the great ridge of the Cordilleras. So it was when the adventurous Spaniards coasted here three centuries ago, and so it had remained ever since. These observations were interrupted by a heavy shower, acceptable for the wind it brought, which filled the idle sails, and moved us towards our haven. And though the rain fell in torrents, it did not deter us from getting soaked, in vain endeavors to harpoon the porpoises that came tumbling in numbers around our bows.

But the shower passed, and with it our breeze, and again the brig rocked lazily on the water, which was now filled with branches of trees, and among the rubbish that drifted past, a broken spear and a cocoa-nut attracted particular attention; the one showed the proximity of a people whose primitive weapons had not yet given place to those more effective, of civilized ingenuity, and the other was a certain index of the tropics. The shower passed, but it had carried us within sight of our port. Those who had previously seen cabins on the shore could not now perceive any evidences of human habitation, and stoutly persisted that we had lost our reckoning, and that we were far from our destined haven. But a trim schooner which was just then seen moving rapidly along under a pouring shower, in the same direction with ourselves, silenced the pretended doubters, and became immediately a subject of great speculation. It was finally agreed on all hands that it must be the B——, a vessel which left New York three days before us, the captain of which had boasted that he would "beat us in, by at least ten days." So everybody was anxious that the little brig should lead him into the harbor, and many were the objurgations upon the wind, and desperate the attempts of the sailors to avail themselves of every "cat's-paw" that passed.

The excitement was great, and some of the impatient passengers inquired for sweeps, and recommended putting out the yawl to tow the vessel in. They even forgot, such was the excitement, to admire the emerald shores which were now distinct, not more than half a mile distant, and prayed that a black-looking thunder-storm, looming gloomily in the east, might make a diversion in our favor. And then a speck was discerned in the direction of the port; and by-and-by the movement of the oars could be seen, and bodies swaying to and fro, and in due time a *pit-pan*, a long, sharp-pointed canoe, pulled by a motley set of mortals, stripped to the waist, and displaying a great variety of skins, from light yellow to coal black, darted under our bows, and a burly fellow in a shirt pulled off his straw hat to the captain, and inquired in bad English, "Want-ee ah pilot?" The mate consigned him to the nether regions for a lubber, and inquired what had become of his eyes, and if he couldn't tell the Francis anywhere; the Francis, which "had made thirty-seven voyages to this port, and knew the way better than any black son of a gun who ever put to sea in a bread-trough!" And then the black fellow in a shirt and straw hat was again instructed to go below, or if he preferred, to go and "pilot in the lubberly schooner to windward." The black fellow looked blacker than before, and said something in an unintelligible jargon to the rest, and away they darted for the schooner.

Meantime the flank of the thunder storm swept towards us, piling up a black line of water, crested with foam, while it approached with a noise like that of distant thunder. It came upon us; the sails fluttered a moment and filled, the yards creaked, the masts bent to the strain, and the little brig dashed rapidly through the hissing water. In the darkness we lost sight of the schooner, and the shore was no longer visible, but we kept on our way; the Francis knew the road, and seemed full of life, and eager to reach her old anchorage.

"Don't she scud!" said the mate, who rubbed his hands in very glee. "If this only holds for ten minutes more, we're in, like a spike!"—and, strange to say, it did hold; and when it was past we found ourselves close to "Point Arenas," a long narrow spit, partly covered with water, which shuts in the harbor, leaving only a narrow opening for the admission of vessels. The schooner was behind us, but here was a difficulty. The bar had changed since his last trip; the captain was uncertain as to the entrance, and the surf broke heavily under our lee. Excitement of another character prevailed as we moved slowly on, where a great swell proclaimed the existence of shallows. The captain stood in the bow, and we watched the captain. Suddenly he cried, "Hard a-port!" with startling emphasis, and "Hard a-port!" was echoed by the helmsman, as he swept round the tiller. But it was too late; the little vessel struck heavily as the wave fell.

"Thirty-seventh, and last!" muttered the mate between his teeth, as he rushed to the fastenings, and the main-sail came down on the run. "Round with the boom, my men!" and the boom swung round, just as the brig struck again, with greater force than before, unshipping the rudder, and throwing the helmsman across the deck. "Round again, my men! lively, or the Francis is lost!" cheered the mate, who seemed invested with superhuman strength and agility; and as the boom swung round the wave fell, but the Francis did not strike. "Clear she is!" shouted the mate, who leaped upon the companion-way, and waved his hat in triumph; and turning towards the schooner, "Do *that*, ye divil, and call yerself a sailor!" There was no doubt about it; the Francis was in before the schooner; and notwithstanding the accident to her rudder, she passed readily to her old anchoring ground, in the midst of a spacious harbor, smooth as a mill-pond. There was music in the rattling cable as the anchor was run out, and the Francis moved slowly round, with her broadside towards the town. The well was tried, but she had made no water, which was the occasion for a new ebullition of joy on the part of the mate.

All danger past, we had an opportunity to look about us. We were not more than two cable-lengths from a low sandy shore, upon which was ranged, in a line parallel to the water, a double row of houses, or rather huts, some built of boards, but most of reeds, and all thatched with palm-leaves. Some came down to the water, like sheds, and under one end were drawn up pit-pans and canoes. Larger contrivances for navigating the San Juan river, resembling canal-boats, were also moored close in shore, and upon each might be seen a number of very long and very black legs, every pair of which was surmounted by a very short white shirt. In the centre of the line of houses, which was no other than the town of San Juan de Nicaragua, was an open space, and in the middle of this was a building larger than the others, but of like construction, surrounded by a high fence of canes, and near one end rose a stumpy flag-staff, and from its top hung a dingy piece of bunting, closely resembling the British Union Jack; and this was the custom-house of San Juan, the residence of all the British officials; and the flag was that of the "King of the Mosquitos," the "ally of Great Britain!"

But of this mighty potentate, and how the British officials came there, more anon. Just opposite us, on the shore, was an object resembling some black monster which had lost its teeth and eyes, and seemed sorry that it had left its kindred at the Novelty Works. It was the boiler of a steamer, which some adventurous Yankees had proposed putting up here, but which, from some defect, had proved useless. Behind the town rose the dense tropical forest. There were no clearings, no lines of road stretching back into the country; nothing but dense, dark solitudes, where the tapir and the wild boar roamed unmolested; where the painted macaw and the noisy parrot, flying from one giant cebia to another, alone disturbed the silence; and where the many-hued and numerous serpents of the tropics coiled among the branches of strange trees, loaded with flowers and fragrant with precious gums. The whole scene was unprecedentedly novel and picturesque. There was a strange blending of objects pertaining to the extremes of civilization. The boiler of the steamer was side by side with the graceful canoe, identical with that in which the simple natives of Hispaniola brought fruits to Columbus; and men in stiff European costumes were seen passing among others, whose dark, naked bodies, protected only at the loins, indicated their descent from the aborigines who had disputed the possession of the soil with the mailed followers of Cordova, and made vain propitiations to the symbolical sun to assist them against their enemies. Here they were, unknowing and careless alike of Cordova or the sun, and ready to load themselves like brutes, in order to earn a sixpence with which to get drunk that night, in concert with the monotonous twanging of a two-stringed guitar!

Our anchor was hardly down before a canoe came alongside, containing as variegated an assortment of passengers as can well be conceived. Among them were the officers of the port, whose importance was made manifest from the numerous and unnecessary orders they gave to the oarsmen, and the prodigious bustle they made in getting up the side. They looked inquiringly at the bright silken flag which one of the party held in his hands, and which looked brighter than ever under the rays of the setting sun. The eagles on the caps of the party were also objects which attracted many inquiring glances; and directly the captain was withdrawn into a corner, and asked the significance of all this. The answer seemed to diminish the importance of the officials materially, and one approached, holding his sombrero reverently in his hand, and said that "Her Britannic Majesty's Consul-General in Mosquitia, Mr. C——, was now resident in the town, and that he should do himself the honor to announce our arrival immediately, and hoped we had had a pleasant voyage, and that we would avail ourselves of his humble services;" to all of which gracious responses were given, together with a drop of brandy, which last did not seem at all unacceptable. I had warm letters of introduction to several of the leading inhabitants of San Juan, and accordingly began to make inquiries as to their whereabouts of a respectable looking negro, who was amongst the visiting party. To my first question, as to whether Mr. S—— S—— was then in town, the colored gentleman uncovered his head, bowed low, and said the humble individual named was before me. I also uncovered myself, bowed equally low, and assured him I was happy to make his acquaintance, delivering my letter at the same time with all the grace possible under the circumstances.

He glanced over its contents, took off his hat again, and bowed lower than before. Not to be behindhand in politeness, I went through the same performance, which was responded to by a genuflection absolutely beyond my power to undertake, without risk of a dislocation; so I resigned the contest, and gave in "dead beat," much to the entertainment of the Irish mate, who was not deficient in the natural antipathy of his race towards the negro. Ben, my colored servant, next received a welcome not less cordial than my own; and my new acquaintance "was glad to inform me, that fortunately there was a new house under his charge, which was then vacant, and that he was happy in putting it at my disposal." The happiness was worth exactly eight dollars, as I discovered by a bill which was presented to me four days thereafter, as we were on the point of leaving for the interior; and which, considering that the usual rent of houses here is from four to five dollars per month, was probably intended to include pay for the genuflections on shipboard. We were impatient to land, and could not wait for the yawl to be hoisted over the side; so we crowded ourselves into the canoe of the "Harbor Master," and went on shore.

The population of the town was all there, many-hued and fantastically attired. The dress of the urchins from twelve and fourteen downwards, consisted generally of a straw hat and a cigar, the latter sometimes unlighted and stuck behind the ear, but oftener lighted and stuck in the mouth; a costume sufficiently airy and picturesque, and, as B—— observed, "excessively cheap."

Most of the women had a simple white or flowered skirt (*nagua*) fastened above the hips, with a "*guipil*," or sort of large vandyke, with holes, through which the arms were passed, and which hung loosely down over the breast. In some cases the *guipil* was rather short, and exposed a dark strip of skin from one to four inches wide, which the wanton wind often made much broader. It was very clear that false hips and other civilized contrivances had not reached here, and it was equally clear that they were not needed to give fullness to the female figures which we saw around us. All the women had their hair braided in two long locks which hung down behind, and which gave them a school-girly look quite out of keeping with the cool, deliberate manner in which they puffed their cigars, occasionally forcing the smoke in jets from their nostrils. Their feet were innocent of stockings, but the more fashionable ladies wore silk or satin slippers, which (it is hoped our scrutiny was not indelicately close) were quite as likely to be soiled on the inside as the out. A number had gaudy-colored *rebosos* thrown over their heads, and altogether, the entire group, with an advance-guard of wolfish, sullen-looking curs, was strikingly novel, and not a little picturesque. We leaped ashore upon the yielding sand with a delight known only to the voyager who has been penned up for a month in a small, uncomfortable vessel, and without further ceremony passed through the crowd of gazers, and started down the principal avenue, which, as we learned, had been called "King street" since the English usurpation. The doors of the various queer-looking little houses were all open, and in all of them might be seen hammocks suspended between the front and back entrances, so as to catch the passing current of air. In some of these, reclining in attitudes suggestive of most intense laziness, were swarthy figures of men, whose constitutional apathy not even the unwonted occurrence of the arrival, at the same moment, of two ships could disturb. The women, it is needless to say, were all on the beach, except a few decrepit old dames, who gazed at us from the door-ways. Passing through the town, we entered the forest, followed by a train of boys and some ill-looking, grown-up vagabonds. The path led to a beautiful lagoon, fenced in by a bank of verdure, upon the edges of which were a number of women, naked to the waist, who had not yet heard the news; they were washing, an operation quite different from that of our own country, and which consisted in dipping the clothes in the water, placing them on the bottom of an old canoe, and beating them violently with clubs. Visions of buttonless shirts rose up incontinently in long perspective, as we turned down a narrow path which led along the shores of the lagoon, and invited us to the cool, deep shades of the forest. A flock of noisy paroquets were fluttering above us, and strange fruits and flowers appeared on all sides. We had not gone far before there was an odor of musk, and directly a plunge in the water. We stopped short, but one of the urchins waved his hand contemptuously, and said "Lagartos!" And sure enough, glancing through the bushes, we saw two or three monstrous alligators slowly propelling themselves through the water. "Devils in an earthly paradise!" muttered B——, who dropped into the rear. The urchins noticed our surprise, and by way of comfort, a little naked rascal in advance observed, looking suspiciously around at the same time, "*Muchas culebras aqui*,"—"Many snakes here!" This interesting piece of intelligence opened conversation, and we were not long in ascertaining that but a few days previously, two men had been bitten by snakes, and had died in frightful torments. It was soon concluded that we had gone far enough, and that we had better defer our walk in the woods to another day. It is scarcely necessary to observe, that it was never resumed.

Returning, we met my colored friend, who informed me that there was a quantity of hides stored in the house selected for my accommodation, but that he would have them removed that evening, and the house ready for our reception in the morning. Regarding ourselves as guests, whom it became to assent to whatever suggestion our host might make, we answered him that the arrangement was perfectly satisfactory, that we could sleep that night comfortably on board the vessel—a terrible fib, by the way, for we knew better—and that he might take his time in making such provision for us as he thought proper. We then sauntered through the town, looking into the door-ways, catching occasional glimpses of the domestic economy of the inhabitants, and admiring not a little the perfect equality and general good understanding which existed between the pigs, babies, dogs, cats, and chickens. The pigs gravely took pieces of *tortillas* from the mouths of the babies, and the babies as gravely took other pieces away from the pigs. B—— observed that this was as near an approach to those millennial days when the lion and the lamb should lie down together as we should probably live to see, and suggested that a particular "note" should be made of it for the comfort of Father Miller and the Second-Advent Saints in general. There was one house in which we noticed a row of shelves containing sundry articles of merchandise, among which long-necked bottles of various pleasant hues were most conspicuous, and in front of which was a rude counter, behind which again was a short lady of considerably lighter complexion than the average, to whom our colored friend tipped his hat gallantly, informing us at the same time that this was the "Maison de Commerce de Viscomte A. de B—— B—— et Co.;" the "Et Co." consisting of the Viscomte's wife, two sons, and five daughters, whose names all appeared in full in the Viscomte's circulars. Had we been told that here was the residence of some cazique with an unpronounceable name, we might have thought the thing in keeping, and passed on without ceremony; but a Viscomte was not to be treated so lightly, and we turned and bowed profoundly to the short lady behind the counter, who rose and courtesied with equal profundity.

We reached the beach just as the sun was setting, where we found our mate with the yawl: "An' it bates any city ye've seen, I'll be bound! It's pier number one, is this blessed spot of dirt where ye are just now; may be ye don't know it! And yonder hen-coop is the custom-house, be sure! and that dirty clout is the Nagur King's flag, bad luck to it! and it's meself who expects to live to see the stripes and forty stars to back 'em, (divil a one less!) wavin' here! Hurrah for Old Zack!—an' it's him that can do it!"

It was clear that our mate, who had not looked at a bottle during the whole voyage, thought a "d'hrap" necessary to neutralize the miasma of San Juan.

"Perhaps ye know what ye'r laughing at, my dark boy; an' it's meself that'll be afther givin' ye a taste of the way we Yankees do the thing, savin' the presence of his honor here," said the mate, dashing his hat on the ground, and advancing a step toward my new acquaintance, who recoiled in evident alarm. We interposed, and the mate cooled at once, and shook hands cordially with the colored gentleman, although he spoiled the amende by immediately going to the water's brink and carefully washing his palms.

While this scene was transpiring, a ghostly-looking individual, wan with numberless fevers, approached us. He was dressed in white, wore a jacket and a glazed cap, and upon the latter, in gilded capitals, we read "POLICE." He took off his cap, bowed low, for he was used to it, and said that Her Britannic Majesty's Consul General presented his respects to the gentlemen, regretted that, being confined to his house by bodily infirmity, he could not wait on them in person, and hoped that under the circumstances the gentlemen would do him the favor to call upon him.

We responded by following the lead of the wan policeman (there was only one other, the rest had run away,) who opened a wicket leading within the cane enclosure of the custom-house, entered that building, and ascending a rough, narrow, and ricketty flight of stairs, we were ushered into what at home would be called a shocking bad garret, but which were the apartments of Her Britannic Majesty's Consul General. A long table stood in the centre, and a couple of candles flared in the breeze that came in at the unglazed openings at either end of the apartment, giving a dim intermittent light, by means of which, however, we succeeded in discovering Mr. C——, the Consul General. He was reclining on a rude settee, and rose with difficulty to welcome us. He apologized for his rough quarters, betraying by his pronunciation that his youth at least had been passed among the haunted glens of Scotland. He had formerly been a member of Parliament, and had been nearly a year on this coast, in a service clearly little congenial to his feelings, and far from being in accordance with his notions of honor and justice. We found him intelligent and agreeable, and as free from prejudices as a Briton could be, without ceasing to be a Briton and a Scot.

The evening passed pleasantly, ("barring" the mosquitos,) and though we were told of scorpions, which are often found when people turn down their blankets, and of numerous lizards, which insinuate themselves over night in one's boots, we were too glad to get on shore to be much alarmed by the recital. Upon leaving, we were pressed to come every day to the consulate to dine; for we were assured, and with truth, that it was impossible to procure a reasonably decent meal elsewhere in the town. The Nicaraguans at the fort above, it was asserted, had bought up all the vegetables and edibles intended for San Juan, having determined to starve the hated English out, and there was not a foot of cultivated ground within fifty miles; consequently the market was poorly supplied, except with ship provisions, and of these we had had quite enough. This was far from being comfortable, for we had expected to find at San Juan a profusion of all the productions of the tropics, concerning which travellers had written so enthusiastically; to be put, therefore, on allowances of ship-biscuit and salt pork, was too much to permit any consideration of delicacy, so we accepted Mr. C——'s generous offer, returning on board to be phlebotomized by a horde of barbarous mosquitos, and to get up next morning feverish and unrefreshed, and only prevented from appealing to the medicine-chest by the happy consciousness that we were near the land.

The cook's nondescript mess to which we had been treated every morning since we left New York, and which had been called by way of courtesy "breakfast," was soon disposed of, and we went on shore, where our colored friend received us with a low bow, informing us at the same time that our house was ready. He led the way to a building not far distant from the "Maison de Commerce," opening upon aristocratic King street. It was constructed of rough boards, and was elevated on posts, so that everybody who entered had to take a short run and flying leap, and was fortunate if he did not miss his aim and bark his shins in the attempt. It was satisfactory to know that the structure was comparatively new, and that the colonies of scorpions, lizards, house-snakes, cockroaches, and the other numerous, nameless, and nondescript vermin which flourish here, had not had time to multiply to any considerable extent. And though there was a large pile of tobacco in bales in one corner, with no other object movable or immovable in the room, the novelty of the thing was enough to compensate for all deficiencies, and we ordered our baggage to be at once brought to the house. By way, doubtless, of indicating the capacity of the structure, our colored friend told us that this had been the head-quarters of a party of Americans bound for California for the space of six weeks, and that forty of the number had contrived to quarter here; a new and practical illustration of the indefinite compressibility of Yankee matter, which surpassed all our previous conceptions. Our friend had provided for us in other ways, and had engaged a place where we might obtain our breakfasts, and proposed to introduce us to the

"OUR HOUSE" AT SAN JUAN.

family which was to furnish that important meal. The house was close by, and we were collectively and individually presented to Monsieur S——, who had been a grenadier under Napoleon, had served in numerous campaigns, had been in many bloody battles, and had probably escaped being shot because he was too thin to be hit. We were also introduced to the spouse of Monsieur S——, who was the very reverse of her lord, and who gave us a very good breakfast and superb chocolate, for which we paid only a dollar each per day. It was a blessed thing for our exchequer that we didn't dine, sup, and lodge there! At the same place breakfasted a couple of Spanish gentlemen, who had come out in the schooner, with a valuable cargo of goods for the interior. Our hostess certainly could not have had the heart to charge them a dollar for breakfast, for they had heard of revolutions and a terrible civil war in Nicaragua, and had been fright-

9

ened out of their appetites. A "bad speculation" at the best was before them, perhaps pecuniary ruin. We pitied them, but our appetites did not suffer from sympathy.

The day was passed in receiving visits of ceremony, arranging our new quarters, rigging hammocks, (which we obtained, at but little more than twice their actual value, at the "Maison de" Commerce of the Viscomte,) and dragging to light and air our mildewed wardrobes. We thought of consigning our soiled linen to the women at the lagoon; but the sturdy blows of their clubs still sounded in our ears, and we trusted to the future; but the future brought rough stones in place of the smooth canoe!

That night we passed comfortably in our new quarters, interrupted only by various droppings from the roof, which the active fancies of sundry members of the party converted into scorpions and other noxious insects. All slept, notwithstanding, until broad daylight next morning, when every one was roused by the firing of guns, and a great noise of voices, apparently in high altercation, combined with the cackling of hens, the barking of dogs, and the squealing of pigs; a noise unprecedented for the variety of its constituent sounds.

"A revolution, by Jove!" exclaimed M——, whose brain was full of the news from the interior; "it has got here already!"

The doors were nevertheless thrown open, and every unkempt head was thrust out to discover the cause of the tumult. The scene that presented itself passes description. There was a mingled mass of men, women, and children, some driving pigs and poultry, others flourishing sticks; here a woman with a pig under one arm and a pair of chickens in each hand; there an urchin gravely endeavoring to carry a long-nosed porker, nearly as large as himself, and twice as noisy; there a busy party, forming a cordon around a mother pig with a large family, and the whole excited, swaying, screaming mass retreating before the two policemen in white, each bearing a sword, a pistol, and a formidable looking blunderbuss.

"They are driving out the poor people," said M——; "it is quite too bad!"

But the manner in which two or three old ladies flourished their sticks in the faces of our wan friend and his companion, betokened, I thought, anything but bodily fear. Still, the whole affair was a mystery; and when the crowd stopped short before our doors, and every dark visage, in which anger and supplication were strangely mingled, was turned towards us, each individual vociferating the while, at the top of his voice, we were puzzled beyond measure. "Death to the English!" was about all we could gather, until the wan policeman came up and explained, under a torrent of vituperation, that he and his companion were merely carrying into effect a wholesome regulation which Her Majesty's Consul General had promulgated, to the effect that the inhabitants of San Juan (which he called Greytown) should no longer allow the pigs and poultry to roam at large, but should keep them securely "cooped and penned," under penalty of having them shot by Her Majesty's servants; and as the aforesaid pigs and poultry had roamed at their will since the time "the memory of man runneth not back thereto," and as there were neither coops nor pens, it was very clear that the wholesome regulation could be but partially complied with. A stout mulatto, behind the policeman, carried a pig and several fowls, which had evidently met a recent and violent end; and we had strong misgivings as to the manner in which the various small porkers and chickens which we had encountered at the consul's table had been procured.

The pale policeman grew pathetic, and was almost moved to tears when he said that, while in the performance of his duty, he was assailed as we saw, and that all his explanations were unregarded, and he was disposed to do as his companions had done—run away, and leave the town to the dominion of the pigs and chickens.

The crowd, which had been comparatively quiet during this recital, now broke out in reply, and gathering countenance from the presence of the Americans, fairly hustled the policemen into the middle of the street, and might have treated them to a cold bath in the harbor, had they not been recalled by the voice of the Viscomte, who mounted a block and declaimed furiously, in mingled Spanish and French, against the "perfidious English," and talked of natural and municipal rights in a strain quite edifying, and eminently French. But as the Viscomte had been instrumental in bringing the English there, he did not get much of our sympathy. He had lost a pet pig that morning, which gave pith to his speech; and we determined to pay our particular respects to it that evening at the consul's.

To the appeals made to us directly, we were, as became us, diplomatically evasive; but the people were easily satisfied, and late that night we were treated to a serenade, the pauses of which were filled in with, "*Vivan los Americanos del Norte;* and next day the news was current that six American vessels of war were on their way to San Juan to drive out the English, whose effective force consisted of the wan policeman and his equally wan companion! And the consul himself did us the honor to hope that we had said nothing to encourage the poor people in their perversity, for he almost despaired of making them respectable citizens! They couldn't discern, he was sorry to say, their own best interests. We might have suggested to him that circumstances here were quite different from those which surrounded the little towns of Scotland, and that which might be "good for the people" in one instance, might be eminently out of place in another; but then it was none of our business.

During the day we paid a visit to the other side of the harbor, where some Mosquito Indians, who came down the coast to strike turtle, had taken up their temporary residence. They were the most squalid wretches imaginable, and their huts consisted of a few poles set in a slanting direction, upon which was loosely thrown a quantity of palm leaves. The

HUT OF MOSQUITO INDIANS.

sides were open, and altogether the structure must have cost fifteen minutes' labor. Under this shelter crowded a variety of half-naked figures, begrimed with dirt, their faces void of expression, and altogether brutish. They stared at us vacantly, and then resumed their meal, which consisted of a portion of the flesh of the alligator and the manitus, chopped in large pieces and thrown into the fire until the outer portions were completely charred. These were devoured without salt, and with a wolfish greediness which was horrible to behold. At a little distance, away from the stench and filth, the huts, with the groups beneath and around them, were really picturesque objects.

One hut had been vacated for the moment; against it the fishing rods and spears of its occupants were resting, and in front a canoe was drawn up; this attracted our particular notice, and I had a sketch made of it on the spot. As we paddled along the shore, we saw many thatched huts in cool, leafy arbors, surrounded by spots of bare, hard ground, fleckered with the sunlight, which danced in mazes as the wind waved the branches above. Around them were dark, naked figures, and before them were light canoes, drawn close to the bank, filling out the foreground of pictures such as we had imagined in reading the quaint recitals of the early voyagers, and the effects of which were heightened by the parrots and macaws, fluttering their bright wings on the roofs of the huts, and deafening the spectator with their shrill voices. Occasionally a tame monkey was seen swinging by his tail from the branches of the trees, and making grimaces at us as we passed.

The habits of the natives were unchanged in the space of three hundred years; their dwellings were the same; the scenes we gazed upon were counterparts of those which the Discoverers had witnessed. Eternal summer reigned above them; their wants were few and simple, and profuse nature supplied them in abundance with all the necessaries of existence. They little thought that the party of strangers, gliding silently before them, were there to prepare the way for the clanging steamer, and that the great world without was meditating the Titanic enterprise of laying open their primeval solitudes, grading down their hills, and opening, from one great ocean to the other, a gigantic canal, upon which the navies of the world might pass, laden with the treasures of two hemispheres!

CHAPTER II.

THE PORT OF SAN JUAN DE NICARAGUA; ITS POSITION; CLIMATE; POPULATION; EDIFICES OF ITS INHABITANTS; ITS INSECTS; THE NIGUA; THE SCORPION, ETC.; ITS EXPORTS AND IMPORTS; POLITICAL CONDITION; IMPORTANCE. PRESENT AND PROSPECTIVE; SEIZURE BY THE ENGLISH, ETC.—MOUTH OF THE RIVER SAN JUAN—THE COLORADO MOUTH—THE TAURO—NAVIGATION OF THE RIVER—BONGOS AND PIRAGUAS—LOS MARINEROS—DISCOVERY AND EARLY HISTORY OF THE PORT OF SAN JUAN.

THE Port of San Juan derives its principal importance from the fact that it is the only possible eastern terminus for the proposed grand inter-oceanic canal, through the territories of Nicaragua, via the river San Juan and Lake Nicaragua; and from the further circumstance of being the only available port of Nicaragua upon the Atlantic. The harbor is not large, yet it is altogether better and more spacious than is generally supposed. The entrance is easy, and vessels of the largest class find little difficulty in passing the mouth, and obtaining within a safe and commodious anchorage. It has been represented that, in consequence of the peculiar make of the land, it is extremely difficult to be found. This is true to a certain extent; but although the coast in the immediate vicinity is low, yet a short distance back the land is high and marked, and cannot be mistaken. With proper charts, correct sketches of the coasts, and with a lighthouse on Point Arenas, every difficulty would be obviated. This is evident even to the unprofessional observer. The harbor is probably adequate to every purpose connected with the proposed canal.

The town of San Juan consists (June, 1850) of fifty or sixty palm thatched houses, or rather huts, arranged with some degree of regularity, upon the south-western shore of the harbor. It is supported entirely by the trade carried on through it; and its inhabitants are dependent upon the supplies brought down from the interior, or furnished from trading vessels, for the means of subsistence. There are no cultivated lands in the vicinity, and excepting the narrow space occupied by the town, and a small number of acres on the island opposite, where a few cattle find pasturage, the primitive forest is unbroken by clearings of any description. The ground upon which the town is built is sandy, and although elevated but a few feet above the water, is, nevertheless, dry. The country all around it is low, and is a short distance back from the shore really marshy, interspersed with numerous lagoons. After penetrating a number of miles into the interior, however, higher land is found, with a soil adapted for every purpose of cultivation.

Although the climate of San Juan is warm and damp, it is exempt from the fevers and epidemics which prevail in most places similarly situated, upon the shores of the Gulf of Mexico and Caribbean Sea. I could not learn that any cases of the yellow fever, or *vomito*, have ever occurred here; and when the cholera, in 1837, (five years after the period of its ravages in the United States,) devastated the interior, and almost depopulated the ports to the northward and southward, San Juan entirely escaped its visitations. It may safely be said that there are few ports, if any, under the tropics of equal salubrity. The nature of the soil, the fact that the malaria of the coast is constantly swept back by the north-east trades, and that good water may be obtained in abundance, at a depth of a few feet below the surface, no doubt contribute to this result. It is, however, a singular circumstance, vouched for by the older residents of San Juan, that the island or opposite shore of the harbor, not more than half a mile distant, and which, from the greater depth of water immediately fronting it, and other circumstances, seems to be the best site for a town, is fatal to those who may attempt to occupy it. A settlement was commenced there a number of years ago, but the inhabitants were decimated within the first two months; after which the rest removed to the other shore. The same cause, it is said, led to the abandonment of the military works which the Spaniards had erected there before the revolt of the colonies. The cause of this difference is not apparent, but no doubt as to the fact seems to exist among the inhabitants. Foreigners at San Juan, however, by observing ordinary and proper precautions, need not, I am convinced, form exceptions to the general good health of the native inhabitants.

The temperature of San Juan varies a little with the different seasons of the year, but is generally pleasant, differing not much from that of New York in the month of July. The range of the thermometer is not, however, so great as it is with us during that month. During my stay in June, 1849, and upon my return in the same month, in 1850, the range was from 74° of Fahrenheit at sunrise, to 85° at the hottest hour of the day. In the evening there is usually a pleasant and invigorating sea-breeze.

The population of the town does not exceed three hundred, having considerably diminished since the English usurpation. Besides what may be called the native inhabitants, and who exhibit the same characteristics in language, habits, and customs with the lower classes in the interior of the state, there are a few foreigners, and some creoles of pure stock, who reside here as agents, or consignees of mercantile houses, and as commission dealers. There are also the English authorities, consisting chiefly of negroes from Jamaica. The inhabitants, therefore, exhibit every variety of race and complexion. Whites, Indians, negroes, mestizos, and sambos,—black, brown, yellow, and fair,—all mingle together with the

10

utmost freedom, and in total disregard of those conventionalities which are founded on caste. In what might be called the best families, if it were possible to institute comparisons on the wrong side of zero, it is no uncommon thing to find three and four shades of complexion, from which it may be inferred that the social relations are very lax. This is unfortunately the fact; and the examples which have been set upon this coast in times past, by Jamaica traders, have not had the effect of improving morals. There is neither church nor school-house in San Juan, nor indeed in the whole of what the English facetiously call the "Mosquito Kingdom." Before the seizure, San Juan was a curacy, dependent upon the Diocess of Nicaragua, but subsequently to that event it was vacated, in consequence of the obstacles thrown in the way of its continuance by the English officials, whose high sense of Christian duty would not permit them to tolerate anything but the English Church, which is, I believe, the established religion throughout the dominions of "His Mosquito Majesty!" Occasionally a priest, in his black robes, is seen flitting about the town; but unless it is desired to find out the residence of the prettiest of the nut-brown señoritas, it is not always prudent to inquire too closely into his movements.

The dwellings of the inhabitants, as already intimated, are of the rudest and most primitive description, and make no approach to what, in the United States, would be regarded as respectable out-houses. They are, in fact, mere thatched sheds, roughly boarded up and floored, or made of a kind of wicker work of canes, sometimes plastered over with mud. The furniture, which seldom consists of more than a hammock, a high table, a few chairs, and a bed, is entirely in keeping with the edifices. Yet, mean and uninviting as these structures are, they answer a very good purpose in a climate where anything beyond a roof to keep off the sun and the rain may almost be regarded as a superfluity. The heavy thatch of palm leaves or long grass is an effectual protection against these, and though it furnishes excellent quarters for scorpions, small serpents, and other pleasant colonists, yet these soon cease to excite apprehension, and, with the mice and cockroaches, sink into common-places. The sting of the domestic scorpion, so far as I am able to learn of its effects from others, never having myself experienced it, is not much worse than that of a wasp or hornet, and seldom produces any serious result. The *alacran del monte*, scorpion of the forest, or wild scorpion, is more to be dreaded; its sting sometimes induces fever, causing the tongue to swell so as to render utterance difficult, or impossible. This latter never inflicts its sting unless pressed upon, or accidentally disturbed by some part of the person. It is quite as common in San Juan as in any part of the country; being brought there probably with the Brazil wood, the knots and crevices of which afford it an excellent lodgment. And, while upon insects, I may mention a kind of a flea, called *nigua* or *chigoe* by the Spaniards, and "*jigger*" by the West Indian English, which generally attacks the feet, working its way, without being felt, beneath the skin, and there depositing its eggs. A small sack speedily forms around these, which constantly increases in size, first creating an itching sensation, and afterwards, unless removed, becoming painful. When small, it may be extracted without difficulty, but when larger, the operation is delicate and often painful; for if the sack is broken, a bad ulcer, extremely liable to inflammation, and sometimes affecting the entire foot and leg, is a probable result. The best surgeon in these cases is an Indian boy, who always performs the operation skillfully, and considers a *medio* (sixpence) a capital fee for his services. He has a sharp eye for "las niguas," and will frequently detect them before they are seen or felt by the strangers in whose feet they are burrowing. It is well to submit one's pedal extremities to his criticism as often as once every three days, while sojourning in San Juan, where this insect is more common than anywhere else in Central America. When to this digression on insects and reptiles, I have added that the harbor is infested by sharks, and that alligators are far from rare both there and in the lagunas near the town, the catalogue of things annoying and disagreeable to be encountered here is nearly complete. But after all, the inconvenience or danger from such sources is chiefly imaginary, and exists more in anticipation than in reality.

From what has been said it will be seen that San Juan has no resources of its own, and derives its present importance solely from the trade which is carried on through it with the interior. A considerable part of the exports and imports of Nicaragua passes here. The exports are indigo, Brazil wood, hides, and bullion, and the imports manufactured goods of every description, suitable for general use. The indigo and bullion go, in great part, to England, by the British West Indian line of steamers, which touches here monthly, and which has already nearly monopolized the carrying of those articles of high value but small bulk, upon which it is desirable to realize quick returns. The Brazil wood and hides, on the other hand, pass chiefly to the United States and Jamaica. By far the greater proportion of the carrying trade is in the hands of Americans, conducted through native houses, and through travelling agents in the interior: and considerably more than two-thirds of the tonnage entering the port is American. An Italian vessel comes once or twice a-year, and a couple of French vessels occasionally, as also some nondescript coasters, bearing the New Granadian or Venezuelan flags. A portion of the trade of Costa Rica, via the rivers San Juan and Serapiqui, is now carried on through this port. There are no means of ascertaining its value, nor that of the general commerce of San Juan, inasmuch as no regular tables have been kept at the Custom House. Previous to the seizure of the port by the English, in 1848, the duties collected here by the Nicaraguan government amounted to about $100,000 per annum; and as the rate of imposts was about 20 per cent., the value of the imports may be approximately calculated at nearly $500,000. Since the English usurpation, the trade has seriously diminished, in consequence of the depression and uncertainty which it has created in the interior, and which have induced many of the native merchants to contract their business. The additional duties levied by the usurping authorities have also contributed to the same results. They have imposed an import and export duty of 2½ per cent. ad valorem, and made other onerous restrictions on commerce. Under these, they have nevertheless lately farmed out the customs at $10,000 per annum, which, as this is apart from the cost of collection, implies a trade of at least $300,000.[1] The actual trade of the port may now be roughly estimated at $400,000, not allowing for the increase which has already followed the general commercial activity induced by the California movement, nor for the direct influences of the partial opening of the Nicaragua route of transit, and the consequent direction of public attention and individual enterprise to that portion of the Central American Isthmus. As the trade of Nicaragua, by way of this port must pass through the river San Juan, the Nicaraguan Customs Establishment has been fixed at the old Fort of San Carlos, at the head of the river, on the lake. The average rate of duty exacted under the Nicaraguan tariff, is about 21 per cent. ad valorem,[2] which, added to the

[1] Since the above was written, the collection of customs at San Juan, from motives of policy, has been *suspended*, but not permanently abandoned, by the British Government.

[2] It should be mentioned, however, that although the Nicaraguan tariff is nominally 21 per cent. ad valorem, yet as one half of the amount of duties may be paid in Government *vales*, or notes, which range from ten to sixty per cent. in value, according to their class and date, it is practically not more than 15 per cent.

British impositions at San Juan, makes the total duty to be paid on articles passing into the interior about 24 per cent.

When the political questions connected with British aggressions in Nicaragua shall have been satisfactorily and permanently adjusted, and the projected canal really commenced, this port will become one of the first importance, if not the most important, on the continent. Its prospective value can hardly be estimated; for apart from its position in respect to the proposed work, it is the only Atlantic port of one of the finest countries under the tropics, possessing inexhaustible agricultural and mineral resources, which recent movements indicate with certainty are destined to a speedy development.

As already observed, this is the only possible Atlantic terminus for the (probably) only possible ship-canal route across the continent. And this is to be regarded as the great and controlling fact which led to its seizure by the English, at the moment when it became certain that California would fall into the hands of the United States, and the question of an inter-oceanic communication became one of immediate and practical importance. The seizure, it is well known, was made under the shallow pretext of supporting the territorial pretensions of a tribe of savages, or mixed negroes and Indians, called Moscos, or Mosquitos, and in virtue of some equivocal relations which the pirates of Jamaica anciently maintained with them. When, however, it is known that this was the principal port of entry of Nicaragua under the Spanish dominion; that for more than three hundred years it was the avenue through which its trade was conducted; that the river flowing past it was defended by massive and costly works, which, although in ruins, are yet imposing; that no Mosquito Indian ever resided here; that all its inhabitants were, and with the exception of a few foreign merchants and the English officials, still are Nicaraguans; and that England herself recognized it as pertaining to

Nicaragua by blockading it as a part of her territories; and when to all this is added the fact, that the Mosquito Indians never, themselves, pretended to any territorial rights here or elsewhere, until induced to do so by British agents, the enormity of the seizure is rendered apparent. But as the facts connected with these and similar encroachments will form the subject of a separate chapter, it is unnecessary to refer further to them here. Since the seizure of the port, and in ludicrous commentary on the assertion of the British Government, that its sole design in taking that step was the "*re-establishment* of Mosquito rights and authority," its municipal and other regulations, not excepting its port charges and customs' rates, have been promulgated and fixed by an officer styling himself "Her Britannic Majesty's Consul," or "Vice Consul;" who has for his executive force a few Jamaica negroes, called, probably in irony, "police." He is, in fact, dictator of the place, and the inhabitants are subject without appeal to his will, for there are no written laws or fixed regulations of any kind. He assumes to dispose of lands, and gives titles under his consular seal; nor does he, ever so remotely, appear to recognize the so-called Mosquito King. Indeed, the only evidence that this farcical character is held in remembrance at all is that a flag, said to be his, is occasionally hoisted in an open space in the centre of the town. The English flag, however, floats over what is called the Custom House, and is the only one for which any degree of respect is exacted. The new tariff, promulgated here in April, 1850, was signed "J. M. Daly, Collector," and did not purport to have been enacted by any superior authority. Indeed, the present situation of the town, overawed as it constantly is by one or two British vessels, is anomalous in the extreme. If, as it is pretended, this port belongs to the supposititious Mosquito King, it is difficult to understand how a second party can exercise sovereignty over it; or upon what principles of international law the consuls of one nation can assume municipal and general administrative authority in the ports of another. The simple fact is, that Great Britain, having secured possession of this important port, under a pretext which deceives nobody, no longer cares to stultify herself by affecting to conform to that pretext. The thing is too absurd to be continued.

The River San Juan reaches the ocean by several mouths. The divergence takes place about twenty miles from the sea. forming a low delta, penetrated by numerous canals, or, as they are called on the Lower Mississippi, *bayous*, and lagunas. The principal branch is the Colorado, which carries off at least two-thirds of the water of the river, and which empties into the ocean some ten or fifteen miles to the southward of the port. There is an almost impassable bar at the entrance, which would preclude the ascent of vessels, even if the depth of water above permitted of their proceeding after it was passed. The little steamer "Orus," nevertheless, after repeated trials, succeeded in passing it in August last. There is another small channel called the *Taura*, which reaches the sea midway between the port and the mouth of the Colorado. The branch flowing into the harbor, the one through which the ascending and descending boats pass, carries off only about one-third of the water of the river. It has also a bar at the mouth, that is, at its point of debouchure into the harbor, upon which, at low tide, there are but three or four feet of water. This passed, the bed of the river is wide and studded with low islands; but excepting in the channel, which is narrow and crooked, the water is very shallow. It has been suggested that the Colorado branch might be dammed, and a greater column of water thrown into the other, or San Juan branch. But this suggestion can only be made by those who are wholly unacquainted with the subject. Allowing it to be possible to build a dam, the stream would find a new channel to the sea; or if it took the direction of the harbor, fill it up, during the first rainy season, with mud, or at once destroy the sandy barriers which now form and protect it. As will be seen, when I come to speak of the practicability of a canal, the utmost that can be done with the river is to dredge out the channel to the Colorado, and remove some of the obstacles at the various rapids above, after which it might be navigated by small steamers. It cannot be made navigable for ships or vessels of any kind, except of the lightest draught, by any practicable system of improvements.

The boats used upon the river for carrying freight and passengers are exaggerated canoes, called *bongos*. Some are hollowed from a single tree, but the better varieties are built, with some degree of skill, from the timber of the *cedro*, a very light and durable kind of wood, which grows abundantly about the lakes. The largest of these carry from eight to ten tons, and draw two or three feet of water when loaded. They are long, and rather deep and narrow, and have, when fully manned, from eight to twelve oarsmen, who drive the boat by means of long sweeps and setting-poles. Sails are seldom if ever used, except upon the lake. The masts are unshipped and left at the head of the river in descending, and resumed again in returning. These boats have a small space near the stern, called the "*chopa*," covered with a board roof, a thatch of palm leaves, or with hides, which is assigned to the passengers. The rest of the boat is open, and the oarsmen, or, as they call themselves, *marineros*, sailors, are without protection, and sleep upon their benches at night, covered only with their blankets, and with the gunwale of the boat for a common pillow. The captain, or *patron*, is the steersman, and occupies a narrow deck at the stern, called the *pineta*, upon which he also sleeps, coiling himself up in a knot, if the boat is small and the pineta narrow. The freight, if liable to damage from exposure, is covered with raw hides, which, between sun and rain, soon diffuse an odor very unlike the perfumes which are said to load the breezes of Arabia the Blest. The usual freight from San Juan to Granada, a distance of one hundred and sixty or one hundred and seventy miles, is from thirty to fifty cents per cwt.; if the articles are bulky, it is more. The boatmen are paid from seven to eight dollars the trip, down from Granada and back, which usually occupies from twenty to thirty days, although with proper management it might be made in less time. Time, however, in these regions is not regarded as of much importance, and everything is done very leisurely. It is only in active communities that its value is considered.

Columbus coasted along the entire eastern shore of Central America, from Cape Honduras to Nombre de Dios, or Chagres, in 1502, and was probably the first discoverer of the Port of San Juan. In 1529, Captain Diego Machuca, residing in the city of Granada, on Lake Nicaragua, undertook the exploration of that lake, discovered its outlet, passed down the San Juan to the port at its mouth, and sailed thence to Nombre de Dios. The principal rapids in the stream still bears his name. We are informed by the historian Gonzalo Fernandez de Oviedo y Valdez, who was in Nicaragua in 1529, and was personally acquainted with Machuca, that the latter projected a colony at the mouth of the river, but was interrupted in his design by Robles, commandant at Nombre de Dios, who contemplated the same enterprise. At how early a date the Spanish made establishments at San Juan, is not known; but it is a historical fact, that early in the seventeenth century a fort existed at San Carlos, which was captured by the English in 1665, but recovered by De Mencos and De Caldas, officers of Spain in the then Kingdom of Guatemala. (*Juarros' History of the Kingdom of Guatemala, Baily's Trans.*, p. 67.) In consequence of this event, a royal decree was issued, commanding that the entrance of the river should be fortified; which order was carried into effect by Don Fernando de Escobeda, who examined the port and river, and built a fort in obedience to his instructions. It is also a historical fact, that at the period of the *rebuilding* of the Fort of San Juan, on the river above, about 1727, a garrison was maintained here. At that time not less than twelve military stations existed on the river; the first was at San Carlos, at the head of the stream; the second at the mouth of the Rio Savalos; the third, a short distance from the mouth of the Rio Poco Sol; the fourth, the Castle of San Juan; the fifth, the Island of Bartola; sixth, a high bank below the Rapids de los Valos, called "*Diamante;*" seventh, at the Rapids of Machuca; eighth, on an island at the mouth of the River San Carlos; ninth, at the mouth of the Rio San Francisco; tenth, at the mouth of the Serapiqui; eleventh, at the point called "Conception," opposite an island of the same name; and twelfth, at the Port of San Juan itself, with an intermediate temporary station called "Rosario."

The commerce of Nicaragua with Europe and the West Indies was always carried on through this port; and we have records of as early a date as 1665, of vessels clearing for the ports of Spain from the city of Granada. San Juan was made a port of entry by royal order of the King of Spain, dated February 26, 1796. By a royal order of the 27th of March following, regulations were made for promoting the settlement of the country in the neighborhood of that port, among which was one authorizing the introduction, in the ports of Spain, of dye and other woods cut there, or of coffee grown there, free of duty. From this period an augmented military force was kept up at San Juan, and in 1821 additional defences were erected for their protection, as may be seen by the order of the Captain-General of Guatemala, of the date of May 2, 1821. Upon the declaration of independence, the royal troops were expelled by the patriots of Nicaragua, by whom the port was indisputably occupied until the British seizure in January, 1848.

CHAPTER III.

THE MAGNATES OF SAN JUAN—CAPTAIN SAMUEL SHEPHERD—ROYAL GRANTS—VEXATIOUS DELAYS—IMPOSING DEPARTURE—ENTRANCE OF THE RIVER SAN JUAN—"PEELING" OF THE MARINEROS—CHARACTER OF THE STREAM—THE JUANILLO—AN IMMEMORIAL STOPPING-PLACE—BONGOS, AND THEIR EQUIPMENTS AND STORES—MEALS—ESPRIT DE CORPS AMONG THE BOATMEN—THE "ORACION"—QUEER CAPRICES—MEDIO—OUR ACCOMMODATIONS—A SPECIMEN NIGHT ON THE RIVER—MORNING SCENES AND IMPRESSIONS—BONGO LIFE—THE COLORADO MOUTH—CHANGE OF SCENERY—THE IGUANA—A SOLITARY ESTABLISHMENT—TROPICAL EASE—THE RIO SERAPIQUI—FIGHT BETWEEN THE NICARAGUANS AND THE ENGLISH—"A FAMOUS VICTORY"—THE RIO SAN FRANCISCO—REMOLINO GRANDE—PICTURESQUE RIVER VIEWS—THE HILLS AND PASS OF SAN CARLOS—THUNDER STORMS—THE MACHUCA RAPIDS—MELCHORA INDIANS—RAPIDS OF MICO AND LOS VALOS—RAPIDS OF THE CASTILLO—ISLAND OF BARTOLA—CAPTURE BY LORD NELSON—THE "CASTILLO VIEJO," OR OLD CASTLE OF SAN JUAN—"A DIOS CALIFORNIA!"—ASCEND TO THE RUINS—STRONG WORKS—CAPTURE OF THE FORT BY THE ENGLISH IN 1780—FAILURE OF THE EXPEDITION AGAINST NICARAGUA; A SCRAP OF HISTORY—PASSAGE OF THE RAPIDS—DIFFERENT ASPECT OF THE RIVER—A BLACK EAGLE—NINETY MILES IN SIX DAYS—THE FORT OF SAN CARLOS—GREAT LAKE OF NICARAGUA—LAND AT SAN CARLOS—THE COMMANDANTE—HEARTY WELCOME—NOVEL SCENES—ANCIENT DEFENCES—VIEW FROM THE FORT—THE RIO FRIO—THE GUATOSOS INDIANS—A PARADISE FOR ALLIGATORS, AND SOME HAPPY INSTITUTIONS OF THEIRS.

MOST small communities have in their midst one or two resident notabilities, who are regarded something in the light of oracles, and to whom general deference is acceded. San Juan is not an exception; and Captain Samuel Shepherd is at once, *per se*, a personage so characteristic and so associated and identified with the place, that no description of San Juan would be complete in which he failed to be a prominent feature. His residence is the most pretentious edifice in San Juan; it is, in fact, the architectural wonder of the place, inasmuch as it is not only a framed building, but has a shingled roof and glazed windows. It was built by Captain Shepherd, in his more prosperous days, when he was the principal trader on the coast from Boca del Toro to Yucatan, and before age had crippled his energies, and reverses dissipated his fortune. He is now old and nearly blind, but hale, cheerful, intelligent, and communicative, and capable of giving more information relative to the coast than any man living. He seldom leaves his hammock, which is swung in the principal room of his house, and in which he receives all his visitors. We called upon him, on the second day after our arrival, and were received with every demonstration of respect. The captain was never more eloquent, and although he had always been classed as an Englishman, yet he said he was born in the United States, and meant to claim its protection as a citizen. He had been appointed "Governor of the Port," or some such nominal and trumpery office, by the British Consul, by way of conciliation, but he was not to be taken in so easily; and as for the orders which had been promulgated in his name, concerning the pigs and chickens, he protested it was altogether the consul's doings; he had shut up neither the one nor the other, and regarded these animals quite as good citizens as the rest; the consul might shoot any of them, (pigs or citizens,) if he dared. And as for the pretended English protectorate, and the authority assumed under it, the one was a fraud and the other an imposition; for whatever title the Mosquito Indians ever possessed, had been formally transferred and secured to him. And the captain here produced, from a very closely locked and substantial case, a variety of parchment grants and conveyances, bearing the "his + mark" of "Robert Charles Frederick," father of the little Sambo boy now wearing the Mosquitian purple, in which it was duly set forth and attested that "upon the 24th of January, 1839, in consideration of the true and laudable services rendered to us by Samuel Shepherd, etc., we, Robert Charles Frederick, King of the Mosquito nation, of our special grace, and of our certain knowledge and free motion, have given and granted, and by these presents, sealed with our seal, do give and grant unto the said Samuel Shepherd, etc., all that tract of land lying between Blewfields River on the north, and San Juan River on the south," etc., etc., in the most approved form, and with royal prolixity, all of which is duly witnessed, together with the peaceable transfer and possession of the territory in question, approved by General Slam, Admiral Rodney, Lord Nelson, and other equally distinguished personages,[1] comprising the august council of the breechless but imperial "Robert Charles Frederick." Several other similar and equally formal documents were produced, in which the various Mosquito potentates had transferred to Mr. Shepherd and his associates about two-thirds of their pretended kingdom. When, in 1841, the English government sent its agents here to secure the country as a dependency on the British Empire, their first act was to procure the revocation of these grants, by the young Sambo, "George William Clarence," which was accordingly done; the act of revocation setting forth, in a most unfilial way, that "his late majesty was not in his right mind when he made them," that is, *was drunk!* But Captain Shepherd protests that the revocation was procured

[1] Like most savages, the Mosquito Indians are exceedingly vain, not less of names than apparel. It is a common thing to see a black fellow, without hat, shirt, or breeches, strutting through the little Indian towns on the coast, in a buttonless military jacket, purchased from a Jew's cast-off clothing shop in Kingston, and given to him by some Jamaica trader in exchange for turtle shells. In nine cases out of ten the wearer proclaims his name to be Lord Wellington, General Wolfe, or Lord Nelson, or some other equally distinguished name, which he has heard the traders mention. The lowest rank thus assumed is that of General.

through the influence of Jamaica rum, that his titles are in no degree impaired by it, and that the "his + mark" of one savage is as good as that of another. He regards the British occupation, therefore, as a direct invasion of his rights and sovereignty, and insists that if the port does not belong to Nicaragua, it certainly does to him; a sequitur which we at once admitted, much to the captain's satisfaction, and to his admiration of American justice, discrimination, and judgment.

Once off from his hobby, the old sailor was more interesting, if less amusing, and talked of matters in general in a manner highly original. His account of the relations which existed between the mixed brood of Indians and Negroes on the coasts, and the Jamaica traders, was given with a directness somewhat startling to persons not yet emancipated from the conventional rigors of the United States, but which constituted the best evidence of its truth. To say that these relations were exceedingly free and easy, is hardly explicit enough, as will be admitted when it is known that the visit of the traders was looked forward to as a kind of festival, when all ages and sexes abandoned themselves to general drunkenness and indiscriminate licentiousness. Every old trader had a number of children at every landing-place or settlement on the coast; and on the occasion of each visit, he impiously baptized all those which he conceived might be his own. This indiscriminate intercourse, it can readily be imagined, has resulted in a complete demoralization of the natives, and has been attended by physical consequences quite as deplorable as those which have followed the intercourse of Europeans with some of the Pacific Islands. These relations were established by the pirates, when they thronged the Spanish main, from Jamaica as a céntre, and they are now referred to, by the British government, as an evidence of ancient alliance, and in support of an assumed protectorate! It was not without a feeling of sympathy for the almost sightless old captain, that we left him swinging in his hammock, where he is doubtless yet to be found, clinging hopefully to his parchment titles.

We remained six days at San Juan, at the end of which time, having witnessed a promiscuous affair called a fandango, not at all spiritualized by the West Indian variations on the none-too-delicate original, and exhausted the limited stock of amusements which the place affords, besides having become completely wearied with the low, monotonous scenery, and not a little disgusted because of the absence of those tropical luxuries of which we had formed so high anticipations, we were anxious for a change. But few boats arrived from the interior, in consequence of an attempted revolution, and these brought accounts of the state of affairs, which we afterwards found were much exaggerated, but which made us especially anxious to proceed on our journey. When, therefore, our baggage and stores had been fished up from the hold of the Frances, and piled in dire confusion in the middle of our partitionless house, no time was lost in preparing for our departure. Through the assistance of my colored friend, we had engaged one of the largest bongos then in port for our exclusive accommodation, paying dearly for the stipulation that no freight beyond our own should be taken,—an unnecessary precaution, by the way, of which our colored friend neglected to inform us, for the troubles in the interior prevented the merchants from shipping goods in that direction, and had it not been for our opportune arrival, the boat must have gone empty. This bongo bore the name of "La Granadina," and looked not wholly uncomfortable as she lay at her moorings, just off the shore. She had a crew of ten stalwart oarsmen, and was particularly commended on account of her *patron*, Pedro, one of the patriarchs of the river, who, amongst his other accomplishments, spoke a little English, of which, for a wonder, he was not at all vain. As soon as the arrangement was completed, our marineros made court to us most assiduously, fairly hustling each other for the honor (worth a *medio*) of carrying the members of our party backwards and forth from "La Grenadina." One of the number, a slight but well-proportioned Mestizo, was a subject for the

OUR BONGO—"LA GRANADINA."

Washingtonians, and won the soubriquet of "Medio," from his frequent applications for sixpence. On these occasions he would gravely take off his hat, and throwing himself in a theatrical attitude, bring his closed left hand with Forrestian force on his naked breast, exclaiming, "*Soy un hombre bueno!*" I am a good man! It was worth the money to witness the relapse from dignity to servility when the coin touched his palm. Medio little thought how strict a parallel he afforded to men in other countries, and loftier spheres of action. Medio's price was sixpence, although he had served as sergeant in the army, and distinguished himself among the "veteranos."

The day of our departure had been fixed for the 12th, at four in the morning, and Pedro had promised faithfully to have all things in readiness. With the anticipation of an early start, we bade all our friends good-bye over night, and retired early, declining any provision for breakfast on shore, lest we might cause delays in the morning. Morning came, but not a sailor was to be seen near the "La Granadina," except the one who had kept watch over night; the rest, he said, would be there "*muy pronto*," very soon; whereupon he dodged beneath the *chopa*, and composed himself for another nap. We waited an hour on the shore; meantime the sun came up, door after door was unbarred, and the people came streaming down to the water to perform their morning ablutions, evidently greatly puzzled to account for our presence there. Their salutations seemed to conceal a vast deal of irony, and I fear were not returned with the utmost amiability. At eight o'clock, after firmly resolving to hold Pedro to a strict accountability for his delinquency, we returned in high indignation to our old quarters, and despatched orders for breakfast. To our infinite surprise, Monsieur S. had already prepared it. He received us with a smile, and when the meal was finished, coolly asked our preferences for dinner! This was rather too severe an enforcement of our first lesson in native delays, and led to an explanation, in the course of which Monsieur told us that he had long since found out the absurdity of attempting to advise Americans in such matters; and ended with the assurance that if we got off by the middle of the afternoon we might regard ourselves as particularly fortunate. We nevertheless returned to the shore, and found part of the crew had assembled, and were collecting wood and arranging their kettles preparatory to making breakfast. Never was anything performed more deliberately; and the meal itself was disposed of with equal deliberation. It was nearly eleven when the kettles were again placed in the boat, and quite twelve when Pedro made his appearance. Fortunately for his sable skin, our impatience had taken the chronic form of dogged endurance, and we sat amongst boxes, trunks, and guns, silent and grim, but cherishing the determination to make ourselves even with the vagabonds before we got through with them. Monsieur S. proved to be right; and it was late in the afternoon before the last straggler was got in, and the signal was given for starting. We severally mounted on the naked shoulders of the men, and were deposited on the *pineta*, a novel mode of embarkation with which we afterwards became familiar. The sailors took their places, and Pedro, with a great conch shell in one hand, gravely stationed himself at the tiller. The sweeps were raised, and every eye was fixed on the Patron, who glanced over the crew, as much as to ask "all ready?" and then, raising the shell to his lips, gave a long, unearthly blast. The sweeps fell simultaneously into the wäter, the men uttered a *hoo-pah*, the crowd on the beach shouted, the women waved their rebozos, while Ben unfurled the American flag at the bow. La Granadina seemed to fly through the water, and our friend, the Consul General, protruded his head from his hospitable garret, and waved his adieus as we swept by. The crew of the little Francis also hurrahed from her shrouds, and altogether, as Pedro, dropping his conch, proudly observed, it was a demonstration worthy of the occasion. He evidently thought it would tell well in the United States!

We were too glad to get off, to care much for anything else; nor did we experience many regrets when we took our last look at the long, low line of huts, and found ourselves shut in by the green banks of the river. Fairly in the stream, and out of sight of the town, the oars were drawn aboard, and every marinero stripped himself of his scanty clothing, which was carefully wrapped up, and deposited in a protected place, nor put on again until we reached the head of the river. This somewhat startling ceremony over, each man lighted a segar and resumed his oar; but the strokes were now leisurely made, and the severe realities of the voyage commenced. For some miles the banks of the river, as also the numerous islands which studded it, were low, covered with canes, and with a species of tall grass called *gamalote*. In places the stream was compressed between the islands, with a rapid current; while elsewhere it spread out in broad, glassy reaches, of great apparent depth, but shallow everywhere except in the channel; which, as the bed of the river is sand, is narrow and tortuous, and constantly shifting. A few miles above the harbor, we came to where the Juanillo,

"Little John," rejoins the river, from which it diverges some twenty-five miles above the mouth. After winding through the low grounds back of San Juan, spreading out into lagunas, and at one place into a considerable lake, it returns to the main stream, purple with vegetable infusions. The Indians sometimes penetrate this channel in canoes, for the purpose of shooting the wild fowl which people its marshy, pestilent borders, and of killing the manitus, which here finds a congenial solitude.

During the rainy season the whole marshy region through which the Juanillo flows is covered with water, as is also nearly the entire delta of the river, which, in the ordinary stages, is nowhere elevated more than a few feet above the river. It was now the commencement of the rains in the interior; the stream was rising, and, as our freight was comparatively light, we were enabled to proceed without much difficulty. We nevertheless sometimes ran aground, on which occasions our men leaped overboard, and putting their shoulders under the boat, lifted it off. The bongos are sometimes obliged, both in ascending and descending, to take out part of their freight, and depositing the remainder beyond the shallower sections of the river, return again for it. This, however, occurs only during the dry season, when the river has probably not more than half the volume which it possesses during the period of the rains.

In the exhilaration of our departure we had quite forgotten the disappointment of the morning, and had abandoned ourselves to the enjoyment of the novelty alike of our circumstances and the scenery. But our day's annoyances were not complete. After paddling for perhaps five miles, we came to where the banks had more firmness, and were a trifle higher than below, and where the canes and long grass gave way to a rank growth of palms; their broad leaves forming a roof impenetrable to the sun. Here, at a place where the undergrowth had been removed, and the trees rose like gothic columns, with evergreen arches, covering cool, dark vistas, our boat was quietly thrust in shore, and we were astonished with preparations for another meal. We remonstrated, but it was of no use; all the bongos had stopped here from time immemorial, and Pedro told us, in broken English, that the *demonio* could not get the sailors by. And Pedro himself sat deliberately down on the *pineta*, and turning up his toes, began a grand hunt for *niguas*. Some of the men followed the example of the Patron, others lifted out the kettles, and still others built a fire.

Every bongo, on leaving the interior, takes on board a large number of plantains, not yet fully ripe, and which are therefore called *verdes*. These are detached from the stalk, "corded up" in the bow of the boat, and constitute the principal reliance of the men. A few, that are nearly or quite ripe, called *maduras*, are also taken on board for immediate use. Besides these, there is a box of jerked beef, or what the Americans ironically call *yard beef*,—i. e. beef cut in long strips and dried in the sun. Some bottles of *manteca* (lard), or a quantity of kidney fat and a bag of rice are added, and then the substantial supplies for the voyage are complete. The cookery is very simple. Stakes are driven in the ground to support the kettle, in which is first put a portion of fat, next a layer of *platanos verdes* from which the skin has been stripped, then a layer of beef cut in small pieces, a calabash of rice, some salt, and so on until the kettle is filled. Water is poured over all, and the whole is thoroughly boiled. While this is going on, the men amuse themselves with roasting bits of meat on the ends of pointed sticks. Nothing can be wilder or more picturesque than a dozen naked, swarthy figures crouched around the fire, in the deep shadows of the forest, protecting their faces from the heat with their hands, and keeping up the while a most vociferous discussion, generally about the merits of this or that bongo, or upon some other subject of equal interest to themselves.

When the mess in the kettle is cooked, each one fills his calabash, and with his fingers or a cocoa-nut spoon disposes of it at his leisure. As the "yard beef" has always a most suspicious odor, I could bring myself to taste the contents of the kettle but once. I must do the marineros the justice to say that it was not an unsavory dish. It is always arranged to have half a kettle full of the compound over, to which the men help themselves at their pleasure.

Besides these common stores, every sailor has a private stock, consisting, generally, of a bag of *tiste*, (parched corn, ground with cacao and sugar,) which is mixed with water, making a nourishing and most delicious beverage. He has also a few cakes of *chancaca*, or, as he calls it, *dulce*, i. e., unrefined sugar, which he eats in its raw state. A few stalks of sugar-cane are almost always to be found stowed away amongst the freight, upon which the men entertain themselves after the anchor is cast for the night. In fact, when they are not sleeping or at the oars, they are eating or smoking, and are as loquacious as a flock of parrots. A stranger would suppose they were constantly on the verge of a general quarrel. Yet, like the *arrieros* of Mexico, these men are, with few exceptions, good-tempered, honest, and trustworthy, and have an *esprit de corps* amongst them which is carefully kept up. They are governed by certain conventional rules, which none dare violate; and their quarrels are generally referred to the decision of the older and more influential individuals of their own number.

It was nearly sunset when the meal was finished; the boat was pushed out in the stream, and we were once more on our way. We had now come to that part of the river where the long, broad reaches commence, and were moving slowly and almost noiselessly along in the shadow of the trees, on the tops of which the sunlight was shining, when suddenly, as if by a simultaneous impulse, the sweeps were raised, and each sailor reverently took off his hat,—the hour of the *oracion* had come. The bowman commenced the evening chaunt, the chorus of which was taken up by the entire crew, with a precision, in respect to cadence and time, which could only result from long practice. There was certainly something impressive in the apparent devotion of these rude men, apart from the effect of the melody itself, caught up as it was by the echoes, and prolonged in the forest solitudes. Yet the impression was destroyed by one of those freaks in which the natives of this country seem to delight, and which constantly outrage the traveller's sense of propriety. No sooner was the chaunt concluded, than all hands gave a shout, and bending to the sweeps, pulled like madmen for a few minutes, and then as suddenly stopped again, and broke out in a paroxysm of laughter.

We afterwards frequently witnessed the same proceeding, but could never discover the reason for it, probably because there was no reason in the case. We came, in the end, to look upon it as a simple ebullition of animal feeling. The fit of laughter over, the men pulled steadily for a couple of hours, keeping time to a kind of round which was certainly not without a degree of melody, but which was chiefly acceptable because it required a full and rapid swing of the sweeps, and was therefore favorable to speed. We always applauded it, and when impatient of our slow progress, exercised our ingenuity to introduce it as frequently as possible without creating suspicion of the object. Our friend "Medio," however, sharper than the rest, detected us; but he was adroit enough to turn his wit to account, by exacting extra allowances of our *ardiente* as the reward of his silence.

It was long after dark when we came to anchor in the midst of the stream, at a point above the *gamalote* islands, which are always densely populated with mosquitoes. For this reason the bongos never stop over night near them, if it can be avoided. The sailors have also a fancy, whether well-founded or otherwise I am unprepared to say, that noise will attract these annoying visitors. The sweeps are therefore pulled on board, and the anchor run out as silently as possible, and all conversation thereafter is carried on in a suppressed voice.

One night on the river is much like all others, and our first may be taken as an "average" example of our nocturnal experiences. The trunks of the party had been packed beneath the *chopa*, with principal reference to a level surface. Upon these were spread ponchos, blankets, and whatever might contribute to relieve the unyielding sub-stratum, while the carpet bags, and gutta-percha pouches were reserved for pillows. A stout cord was fastened close under the roof, over which were hung a change of linen, and a few necessary articles of dress. Here too were slung, in easy reach, and with special regard to convenience in case of necessity, our guns, pistols, and bowie knives, with the requisite ammunition. A few books and materials for drawing were bestowed on a shelf beneath the *pineta*, where also Ben had established the commissariat department,—one which, above all others, is not to be neglected in ascending the San Juan. It was barely possible to sit erect beneath the *chopa;* and excepting the narrow space between it and the first bench, there was no room to stand, unless we encroached upon the Patron's *pineta*,—which, it may be mentioned, we were not scrupulous in doing. Here, notwithstanding the heat of the sun, I passed most of the day, to the thorough embrowning of every exposed part of the person. The thatched *chopa*, a paradise for insects, was covered with raw hides, and two immense ones were fixed at either end. When it rained, these were let down, converting the interior into a kind of oven, intolerably close and hot. After one or two trials, we preferred to take the risk of getting wet to that of being suffocated by the heat, and would not allow them to be lowered. In fact, after repeated wettings, their stench became unendurable, and we had them removed entirely, much to the astonishment of Pedro, who really seemed to relish the smell of putrescent hides! In the first class bongos, which have board roofs, with close joints, this annoyance is obviated. In these the traveller also finds a refuge on the top of the *chopa*, from the discomforts of the interior.

We sat up late, watching the men, who gathered in a group near the bow of the boat, each with a cigar in his mouth, a handkerchief bound round his head, and a blanket thrown over his shoulders. There they sat for hours, keeping up conversation in a low tone, and with every appearance of great earnestness. Finally, however, they broke off one by one, and stretched themselves each on his own hard bench. Ben, too, who had been with Fremont across the continent, had travelled all over Mexico, and was consequently a philosopher after his way, took to the only vacant bench, while Pedro coiled himself in a heap on the *pineta*. The night was threatening, no stars were visible, and we could only discern the dark water sweeping past us, by the light of the "fire-fly lamps." An alligator occasionally plunged heavily in the stream, but excepting the water rippling under the bow, all else was silent.

It was past midnight when the drops of an approaching shower warned us to seek the shelter of the *chopa*. We found our quarters sufficiently narrow, and the trunks, spite of ponchos and blankets, portentously hard. Yet, thanks to former experiences, I was soon asleep, and slumbered soundly until morning. A few straggling mosquitos, however, had disturbed my companions, who were up long before me, unrefreshed and complaining. Although it was hardly sunrise, we had been moving for two or three hours, and were past the Tauro mouth of the San Juan, and approaching the point of divergence of the Colorado. And although the banks were little if any higher than before, yet the feathery palms, of which I have spoken, were interspersed with other varieties of trees, some of which were of large size, and draped all over with vines, that hung in rich festoons over the water. Birds of varied plumage glanced in and out of the forest, and cranes and other water-fowl paced soberly along the sand bars, or flew lazily up the stream as we approached. Occasionally a pair of green macaws,—the macaw is never seen except in couples,—fluttered slowly over our heads, almost deafening us with their discordant notes. The air was cool and fresh, reminding me of a morning in June at home, and I experienced a degree of exhilaration in performing my morning ablutions which completely put to flight all my previously conceived notions of tropical lassitude. Mists lurked here and there in the bends of the river, and in shadowy nooks, but they gradually dispersed, and at eight o'clock, when the boat was moored under the shadow of a gigantic tree, the sun shone brilliantly upon a scene as luxuriant as the imagination can portray. Ben boiled his coffee at the sailors' fire, and we made our first breakfast on the river with a degree of satisfaction which, even at this distance of time, it is pleasant to recall.

At ten o'clock we were once more in motion, and shortly after came to the Colorado. At the point of junction, fourteen miles above the port, there is a broad reach, and the river at once assumes a more majestic character. As I have already said, the Colorado carries off fully two-thirds of the water of the river, so that no adequate idea of its size and beauty can be formed until the traveller has reached the main body of the stream. Here the banks become higher; the low islands disappear; and the river is walled in by a dense forest. To avoid the strength of the current, the boat was kept close along the shore, and the long vines, loaded with gay and fragrant flowers, trailed over the *chopa* as it passed beneath them. Brilliantly-colored birds sparkled in the cool, green coverts, and, for the first time, we saw the ugly iguanas looking curiously down upon us from the projecting limbs of the trees. They fully answered to Ben's description of very ugly snakes, which Nature, after forming the head and tail, had neglected, until it was too late, to roll into shape, giving them afterwards four legs, by way of compensation for her oversight. They abound in Central America, and are to be met with in almost every locality, but are particularly abundant on the San Juan, where they attain to great size. They are of a variety of colors, and the different species (of which there appear to be several,) are distinguished by other peculiarities. Hundreds of small size and bright-green color might be seen clinging to every little branch, or sunning themselves on every old trunk which projected into the stream. When disturbed, they would dash for the shore with great swiftness, literally walking the water. We shot many in our passage, but recovered few, as they are very tenacious of life, and often cling to the trees after they are killed. They are esteemed delicious food, and are eagerly sought by the marineros. I could never bring myself to taste them, although the flesh, after being cooked, looked sufficiently delicate and inviting. I do not know how close an anatomical affinity they sustain to the alligator, but their jaws and teeth are much the same, in miniature, and like the alligator they take to the water if closely pressed, when there is no hole or tree in which to find refuge. Their general ugliness is unnecessarily heightened by a kind of crest or integument which runs along the back, from the root of the neck to the tail, and which is elevated when the animal is frightened or enraged. I never overcame my aversion to these reptiles, although I afterwards brought myself to tolerate a colony of them, which had taken up their quarters in the adobe walls of my court-yard in Leon.

During the day we passed an island near the place of divergence of the Juanillo, upon which an adventurous Nica raguan from the interior had established a plantain-walk. His house was nothing more than a shed, and under it was strung a couple of hammocks, in which the master and his spouse swung slowly to and fro, complete impersonations of idleness and ease. A couple of naked children were rolling in the sand of the shore, upon which was drawn up a graceful canoe, the whole constituting a picture of primitive simplicity, to be found nowhere except under the tropics. Our men shouted, and were answered by a couple of wolfish-looking dogs, while the children scampered for the hut in apparent alarm, but neither father nor mother took the trouble to rise. Why should they?

That night we came to anchor a few miles below the mouth of the Serapiqui, and next morning passed the spot where the Nicaraguan boatmen had made their stand against the English, after the capture of San Juan. The position was well chosen, at the head of a long reach, where the river takes a sudden bend, and where the hills, for the first time, come down to the water. Here they had cleared off the trees, and with their trunks had constructed a hasty breastwork, fronting the river. This rude fortification was manned by about one hundred and twenty men, some armed with old fowling-pieces, but others having no weapons except their machetes. They had also one or two rusty pieces of artillery, which none of them knew how to use, and with these preparations they awaited the ascent of the English. The latter, made up of three hundred picked men, from the vessels-of-war "Alarm" and "Vixen," in launches carrying guns at their bows, reached this place on the 12th of February, 1848. There could, of course, be but one result. The Nicaraguans were dislodged, with the loss of some fifteen or twenty killed, and about the same number wounded. With an equal force and equipments, the issue might have been different. The English commander reported his loss at two killed and fourteen wounded, but the Nicaraguans protest that it was four or five times that number, and the men were anxious to convince us of the fact by opening the grave where the English had buried their dead. We did not, however, take interest enough in the matter to stop, and were consequently obliged to keep our doubts, if we entertained any, to ourselves. Certain it is, that the British commander did not include in his statement the loss of Mr. Walker, "British Consul and General Agent on the Mosquito shore," who, with a boon companion, was reported "accidentally drowned." Walker was the most effective agent in getting up the attack on San Juan, and in organizing the British pretensions, being always at hand to manufacture "historical evidence," and his death almost consoled the Nicaraguans for their defeat. Captain Loch was, I believe, promoted for his gallantry, in what the Admiralty termed "the brilliant action of Serapiqui." The whole affair was a wanton act of aggression, and worthy only of pirates. No wonder the sailors hissed "death to the English" through their closed teeth, as we swept past the scene of their humiliation.

The Serapiqui is a large stream, taking its rise at the base of the great volcano of Cartago, in Costa Rica. It is navigable by bongos for the distance of thirty miles, and is one of the avenues through which the inhabited part of Costa Rica is reached from the coast. Flowing wholly to the eastward of the mountains, where the rains fall during the entire year, the volume of water in this river is very constant. It is probably the largest tributary of the San Juan. There is a small spot of ground partially cleared at its mouth, where some families had established themselves previous to the English troubles. Upon the seizure of San Juan, they abandoned their plantations and moved into the interior; and so rapid is the progress of vegetation and the course of decay, that their rude dwellings have entirely disappeared, and no trace of former occupation is left, except a few plantain trees struggling above the rank grass and undergrowth which have since sprung up.

We passed the mouth of the Rio San Francisco during the

afternoon, and spent our third night above "Remolino Grande," where rock first appears in the bank of the river. This name is given to a whirlpool caused by the abrupt turning of the stream, which is here somewhat confined by its unyielding banks. Up to this time we had accomplished only about thirty miles of our voyage, and the easiest portion, for the current above is stronger, and we were now approaching the rapids, where progress against the stream is slow and difficult.

VIEW ON THE SAN JUAN; THE HILLS OF SAN CARLOS.

The next day we came to where the banks of the river were higher than we had yet seen, and where the scenery became, if possible, more beautiful than before. I never wearied in gazing upon the dense masses of foliage that literally embowered the river, and which, in the slanting light, produced those magical effects of shadow on water, which the painter delights to represent. We this day caught occasional glimpses of the high hills at the junction of the San Carlos with the San Juan, where the latter breaks through the barrier which shuts in the great basin of Nicaragua on the east. The afternoon was rainy, and heavy thunder-storms swept over as we approached the highlands. The marineros, nevertheless, seemed to relish the change, and pulled at the oars with renewed vigor. Just before sunset, however, the rains stopped, and as the atmosphere cleared, we found that we were at the mouth of the San Carlos, a broad and long stream, which, like the Serapiqui, takes its rise at the base of the volcano of Cartago, in Costa Rica. This stream, Pedro informed us, brings down immense quantities of volcanic sand, ashes, and decomposed scoriaceous materials, which it deposits at various points, forming what appear to be smooth sand-bars. The material, however, is so soft and yielding, that whoever ventures upon it, sinks at once to his middle. Near the mouth of this stream is one of the largest and most beautiful islands to be found in the river; and, as we approached, two manitees, feeding amongst the grass on its shores, plunged their unwieldy bulks heavily in the water. Above the island is the pass in the hills to which I have alluded, and which reminded me of the entrance of the highlands of the Hudson from the north. The mountains, upon the left, come boldly down to the water, and their tops were wrapped in clouds, lending to them the grandeur which in some degree always pertains to the vague and unknown. Here the river is much compressed, and the current deep and strong, requiring the utmost exertions of the men to carry the boat against it. With darkness came the rain again, and thunder-storm after thunder-storm rolled heavily along the heights of San Carlos. At times the mountain summits were literally wrapped in fire, and they seemed trembling to their very bases under the reverberating peals of thunder. None but those who have witnessed a tropical storm can fully appreciate Byron's magnificent description, or understand the terrible majesty of this elemental warfare. I slept but little that night, and shall never forget the excitement, novel and pleasurable, which I experienced under these new and singular circumstances. Towards morning I fell asleep, and was only awakened by Ben's call to breakfast,—broiled ham, fried plantains, bread, and chocolate.

From the mouth of the San Carlos to the first rapids, those of Machuca, the river seemed to increase in beauty. The banks were higher and firmer, and hills appeared, at intervals, in the background. The country here is evidently one well adapted for cultivation, and must ultimately become populated. At present a few Melchora Indians roam through its forests, deriving their support from the river and its tributaries. They are generally very shy of the boats, and retire upon their approach. One or two families, however, have overcome their fears, and from their communication with the boatmen, have picked up sufficient Spanish to enable them to carry on a broken conversation. Two of these Indians, an old man and a boy, came to us in their canoe, and offered some dried pieces of a large fish, which abounds in the rivers, called *Savalo*, in exchange for bread, plantains, or any other articles which the sailors might have to spare. Both were naked, and the old man was wrinkled and drooping, his gray hair matted on his head and shoulders, while the boy was lithe, bright, and sleek as a young panther. They looked curiously at our party, and frequently exclaimed, *blancos*, *blancos*, whites, whites! I gave them some fish-hooks, in return for which they insisted on my receiving a portion of their dried fish. Pedro endeavored to make them understand that we were from "El Norte,"—but they knew nothing of El Norte, and only shook their heads. They stand in great dread of firearms, as they have been wantonly shot at by passengers ascending or descending the river. And when they glanced under the *chopa*, and caught sight of our armament, they pushed off hastily into the stream; the boy standing in the bow, and striking with his paddle alternately on one side and the other, while the old man guided the boat. I did not succeed in procuring any words of the vocabulary of these Indians, but they are undoubtedly of Carib stock.

The rapids of Machuca, which derive their name from Capt. Diego Machuca, who explored this river in 1529, are the first and most formidable on the river. The bed of the stream, for nearly a mile, is full of rocks and stones, between which the water rushes with great force. The boats, in ascending, are kept close in the right shore, and are poled up, slowly and with great difficulty. In descending they are often kept near the middle of the stream, down which they come, glancing between the rocks with the rapidity of an arrow. In descending, in June, 1850, my bongo, which obeyed the rudder very imperfectly, struck with immense force, and got jammed between the rocks, with its broadside to the current, where we remained for thirty hours, until literally dragged out by the united crews of six boats, after half a day of incessant labor. The boat was of great strength, or it must inevitably have gone to pieces. Such accidents are not of frequent occurrence, as the marineros are extremely expert in the management of their bongos. We were four hours in passing the Machuca. From thence to the Rapides del Mico and los Valos, the current is strong, but the channel is free. These rapids are short, and less difficult to overcome than those of Machuca. It is nevertheless a slow and laborious task to make their ascent; and until they are improved by art, they must always be great obstacles to the navigation of the river. At present the steamer "Orus," sent out by the "American Atlantic and Pacific Ship Canal Company," lies a wreck on the rocks of Machuca.

On the morning of the 17th of June we made the Rapides del Castillo, commanded by the ancient fort of San Juan,

"CASTILLO VIEJO," OR OLD FORT OF SAN JUAN.

now called the Castillo Viejo, "Old Castle," We had looked forward to our arrival here with great interest, not less on account of the historical associations connected with the place, than because, from hence to the lake, the passage is quick and comparatively easy. The morning was wet and gloomy, and altogether the most forbidding of any we had yet encountered, hardly excepting that on which we had made the coast, in the execrable little Francis. I nevertheless put on my water-proof poncho, and took my seat by the side of Pedro, on the *pineta.*

A league below the fort we passed the island of Bartola, on which, beneath the dense verdure, we could discover traces of the ancient advance works of the fortress. It was here the English buried their men who were killed, or died of disease during the memorable but fruitless expedition against Nicaragua, in 1780, under the command of Colonel Polson, and Captain, afterwards Lord, Nelson. This island was carried by Nelson, who here distinguished himself for the first time.

Passing the island, we came to a broad and beautiful reach in the river, at the head of which, upon a commanding eminence, rise the walls of the Castillo. The hill resembles that of Chapultepec, near Mexico; is equally bold, and has been scarped to the steepness and regularity of the pyramids. The sides are now covered with bushes, and matted over with vines, but the walls still frown gloomily above the mass of verdure. At the foot, and nearly on the level of the water, is what is called the "*Platforma,*" where were the ancient water-batteries. It is now occupied by a few thatched houses,—the quarters of a small garrison kept here by the Nicaraguan government, as an evidence of occupancy, and to assist boats in passing the rapids of the Castle, which, although narrow, are very powerful, and better deserving the name of falls than rapids. Here the boats have to be "tracked up" by sheer force; and it is usual for all passengers to land, and to lighten the boat in every way possible. It is often necessary to take out a considerable part of the freight, or to wait for the arrival of another boat, so as to join forces in making the ascent.

Arrived in the eddy below the "Platforma," M. and myself bestrid the shoulders of our men, and were deposited on shore. We started at once for the castle, by a path which the garrison, under express orders from the government, kept clear of bushes. I glanced into one of the huts as I passed, but saw nothing beyond a very pretty yellow girl, swinging slowly to and fro in a hammock, with one naked leg hanging indolently over the side. She threw aside her long black curls, but, without changing her position, exclaimed, "Adios, California!" A party of outward-bound Californians had spent a number of days here, a few weeks previously, and had evidently been on familiar terms with the señora.

The ascent to the castle was very steep and slippery from the rain, which had fallen uninterruptedly all the morning. A wide and deep fosse ran around the brow of the hill, with perpendicular escarpments, which we crossed on a narrow causeway, evidently of comparatively recent construction. If the work seemed imposing from the river, how much more impressive was it when we looked down from its walls into two tiers of chambers sunk in the rock, and in which tall trees were growing, their topmost branches scarcely reaching to the level on which we stood. We descended by a bomb-proof stairway to the bottom, into what had been the magazine, and into the rocky chambers where the ancient garrison had been quartered, more than ever impressed with the daring and energy of those iron men who had subverted the empires of Montezuma and the Incas; and who, within fifty years after the Discovery, had traversed every part of the continent, from California to La Plata. We went into the chapel; there was the niche in which had stood the cross, and an effigy of "Nuestra Madre de Mercedes," "Our Mother of Mercy," and beneath it was the font for holding the holy water. By a passage, protected from shot, we ascended to what is called the tower,—a solid mass of masonry, rising some sixty feet above the lower works, with a parapet embrasured for twelve guns, and now almost as solid and substantial as if built but yesterday. In this climate, where the great corrodent, frost, never reaches, the durability of good masonry is almost incredible. The floor of the tower, with the exception of the centre, which had been broken, probably under the impression that treasure might be concealed there, was as smooth and firm as ever. Upon the western side of the work was the main entrance, the massive buttresses which supported the drawbridge, and a glacis, subsiding to a terrace, which had been the parade ground, garden, and cemetery of the garrison. All around the work on this side was an arched way, and immediately facing the draw, and firmly imbedded in the masonry of the tower, a block of stone, bearing a long inscription, but too much defaced to be perfectly made out. Its purport, however, is, that the castle was *reconstructed*, under royal orders, by the Governor Intendant of Nicaragua and Costa Rica, for the defence of the river, in 1747. How long previously works had existed there is now unknown,—probably from the middle of the sixteenth century. Great but ineffective efforts had evidently been made to dislodge or remove this stone, which bears too potential evidence against the pretensions of one "J. Bull," to be regarded with favor by any in his interest.

On the north-western bastion of the fort and looking both up and down the river, stands a sentinel's box of stone, and close beside it, firmly fixed in the walls, the stump of the ancient flag-staff. Within the box were yet to be seen the grooves which the muskets of the sentinels had worn in the stone. We thrust our heads through the windows, but saw nothing except Pedro and his men, some to their shoulders in the water, pushing up "La Granadina," and others tugging at the rope attached to her bows.

This fort was captured by the English on the 29th of April, 1780. The plan of the expedition was formed by Gen. Sir John Dalling,[1] and had for its object to get possession of Lake Nicaragua, and the cities of Leon and Granada, and thus to cut

SENTINEL'S BOX AT THE CASTILLO VIEJO.

off communication between the northern and southern Spanish possessions in America. The land forces were commanded by Colonel Polson, under whose orders Captain Nelson, then in command of the ship "Hinchinbrook," acted. The Span-

[1] Clark and McArthur's Life of Nelson, vol. p. 32.

ish garrison consisted of two hundred and twenty-eight men, under the command of Juan de Ayssa. Nothwithstanding the overwhelmingly superior force of the English, the siege was a protracted one. The castle was finally brought to terms by the English obtaining possession of a hill commanding it in the rear. By the terms of capitulation, "in consideration of the gallant defence of the fort," the garrison was permitted to march out with colors flying, drums beating, with lighted matches, muskets and sidearms, and to be furnished with vessels and provisions to convey them to any port of Spain in America which might be agreed upon.[1] This triumph was dearly purchased, and was productive of no good results. The entire expedition was a failure, and is passed over very lightly in the English annals. Of the two hundred men comprising the crew of Nelson's vessel, but ten survived the expedition, and he himself narrowly escaped death. In January, 1781, the English abandoned the castle, and withdrew to Jamaica. Collingwood apologises for the failure of the expedition, on the ground that "it was formed without a sufficient knowledge of the country, and presented difficulties not to be surmounted by human skill and perseverance. It was dangerous to proceed on the river, from the rapidity of the current, and the numerous falls over rocks which intercepted the navigation; the climate, too, was deadly, and no constitution could resist its effects."[2]

Some conception of the difficulty of ascending the rapids of the Castillo may be formed from the fact, that it required the utmost exertion of our men, for nearly three hours, to get "La Granadina," with no freight, past them. The boat once up, the crew made breakfast; and after glancing over the list of the Californian party, who had not neglected to

[1] Beatson's "Naval and Military Memoirs of Great Britain," vol. v. p. 97, and vol. vi. p. 230.

[2] Memoirs, 5th ed., vol. i. p. 10.

inscribe their names conspicuously on the walls of the fort, we descended, thoroughly drenched with the rain. I had the toothache, and M—— the rheumatism, for a week, "by way of improvement" on our visit to the Castillo. The commandant of the garrison, having found out who were his visitors, was there to receive us; and from him we learned that we were expected in the interior, and that instructions had gone out from the government to all its officers to treat us with every possible respect, and to afford every facility to our progress. He had accordingly come to put himself "at our disposition." Being hungry, the colloquy took place, on the part of the representative of El Norte, in the intervals which could be spared from Ben's broiled ham and coffee. For an appetite, and a corresponding contempt for etiquette, I recommend a three hours' visit to the Castillo Viejo, before breakfast.

A few miles above the Rapides del Castillo, are the Rapides del Toro, which, however, are not strong, and are easily passed. Beyond these the river becomes of very nearly uniform width, and flows with a deep, regular current. This part of the stream is, in fact, a kind of estuary, or extension of Lake Nicaragua. The banks are low, and the feathery palm again appears lining the shores. The whole country on both shores, for a long distance back, is swampy, and in parts covered with water in the rainy season. Quite a number of sluggish streams, nevertheless, flow through it, whose names indicate the character of their banks and the surrounding country. There is the Rio Palo del Arco, "Arched with Trees;" the Rio Poco Sol, "Little Sun;" Rio Roblito, Mosquito, etc.

It was on the morning of the sixth day after our departure from San Juan, that the boat was pushed in to the low bank for breakfast, at a point but five miles below the Fort of San Carlos, situated at the head of the river, on the lake. Myriads of water-fowl lined the shores, and never so much as moved from the trees above us while we breakfasted. Among them Ben discovered a majestic black eagle, which he shot. The bird fell near us, but as we approached him, he threw himself on his back, with open beak, fierce eye, and threatening talons, defiant to the last. I would have given more than one hard dollar to have undone the wanton act, and sent the proud bird unharmed once more, free to his native mountains.

Although the novelty of our ascent, (ninety miles in six days, think of that, ye voyagers on the Hudson or our western rivers!) had in some degree compensated for its tediousness, and we had "put in" the time rather agreeably than otherwise, yet it was with unqualified satisfaction that we learned that we had nearly passed the river. We were impatient to look upon the great lake, of which the world had heard so much but knew so little, and thought our progress, over the intervening five miles, unaccountably slow. At eleven o'clock, however, upon passing a large island, the river opened in a broad reach, and we saw before us the waters of the lake. A commanding eminence, cleared of trees, and surmounted by a few houses and a flag-staff, rose where the lake terminated and the river commenced. The men seemed hardly less pleased than ourselves; but after pulling with great energy for a few minutes, suddenly stopped, and simultaneously plunged overboard. We had become accustomed to all sorts of fantastic freaks, and contented ourselves with looking on without asking questions. After paddling about for a while, they clambered aboard, and then commenced a grand hunt for the clothes which had been so summarily laid aside when we left San Juan. These were dragged to light from all conceivable out-of-the-way nooks, and directly the whole crew was dressed in clean attire, which made us quite ashamed of our soiled garments. The economy, not to say the convenience, of going naked, for the purpose of keeping one's clothes clean, was never more manifest. Pedro insisted on having the flag unfurled from the *pineta*, and before we had got within a mile from the fort, produced his conch-shell, and blew an awful blast upon it. A few figures appeared on the hill near the flag-staff, and directly the blue and white flag of Nicaragua, with an oval in the centre, containing three volcanoes and the rising sun, was run to its top. The roll of a drum, and the glancing of polished arms in the sun, showed us that we were recognized, and made us more than ever ashamed of our shabby exteriors. But what was to be done? Our trunks were wedged immovably beneath us, and if once dragged out, to our future eminent discomfort, where and how could we make our toilet? Besides we had no time for operations, the men were pulling with all their force, and we were rapidly nearing the fort. M——, with one foot wrapped in a napkin, (a nigua had unluckily escaped detection at San Juan,) proposed that we should throw our gutta percha ponchos over our garments, and decline going on shore, as the only feasible means of keeping up appearances. This was hardly agreed upon and done, before "La Granadina" dashed round the point, and up to the landing of San Carlos. The commandante and his subordinates, in full uniform, the officers of the Aduana or Custom-House, and a large deputation of the people, were all on the beach to receive us, which they did with a storm of vivas, and before we had well recovered from our surprise, a canoe was placed alongside, and the first Alcalde desired us to land. We were, of course, extremely obliged, but preferred to remain on board, as we should proceed at once. Pedro spoiled this by saying that he must ship his masts here, and that his men must eat, and we knew this double performance was good for five or six hours. So, trusting to the impenetrable ponchos, we got into the canoe, and were guided to the shore. We did not feel particularly imposing while receiving the congratulations of our new friends, and at once accepted the proposal of the commandante to go to his house, which was airily situated at the top of the hill, and within what had been part of the ancient defences. Here about twenty-five men, composing the garrison, were drawn up, who presented arms as we passed.

The commandante's house, like all the rest, was composed of a substantial frame-work of timber; the sides were made of canes netted together, the roof was thatched, and the floor the natural earth, excepting that of one room, which was paved with brick tiles. A number of pigeons were billing and cooing in a snug place under the eaves; an exceedingly quiet hen sat brooding beneath a table in one corner of the principal room, and through an opening in a cloth partition, we caught sight of a pretty bed, with snow-white curtains, with a gaudy palm mattress spread in front, on which a full-sized, voluptuously-shaped young woman was playfully tossing a naked infant, some six months old, which crowed in very glee, while a young, clumsy little dog leaped around the child, and barked asthmatically from sheer sympathy. The cool wind rustled amidst the palm thatch, while the sunlight stole in checkered mazes between the woven canes. Altogether the scene, combining so much of simplicity and novelty, impressed me more than any I had ever witnessed. I forgot, for the moment, that I was keeping my host standing, and that the servant was holding the hammock, which invariably swings in every dwelling, open for my reception. I apologized, while the little garrison, bringing their arms to shoulder with a clang, defiled before the door, the officer saluting us in a most formal manner. Our host was anxious to have us remove our ponchos, and seemed puzzled at our pertinacity in keeping them on. By-and-by, however, they became insupportably hot, and, as the best way of getting out of them and a scrape together, I frankly told the whole story of our dilemma, and dragged off the abominations. I fear "El Norte" did not cut a very imposing figure, under the close scrutiny to which he was subjected.

The commandante insisted on our dining, and we had no indisposition to do him the favor,—particularly as we had ocular demonstration, in the flitches of dried meat, the luscious-looking plantains, and other edibles, which hung from the rafters, (not less than in the person of our rotund host, whose uniform was strained to the utmost limit in the buttoning,) that his larder was well supplied, and the wants of the inner man properly cared for. Preparatory to taking a walk through the little village, which the commandante told us was "muy pobre," very poor, we all took a drop of brandy, to his toast complimentary to us, and "to the President of the United States," "El Esclarecido General Taylor."

I have said that the house of the commandante stood within the ancient outworks of the strong fort of San Carlos. The rocky summit of the point had been smoothed, and the slopes scarped, so as to render ascent difficult, if not impracticable. A battery, which raked the river for a mile, once existed here; but the few rusty guns which remain are more formidable in appearance than in fact. The fort itself, which formerly communicated with this battery by a covered way, stands some distance back, on the highest point of land in the vicinity. It was very strong, but is now in complete decay, and covered with large trees and bushes, so as to be entirely hidden from view. Within it we observed many very heavy pieces of ordnance, some of which were cast in Manilla, and trees were growing up through heaps of rusty cannon-balls. The position completely commands the entrance to the lake, and from the nature of the surrounding country must have been nearly impregnable.

The present town of San Carlos consists only of some twenty cane or board houses, occupied chiefly by the officers of the customs, and the soldiers with their families. Since the seizure of San Juan, the customs on goods entering the State, via that port, have been collected here. This circumstance, together with the fact that all the boats passing through the river stop here to unship or resume their masts, and renew their supplies, makes it a place of some importance. It is delightfully situated, and from the corridor of the commandant's house, one of the finest views in the world is presented to the traveller. The broad lake spreads like a mirror in front, its opposite shores marked by the regular volcanic peaks of Orosi, Madeira, and Ometepec, capped with clouds, which rise dim and blue in the distance. Nearer lie the fairy-looking islands of La Boqueta, golden under the tropical sun, while in the foreground the emerald shores stretch their wide arms on either side, a fit setting for so gorgeous a picture. Immediately opposite the town, flowing into the lake, within a few rods of where the San Juan flows out, is the Rio Frio, Cold River, whence the water for consumption in the village is brought. The sources of this river have never been explored, but they are supposed to be somewhere in the mountains of Costa Rica.

A tribe of Indians, called the *Guatosos*, who hold no communication with the whites, inhabit its banks, and resist all attempts at exploration. The late commandante of the fort, Don Trinidad Salazar, endeavored to ascend the stream a few months previously to our arrival; but on the sixth day he was interrupted by a large body of Indians, and after a sharp contest, in which he was severely wounded, was compelled to retreat. He subsequently gave me a glowing account of the beauty of the stream, and the fertility and luxuriance of its shores. It has a depth of two fathoms of water, for a distance of forty miles above its mouth, and from his account, it could probably be navigated by steamers for twice that distance. The fact that a stream of this size, and the wide extent of country around it, are wholly unknown, would seem to show how much remains to be discovered in Central America, and how broad a field it holds out for enterprise and adventure.

Between the mouth of the Rio Frio and the source of the

San Juan, is a broad sand-bar, which seems to be a grand sunning-ground for alligators. Hundreds congregate here during the dry season, when the bar is exposed, and they appear to have an exceedingly good time of it. We could distinctly see their ugly, black carcasses from the commandante's corridor; and our host showed us a basket of their teeth, which he had picked up on the bar, and which were more pleasant to contemplate in that condition, than when adorning the jaws of the living reptile.

A French officer, in the Nicaraguan service, (who was foolish enough to take part against the government in an attempted revolution shortly after, and got shot for his pains,) gave us some facts relative to alligators, of which we were previously ignorant. Those most satisfactory were that they occasionally have terrible fights among themselves, in which many get killed, and that the males destroy all the eggs of the females they can find, besides, Saturn-like, eating up all the young ones they can catch. We only regretted that they were not more successful in their amiable attentions to their own progeny.

THE IGUANA.

CHAPTER IV.

SAN CARLOS—DINNER AT THE COMMANDANTE'S—INTRODUCTION TO "TORTILLAS Y FRIJOLES"—A SIESTA—NEWS OF THE ATTEMPTED REVOLUTION—ANTICIPATING EVENTS, AND WHAT HAPPENED TO THE COMMANDANTE AFTER WE LEFT—DEPARTURE UNDER A MILITARY SALVO—VIEW OF SAN CARLOS FROM THE LAKE—LAKE NAVIGATION—CARD PLAYING—GORGEOUS SUNSET—A MIDNIGHT STORM—SAN MIGUELITO, AND THE "BATH OF THE NAIDES"—PRIMITIVE SIMPLICITY—A DAY ON THE LAKE—"EL PEDERNAL"—A BATH WITH ALLIGATORS—AN "EMPACHO"—A TRIAL AT MEDICINE, AND GREAT SUCCESS—SECOND NIGHT ON THE LAKE—THE VOLCANOES OF MOMOBACHO, OMETEPEC, AND MADEIRA—VOLCANIC SCENERY—THE COAST OF CHONTALES—THE CREW ON POLITICS—"TIMBUCOS" AND "CALANDRACAS," OR A GLANCE AT PARTY DIVISIONS—ARRIVAL AT "LOS CORALES"—SOME ACCOUNT OF THEM—ALARMING NEWS—A COUNCIL OF WAR—FAITH IN THE UNITED STATES FLAG—THE ISLAND OF CUBI—MORE NEWS, AND A RETURN OF THE "EMPACHO"—DISTANT VIEW OF GRANADA—MAKING A TOILETTE—BEES—ARRIVAL AT THE RUINED FORT OF GRANADA—HOW THEY LAND THERE—SENSATION AMONGST THE SPECTATORS—ENTRANCE TO THE CITY—THE ABANDONED CONVENT OF SAN FRANCISCO—THE HOUSES OF THE INHABITANTS—FIRST IMPRESSIONS—SOLDIERS AND BARRICADES—THRONGED STREETS—SENOR DON FREDERICO DERBYSHIRE—"OUR HOST"—A WELCOME—OFFICIAL COURTESIES—OUR QUARTERS—FIRST NIGHT IN GRANADA.

Two hours sufficed to exhaust the lions of San Carlos, including the arsenal, which was a cane hut, with a quantity of powder in kegs, piled in the middle and covered with hides; two pieces of artillery, and a hundred stand of arms, over all of which a single sentinel kept watch, and the public warehouse or *bodega*, which was nothing more than a great shed, with convenient hammocks for its idle guardians,—we saw all these before two o'clock, at which hour dinner was served in the commandante's house. The table-cloth was unimpeachably white, and the service altogether neat and ample. It was clearly the intention of our host to do his best; even the pigeons seemed impressed with the idea that something extraordinary was going on, and the hen in the corner was nervous with excitement in view of the display. All the juvenile population of the place, if possible still more airily dressed than the urchins at San Juan, crowded round the doors, (they had followed us, at a distance, during our peregrinations), and regarded the whole affair with evident admiration. A number of their seniors, comprising the more respectable part of the inhabitants, arrayed for the occasion, in snow-white shirts and pantaloons, each with white buck-skin shoes, and a red sash, now made their appearance, and were collectively and individually introduced, to the renewal of our mortification on the score of dress.

We sat down at the table, which was placed so as to give me the seat of honor in the hammock, while the commandante and his lieutenant, took, respectively, the head and foot. They declined to eat, devoting themselves wholly to supplying their guests. This, we afterwards learned, was Nicaraguan etiquette, when special distinction was intended to be conveyed. We were now, for the first time, introduced to the eternal *tortilla* and the omnipresent *frijoles*, to say nothing of the endless variety of *dulces* (sweetmeats), for which all Spanish America is famous. We commenced with beef, culminated over chicken, and finished with oranges, bananas, coffee, and cigars; with a pleasant stomachic conviction that good dinners were not incompatible with cane-huts, brooding hens in the corners, and amative pigeons under the eaves! We were anxious to see the señorita, of whom we had had a glimpse on our arrival, and whose low, laughing voice we occasionally heard through the cloth partition; but this was a delicate point, which we were cautious in touching upon, since M—— had found out that the commandante was a bachelor. Ah, commandante! I may have been mistaken, but I feel very sure it was a large black eye which I caught merry glances of through a small rent in that cloth partition!

A siesta was strongly commended to us after dinner, and hammocks were strung for the whole party. It was indispensable, our host told us, in this climate, and he wondered how it could be omitted in El Norte. Life, in his opinion, without a siesta after dinner, must soon become a wearisome affair,—and he quoted some verses from a native poet which were conclusive on the subject; so we yielded, and lay down; the people left, the doors were closed, and all was silent—even the pigeons were still. Two hours passed in a dreamy, pleasurable way, with just enough of consciousness to enjoy the mingled sensation of novelty and ease, when Ben came to apprise us that the boat was ready, and the crew on board. Our host pressed us to stay until the next morning, but the wind and weather were fair; and, although the temptation was strong, we adhered to our first intentions, and were deaf to argument. Before leaving, I inquired about the revolution of which we had heard so much at San Juan, but got no very satisfactory information. There had been an "escaramúza," a scrimmage, at Granada, and a lawless, reckless fellow, under proscription for murder, named Somoza, had collected together a party of adherents, and sacked the city of Rivas or Nicaragua. The commandante was certain that peace and order were by this time restored; but if they were not, our arrival would certainly produce quiet. The commandante hardly thought that the same robber chief, of whom he spoke so lightly, would pay him a visit within a fortnight, and carry him off a prisoner! But so it proved to be; and although our commandante effected his escape, at imminent peril, through a wilderness, unarmed and alone, yet he was suspected of cowardice, imprisoned, and court-martialed. He came out safely, however, a shade less rotund perhaps, "a wiser if not a better man;" and before I left the country I had the satisfaction of seeing him reinstated at the fort, fat, happy, and hospitable as ever. The dark-eyed señorita was there too.

At five o'clock we embarked, for the first time, on Lake Nicaragua. The people all came to bid us good-bye; and one old man insisted upon a parting embrace. Like the prophet of old, he said he was now ready to die, for he knew that his country was safe beneath the guardianship of the Republic of the North. We pushed off under a torrent of *vivas*, and a *feu de joie* was fired by the little garrison, which Ben efficiently returned with his double-barrelled gun, while Pedro blew another nerve-cracking blast on his conch—that awful conch! The view of San Carlos, from the lake, was picturesque in the extreme, and the accompanying sketch of it will be sufficiently curious twenty years hence, when it shall have become, as it inevitably will, a large and important town. Already a steamer plies regularly between San Carlos and Granada; and the alligators, disturbed in their slumbers on the sand-bar, by its plashing wheels and noisy engine, are meditating a grand migration into the country of the Guatosos.

The faintest of all zephyrs was dying away on the lake when we started, yet we had not gone half a mile before the oars were drawn aboard, and a huge triangular sail spread from the newly-rigged mast. The breeze was hardly strong enough to fill it; and the boat dawdled, rather than moved, through the water. We expostulated with Pedro; but it was useless; the marineros never did row while there was the least apology for a wind abroad, and the "demonio" himself couldn't make them. So Pedro lit his cigar, while the men produced a pack of cards, and commenced a game, novel enough to us, in which it was the privilege of the winner to pinch, beat, and otherwise maltreat the loser, who was obliged to submit without resistance, until the spectators pronounced "bastante," enough. One fellow, who was a

SAN CARLOS—OUTLET OF LAKE NICARAGUA.

little rebellious, was incontinently thrust overboard, to the great damage of a gaudy bandana handkerchief which he wore about his head, and to the manifest delectation of the crew, who jibed him unmercifully as a "ladron," and "picaro," "a rascal" and "a loafer."

The sun went down that night directly behind the purple peak of Orosi. The body of the volcano appeared to be a nucleus, whence fan-like rays radiated up to the very zenith, while the yellow light streamed past the mountain upon the lake, in a dazzling flood, in which the islands of Solentenami and La Boqueta seemed to float as in liquid gold. As the sun sank lower, the hues of the heavens changed to crimson, bringing out the palm-trees on the islands in high relief against the sky; then to purple, and finally to the cool gray of evening, through which the stars shone down with a strange and almost unnatural lustre. The transition was rapid, for here the lingering twilight of northern latitudes is unknown. Our boatmen were not insensible to the almost unearthly beauty of the scene; and when it all was passed, they began the evening chaunt,

"Ave Maria purisima," etc.

the echoes of which were repeated from the shores, until they died away in murmurs in the distance.

The night was wonderfully still. We could distinctly hear the tinkling of guitars at the fort, at least three miles distant, interrupted by bursts of gay laughter, until a late hour. Before I slunk under the *chopa*, however, clouds began to gather in the north-east, lighted up momentarily by flashes of lightning, while fitful gusts of wind, veering in every quarter, betokened the approach of a thunder-storm. I nevertheless went to sleep while listening to the distant mutterings of thunder and the dismal howlings of the "mono colorado," or howling monkey. A little past midnight, however, we were all roused in a summary manner by a dash of water full in our faces, followed the next instant by the lurching of the boat, which tumbled passengers, arms, books, and whatever was movable, all in a heap together. I disengaged myself in a moment, and scrambled out upon the pineta, where Pedro, clinging to the tiller, was calling frantically to the men, who in a confused, shouting mass were clustered around the swaying mast, vainly endeavoring to take in the sail. We were before the wind, which was blowing a hurricane, and going with immense velocity, the hissing waters rising under our stern, almost to the level of the pineta. Broad sheets of blinding lightning fell around us, followed by deafening peals of thunder, drowning for a moment the roar of the tempest. I had hardly time to comprehend the peril of our situation, with the sail entangled in the ropes, and swaying from side to side, when a flash of lightning revealed to me Ben's stalwart form amongst the frightened marineros. I saw his short Roman sword glance for an instant above their heads,—he had cut the ropes. The sail fell, but was at once dragged aboard, while the relieved boat scudded steadily before the storm, which soon exhausted itself, leaving us drenched and uncomfortable, tossing roughly amongst the waves. The men took to the oars without an order, and in evident relief pulled back towards the course from which we had been driven. All that night, thunder-storms, like invading columns, swept over the lake around us, but we fell in the course of none of them. They all seemed to linger against the high volcanoes on the opposite shores of the lake, as if they would level in their wrath the daring rocks which opposed their progress.

The men slept no more that night, but pulled steadily and silently at the oars. Towards morning I crept again under the *chopa*, and slumbered until roused by the bellowing of cattle, and by the sun shining brilliantly in my face. It was after nine o'clock; we had passed the islands of La Boqueta, which lay within view, fresh and inviting, exposing under an archway of trees one or two picturesque huts, with canoes drawn up in front of them. We were within a snug little bay, in front of a broad sandy beach, on which the men were kindling fires preparatory to breakfast, while a herd of sleek-looking cattle wandered along the shore, here stooping to drink, and there engaging in mimic fights. Beneath the trees wound back a broad, well-beaten pathway, and beyond we could see the golden tops of palm-trees, the thatched roofs of houses, and hear the crowing of cocks, and the merry sound of infant voices. We were in the "Bahita de San Miguel," the little bay of San Miguel, distant about twenty miles from San Carlos, on the northern shore of the lake. The storm of the preceding night seemed almost like a dream; could it be possible that a few hours had wrought such a change? But the tattered sails, and the saturated blankets beneath the *chopa*, bore testimony to the reality of the storm. In fact, Pedro was yet full of wrath at what he called the stupidity of his men—they were "tontos" all, fools and brutes. I had been as indignant as himself, but was too glad to get out of the scrape safely, to nurse my wrath; so I poured out for Pedro a gill of brandy in his calabash, which he drank to our good health, and smacking his lips, straightway recovered his temper.

Directly, a little troop of girls, with purple skirts and white guipils, their long black hair dangling loosely to their waists, and balancing red water-jars on their heads, came laughing down the pathway for water. They appeared to be old friends of our crew, who hailed them gayly with "à Dios, mi alma!" "buena mañana, mi corazon!" adieu my soul!" "good morning, my heart!" to which they replied with "como estan, mis negritos?" "how are you, my darkeys?" and other railleries, very much, to our thinking, of the Bowery order. They passed along the shore a little distance, to a clump of bushes, and the next instant we saw them plashing like mermaids in the water; while some of our crew, who were throwing a net "for a fry," as Pedro said, tried to frighten them by shouting "lagartos, lagartos!" "alligators, alligators!" and affecting to make great efforts to escape to the shore. But the girls were not to be "sold" so easily, and only laughed the louder, and splashed water in the faces of the jesters as they ran by. Upon discovering us, instead, as the reader might suppose, of making for the shore in confusion, they paddled boldly up to the boat, their long hair trailing like a veil on the surface of the water. They looked laughingly up in our faces for a moment, exclaiming, "California," then ducked under, and were away. It seemed to us, while they stood drying their wet locks on the beach, that no sculptor could desire fairer models for his studio; nor the painter a more effective group for "the Bath of the Naides." We were there in an auspicious period; those days of primitive simplicity are passing away, if, indeed, they are not already past.

After drying ourselves in the sun, we took our guns and went on shore. We followed the inviting path to which I have referred, for a short distance, when we reached a brisk little brook which came murmuring among the stones with a familiar New England accent, here rippling over the bright sand, and there widening into broad, transparent pools. In one of them a whole bevy of little naked children were tumbling about, who took to their heels, like young ducks, upon our approach. Here we met Ben, coming down from the rancherias with two foaming calabashes of fresh milk, one of which was drained on the spot, the other reserved for our coffee. I shot a few strange water-birds and a parrot amongst the bushes, and strayed back to the shore just in time for broiled fish, crisp and hot from the fire.

Every step into this strange country had been full of novelty; and although our interest never flagged for an instant, yet we thought San Miguelito more interesting than any place we had encountered, and at first entertained some vague notions of stopping there for the day. But when the freshness of the morning had passed, which it did before we had finished breakfast, when the cattle had all gone off in the woods, and no more amphibious girls came down for water, we were not only ready but anxious to depart, which we did a little before noon. I shall never forget our breakfast at San Miguelito.

The day was still and sultry: Nature seemed wearied of the elemental war of the preceding night, and anxious for repose; the branches on the palm trees on the shore appeared to droop languidly; while the men, under plea of previous extra labor, paddled along at what Ben piously denominated "a poor, dying rate." The north-east trades sweep entirely across the continent in Nicaragua, and this wind, for boats bound from San Carlos to Granada, is therefore exceedingly favorable. They keep close under the northern shore, following its bendings, until they get nearly opposite Granada, and then stretch boldly across the lake. This is done because, with their imperfect sailing gear, venturing into the mid-lake would almost infallibly end in being blown over to the leeward shore, whence they could only be relieved by long and toilsome rowing against a cross sea—for on that shore the waves roll with almost the strength and majesty of those of the ocean. The later-built boats have something of a keel, and are schooner-rigged. These make the passage from the fort more directly. But our sails were, I suppose, a perpetuation of those used by the Indians before the Discovery, and quite indescribable. Pedro said they were "no good," except before the wind, and there they would make the boat fly, to use his own words, "like devil." The vision of the night recurred to me, and I yielded a full assent to the remark.

We spent nearly the whole day in vain trials to catch the ghosts of breezes, which came drowsily over the water, in our sails. I presume they were raised a score of times during the afternoon, but they only fluttered for a moment, and then dropped around the masts. This went on until the men felt hungry, and then we put in again at "El Pedernal," the landing-place for the cattle estate of Don Frederico Derbyshire, a merchant residing in Granada, the owner of "La Granadina," and to whom we bore letters of introduction from his correspondents in the United States. The place is not inappropriately named "The Flint." It is the very reverse of San Miguel; there is no smooth sandy beach, but instead, the whole shore is piled with rugged black basaltic or trachytic rocks, blistered with heat, among which grow some stunted trees. A narrow path winds amongst the rocks to a little cove, in which our boat was run. A man was despatched to the estate, which is situated a mile or two inland, to know of the mayor-domo if any of the products of the farm were to be sent to the city. Meanwhile the men went deliberately through the usual tedious process of dinner-making, and we got over the side for a bath. Notwithstanding the rocky shore, the bottom is a soft black mud, in which we sank to the knees. This was neither expected nor pleasant, and when I discovered an alligator slowly rise to the surface not two rods distant, I clambered aboard with more expedition than grace, and gave the monster the contents of my gun, in return for the courtesy of his appearance.

It was nearly sunset, dinner had been finished, and the kettles had been towed on board again, when we heard voices, and suddenly turning round the point of rocks there came three horsemen, each carrying, in net-work sacks, four large square cheeses, of the weight of two arrobas (fifty pounds) each. The horses were ridden up to the side of the boat, and the cheeses carefully placed in the centre. This finished, a breeze having meantime sprung up, we hoisted sail, and glided away from "El Pedernal," not at all dissatisfied to leave its rocks and alligators to their own pleasant company.

One of my companions, who had been growing silent and pale for several hours, now gave signs of an approaching crisis of some sort. Pedro pronounced him laboring under an "empacho," and recommended brandy—that was his universal specific for everything, from a sprained ankle to the toothache. But the patient protested against the medicine, as an abomination which made him only the worse to think of. I thought it a capital opportunity to bring out the medicine-chest, which had been packed with an extensive regard to all sorts of contingencies at "Rushton and Clark's," and Ben began a grand rummage for it, to the utter distraction of everything in the boat. Meantime, as became a learned practitioner, I propounded the question usually asked by anxious mammas of complaining children, "what have you eaten?" It turned out that, besides half a calabash of fresh milk, fried fish, three eggs, a slice of ham, and bread and coffee *ad libitum*, the patient had "put in" the afternoon with raw plantains, and "*dulce*"—sugar! I comprehended that "empacho" meant something like surfeit, and to disguise the dose, mixed a little tartar emetic with magnesia, which wrought a wonderful cure—much to my elevation in the eyes of the crew, who set me down at once as a great *medico*. I had immediate applications on behalf of ailing wives, scalded babies, and feverish boys, for all of which I prescribed, after deliberate consultation of the "Pocket Physician." While this was going on night fell, and I lost the sunset,—a circumstance for which, as he is thereby spared the description, the reader is no doubt properly thankful.

As the evening progressed, the breeze continued to freshen, and about midnight, Pedro, calculating that we were sufficiently to the windward, laid the course of the boat direct for Granada. I went to bed early, and owing to the disturbance of the previous night, slept soundly. When I woke, we were in mid lake, and might have been in mid sea, for all the difference discoverable in the appearance of the waves and water. The wind was strong, cool, and damp, and the men had their handkerchiefs bound round their heads, and their blankets wrapped over their shoulders. My ailing companion looked sentimental, and professed not to have wholly recovered from the "empacho," but as I felt qualmish myself, I pronounced it sea-sickness, which, as every traveller knows, never entitles the sufferer to sympathy.

We were at least thirty miles from land, yet the shores appeared wonderfully distinct and near. We now, for the first time, felt the majesty of the giant volcanoes of Ometepec and Madeira, which had hitherto seemed so dim and distant. There they rose clear and bold against the sky, regular as works of art, the moving clouds casting their sides in shadow, and clasping their summits as they passed, then sweeping away to the distant islands of the great Pacific. Between us and the shore was the high, uninhabited island of Zapatero, its outline changing every moment with our position, while directly in front, distinguished by the towering edges of its vast and ragged crater, rose the extinct volcano of Momobacho, at the foot of which stands the ancient city of Granada. High above the forests of the shore, are some conical hills, of light green, bordering on yellow, which seemed to be cleared, and which puzzled us exceedingly. We became familiar with them afterwards, and I presume they are common in all volcanic regions. They are the cones of scoriæ, sand, and ashes, which are heaped up during eruptions. On these, trees rarely take root, but in their place a species of long, coarse grass weaves a net-work of verdure over their smooth sides. This grass is of a lively green during the rainy season, but becomes yellow in the dry, when the hills are burned over, after which they change to deep sable. Thus forever varying, they constitute remarkable and characteristic features in a Nicaraguan landscape. Upon the northern shore of the lake we saw only the broken volcanic mountains of Chontales, patched with trees, here black with lava, and there red and white with scoriæ and sand. It should be observed that it is only that part of Chontales bordering the upper portion of the lake, which presents this burned and broken aspect. Elsewhere the shores are comparatively low and undulating, with extensive savannas, which furnish abundant pasturage. The whole district is well adapted for grazing purposes.

While we were occupied with the novel and beautiful scenery of the lake, our men, collected around the foot of the mast, were engaged in a low but earnest discussion, which we soon discovered related to politics, and especially to the attempted revolution of which we had heard so much. They made frequent use of the terms "Timbucos" and "Calandracas," which were about as significant to us as "Coons" and "Locofocos" probably were to strangers on our own shores, during certain presidential elections. We had abstained from asking questions about politics, not from want of interest, but from motives of policy; but took occasion to hear all that might be said upon the subject. We had thus contrived to get some imperfect notions of the partisan divisions of the country; the bases of which, though very trivial to the impartial traveller, were probably quite as important in fact as those which we had seen sustained with so much vehemence and virulence at home. It was easy to discover that our crew were unanimously "Timbucos," or of the government party, while the "Calandracas" were the disaffected portion of the people. They, however, appeared to have but a sectional importance, and were far from numerous, except in the southern departments of the Republic. The robber-chief, Somoza, had turned this partisan feeling to some account by professing to be its champion, and having collected a few hundred reckless and ignorant men around him, made a sudden and successful attack on Rivas, or Nicaragua, which was defended by a small garrison of only forty soldiers. In the attack he burned a number of houses, and committed some cruel murders, besides pillaging and robbing on every hand. According to the accounts which had reached us, however, the entire city had been burned, and the inhabitants slaughtered indiscriminately and without mercy. These stories, as well as those relating to the number of his forces, proved, in the end, to be gross exaggerations,—as the reader will discover in due course.

It appeared, from what was said, that there had been a vague rumor at San Carlos, to the effect that Somoza, at the head of three thousand men, had set out some days previously for an attack on the city of Granada; and the probabilities of its truth, and the course to be pursued in the event he should have reached there, were now, as we approached the city, subjects of increasing interest with our men. The circumstance that we had, on the day preceding, seen a number of boats, making what appeared to be a forced trip in the direction of San Carlos, but too far distant to be hailed, was dwelt upon as exceedingly significant. In short, it was evident enough that the feeling of excited suspense amongst the men was every moment increasing. Pedro was silent, and answered our questions evasively, but listened earnestly to all that was said. He seemed to be oppressed by a sense of responsibility of some kind; but whether on account of himself, his boat, or his distinguished passengers, we could not make out.

By the veering of the wind, or the "falling off" of our keel-less boat, instead of making the northern islands of the group called the "Corales," rising, hundreds in number, at the foot of the volcano of Momobacho, we found ourselves, at about two o'clock in the afternoon, at the almost extreme southern part of the archipelago. The approach to these islands was exceedingly beautiful; but when we were amongst them, out of the rough waves into the smooth water, they were really enchanting. They are of volcanic origin, elevated in the form of cones, to the height of from twenty to one hundred feet. The sides are steep, and composed of immense volcanic rocks, black and blistered by fire; but their summits are covered with verdure, and long vines hang trailing over the stones, blushing with strange flowers, almost to the edge of the water. Some of them, upon which there is a sufficient accumulation of soil, are inhabited by Indians; and their thatched huts, shaded by tall palms, with a dense background of plantains, are the most picturesque objects that can be imagined.

Within these islands the sail was dropped, and the oars resumed. Everybody was now anxious to hear the news, but the huts on the islands seemed to be deserted; at least no one appeared, although the men shouted to the inmates at top of their voices. Very soon a canoe, containing a boy and a woman, shot across our course, from between two little islands, just in advance. For a moment they showed evidences of alarm, and a disposition to retreat; but recognising Pedro, they came alongside, under a shower of confused and eager questions, which completely confounded us, and prevented anything like an understanding of what was said. We conjectured that the news was of an exciting kind, from the earnest faces and violent gestures of the crew. By-and-by the canoe pushed off, but it was full a quarter of an hour before the men took up the oars, during which time there was a warm discussion as to whether the boat should proceed at once to Granada, or remain concealed amongst the islands until the issue of affairs at the city could be ascertained. The opinion, however, seemed to be pretty decided, that we should go ahead, at whatever hazard. This decision was based, as we afterwards discovered, on the faith reposed in "la bandera del Norte America," the flag of the United States; which they all believed neither man nor devil dared disregard. It appeared that the woman and boy of the canoe had told an alarming story of the approach of Somoza, the flight of the inhabitants, and the probable capture of the city. But Pedro, more cautious than the rest, was of the opinion that their tale had but little better foundation than their fears; and expressed great faith in the ability of the little garrison of "veteranos," stationed in the city, to prevent its being carried by Somoza. His faith was somewhat shaken, however, on learning, a few minutes thereafter, from an Indian, lurking on one of the islands, that there had been a great firing in the city the previous night and this morning; and that all the boats had left the landing and made for the opposite shore of the lake.

There is pleasure in all kinds of excitement, which is rather enhanced than diminished by the presence of danger. And so far from being alarmed by these accounts, I was only the more anxious to get to Granada. I had been told that Somoza, notwithstanding his crimes, cruelty, and contempt for the laws, had much of the cavalier in his composition; gay, gallant, generous, and withal the finest looking and most dashing fellow in all Nicaragua. No man rode such fine horses, or could rival him in wielding the lance. Indeed, the commandante at San Carlos had intimated that he owed it to the place which he held in the good graces of the señoritas of the country, that he had so long baffled justice and defied pursuit. Altogether I had pictured him something like the gentlemanly cut-throat of the Apennines and Sierra Morina, or the amiable bandits of the Peninsula, and almost considered myself fortunate in the prospect of an adventure, at my very first step in the country.

Two hours of steady rowing amongst the fairy "Corales" brought us to the little island of Cubi, when a broad bay, with a white beach, and an old castle on the shore, opened before us; while beyond a belt of woods, on higher ground, rose the towers of Granada. We could distinguish little of the town except the red, tiled roofs of the houses; and though from this distance it was far from imposing, yet we had so long looked forward to our arrival here, that had dome been piled on dome, and palace risen above palace, in long perspective, we could not have experienced greater satisfaction than we now did in gazing, for the first time, upon this ancient city. At the island, we found several huts, and a number of boats drawn into little nooks between the rocks, while beneath the trees were clusters of women and children, and here and there groups of men, absorbed in playing some noisy game of cards. With a vivid recollection of the indifferent figure we had cut at the fort, we had arranged with Pedro to stop here, in order to replace our stained and tattered garments; an operation which we soon discovered must be performed in face of the assembled population of Cubi, unless we preferred to encounter the fleas which we fancied must infest the dirty, dog-stocked huts on the shore. We chose the former alternative; but had hardly commenced the disruption of trunks and boxes, and the overhauling of carpet bags, before we heard a cannon in the direction of the city, followed very soon by what appeared to be a rolling discharge of musketry; and looking in that direction, we could see a volume of smoke rising from the centre of the town. Our invalid had a violent recurrence of his "empacho," refused tartar emetic, anticipated a fever, and was altogether too ill to leave the island. So he was led up to one of the huts, and deposited in a hammock. Meantime the fusilade ended with one or two more discharges of cannon, while a white cloud rose slowly over the city. Our first impression was that Somoza had arrived, and that a fight was already in progress. The people of the island were also somewhat startled, and for a time watched the town with evident anxiety; but in the end quietly resumed their amusements. Pedro also seemed to be relieved; and after listening for a while, finally exclaimed that all was right:

the day, he said, was a *fiesta*, and what we had supposed a discharge of firearms, was only the explosion of "*bombas*" or rockets,—" in point of fact," fireworks. I cannot say that I was particularly gratified with the information, after having prepared myself for a siege at least, if not an assault.

Myriads of bees, attracted by the sweets in the boat, swarmed around us while making our toilet. Their first onset fairly drove us out on the rocks, but Pedro quieted us with the assurance that they were stingless, when we returned and completed our arrangements. It was late in the afternoon, the wind blowing fair, when we again put up sail, and steered for the landing of Granada. As we approached, we discovered hundreds of people on the shore and in the water, some in groups, and others in gay trappings dashing about on horseback,—a picture of activity and life. On the gray walls of the old castle we also discerned soldiers, their muskets glancing in the sun; and, anchored a little distance from the shore, was an odd-looking craft, in two pieces, resembling some awkward canal-boat, which we afterwards discovered had been built to receive the engine and boiler which we had seen in San Juan. In this rude, unwieldy affair, with infinite trouble, and after three weeks of toil, a party of some seventy-five outward-bound Californians had ascended the river and passed the lake to this place,—the pioneers on this line of transit.

In an hour after leaving Cubi, we cast anchor under the walls of the old castle. Our flag attracted immediate attention, and the people crowded upon the walls of the fort to look at us. Some called to Pedro, with a multitude of gesticulations; but the noise of the surf was so great that we could not make out what was said. The question which presented itself most strongly to us was, how are we going to land? for a surf like that of the ocean broke on the shore. We had a practical answer, however, very shortly. The cable was let out, so as to bring us as far in shore as was safe, and then three or four sailors leaped overboard, their heads and shoulders just appearing above the water, and invited us to get on! Get on what—where—how? Pedro explained that we were to put our feet on the shoulders, and seat ourselves on the head of one, and hold on with our hands to the hair of another just in advance. After a number of awkward attempts, which excited great merriment, and at the expense of wetted feet, we finally got into position, and were duly deposited on shore, amidst a swarm of boys and women. Some of the former pressed forward, exclaiming "California," or "goode by," and then disappeared laughing amongst their companions. It was very evident that our countrymen had created a great sensation in their progress. Probably no equal number of strangers had passed through the country for a century.

Pedro slipped off his clothes, and holding them above his head, also came on shore, in ecstatic spirits to find the town standing and all safe. He dressed with great expedition, and with much dignity put himself in advance, to escort us to the town. Not at all sorry to get out of the crowd of gazers, we followed along a broad, well-beaten road, with elevated foot-paths on each side, in the direction of the city. The ascent seemed to be by terraces; the faces of which were paved with stone, and guarded by masonry, to protect them from the wasting action of the rains. Palms, plantains, orange and other tropical trees lined the road on either hand, shut in by a hedge composed of a species of cactus, bearing brilliant red flowers. We met troops of laughing girls, of every shade of complexion, from pure white to ebon black, fancifully attired, with water-jars on their heads, on their way to the lake. They were as straight as arrows, and seemed to have an infinite fund of animal spirits. Most of them passed us with a side glance, half of curiosity and half of mischief, while others more bold, turning full round, exclaimed gayly, "Adios, caballeros!" to which we responded, "Adios, mi alma!" much to their apparent entertainment.

It was full a third of a mile to a steep terrace, ascending which we found ourselves amongst the neat cane huts composing the suburbs of the city, and in which reside the poorer portion of the population. Most of these, like those at San Carlos and San Juan, were built of canes and thatched with palm leaves or grass, while others were plastered with mud, and whitewashed. A clump of fruit-trees overshadowed each, and within the doors we could discover women spinning cotton with a little foot-wheel, or engaged in grinding corn for tortillas. On almost every house were one or two parrots screaming at each other, or at some awkward looking macaw, which waddled clumsily along the crown of the roof. Around all, dogs, chickens, and children mingled in perfect equality.

Beyond these huts commenced the city proper. The buildings were of adobes, on cut stone foundations, and roofed with tiles. The windows were all balconied, and protected on the outside by ornamental iron gratings, and within by painted shutters. They were, with scarcely an exception, of one high story. The principal entrances were by arched and often elaborately ornamented gateways, within which swung massive doors, themselves containing smaller ones, all opening into the courtyards. Besides these, there were, in some instances, other entrances, opening directly into the grand sala of the house. The eaves of all the houses project several feet beyond the walls, serving the double purpose of protecting the latter from the rains, and sheltering the foot-passenger from the sun and the elements. The side or foot-walks were all raised one or two feet above the street, and flagged, but barely wide enough to admit persons meeting each other to pass. Towards the centre of the town some of the streets are paved, like those of our own cities, with this difference, that instead of a convex, they present a concave surface, so that the gutter is in the centre of the street.

As we progressed, we met a number of well-dressed people, of both sexes, who, seeing that we were strangers, bowed respectfully to us as we passed. Evidences of comfort, not to say elegance, now began to appear, and through an occasional open door we caught glimpses of sofas and easy chairs, and beds which a Sybarite might envy. Occasionally there were niches in the walls of the houses, in which were placed crosses, covered with faded flowers; in some instances the crosses were simply fastened to the walls, or planted at the corners of the streets. Advancing further, we found ourselves in the shadow of a large and massive stone building, with terraces, domes, and towers, half Moresque, and altogether an architectural incongruity. It appeared to be very ancient, and I stopped Pedro, who strode ahead with the gait of a conquering hero, to inquire what building it might be. He said it was the ancient and now abandoned convent of San Francisco, and showed us the gratings through which its former inmates had intercourse with the world, and pointed out the wooden cross in front, made of cedar from Lebanon. I do not know how long Pedro would have run on, had I not cut his story short, by saying I would hear the rest to-morrow. Just then a party of soldiers defiled across the street in front of us. They were bare-footed, and wore white pantaloons and jackets, with funny little, black caps, banded with metal, and having little, round, red cockades stuck saucily in front. A dashing young officer rode at their head, who lifted his hat gracefully to us. It was a scouting party just coming in. We followed them with our eyes down the street, and saw that sentinels were stationed at the corners, but two squares distant, and that the streets near the plaza were barricaded with adobes and timbers, with a single embrasure in the centre, through which a cannon looked grimly towards us. We now observed that soldiers were stationed on the walls of the convent, and in the towers of the parochial church, which had just come in view. It was evident that the government and military were on the alert, and prepared for any emergency. We found the streets more animated, and the houses better built, as we approached the centre of the town; women were moving hither and thither with trays, vegetables, bottles, and a hundred other commodities on their heads, and babies on their hips, and men with slouched hats, and breeches turned up to their knees, bare-footed, or wearing sandals, and carrying a large machete in their hands, were driving meek-looking horses, bearing loads, through the streets before them, or else with a long, iron-pointed pole, pricking on little compact oxen, fastened by the horns to long, heavy, awkward carts, with solid wheels cut from the mahogany tree. Amongst these flitted now and then a priest, with his black robe, preposterous bell-crowned, fur hat, and gaudy umbrella. There were quiet señoritas, also, moving slowly along, with a grace and dignity of motion seldom or never seen in our cities; and gay fellows on fiery little horses, who dashed at a break-neck pace through the streets. It was a novel scene, and we had hardly taken in its more striking features, when Pedro stopped before a large arched gateway, or *portada*, as it is called here, and told us this was the "Casa del Señor Don Frederico." He unlatched the small door within the larger, and entering, we found ourselves in a broad corridor, completely surrounding a court, in which were growing a number of orange, marañon, and other fruit trees, fragrant bushes, and clumps of flowers. On one side was the store, filled with bales and boxes, and in front of it were huge scales for weighing commodities; while the sala, dining, and private rooms occupied the remaining two sides of the court. In one corner of the corridor were two or three movable desks, where Don Frederico's children were engaged in their afternoon lessons with their tutor, a pale, intellectual looking young man; and just beyond, reclining in a hammock, was the portly form of Don Frederico himself. Pedro approached him, hat in hand, and with profound reverence, announced us. Our host immediately rose, and in due course I delivered my letters, which were honored in a spirit of the most enlarged and liberal hospitality. A part of a spacious and commodious house immediately opposite, which was occupied by the children of Don Frederico and their governess, was at once ordered to be prepared for our accommodation, while a couple of carts were despatched to the shore for our luggage. Our reception was so warm and cordial, that I felt at once perfectly at home, and was delighted with the neatness and comfort of everything around us. Don Frederico was born in Jamaica, but had resided for thirty years in the country, where he had married, become a citizen, and accumulated a large fortune. Entertaining the respect and confidence of all parties, he had passed safely through all the troubles to which the country had been subjected. He seemed very little alarmed at the threatened attack on the city, and felt confident that the insurgents would ultimately be put down. Still, unless reinforcements speedily arrived from the government, he anticipated that trouble might ensue, and perhaps an assault be attempted, because Somoza was as daring as he was unscrupulous. But even then it was only necessary to barricade the doors, and every house became a fortress. He had gone through several revolutions, securely locked in, eating and sleeping as usual. When the affair was over, he opened the portada again, and things went on as before.

As we had eaten scarcely anything during the day, our host gave us a cup of chocolate, pending the preparation of dinner. While thus engaged, we were surprised by the appearance of an officer bearing a note from the commandante of the Plaza, congratulating us upon our safe arrival, and very considerately proposing that some time should be named, when we were recovered from our fatigues, to enable him to pay his respects in person. He also placed a guard at our disposition, which I of course declined. Hardly had this messenger been despatched, before another, from the Prefect of the Department, made his appearance. The next day at noon was named for receptions, and meantime we instructed the *portero* or gatekeeper to report us to all visitors as engaged.

The evening passed delightfully with our host. It was a great rélief to stretch one's legs once more beneath a table spread like our own at home; a pleasure not slightly enhanced by the presence of entirely new and curious dishes, upon the merits of which we successively passed summary, and generally favorable, judgments. A gentle shower meanwhile pattered upon the tiled roofs, cooling and purifying the air; and we experienced, for the first time, the pleasures attending life in a well-appointed residence beneath the tropics. After the bell struck eight, we heard every five minutes the word "*Alerte!*" caught up in succession by the guards, in evidence that they were all awake, and keeping a bright lookout. Occasionally the "*Quien vive?*" or challenge of the sentinel stationed at the corner of the street below us, was given with an emphasis which fell startlingly upon our unaccustomed ears. Our host was used to it. We were really in the midst of war and "its alarums," and felt all the better for it. We retired early to our new quarters, which consisted of a large sala, in which were a piano, mahogany tables and chairs, with sleeping apartments attached. Here we found that Ben, with an eye to all our wants, had arranged everything necessary to our comfort. Forty nights in close, narrow berths, in hammocks, and on the tops of boxes and trunks, had qualified us to enjoy the delightfully cool and scrupulously neat *camas* which that evening invited us to slumber. I bestowed myself in one without ceremony, and in less time than I am writing it, went to sleep, to dream of Somoza, storms on the lake, and a thousand incongruous matters. Nor did I wake until Ben, utterly renovated, and looking wonderfully genteel, came to announce that breakfast was ready. It was some seconds before I could comprehend clearly where I was; but once awake, I found myself thoroughly refreshed, and ready for any turn of events,—breakfast or revolutions.

THE PLANTAIN TREE.

CHAPTER V.

RECEPTION-DAY—GENERAL RESPECT AND ADMIRATION FOR THE UNITED STATES—AN EVENING RIDE—THE PLAZA—CHURCHES—HOSPITAL—THE "JALTEVA"—DESERTED MUNICIPALITY—MELANCHOLY RESULTS OF FACTION—THE ARSENAL—NATURAL DEFENCES OF THE CITY—"CAMPO SANTO"—AN EX-DIRECTOR AND HIS "HACIENDA"—SHORE OF THE LAKE IN THE EVENING—OLD CASTLE—THE "ORACION"—AN EVENING VISIT TO THE SENORITAS—OPERA AMIDST ORANGE GROVES—"ALERTAS" AND "QUIEN VIVAS?"—THE GRANADINAS AT HOME—AN EPISODE ON WOMEN AND DRESS—MR. ESTEVENS—"LOS MALDITOS INGLESES"—A FEMALE ANTIQUARIAN COADJUTOR—"CIGARITAS"—INDIAN GIRLS—COUNTRYMEN—AN AMERICAN "MEDICO"—NATIVE HOSPITALITY TO STRANGERS—THE WAYS INFESTED BY "FACCIOSOS"—AN AMERICAN TURNED BACK—EXPECTED ASSAULT ON THE CITY, AND PATRIOTIC RESOLVES "TO DIE UNDER THE AMERICAN FLAG"—A NOTE ON HORSES AND SADDLES—VISIT TO THE CACAO ESTATES OF THE MALACCAS—THE CACAO TREE—DAY-DREAMS—AN ADVENTURE ALMOST—GRIEVOUS DISAPPOINTMENT—SOMOZA, THE ROBBER CHIEF—OUR ARMORY—FEVERISHNESS OF THE PUBLIC MIND—LIFE UNDER THE TROPICS—A FRIGHTENED AMERICAN, WHO HAD "SEEN SOMOZA," AND HIS ACCOUNT OF THE INTERVIEW—SOMOZA'S LOVE FOR THE AMERICANS—GOOD NEWS FROM LEON—APPROACH OF THE GENERAL IN CHIEF, AND AN ARMED AMERICAN ESCORT—CONDITION OF PUBLIC AFFAIRS—PROCLAMATION OF THE SUPREME DIRECTOR—DECREES OF THE GOVERNMENT—OFFICIAL ANNOUNCEMENTS, AND PUBLIC ADDRESSES—HOW THEY EXHIBITED THE POPULAR FEELING—NICARAGUAN RHETORIC—DECISIVE MEASURES TO PUT DOWN THE INSURGENTS—GENERAL CALL TO ARMS—MARTIAL LAW—PUBLICATION OF A "BANDA"—GREAT PREPARATIONS TO RECEIVE THE GENERAL IN CHIEF AND HIS "VETERANOS"—NO FURTHER FEAR OF THE "FACCIOSOS"—A BREAK-NECK RIDE TO THE "LAGUNA DE SALINAS"—A VOLCANIC LAKE—DESCENT TO THE WATER—HOW CAME ALLIGATORS THERE?—NATIVE "AGUARDIENTE" "NOT BAD TO TAKE"—RETURN TO THE CITY—A RELIGIOUS PROCESSION—THE HOST—INCREASING TOLERANCE OF THE PEOPLE—PREPARATIONS FOR "LA MANANA."

At noon, agreeably to appointment, we were waited upon by the dignitaries of the city, and the commander of the garrison, together with a large number of the leading inhabitants. They all exhibited the same cordiality with the ruder portion of the population, and a degree of refinement and courtesy which would have done credit to more pretending capitals. We were a little startled by the somewhat exaggerated tone of compliment, both in respect to ourselves and our country, which ran through their conversation, and which seems characteristic of the Spanish people wherever found, in the Old World or the New. All concurred in representing the present unsettled state of public affairs as in a great measure due to foreign intervention and intrigue; and referred to the seizure of San Juan, and the English encroachments on their territories, in a tone of indignation and reproach, commensurate with the indignity and outrage to which they had been subjected. They seemed to entertain the highest hopes from the opening of more intimate relations with the United States; but, unacquainted with the nature, constitutional powers, and the policy of our government, these hopes were, as a matter of course, somewhat vague; yet it was not unnatural that, distracted within, and subjected to unscrupulous aggression from without, the United States should be looked to as a conciliator of intestine factions, as a friend, and a protector. I was deeply impressed with the feeling which they manifested, and was convinced that if once treated with consideration, and taught to respect themselves as a nation, there was no reason why the States of the Isthmus should not take a respectable rank amongst the republics of the continent. The interview was highly interesting, and gave me more elevated views of the temper of the people of the country than I had gathered from what had been published concerning them; an impression which a further and more intimate acquaintance only tended to confirm.

Towards evening, in company with Col. Trinidad Salazar, the commandant of the Plaza, we took a ride through the city and its environs. We found that with the exception of the Church of La Mercedes, and the Convent of San Francisco, already mentioned, there were few buildings at all remarkable or imposing. The Parochial Church, on the plaza, is very ancient, and distinguished as containing the bones of several of the first bishops of Nicaragua, which was established as a diocess as early as 1532. The interior was far from imposing. It had some paintings, too ancient to be distinguished, with some indifferent prints of saints, and scenes in the life of Christ and the apostles. Upon one side of the plaza is the façade of the unfinished church of San Juan de Dios, which was designed to be the most beautiful in the city, but for some reason was never finished. The façade is very elaborate, and profusely loaded with ornament. It has been standing in its present condition for more than a hundred years. A hospital has been erected in the area it was intended to occupy, which is supported by a small market tax and voluntary contributions. Buildings of one or two stories, with spacious corridors in front, extend round two sides of the square, in which are some of the principal retail "*tiendas*" of the city. The wares of the shopkeepers were as conspicuously displayed as in some of the minor streets at home; while in front were the market-women, with fruits, cacao, maize, and all the various edibles of the season. These were generally placed in baskets, or spread on a white sheet on the ground, in a style probably very little different from that practised by the aborigines at the time of the Conquest. All the streets leading from the plaza were barricaded, and we found advance posts of troops in every part of the city.

From the grand plaza we rode through the narrow streets, between long rows of substantial houses, in the direction of the municipality of Jalteva.[1] Dashing up a broad causeway,

[1] This municipality is mostly made up of Indians. The present name, "*Jalteva*," is probably a corruption of the Indian "*Salteba*," the name

with heavy flanking walls, surmounted by urns, we came at once into the second grand plaza. Here we found the buildings more scattered, and of a poorer character; huts of canes alternating with adobe houses and open lots of ground. The plaza was deserted, and as we rode along we observed that the whole quarter seemed depopulated. We found, upon inquiry, that this municipality was the stronghold of the "Calandracas," and hereditarily jealous of the city proper. This hostility led to the collision of which we had heard, in which the disaffected party had suffered a defeat; whereupon, either from fear, or with a design of organizing for sharper work, they had chiefly fled "*al monte*," to the fields. Those who remained, with scarcely an exception, had moved, for greater security, within the city. The silence and desolation which reigned in this deserted quarter was a mournful commentary on partisan feuds. A few dogs and unclaimed cattle wandered despondingly amongst the houses, as if in search of their masters; but beyond these there were no signs of life.

Passing the Jalteva, we came into the broad open road leading to Leon, and soon reached a square compact building, which was the arsenal. It was surrounded by a high wall, and at the corners were erected towers, looped for musketry, each containing a guard of soldiers. A cannon looked morosely through the open gateway, around which was a company of lancers, just returned from some expedition. Their lances, to each of which was hung a little red streamer, flashed in the sun as they fell into line on the approach of the commandante; while the guards, on the tap of the drum, leaped to their feet, and presented arms. Just beyond the arsenal is what the commandante called the natural defence of the city. It is a deep, narrow ravine,

of the aboriginal town which occupied the site of Granada before that city was built.

with absolutely precipitous walls, worn by the rains through the volcanic or calcareous breccia upon which the city is built. It extends on three sides of the town, and can be passed only in one or two places, where lateral inclined planes have been artificially cut from the top to the bottom on one side, and from the bottom to the top on the other. It is a feature of some importance in calculating the means of defending the city, and probably had something to do in determining its site.

From the arsenal we turned off to the left, following a broad, well-beaten path, which wound beneath a complete archway of trees, vines, and flowers, in the direction of the "*Campo Santo*," or burial place of the city. This is an area of several acres of ground in extent, surrounded by a high wall of adobes, neatly whitewashed, and entered beneath a lofty gateway, surmounted by a cross, and bearing a Latin inscription, which I have forgotten. There was little to see; and, as the gates were shut, we could not enter; so, turning in the direction of the lake, we galloped to the hacienda of Don Jose Leon Sandoval, passing on the way, in a picturesque glen, shadowed over with trees, the "corral" or cattle yard of the estate. A brisk ride through the bushes brought us to the house, built upon a high terrace, overlooking the lake and city, and embowered in palm, marañon, orange, and jocote trees. The proprietor was out somewhere on the estate, and we started to find him, which we soon succeeded in doing. He was mounted on a splendid mule, and just returning from inspecting the day's work of the "*mozos*," or what in New England would be called "hired help." Don Jose proved to be a plainly dressed, substantial person, bearing a close likeness to General Taylor. Upon my mentioning the fact, he bowed low, in acknowledgment, and said that he knew the General was a farmer-soldier and a citizen-President; and he only hoped that the resemblance might extend from person, which was of little, to character, which was of greater, consequence. Don Jose had once been Director of the State, but had resigned the office, preferring, he said, to be a good farmer rather than a poor director. We followed him over various parts of the estate to his indigo vats and drying houses, and to his plantain and cacao walks and corn-fields, all of which we found to be in capital order, and bearing the evidences of intelligence, enterprise, industry, and care.

After a pleasant interview of half an hour, we bade Don Jose "*buena tarde*," and descended to the shores of the lake, just as the sun was setting, throwing the whole beach in the shade, while the fairy "Corales" were swimming in the evening light. The shore was ten-fold more animated than when we landed the previous day; men on horseback, women on foot, sailors, fishermen, idlers, children, and a swarm of water-carriers, mingling together, gave life to the scene; while boats and graceful canoes, drawn up on the beach, bongos rocking at their anchors outside, the grim old fort frowning above, and the green border of trees, with bars of sunlight streaming between them, all contributed to heighten and give effect to the picture. We rode up the glacis of the old castle, through its broken archway, into its elevated area, and looked out beyond the broad and beautiful lake, upon the distant shores of Chontales, with its earthquake-riven hills, and ragged, volcanic craters. Their rough features were brought out sharply and distinctly in the slanting light which gilded the northern slope of the gigantic volcano of Momobacho, while its eastern declivity slept in purple shadow. We were absorbed in contemplating one by one these varied beauties, when the bells of the city struck the hour of the "oracion." In an instant every voice was hushed, the horseman reined in his steed, the ropes dropped from the hands of the sailor, the sentinel on the fort stopped short in his round, even the water-jars were left half-filled, while every hat was removed, and every lip moved in prayer. The very waves seemed to break more gently on the shore, in harmony with the vibrations of the distant bells; while the subdued hum of reverential voices filled the pauses between. There was something almost magical in this sudden hush of the multitude, and its apparently entire absorption in devotion, which could not fail deeply to impress the stranger witnessing it for the first time.

No sooner, however, had the bells ceased to toll, and struck up the concluding joyful chime, than the crowd on the shore resumed its life and gayety, while we put spurs to our horses, and dashed through their midst, on our return to the city. The commandante and his companions would only leave me at my door, where we were saluted by our host with "Saved your distance, gentlemen; dinner is ready!"

An evening visit to the Señorita Teresa finished our first entire day in Granada. This young lady had been educated in the United States, spoke English very well, and was withal a proficient in music,—accomplishments which we never before learned to estimate at their true value. It was worth something to hear well executed passages from familiar operas, amidst tangible and not painted orange trees and palms, and in an atmosphere really loaded with tropical perfumes, instead of the odors of oil-pots and gas-lights. Eight o'clock was the signal for general withdrawal from the streets, for then commenced the rigors of the military police, and the city became at once still and quiet. The occasional barking of a dog, the tinkling of a distant guitar, the soughing of the evening wind amongst the trees of the court-yard, the measured tread and graduated "alertas!" of the sentinels, were the only interruptions to the almost sepulchral silence. While returning to our quarters, we were startled by the "Quien vive?" of the sentinel, uttered in a tone absolutely ferocious, and as these fellows rarely parleyed long, we answered with all expedition, "La Patria," which was followed on the instant by "Que gente?" "Americanos del

Norte." This was enough; these, we found, were magic words, which opened every heart and every door in all Nicaragua. They never failed us. We felt proud to know that no such charm attached to "Ingleses," "Alemanes," or "Franceses."

The day following, in accordance with the "costumbres del pais," the customs of the country, we returned the visits of the preceding day, and began to see more of the domestic and social life of the citizens of Granada. We found the residences all comfortable, and many elegant, governed by mistresses simple, but graceful and confiding in their manners. They were frank in their conversation, and inquired with the utmost *naïveté* whether I was married or intended to be, and if the ladies of El Norte would probably visit Granada, when the "Vapores grandes," the great steamers, came to run to San Juan, and the "Vaporcitas," steameretts, to ply on the lake and river. They had heard of a Mr. Estevens, (their nearest approach to Stephens,) who had written a book about their "pobre pais," their poor country, and were anxious to know what he had said of them, and whether our people really regarded them as "esclavos y brutos sin verguenza," slaves and brutes without shame, as the abominable English (los malditos Ingleses) had represented them. They were also very anxious to know whether the party of Californians which had passed through were "gente comun," common people, or "caballeros," gentlemen; upon which point, however, we were diplomatically evasive, for there was more in the inquiry than we chose to notice. One lady had heard that I was a great antiquarian, and anticipatory to my visit, had got together a most incongruous collection of curiosities, from "vasos antiguos," fragments of pottery, and stone hatchets, down to an extraordinary pair of horn spectacles, and a preposterously distorted hog's hoof,—all of which she insisted on sending to my quarters, which she did, with some rare birds, and a plate of *dulces!* At every house we found a table spread with wines and sweetmeats, and bearing a little silver brazier filled with burning coals, for the greater convenience of lighting cigars. I excited much surprise by declining to smoke, on the ground that I had never done so; but the ladies insisted on my taking a "cigarito," which they said wouldn't injure a new-born babe, and paid me the compliment of lighting it with their own fair lips, after which it would have been rank treason to etiquette, and would have ruined my reputation for gallantry, had I refused. I at first endeavored to shirk the responsibility of smoking by thrusting it into my pocket, but found that as soon as one disappeared another was presented, so I was obliged "to face the music" in the end. In every sala we found a large hammock suspended from the walls, which was invariably tendered to the visitor, even when there were easy chairs and sofas in the room. This is the seat of honor.

The women of pure Spanish stock are very fair, and have the *embonpoint* which characterizes the sex under the tropics. Their dress, except in a few instances where the stiff costume of our own country had been adopted, was exceedingly loose and flowing, leaving the neck and arms exposed. The entire dress was often pure white, but generally the skirt, or *nagua*, was of some flowered stuff, in which case the *guipil* (*anglice*, vandyke) was white, heavily trimmed with lace. Satin slippers, a red or purple sash wound loosely round the waist, and a rosary sustaining a little golden cross, with a narrow golden band or a string of pearls extending around the forehead and binding the hair, which often fell in luxuriant waves upon their shoulders, completed a costume as novel as it was graceful and picturesque. To all this, add the superior attractions of an oval face, regular features, large and lustrous black eyes, small mouth, pearly white teeth, and tiny hands and feet, and withal a low but clear voice, and the reader has a picture of a Central American lady of pure stock. Very many of the women have, however, an infusion of other families and races, from the Saracen to the Indian and the Negro, in every degree of intermixture. And as tastes differ, so may opinions as to whether the tinge of brown, through which the blood glows with a peach-like bloom, in the complexion of the girl who may trace her lineage to the caziques upon one side, and the haughty grandees of Andalusia and Seville on the other, superadded, as it usually is, to a greater lightness of figure and animation of face,—whether this is not a more real beauty than that of the fair and more languid señora, whose white and almost transparent skin bespeaks a purer ancestry. Nor is the Indian girl, with her full, lithe figure, long, glossy hair, quick and mischievous eyes, who walks erect as a grenadier beneath her heavy water-jar, and salutes you in a musical, impudent voice as you pass—nor is the Indian girl to be overlooked in the novel contrasts which the "bello sexo" affords in this glorious land of the sun.

We called upon several French and Italian families resident in Granada, but found that a long period of naturalization had completely assimilated them to the natives of the country, with whom they had largely intermarried. But what surprised us most was, that in the best houses it was no uncommon thing to find a shop occupying the "esquina," or corner, or a room on one side of the court, in which few of the ladies thought it derogatory to their dignity or a violation of propriety, to preside on any necessary occasion. In fact, these shops were generally superintended by the wife of the proprietor, seated with her sewing in her lap, in an easy chair, behind the low counter. And even in entertaining her visitors in the grand sala, it was common for the lady to keep an eye to what was passing in the "tienda," through a convenient, open door. In the larger establishments, however, there exists all the paraphernalia of clerks and attendants which we find at home.

When we returned from our visits, we found a party of three Americans waiting for us. One was Dr. S., who had resided for many years in the country, where he held the first place as a "medico," and was a universal favorite amongst all classes of the people. By him we were introduced to the others, both of whom had come out with the company of Californians to which I have alluded. Mr. P., who was to have acted as engineer of the preposterous craft which was anchored off the Castillo, was reduced by illness, and being unable to accompany the party, had abandoned it, and was thus far on his return to the United States; but sick and destitute, was now anxiously awaiting my arrival, to procure the means of reaching home. He, however, was comfortably situated, having been generously and hospitably received by Señor Lacayo, a prominent native merchant, who had, in the current phrase of the country, placed "his house at the disposition" of the stranger. The third person was a young physician from New Haven, from whom we learned that the Californians were still detained at Leon and Chinandega, waiting for a vessel to take them off, in great impatience and discontent. Wearied of the delays, this gentleman had returned on a flying visit to Granada, where he had been staying for a fortnight. Meantime, the disturbances in the country had come to a crisis, and the day of our arrival he had attempted to return to Leon, but was turned back by armed parties on the road, who gave him the unsolicited pleasure of looking down their presented musket-barrels, by way of enforcing their wishes. The doctor, who had met Somoza in times past, and entertained a good deal of faith in his personal influence and prowess, informed us that the rebel chief had once been imprisoned in Granada, and owed it a special spite. He had sworn to burn the city, and the doctor was of opinion that he would keep his word. He thought we might, any night, have an attack; but felt confident that foreigners, keeping out of the way, would sustain no injury. At any rate, if the worst came to the worst, we could all collect together, under the American flag, and between revolvers, rifles, and what not new invention, make a respectable fight against the poorly armed assailants. And by way of encouragement, the doctor gave us an animated account of a party of foreigners, but five or six in number, who some years before had sustained a siege of three days, in this very city, and kept their assailants at bay, until they were dispersed by the troops of the government.

I had arranged that afternoon to ride to the cacao estates called the "Malaccas," distant about five miles from Granada; and although the city was full of stories about the "facciosos" who infested the country, I persisted in my determination to go. My companions thought they could entertain themselves very well in the city; so I armed Ben, and with an English creole merchant resident here, who kindly furnished horses, started for the Malaccas. We had already discovered that the horses of Nicaragua were of the Arabian stock; and although like the Arab horses small, they were compact, fleet, good tempered, spirited, and of excellent bottom. As all travelling here is performed on horseback or on mules, great care is used in breaking and training saddle beasts, while their price depends less upon their beauty than upon their training. They are all taught a rapid but exceedingly easy gait, between trotting and pacing, called the *paso-trote*. A well-trained horse strikes at once into this gait, and keeps it steadily from morning to night. I have ridden them from twenty to forty miles at a heat, without once breaking the pace, and with less fatigue than would be occasioned in riding the best saddle-horses in the United States for a distance of five miles. At this gait the horse gets over the level roads of Nicaragua, at from six to eight miles the hour. The same animal is frequently taught several gaits, and may be forced into one or the other by a peculiar pressure on the bit, which is very different from those used in the United States, and gives the most perfect control of the animal to the rider. Besides the *paso-trote*, which may be called the ordinary gait, the horses are taught an easy amble, the *paso-llano*, which is very rapid, and yet so gentle that, as observed by a recent Peruvian traveller, the rider may carry a cup of water in his hand without spilling a drop, while going at the rate of six miles an hour. There are also other gaits taught to different horses, which have each their advocates; among them the *paso-portante*, in which the horse raises the fore and hind foot of each side simultaneously, causing a rapid see-saw motion, not agreeable to riders generally.

The saddles are modifications of the Mexican saddle, with high peaks, over which are thrown gaudily colored sheep-skins, here called "pillons," or "pellons." The equipment is not complete without a pair of holsters and pistols; and a Nicaraguan "caballero" is never so much in his element as when mounted on a spirited, champing horse, with a fanciful "pillon," jingling bit, and portentous spurs, his sombrero, covered with oiled silk, set jauntily on the side of his head, with a señora or two in a neighboring balcony to whom he may lift his hat as he passes by. The ordinary saddle, or "albarda," is a very cheap affair, and will hardly admit of a description which shall be comprehensible to the uninitiated reader. It is sometimes used from preference, but my experience would never lead me to recommend it to any but an inveterate enemy.

The road to the Malaccas passed through an unbroken forest, into which we struck almost as soon as we left the city. It was level, completely arched over with trees, whose dense foliage shuts off the sun; while cactuses, and shrubs whose fragrant flowers almost compensated for the thorns which pricked one's legs, and scratched one's hands in endeavoring to pluck them, fenced in the path with a wall of verdure. Here and there we caught glimpses of the lake through a vista of trees, while at intervals, narrow, well-beaten paths branched off to the "hattos" and haciendas which were scattered over the country, away from the principal thoroughfares. We met men and boys driving or riding mules loaded with corn, *sacate* (grass), fruits, wood, and all the various articles of common use in the city, and occasionally a woman going in with a basket of chickens, sausages, coffee, or cacao, to be offered the next morning in the market. The entire stock, in some instances, was hardly worth a *medio* (sixpence), but this, it should be remembered, is no insignificant sum, in a country where a *rial* (twelve and a half cents) is the daily wages of a working man. All these people bowed with the grace of courtiers as we rode by; for all, from the highest to the lowest, from the little Indian boy who clasps his hands before him and says "buena dia, señor," to the lady who inclines her fan to her lips in token of recognition, have an apparently instinctive sense of politeness.

After riding some miles, we came to open fields, and passed by several fine estates surrounded by ditches and cactus fences in full bloom. The fourth was that which we came specially to visit. A man opened the gate, and we rode in and dismounted under the corridor of the house, which was a large, square structure, built of adobes, and tiled. The proprietor was not at home, and the family, in the unsettled state of the country, had retired to the city. We were nevertheless received with the greatest civility by the mayor-domo, who insisted that we were hot and thirsty, and wanted "*algo fresco*," and incontinently despatched a boy to get some fresh cocoa-nuts, the milk of which, when the nut is not too much matured, is transparent as water, and makes a cool and delightful beverage,—especially when a drop of brandy is mixed in "to take off the edge," and prevent fevers! The mayor-domo complained loudly of the condition of public affairs; now was the time for collecting the cacao, but no men were to be had; a few of those who had been employed on the estate were implicated in the insurrection, others had been pressed into the army, and still others had fled to the seclusion of the fields, to avoid the same fate. He had only half a dozen boys and some women to assist him, and they were "sin valor, nada," of small account. He showed us a large square space where the ground was beaten hard and swept clean, in which the nuts, after being removed from the husks, were spread on skins to dry. They required to be turned often to prevent moulding, and after becoming thoroughly dry, had to be carefully assorted, one by one, and packed in skins.

After resting awhile, we mounted again, and riding through a long gravelled walk, completely fenced in and arched over by magnificent mango trees, now literally golden with fruit, and through a vista of orange trees beyond, flanked by marañons, we entered the cacao plantation. It is difficult to describe these plantations; they more resemble beautiful parks of large trees, with broad walks running in every direction, all kept scrupulously neat and clean, than anything else in the United States with which they can be compared. The tree producing the fruit is known to botanists by the generic name of *Theobroma*, from the Greek, and signifying food for a god. It seldom rises higher than twenty feet; its leaves are large, oblong, and pointed, somewhat resembling those of the cherry tree, but infinitely larger; flowers small, and of a pale red color: they are surrounded by oval-pointed pods, grooved like a musk-melon, although much smaller; the nuts are very numerous, some pods containing as many as fifty; it produces two crops a-year, but is never without some pods on it. The trees are planted about fourteen feet apart, in a good soil. It is peculiarly necessary to defend this tree from the scorching rays of the sun, and at the same time sufficient warmth should be afforded for vegetation; this is done by shading it with the plantain tree and the Erythrina. As the cacao advances in size, the plantain is cut down, the Erythrina, or *coral tree*, or as it is sometimes called "*cacao madre*," mother of the cacao, having attained sufficient height to protect it from the sun. It begins to bear at seven years old, and comes to perfection in about fifteen years. The coral tree grows to about the height of sixty feet, and entirely drops its leaves (in Nicaragua) about the end of March and beginning of April, and then becomes covered with flowers of a bright crimson, and shaped like a cimetar. At this season an extensive plain, covered with cacao plantations, is a magnificent object, when viewed from a height. The tops of the far-stretching forests of Erythrina then present the appearance of being clothed with flames. The cacao, it may be added, is indigenous to America, and became early an article of general consumption by the Spanish Americans, as it had been of the Indians from time immemorial. Subsequently to the Discovery it was introduced into the Canary and Phillipine islands by the Spaniards. It was called *tlalcacahuatl* by the ancient Mexicans; amongst whom, as also among the natives of Central America, New Granada, and Peru, it was used as money, or a medium of exchange. It is still used as such in the markets of the cities of Granada and Leon. One hundred and fifty of the nuts were formerly valued at a dollar, which is, I believe, their present valuation. The cacao of Nicaragua is regarded as second to none, unless to that of Soconusco, which, during the Spanish dominion, was a monopoly of the crown. It is almost entirely consumed in the country, where it commands double the price of the Guayaquil, that which usually reaches the United States.[1] The taste for chocolate grows with its use, and

[1] Great confusion exists in the popular mind in respect to *Cocoa*, *Cacao*, and *Coca*, which are very generally confounded with each other, although differing as widely as almost any three products which it is possible to mention. *Cocoa* is the name given to a species of palm, producing the

hardly any person resides under the tropics for any length of time, to whom it does not become more an article of necessity than luxury. "He who has drunk one cup," says Cortez, in one of his letters, "can travel a whole day without any other food, especially in very hot climates; for chocolate is, by its nature, cold and refreshing." And the quaint old traveller in Central America, Gage, devotes a whole chapter to its praise, the manner of its use, and its effects on the human system. He asserts that *chocolate* "is an Indian name, compounded from *atl*, which in the Mexican language signifies *water*, and *choco-choco-choco*, the sound which water makes when stirred in a cup." He claims for it a most healthful influence, and bears his testimony as follows: "For myself, I must say, I used it for twelve years constantly, drinking one cup in the morning, another yet before dinner, between nine and ten of the clock; another within an hour or two after dinner, and another between four and five in the afternoon; and when I purposed to sit up late to study, I would take another cup about seven or eight at night, which would keep

cocoa-nut, which is too well known to need description. *Cacao*, the fruit of the cacao-tree, (*Theobroma cacao*,) described in the text. This fruit is described in the scientific books "as a large coriaceous capsule, having nearly the form of a cucumber, from the seeds of which the buttery and slightly bitter substance called cacao, or chocolate, is prepared." *Coca* is the name given to a shrub,(*Erythroxylon coca*,) which grows on the eastern declivities of the Andes of Peru and Bolivia; and is, to the natives of those countries, what opium and betel are to those of Southern Asia. Its leaves, which are chewed by the Indians, have such an effect in allaying hunger and thirst, that those who use them can subsist several days without any other nourishment. The shrub grows about six feet in height, with bright green leaves and white blossoms. When the leaves are ripe, that is to say, when they crack on being bent, they are gathered and dried. They are chewed or eaten with a little unslacked lime, to give them a relish. When constantly used, they produce some of the deleterious effects of opium.

me waking till about midnight. And if by chance I did neglect any of these accustomed hours, I presently found my stomach fainty. And with this custom I lived for twelve years in these parts, healthy, without any obstructions, or oppilations; not knowing what either Fever or Ague was." He, however, warns against the use of the cacao before preparation, for the reason that the simple nut, when eaten, as it often is by the Creole and Indian women, "doth notably obstruct and cause stoppings, and makes them look of a pale and earthy color, as do those that eat earthenware and pieces of lime wall."[1]

As I have already said, the cacao tree is so delicate, and so sensitive to exposure, that great care is required to preserve it during the early periods of its growth. It commences to bear in seven or eight years, and continues productive for from thirty to fifty years. Capital and time are therefore required to start an estate; but once established, it is easily enlarged by annual additions. One man, it is calcu-

[1] After giving expression to his enthusiasm on the subject of Cacao, Gage becomes philosophical, and discourses thus lucidly upon what, in these transcendental days, would be called "the dual nature, harmoniously blended," of this wonderful product:

"Cacao, although a Simple, contains the Quality of the four Elements; yet it is held to be cold and dry, *à prædomino.* It is also in the substance that rules these two Qualities, restringent and obstructive, of the Nature of the Element of the Earth. And as it is thus a mixed and not a Simple Element, it hath parts correspondent to the rest of the Elements; and particularly it partakes of those which correspond with the Element of Air,—that is, heat and moisture, which are governed by unctuous parts; there being drawn out of the *cacao* much Butter, which I have often seen drawn out of it by the Criolian women to oint their faces. * * And this is very conformable to reason, if we consider that every Element, be it never so simple, begets and produceth in the liver four Humors, not only differing in temper but substance; and begets more or less of that Humor, according as the Element hath more or fewer parts corresponding to the substance of that humor which is most ingendered."—*A New Survey of the West Indies*, p. 239.

lated, is able to take care of a thousand trees, and harvest their crop. As a consequence, cacao estates are more valuable than those of sugar, indigo, cotton, or cochineal. A good plantation, with fair attention, will yield an average annual product of twenty ounces of cacao to every tree, which for one thousand trees equals twelve hundred pounds. At the usual market rate of twenty-five dollars the quintal, this would give three hundred dollars per annum to each thousand trees and each laborer. Owing to a variety of causes,—some of the most important are obvious enough from what I have already said,—this yield is seldom obtained in Nicaragua; but may be when order is fully restored, and labor and its wages properly organized. No means exist for obtaining even an approximate estimate of this branch of production in Nicaragua, and I shall not therefore attempt to present any statistics on the subject, but proceed with my narrative.

I was delighted with the plantation, and after riding for an hour, until we got bewildered amongst the cross-walks and avenues, we began to thread our course back again. This was no easy matter, and we marched and countermarched for a long time before we struck the right path. This will not appear so surprising when I say that the plantation contained ninety-five thousand trees, which are valued at one dollar each.

Once in the main road, we paced slowly along on our return to the city, with that feeling of satisfaction which is always experienced after visiting an object that more than realizes the anticipation. I began to indulge the pleasing fancy that I might yet come to have a cacao plantation, which would be just the thing for a student or a man who loved his ease. It would require no expensive machinery, no long practice in manipulation of any kind; a boy could go through all the simple processes, and the whole might be left for a year or two without suffering the deterioration of sugar, rice, or cotton plantations. The summers in El Norte, and the winters here amidst the cacao and orange, with only a few days of steaming between,—of course the thing was feasible.

While indulging such reveries as these, my horse, which was the fastest walker, had carried me some distance ahead of my companion, when turning a sharp corner, I came abruptly upon a party of armed men, reclining in easy attitudes under a large cebia tree. I at once drew rein, and they as suddenly leaped to their feet and formed in line. My companion at that moment coming up, hurried past me, in evident anxiety as to the character of the party, and I followed close at his heels. One who seemed to be in command, stepped forward as we approached, exclaiming, "Quien vive?" "Amigos," friends, replied my companion, cautiously avoiding the pass-word of the government, until he knew whether the party was a strolling band of "facciosos," or regular troops of the State. Meantime we continued to approach, as if in perfect confidence, until ordered to stop by the person in authority, who advanced a few steps and scrutinized us for some moments, and then, with the air of a man satisfied, motioned us to go on. As I passed, he lifted his hat in recognition, exclaiming, "Adios, Señor Ministro!"

It was a disguised scout from the garrison, on the lookout for a party of insurgents which was reported to be committing some excesses in this direction. I had been quite excited with the prospect of an adventure, and even indulged a vague hope that the one in command might prove to be Somoza himself; the upshot was, therefore, something of a disappointment. An interview with the robber chief, whose name carried terror through the whole country, and a handsome villain withal,—what a paragraph it would have made in these "Incidents of Travel!" I was clearly not in luck, but comforted myself with the possibility of a night assault upon the city, in anticipation of which Ben daily examined our armory, re-capped each formidable Colt, and had even prepared the proper timbers for barricading our house at a moment's notice. I tried to work myself into a state of excitement, anxiety, and suspense, but it was of no use; we ate and drank inordinately, slept soundly, and altogether voted insurrections to be humbugs and bores.

There was great anxiety for the arrival of the commander-in-chief of the forces of the State, General Muñoz, with reinforcements, and we were amused for a week with rumors that he had just started from Leon with a thousand men,—was within two days' march,—and then that he had not started at all, that there was trouble in other departments,—in short, the city was in a fever, and full of reports; to which, after a few days, we ceased to listen, or listened only to laugh at them. We almost concurred with the Señorita Teresa in the wish that Somoza or General Muñoz would come,—she didn't care much which; for in either case this chronic state of alarm would be terminated. Upon the whole, she would rather prefer that the General should arrive, for he was the most polished man in the country, and withal would bring his military band, and then there would be no end to the evening music in the plaza, and the "*tertúlias*" and balls afterwards!

Between baths in the lake at early dawn, delicious snoozes in hammocks at noon, rides on the beach in the evening, dinners, visits, and a general overhauling of books, papers, and baggage, time passed rapidly and pleasantly enough for a week. During that period, I had put our sick countryman in funds, and he had started from Los Cocos, at the head of the lake, in a bongo owned at San Juan, for that port, there to wait a vessel for the United States. He came one afternoon to bid us good-bye, and as I looked in his pale face, momentarily flushed with the excitement of starting for home and friends, and heard his low, weak voice, I could not help thinking that the poor fellow would never reach his native land, and little supposed then that I should ever see him or hear from him again. But what was our surprise when, some five or six days thereafter, he came trotting into the court on a sorry mule, and in most woful plight. His eyes were very large, and his whole appearance that of a man who bears important news. He did not wait to be questioned, but started off at once with "I've seen him, I've seen Somoza!" His voice had all come back again. We got the whole of the story directly, told with a *naïveté* and earnestness which in themselves, apart from the incidents, were convulsing. He had embarked in a small bongo, with a colored gentleman, his wife, and two children, as passengers,—catalogued in the recital as "an old nigger, a fat wench, and two naked picaninnies." The narrow *chopa* he had the satisfaction of sharing with these pleasant companions; but after one night's trial, he had arranged that he might occupy it alone in the afternoons, on condition that his fellow-passengers should have exclusive possession of it the rest of the time. The second night, therefore, he watched the stars and kicked his heels in the bow, and had only just commenced his afternoon's lease on the succeeding day, and began dreaming of home, when he was aroused by a great commotion and loud words. He found the sails all taken in, a boat full of armed men, with a swivel at the bow, alongside, and a number of others similarly manned close by. His colored companion was dumb, and of a dull ashy color, while the spouse, with a child in each arm, was prone and sobbing in the bottom of the boat. The crew were in a like plight, their teeth fairly chattering with alarm. Standing beside the mast was a tall, graceful man, with a feather in his hat, a red Spanish cloak hanging over one shoulder, a brace of naked pistols stuck in his belt, and a drawn sword in his hand, with its point resting on the rower's seat beside him,—who was questioning the trembling patron, with bent brow and eagle eyes, in a tone which our friend said would have drawn the truth from a stone. He comprehended at once that this was Somoza, and at first had a notion of taking a shot at him, but thought better of it on the whole, and concluded to watch the turn of events, and so lay down again. The questioning was kept up for a very long time, as it appeared to him, while pretending to be asleep, but nevertheless keeping a sharp lookout. When he had finished, Somoza gave some order to his men, and stepped towards the *chopa.* Our poor friend thought it all up with him, but the insurgent chief only stooped down and took his arm, exclaiming, with a smile, in broken English, "How do, me amigo Americano?" Greatly relieved, our friend got up, whereupon Somoza dropped his sword, and throwing his arms around him, gave him an embrace, *la Española,* which made his back ache even now to think of. This was repeated several times, until the pain, overcoming all alarm, he cried in very agony, "No mas, señor, no mas!" No more, sir, no more! But this infliction only terminated to give place to another; for, taking both of our friend's hands in his own, with the gripe of a vice, he shook them until his arms were on the point of leaving his shoulders; delivering, meantime, an energetic oration, perfectly unintelligible to his auditor, who could only ejaculate, in broken syllables, "Si, señor! si, si, señor!!" yes, sir! yes, yes sir!!" This finished, Somoza took a splendid ring from his finger, and insisted on placing it on the hand of our friend, who, however, looking upon it in the double light of stolen property and a bribe, sturdily refused to accept it. He gathered that Somoza was going to attack San Carlos, and thus get possession of the arms and ammunition stored there, and of which he stood in much need. Somoza parted from him with much kindness, and after giving some orders in a threatening tone to the patron, retired to his own boat; whereupon the patron and his crew picked up their oars and pulled like mad, on the back track towards Granada. The last glimpse that was had of Somoza, he was standing in the stern of his boat, conspicuous amongst his half-naked men, from his red cloak and dancing plume, worn after the fashion of the mailed conquistadors.

Somoza, we afterwards learned, affected great attachment to the Americans, and at an early stage of his operations, had sent a courier to our Consul, bearing a letter full of assurances of good feeling, and expressing his determination after "regulating the Government," of proceeding to San Juan to expel the English "ladrones." He was nevertheless accused of being in the English interest, and acting directly or indirectly under British instigation.

I have, in a preceding chapter, anticipated the result of Somoza's visit to San Carlos, in its capture and that of our fat friend the commandante. The capture was made without firing a gun, nor was it attended with excesses of any kind.

With the information thus obtained of the whereabouts and destination of Somoza, the long-expected attack on the city receded in the distant perspective, and I resolved to proceed at once to Leon, especially as I began to entertain suspicions that the obstacles in the way had been magnified with a view of keeping us in Granada as pledges for its safety. That afternoon, however, a courier, which I had despatched to Leon, returned, bringing positive intelligence that General Muñoz was on the road, and at that moment at the large Indian town of Masaya, half a day's march distant, where he had arrested a number of persons implicated in the insurrection, and, in virtue of extraordinary powers, conceded by Government, was engaged in trying them by the summary process of martial law. He brought advices from Mr. Consul Livingston, that a party of twenty-five volunteers from among the Californians stopping in Leon had been furnished with horses by the Government, and would set out in a day or two for Granada, to escort the Legation to the capital. He also brought a number of the Governmental decrees and proclamations, showing that the state authorities were taking the most efficient means in their power to put down the insurgents and restore the peace of the State. Perhaps the mode of precedure cannot be better shown than by the following proclamations, decrees, and announcements, from the official bulletins, which will also serve to give an insight into the nature of the troubles which afflicted the State, and illustrate the style of composition, and the character of the appeals made use of by those in public station. The latter were of necessity adapted to touch the popular mind, and must therefore, give us some idea of its bent, the principles which it regarded as most important to be sustained, and the dangers most essential to be arrested. I have already intimated that the existing troubles had their primary origin in the virulence of the parties which divided the State; but that the proximate cause of the insurrection was the malefactor, Somoza, who had gathered a considerable number of reckless characters around him, and set all law at defiance. At first, and until overt acts were committed, such was the strength of party feeling, it is not impossible that the opposition to the Government was disposed to regard the movements of Somoza with indulgence, if not positive favor. But when it became apparent that his blows were aimed at all order, and that his real objects were revenge and plunder, party distinctions were forgotten; the opposition no longer looked upon his acts in the simple light of being embarrassing to the Government, but as directed against themselves and the body politic, and, forgetting all their previous predilections, heartily seconded the measures which were adopted to restore the public peace.

In one of the public papers of the time it was said:

"In every republic, parties have always existed, and always will exist. It is right and necessary that they should, in order to act as checks one on the other, and thus protect the public welfare. Honestly differing in their views of certain measures of national policy, and in the decision of which every citizen must feel the deepest interest, we have long had, in

Nicaragua, two parties, bearing the somewhat extraordinary names of '*Timbucos*' and '*Calandracas*.' So far from regarding this circumstance as a thing to be deplored, the well-wishers of the State have witnessed it with satisfaction, as showing that the people at large comprehended the nature of republican institutions, and the necessity of deciding for themselves, upon whatever, of a public nature, might affect them or their interests. We have seen one of these parties, after a long struggle, in which arguments were substituted for bayonets, and ballots for bullets, succeeding the other, and reforming the fundamental law of the State, while the other, as in duty bound, yielded peaceably to the will of the majority. The laborer pursued his avocations undisturbed while this peaceable revolution was going on; the merchant continued his legitimate business; no blood was spilled, no women widowed, or children rendered fatherless.

"The monstrous faction which now threatens the State belongs to no party; it is a Vandalic horde, aiming, by vile means, at unwarrantable ends, and directing its efforts against the Government, not because of the policy of that Government, but because it is charged with the execution and vindication of the laws which this faction would annul and destroy! It is made up of enemies of order, of liberty, and of humanity. Let not former differences of opinion blind men to the real enormity of the insurrection; let no party favor this attempt to overturn not only the existing, but all governments, and plant anarchy in the soil of peace. When the country is threatened, we are neither 'Timbucos' nor 'Calandracas,' but Nicaraguans. We cannot believe that this faction, which has no principles, no policy, no moral incentives to action, and whose constant object is the destruction of society, can find sympathy or support, except amongst assassins and robbers."

The first step taken by the Government, upon ascertaining the formidable character of the insurrection, is indicated below.

OFFICIAL BULLETIN.

LEON, JUNE 19, 1849.

"No man shall be molested or persecuted on account of his opinions, of whatever nature they may be, provided that he does not by any overt act infringe the laws."
—*Art*. 30 *of the Constitution*.

"Every one has seen with horror the devastation which has followed in the steps of the barbarous Bernabe Somoza since his arrival in the town of St. George, in the Department Meridional. He burned and desolated its haciendas, and gave the city of Rivas to the flames, at the same time that, with the horde that follows him, he attacked the garrison of the line, and the various patriots assembled there, who, after having sustained a siege of eleven days, in the most heroic manner, were compelled to retreat;—therefore, the Supreme Government, in discharge of the duties imposed upon it by humanity, religion, and the country, has issued the following extraordinary decrees:

"God, Union, Liberty."

Department of War;
House of the Government, Leon, June 19, 1849.

"*To the General-in-Chief, Commanding the Regular Forces of the State:*

"Sir: The Supreme Executive Power has ordered me to communicate to you the following decrees for execution: BUITRAGO."

No. 1.

"It having become necessary to the well-being of the State to put an end to the anarchical movements which threaten with destruction the persons and properties of the Departments Oriental and Meridional, and which now disturb the general peace, therefore, in view of this peremptory exigency, and in order to save the liberty of the people, and to put the State in a position to defend its independence and integrity, now placed in extreme danger by the refusal of the British Government to listen to our claims of redress against the usurpation of the most precious part of our territories, in conformity with Art. 48, Sec. 9, of the Constitution, it has been and is

DECREED:

"Art. 1. All citizens of Nicaragua, from the ages of sixteen to fifty years, are required by the fundamental law to take up arms in support of the public order and territorial integrity of the State, excepting only the clergy, and those who, by some physical defect, are absolutely incapacitated for military service.

"Art. 2. They are therefore required to present themselves for enrolment, with their equipments, and all horses and mules which they may possess, before the chief of the forces of the line in this city, or before the legionary commanders in the departments.

"Art. 3. The horses and mules as aforesaid of those who do not present themselves, are liable to be seized by detachments of troops sent out for that purpose, and the owners will incur the penalty, in case they are lost, of being excluded from recovering their value, as provided by Art. 173, Sec. 1, of the Constitution, besides being themselves subject to the penalties prescribed by Art. 104 of the penal code.

"Art. 4. The forces which may be enrolled shall hold themselves in readiness to move whenever and wherever required.

"Given in Leon this 19th of June, 1849.

"NORBERTO RAMIREZ."

No. 2.

"To save the State from anarchy, and to enable it to defend its territorial integrity, in compliance with duty, and in use of constitutional power, it is

DECREED:

Art. 1. That the General in Chief, Don Jose Trinidad Muñoz, is fully authorized to put an end to the existing insurrection, and to restore complete order, as also to place the State in an attitude to defend its territorial integrity; his orders are therefore to be punctually executed by the legionary commanders, and exactly complied with by the commissaries, not only for ordinary but extraordinary expenses.

Given in Leon, this 19th of June, 1849.

NORBERTO RAMIREZ.

Decrees were also issued for the collection of an extraordinary tax, and requiring persons entering the various towns to procure passports. The proclamation of the Supreme Director, Ramirez, was a well written appeal to the patriotism of the people, concluding as follows:

"No good object can be attained by disturbing the public peace, and the misguided men who have joined in these lawless movements forget that their interests are identical with those of all other citizens; forget that their conduct must destroy every social and civil privilege, and plunge society into its savage, chaotic state, when might shall subvert right; and when life, liberty, nor possessions are secure. Hatred begets hatred, and vengeance, vengeance; and they who strike against the wholesome restraints of law, will themselves be stricken down in its fall.

"People of Nicaragua, by your choice I have been placed in a position where my authority is individually greater than yours; but your blood has as much value as mine; my interests are yours, and those of the nation. Let me then, both as a magistrate and a citizen, conjure you, in the name of humanity, by our hopes of future prosperity, and on behalf of our country, to rally to the support of the constitution and the laws, and thus confound our enemies, and realize the blessings which shall flow from peace and the maintenance of public order."

The address of the General in Chief of the State to his soldiers, furnishes a very favorable example of the style of such documents in Central America; and its introduction will, in this respect at least, prove interesting.

"SOLDIERS!

"The honored standard of order, which you have hitherto so gloriously sustained, is again attacked. Forty intrepid men of your number covered themselves with glory, in maintaining the city of Rivas against overwhelming numbers; yielding only with their lives the trust confided to their care. Since their lamented fall, over which a bereaved country is still weeping, there has been no check on the wanton atrocities of the robbers and Vandals who overcame them. The devastation which moves with the insurgents will extend all over the State, if not opposed by the honor, valor, and patriotism you have so conspicuously exhibited in other days. What will become of our beautiful country, companions in arms, if this turbulence, which finds its food in blood and ashes, does not encounter, in its savage progress, the invincible obstacle of your courage?

"You are called upon to guard the supreme powers of the State, as you have sworn to do at the foot of your flag. Your loyalty and heroism have been and are still the shield of the country, not less than the terror of those who compass its destruction and your enslavement. The soul of the hero of Rivas, the valiant Martinez, will glory in your triumph over the enemies of the country for which he died!

"FELLOW CITIZENS, FRIENDS OF SOCIETY!

"Social order is attacked; the lava of sanguinary destruction threatens to overflow our dearest interests. The assassin of the honored Venerio, and of the innocent Solorio, the destroyer of the pacific Rivas, and the hated cause of innumerable other misfortunes, has seduced a portion of the unreflecting people of the department Meridional from their allegiance, and is leading them into the direst iniquities, while, like another Nero, he revels above the ruins of the capitol of that unfortunate department. But if your valor and patriotism unite to support the cause of order, they will interpose an efficient obstacle to the dangers which threaten us, and turn back in confusion the enemies of the State.

"The supreme government, the centre of order, has invested me with the largest authority to act for its support; and with your effective aid, I go with my soldiers to fulfill the duties with which I am charged. The country asks, if it need be, the lives of her sons; our wives, mothers, and children look to you in this emergency for the security of their liberty and lives!

JOSE TRINIDAD MUNOZ.

"HEAD-QUARTERS, JUNE 21, 1849."

The subjoined is also a specimen of the announcements and appeals made by the editors of the official Bulletin, with the view to rouse the patriotism of the people, and concentrate their indignation against the insurgents.

"We denounced before the people, in a previous number, the incendiarism, pillage, and bloodshed, with which that most ferocious barbarian, (*antropofago*,) Bernabe Somoza, had desolated the department Meridional; but those crimes were as nothing in comparison with the most unheard-of outrages and unparalleled barbarisms which he has more recently committed in that important section of the State. He has spared neither age nor sex, not even the unresisting wounded, nor the corpses of the dead; and with impious hand has seized upon the sacred vessels in the temple of the God of Justice, who, penetrating at a single glance the hearts of men, and always as just as inexorable in the end, will as assuredly save the virtuous, as he will, with his terrible lightnings, strike down the wicked and the criminal. In evidence of the new and almost incredible horrors which have filled up the cup of sorrow, for all those who possess souls and human sympathies, we publish the following account, communicated by Don Trinidad Salazar, commandant in the department Oriental, to the General-in-chief:

"'I have positive news from Rivas, that Somoza is still in that city, perpetrating every excess. He has shot all the wounded; robbed even the sacred vessels in the churches, and is on the eve of entirely burning the city. He has disinterred the body of Lieut. Col. Martinez, and dragged it naked through the streets. In short, these are but few examples of the thousand horrible acts committed by this barbarous man. Within an hour has died in this city, from the effects of his wounds, our friend, the brave Capt. Santos Ramirez, notwithstanding every means were exhausted to save him; and it only remains for me to pay his remains their last sad honors.'

"How terrible to the imagination, how disgraceful to humanity, are deeds like these, committed on the spot consecrated by the blood of the hero and Christian, the honored Don Manuel Antonio de la Cerda, first chief of Nicaragua, whose sacred corpse was also thus outraged in those days of barbarism which have been looked back to with horror, but which bear no parallel to those now passing in that unfortunate department.

"But those noble soldiers, the brave Martinez and Ramirez, shall receive the rites of sepulchre in our hearts. There we will engrave deep their memories. Their conduct shall be forever an example to our soldiers, to the friends of humanity, and the admirers of true honor. Our breasts shall be the temples where they shall receive the tribute of our gratitude, and immortal glory. God's justice and the sword of the violated laws have gone forth to avenge their blood!"

Having received these documents and the information accompanying them, I relinquished the idea of an immediate departure, and determined to wait for the arrival of the Californian escort. The news of the General's approach created great joy; and the bells were rung and guns fired in token of satisfaction. He was expected to arrive the next day; and that evening a "banda" was published, requiring the houses on the principal streets and on the plaza to be decorated, and everything put in order to receive him. The publication of the "banda" was a novelty to us. It was done in this wise: a party of soldiers, preceded by a drum and fife, and a municipal officer, marched through all the principal streets, stopping at each corner, when the music ceased, and the officer took off his hat and read the proclamation aloud, while the people thrust out their heads and listened. We laughed at first at this new mode of publishing the laws, but in the end came to regard it as not a bad idea.

That evening, there being no longer fear of the "facciosos," we had no difficulty in making up a large riding party for the Laguna de Salinas, distant about four miles from the city, which was represented to us as being lower than lake Nicaragua, salt, and shut in by perpendicular rocks. We followed the "camino real," in the direction of Leon, for a short distance, and then turned off on a narrow mule path, amongst the trees and bushes. It was very evident that the "caballeros" who accompanied us were determined to show us a specimen of their horsemanship, and rode at breakneck pace, keeping a bright lookout for the trunks and branches of the trees, now bending to their horses' necks to escape the latter, and now throwing their feet dextrously out of the stirrups, to avoid hitting the former. Thanks to early habits of life, this was no very severe trial to me, and I kept even pace with the rest, to their evident surprise, and the strengthening of their conviction that the Yankees were "up" to everything. We passed, here and there, a cane hut, surrounded by plantain trees, corn-fields, and patches of yucas, over ridges of volcanic scoriæ, covered only with grass, down into ravines with a scramble, and out again with a leap, and in half an hour came to the brink of the lake. I dismounted, and pushed through the trees and bushes to the edge of the precipice, and saw, far down, hundreds of feet below me, the glistening waters of the lake, surrounded on all sides by the same bare, blistered, black walls, with a rim of verdure skirting the water's edge. Mounting again, we rode a little further, to the sole place of descent, in part natural, but chiefly artificial. A narrow path, half-cut, half-worn, in the rock, wound down before us, something after the manner of the winding stairways in monumental columns, only not so wide. The horses picked their way cautiously, avoiding the loose stones, while the rider had enough to do to prevent his legs from being jammed against the wall of rock on either hand. A man had previously been sent ahead, to see that the way was clear, for there is no turning around in this narrow passage, which no doubt owes its origin to the aborigines, and is hardly wide enough to admit the passage of a horse. This cut passed, we came to a place where the fallen debris and rocks made a kind of shelf or terrace. Here we left our horses, the declivity below being very steep, and the rocks slippery withal, and proceeded on foot,—leaping from one stone to the other, and catching at bushes and saplings to check our descent. We soon came to the shore of the lake, where, beyond a line or belt of bushes, was a narrow beach of fine sand. The water was very clear and limpid, but had a sulphury or yellowish green color where it was deeper, a little distance from the shore. It was slightly salt to the taste, from the minerals held in solution. We observed some small fishes, and were told that there were alligators, but how they got here was a mystery; as I have already said, the lake is surrounded by absolutely precipitous walls of rock, several hundred feet in height, with no practicable descent for man or beast, except at this point. It was evident enough that the lake was of volcanic origin; but in what way formed, was not so clear. The black and frowning rocks seemed to imply that it was an ancient crater; but this conclusion was somewhat shaken by the fact that, from the plain, upon the western side of the lake, rose a conical hill, or small mountain, which had been a volcano, and exhibited a crater. Had the earth sunk suddenly here, during some terrible convulsion of nature? "Quien sabe?" We afterwards found numerous other lakes, equally extraordinary, and some of considerably larger size. This one, called in the aboriginal language, Lendiri, was, I should think, about three miles in circumference.[1] The trees grew to the very edge of the precipice, and vines and creepers hung in waving festoons down its rugged sides; altogether forming an impressive picture. Our appreciation of it was not a

[1] Oviedo (1529) says of this lake, "In the province of Diria is another lake, the water of which is salt, like that of the sea; and the flavor of the fish, which it produces in abundance, is far superior to that of the other fresh water lakes of which I have spoken. It is about a league and a half, or two leagues, from Granada, or Salteba."

little enhanced by the feeling, half of curiosity and half of awe, which every one must experience upon witnessing, for the first time, the terrible effects of volcanic forces, and which no familiarity ever materially weakens.

We were hot, weary, and thirsty, when we had clambered again to where our horses were fastened, and emptied a flask of "agua ardiente" and water, with which one of the party had considerately supplied himself, in much less time than it takes me to make the confession, and with a satisfaction which I shall not attempt to describe. We returned leisurely, for the shades of evening were falling, and the narrow path was much obscured by the trees. It was late when we reached the city, which had now recovered from the chilling influences of impending danger, and was gay and cheerful. The streets were thronged with noisy children, and the señoras and señoritas were all seated in the doorways or in the balconied windows, in quiet enjoyment of the cool evening breeze, which swung the lamps, suspended in front of each house, slowly to and fro. There seemed to be a sense of the luxury of mere existence among the inhabitants, which the traveller looks for in vain except under the tropics, and which there appears to be in perfect harmony with nature.

We had scarcely entered the main street, when my companions suddenly stopped short, and taking off their hats, turned back again. Without comprehending fully the reason, I did the same. The next moment, however, I heard the tinkling of a bell, and looking around the corner, saw a procession of persons with uncovered heads, each bearing a light, preceded by a boy ringing a bell, who was followed by some men playing on violins, and a guard of soldiers surrounding four persons who supported, with silver rods, a crimson silken canopy, over a priest dressed in his robes, and carrying the host. The children fled to the sides of the street and fell on their knees, as did also all the inhabitants, upon the approach of the procession, which was proceeding to the house of some one dangerously ill, or dying. We stood in the cross street, with uncovered heads, as it passed by. It was only a few years before that a party of foreigners had been torn from their horses and otherwise maltreated, because they did not dismount and kneel on an occasion like this. The people, however, had now become comparatively enlightened and liberal, and exacted nothing beyond a decent respect for their religious notions and ceremonies. It looked rather strangely to see a file of soldiers, with glancing bayonets, surrounding a priest bent on such a mission; but either to insure proper respect, or to show it, the guard is never omitted, if men and muskets are, by any possibility, to be found. Sometimes the priest rides in a lumbering carriage, or is carried in a litter or chair, on men's shoulders.

That night, until eight o'clock there was a firing of "bombas" in the plaza, and general demonstrations of satisfaction everywhere, to say nothing of great preparations for the morrow, the day announced for the arrival of General Muñoz and his veteranos. Preceding that event, and the recital of what followed, it will not be uninteresting to turn for a moment to the early history of Granada, which was a city grown, long before the Pilgrims landed at Plymouth, and before Hudson entered the bay of New York.

CHAPTER VI.

DISCOVERY OF NICARAGUA IN 1522; GIL GONZALES DE AVILA, AND HIS MARCH INTO THE COUNTRY; LANDS AT NICOYA; REACHES NICARAGUA AND HAS AN INTERVIEW WITH ITS CAZIQUE; IS CLOSELY QUESTIONED; MARCHES TO DIRIANGA, WHERE HE IS AT FIRST RECEIVED, BUT AFTERWARDS ATTACKED AND FORCED TO RETREAT; PECULIARITIES OF THE ABORIGINES; THEIR WEALTH; ARRIVAL OF FRANCISCO HERNANDEZ DE CORDOVA; HE SUBDUES THE COUNTRY, AND FOUNDS THE CITIES OF GRANADA AND LEON; RETURN OF GONZALES; QUARRELS BETWEEN THE CONQUERORS; PEDRO ARIAS DE AVILA THE FIRST GOVERNOR OF NICARAGUA; HIS DEATH; IS SUCCEEDED BY RODERIGO DE CONTRERAS; HIS SON, HERNANDEZ DE CONTRERAS, REBELS AGAINST SPAIN; MEDITATES THE ENTIRE INDEPENDENCE OF ALL SPANISH AMERICA ON THE PACIFIC; SUCCEEDS IN CARRYING NICARAGUA; SAILS FOR PANAMA; CAPTURES IT; MARCHES ON NOMBRE DE DIOS, BUT DIES ON THE WAY; FAILURE OF HIS DARING AND GIGANTIC PROJECT; SUBSEQEUNT INCORPORATION OF NICARAGUA IN THE VICE-ROYALTY OF GUATEMALA.—THE CITY OF GRANADA IN 1665, BY THOMAS GAGE, AN ENGLISH MONK; NICARAGUA CALLED "MAHOMET'S PARADISE;" THE IMPORTANCE OF GRANADA AT THAT PERIOD; SUBSEQUENT ATTACK BY THE PIRATES IN 1668; IS BURNT; THEIR ACCOUNT OF IT; THE SITE OF GRANADA; ELIGIBILITY OF ITS POSITION; POPULATION; COMMERCE; FOREIGN MERCHANTS; PROSPECTIVE IMPORTANCE.—LAKE NICARAGUA; ITS DISCOVERY AND EXPLORATION; INTERESTING ACCOUNT OF IT BY THE CHRONICLER OVIEDO, WRITTEN IN 1541; ITS OUTLET DISCOVERED BY CAPTAIN DIEGO MACHUCA; THE WILD BEASTS ON ITS SHORES; THE LAGUNA OF SONGOZANA; SHARKS IN THE LAKE, THEIR RAPACITY; SUPPOSED TIDES IN THE LAKE; EXPLANATION OF THE PHENOMENON.

THE first Spaniard who penetrated into Nicaragua, was Gil Gonzales de Avila, in the year 1522. He sailed from Panama, and landed somewhere upon the shore of the Gulf of Nicoya, probably in the southern department of Nicaragua, now bearing the name of Nicoya, or Guanacaste. With four horses and a hundred followers, he advanced to the northward over land, meeting in his progress with several petty chiefs, and finally came to the territories of a powerful cazique called *Nicoya*, who, says Peter Martyr, "courteously entertained him, and gave him fourteen thousand pieces of eight in gold thirteen carats fine, and six idols of the same metal, each a span long," in return for which, adds Herrara, Gonzales "gave him some Spanish toys, and baptized him and all his subjects, being six thousand in number."

Here Gonzales heard of a powerful chief named Nicaragua, and proceeding fifty leagues to the northward, arrived in his territories, which were between the lake of Nicaragua and the sea, comprising the district of which the city of Nicaragua or Rivas is now the capital, and which occupies the site of the aboriginal town. To this chief, Peter Martyr tells us, De Avila sent the same message which "our men were wont to deliver to the rest of the Indian kings, before they would press them, that is to say, that they should become Christians, and admit their subjection to the King of Spain, if they did not which, then war and violence would be used against them." But Nicaragua, it appears, had heard of the "sharpness of the Spanish swords," and received Gonzales courteously and with great state, presenting him with "twenty-five thousand pieces of eight in gold, many garments, and plumes of feathers." Gonzales prevailed upon him to be baptized, as he accordingly was, with nine thousand of his subjects. Their sole objection to the rite was the prohibition of making war, and "of dancing when they were drunk," alleging that "they did nobody harm thereby, and that they could not quit their colors, weapons, and plumes of feathers, and let the women go to war, whilst they applied themselves to spin, weave, and dig, which belonged to the females and slaves." Nicaragua asked many shrewd questions of the Spaniards, one of which was, "why so few men coveted so much gold?" "Gonzales being a discreet man," observes Herrara, "gave such answers as satisfied him," although they have not been preserved.[1]

After much persuasion Nicaragua consented that "the idols which he worshipped should be cast down, and a cross set up in the temple, which was hung with fine cotton cloths; and thus the country was converted!"

From the territories of this chief, Gonzales, being everywhere kindly received, penetrated the country in various directions, and saw many towns, which, says Herrara, "though not large, were good and populous;[2] and multitudes flocked along the ways to see the Spanish beards, and habits, and their horses, which were so strange to them." While thus engaged, he encountered a warlike cazique, called *Diriangan*, a name that is perpetuated in that of the existing towns of *Diriambi*, *Diriomo*, and *Nindiri*, situated about fifty miles to the north-westward of Nicaragua. This chief was attended by five hundred men, with seventeen women, who wore many gold plates. They were drawn up in order, but

[1] Old Peter Martyr gives quite a minute account of the interview between Gonzales and Nicaragua, calculated to give a very high opinion of the shrewdness of the latter. He inquired about a flood, and how the Spaniards got their information on religious matters from heaven, who brought it, and whether he came down on a rainbow or otherwise; about "the sun, and moon, and stars, and of their motion, quality, distance, and effects!" All these things were noted down on the spot, by Cerezeda, the king's treasurer, who also affirms that Nicaragua was curious about the cause of day and night, and the blowing of the winds, "which Gonzales answered to the best of his ability, commending the rest to God." Gonzales had a long argument with him to prove that his idols were representatives of devils, and warned him in a style not yet wholly obsolete, to avoid them, "lest he should be violently carried away by them from eternal delights to perpetual torments and miserable woes, and be made the companion of the damned." To all of these things the Indians did not offer particular objection, but when they came to talk about temporal affairs, "they made a wry mouth."

[2] Peter Martyr says that he found "six villages, every one of which had two thousand houses a-piece."—"*De Novo Orbe*," *Decade* vi. p. 237.

without arms, "with ten colors, and trumpets after their fashion." When Gonzales came near, the colors were spread, and the cazique touched his hand, as did also each of his followers; every man presenting him, at the same time, with one or two turkeys, and each woman with "twenty golden plates, fourteen carats fine, each weighing eighteen pieces of eight, and upwards."

Gonzales endeavored to persuade Diriangan to become a Christian; but the chief demanded three days to consult upon the subject "with his women and priests." The Spaniards soon suspected that this was a *ruse*, and that it was his design to gather forces to attack and destroy them. In this they were not mistaken, for on the 17th of April, 1522, a body of several thousand Indians, "armed after their manner with cotton armor, head pieces, targets, wooden swords, bows, arrows, and darts, fell upon the Spaniards," and had it not been for the timely notice of a confederate Indian, would inevitably have destroyed them. The strangers returned to the market place, and received the onset of the Indians there. Several of the Spaniards were knocked down; for it seems that here, as in Mexico, it was rather the desire of the natives to capture than kill their enemies, in order to offer the prisoners as sacrifices to their gods. The Spanish horse, in this, as in a thousand other instances, saved them from defeat, driving back the Indians in great terror.[1] Gonzales, considering the smallness of his force, resolved, upon this event, to retire from the country. In passing the town of their former entertainer, Nicaragua, they were however attacked, but nevertheless succeeded in making good their retreat. "The

[1] Peter Martyr tells us that the Indians were not less afraid of men with beards than of the horses, and that therefore, to produce the greatest possible effect, Gonzales made artificial beards "from the powlinges of their heads, for twenty-five beardless youths which he had with him, to the end that the number of bearded men might appear the more, and be the more terrible to the barbarians."—"*De Novo Orbe*," *Decade* vi. p. 240.

Spaniards," adds Herrara, "gave a mighty account of the country upon their return to Panama; for which reason Pedro de Arias, resolved to found a colony there." He accordingly soon after despatched Francisco Hernández de Cordova, who, in 1522, founded the city of Granada upon the Lake of Nicaragua, and subsequently, in the same year, the city of Leon, upon the Lake of Leon, or Managua. Cordova erected a fort at Granada for its protection, but it is hardly to be supposed that the ruined works on the shore of the lake are the remains of this structure.

Gonzales, who had gone to Spain soon after his discovery, to procure the means of conquering and settling the country, finding himself anticipated by Cordova, raised a force and entering Honduras by the valley of Olancho, from the Bay of Honduras, marched upon the towns established by the latter. The consequences were many battles, and much disturbance and turmoil, exceeding anything which had previously resulted from the jealousies and rivalries of the conquerors, in America. Very little regard was paid to the mother country or its directions; in fact, after the death of Pedro Arias de Avila, who was the first governor of the country, Rodrigo de Contreras, his son-in-law, who succeeded him, openly disregarded the order of the crown, which prohibited its officers from holding the Indians as property. For this charges were preferred against him, and he went to Spain to vindicate himself in the "Audiencia Real." In his absence, his son, Hernández de Contreras, resenting his father's treatment, openly revolted. Their first victim was Antonio de Valdivieso, the bishop of Nicaragua, whose portrait is still preserved in the great cathedral at Leon. The insurgents were successful in gaining complete possession of the country; but not satisfied with this, they seized some vessels in the port of Realejo, and embarked for Panama, with a view of extending their conquests in that direction, and ultimately of seizing upon Peru. Hernández, in short, conceived the idea of becoming king of the continent, and ruler of the South Sea. He attacked and captured Panama; but on his way to reduce Nombre de Dios, encountered misfortunes which ended in his death. Thus terminated this bold and magnificent design; the magnitude of which appalled the King of Spain, and which, at one moment, seemed on the eve of a successful consummation. The anniversary of Hernández's death, on the 23d of April, 1549, was celebrated with great solemnity in the Cathedral of Panama, until the period of the independence from Spain.

It is not necessary, nor would it be particularly interesting, to trace the early history of Nicaragua further. In due time, it was organized as a province in the Kingdom or Captain Generalcy of Guatemala, and governed by a Governor Intendant, appointed by the crown, but subject to the Captain General of Guatemala, and so remained until its emancipation in 1823. At that time Granada was among the first cities to declare in favor of republicanism, and has always, in the partisan struggles which have followed, been on the liberal side, as opposed to the servile, oligarchical, or monarchical faction, whose machinations have kept the country in a state of constant alarm, and which is still the enemy of its peace.

Thomas Gage, an English monk, who went through Nicaragua in 1665, has left us a brief but interesting account of the country, which he calls "Mahomet's Paradise, from its exceeding goodness." At that time there were in the city of Granada two cloisters of Mercenarian and Franciscan friars, and "one parish church, which was a cathedral, for the Bishop of Leon did almost constantly reside there." The houses, he says, were fairer than those of Leon, and the merchants enjoyed great wealth. They carried on trade directly with Guatemala, Honduras, and San Salvador, as also with Panama, Carthagena, and Peru. At the time of sending away their vessels, ("frigats," as Gage calls them,) the city was one of the richest in all North America. The king's treasure from Guatemala and Mexico was often sent this way, when the Hollanders and other enemies infested the Gulf of Mexico. Gage tells us that while he was there, "in one day there entered six *Requas*, (which were each at least three hundred mules,) from San Salvador and Honduras alone, laden with indigo, cochineal, and hides; and two days after from Guatemala came in three more, one laden with silver, (which was the king's tribute,) another with sugar, and the other with indigo."[1] Respecting the "frigats" of which Gage speaks, we shall have more to say elsewhere. They generally sailed for Carthagena, but sometimes directly for Spain. They were occasionally intercepted by English and Dutch vessels cruising around the mouth of "El Desaguadero," or the San Juan, and the fear of this, observes the quaint old traveller, "did make the merchants tremble and sweat with a cold sweat."

Granada, in common with all the Spanish cities on the Pacific declivity of the continent, suffered much, at a later period, from the pirates. In 1686 it was attacked by a party from the combined French and English bucaneers then in the South Sea, and sacked. They landed on the seventh of April in that year, on the coast of the Pacific, in number three hundred and forty-five men. They travelled only at night, with a view of surprising the town. De Lussan, who was of the party, records the adventure. He says that on the ninth of the month, two days after their departure from the coast, the fatigue which they had undergone, and the sharp hunger which pressed them, obliged them to halt at a great sugar plantation, about four leagues from Granada, and on the way thither. It belonged to a Knight of St. James, who, however, escaped being taken prisoner, for the excellent reason assigned by the chronicler, viz.: "our leggs at

[1] "A New Survey of the West Indies," p. 421.

that time being much more disposed to rest than run after him." Upon coming near to the town, they discovered that their approach was known, and saw what De Lussan calls "two ships upon Lake Nicaragua," laden with the effects of the retreating inhabitants. They now proceeded with more caution, and upon capturing a prisoner found out that a portion of the inhabitants remained, and had entrenched themselves in the Place of Arms, or Plaza, which was guarded with fourteen pieces of cannon, and " six petereroes." This information, continues the worthy De Lussan, " would doubtless have terrified any but freebooters, but did not retard our design one minute, nor hinder us. About two in the afternoon of the same day, we came up to the town, where at one entrance into the suburbs we met a strong party lying in ambush for us, whom, after an hour's engagement, we fell with that fury on, that we made our way over all their bellies, with the loss of but one man on our side, and from thence entered the town, where we made a halt to wait for the answer of several of our company, whom we had detached to go round and take observation of a fort which we saw in a direct line with the street by which we entered." The reconnoitering over, and the plan of attack laid out with all military precision, the freebooters " exhorted each other to fall on bravely, and advanced at a good round pace to the attack." When they had got within cannon shot of the works, they were fired on, but at every discharge the pirates "saluted them down to the ground, by which means the shot went harmlessly over." This excellent practical joke the Spaniards met by false priming, "to the end that the pirates might raise their bodies after the sham was over," and then receive the real discharge. The pirates then broke into the houses and made their approaches through the walls, from one to the other; and finally came sufficiently near to use their fire-arms and hand grenades, and being superior in numbers, and withal well used to hard fighting, they soon succeeded in making themselves masters of the work. Upon the side of the pirates four men were killed and eight wounded, which, De Lussan complacently observes, "was in truth very cheap." They then went to the great church and piously sang the *Te Deum*, fixed their sentinels, and the Court of Guard, (which was probably some kind of commission to take charge of the plunder,) in the strong-built houses," and afterwards went out to gather in the booty. But their victory was a barren one, for they only found "a few goods and some provisions."

Much disappointed, they sent out parties to collect the treasures which they conceived might be hidden on the estates outside of the city, but with no better success, for they came back, as De Lussan classically observes, "*re infecta.*" They then caught a woman, whom they sent to the Spaniards with a demand for a ransom for the town, and a threat of burning the same in case their requisition was not complied with. The inhabitants were not so easily frightened, and did not trouble themselves to give an answer, whereupon the pirates "set fire to the houses out of mere spite and revenge."

While here, the pirates, wearied of their laborious and perilous life, indulged hopes of returning, through Lake Nicaragua, to Europe. But, in their own words, "the term of dangers and miseries which their destiny had in store for them was not yet come, and they could not take advantage of the favorable opportunity which now offered to get out of these parts of the world, which, though very charming and agreeable to those who were settled there, yet did not appear so to a handful of men, without shipping, the most part of the time without victuals, and wandering amidst a multitude of enemies, against whom they were obliged to be continually on their guard." So they fell back, with infinite trouble and danger, to the coast, being obliged to contest every foot of the ground. They embarked again and sailed for Realejo, which they captured, and subsequently took Pueblo Viejo and Chinendaga, and even made a descent on Leon. These same men, after further exploits on the coast, made a forced march across the continent, from the Gulf of Fonseca to Cape Gracios a Dios, through the northern department of Nicaragua (Segovia) and Honduras.

De Lussan describes the city of Granada, at the time of his visit, as a large and spacious town, with "stately churches and houses, well enough built, besides several religious establishments, both for men and women." Around the city "were a great many fine sugar plantations, which were more like unto so many villages than single plantations."

The site of Granada is admirably chosen. It occupies a gentle slope, descending towards the lake, which here forms a beautiful and partially protected bay, called the bay of Granada. Upon one side rises the great volcano of Momobacho, while behind are the undulating hills and ridges of land which intervene between the lake and the Pacific. The position is, in fact, the only eligible one on the western shore of the lake, near its head, where any considerable town could be built, due regard being had to space, salubrity, and convenience for trade. And while Leon, from the circumstances that it was almost immediately established as the seat of government, and was built in a more fertile and populous district, has preserved a larger population and a greater number of imposing public edifices, Granada has always held a higher place in respect of trade. Through it, from the earliest period, has been conducted the principal part of the commerce of the country, besides a portion of that of the adjacent provinces and States. It has not suffered so much from violence as the political capital; and although subject to the same influences which have depressed the country at large, it has felt them less. Wealth has, in consequence, concentrated here to a considerable extent, and its commercial relations have led to the introduction of many foreign customs, without, however, materially changing its essential Central

American type. More foreigners have, from time to time, established themselves here, than in all the rest of the State. Some of them, after accumulating large fortunes, have returned to their native lands, while others, from habit or inclination, have remained, and almost entirely assimilated themselves to the native population.

The population of Granada is now estimated at from twelve to fifteen thousand inhabitants. This estimate may, however, be considerably wide of the truth. When Juarros wrote, the population was calculated to be 863 Europeans, Spaniards and Creoles; 910 Mestizos; 4,765 Ladinos; and 1,695 Indians. Total, 8,233.

No means exist whereby its trade can be accurately estimated. With the exception of some direct trade with the city of Rivas or Nicaragua, situated on the lake forty-five miles below Granada, the entire commerce with San Juan is conducted through this city. Here are owned nearly all the boats used in the navigation of the lake and river, and here also reside the principal part of the "marineros," or men employed in managing them. There are several wholesale mercantile houses, trading directly with New York, London, Liverpool, some of the French, Spanish, and Italian ports, and Jamaica. The principal supplies of the merchants have, for a number of years, been obtained from the island last named, where their credit is said to be better than that of the traders from any of the other Spanish States. The transactions are often, if not generally, cash, or what is equivalent, remittances in bullion, indigo, or other staples of high value and little bulk. Advances are often made, however, on prospective crops, which seldom fail. Iron, copper, and China wares, silks, calicoes, cottons, etc., are the principal imports; while, as I have already said, the exports consist of indigo, bullion, hides, Brazil wood, and coffee. As it is almost impossible to limit the production of tropical staples in Nicaragua, such as indigo, coffee, cacao, cotton, rice, sugar, and tobacco, not to mention hides, dye-woods, and medicines, the wealth and importance of Granada must go on increasing, as the country becomes developed by the introduction of enterprise and capital, both of which are rapidly taking that direction. This remark will hold true, even though the prospective canal, or the projected route of transit between the oceans, should not pass through or near it; for it is really the only eligible position for a large town on the south or western shore of the lake, and is, and must ever remain, nearer than all others to the great centres of population and production. Several American hotels and mercantile houses are already established there, and it is becoming better known than any other city in all Central America. A small steamer now plies between it and San Carlos, at the outlet of the lake. A short wharf or two alone are wanted to facilitate landing, and secure vessels from the waves of the lake, which sometimes roll in here with almost the force and majesty of those of the ocean.

The lake of Nicaragua, called by the aborigines *Cocibolca*, which gives to Granada its importance, and which is the most remarkable natural feature of the country, has already been described, in general terms, in the second chapter of this book. It, of course, attracted the first attention of the Spanish adventurers, who made many wonderful reports of it, which, reaching Spain, excited much speculation as to the probability of a water communication between the two oceans. Indeed it was confidently announced by some that straits opened from it to the South and to the North Seas; but it was not until 1529 that it was fully explored. In that year, we are informed by the historian Oviedo y Valdez, (who was in the country at the time of which he writes, but whose chronicle remained in manuscript until 1840, and has not yet, in any part, been published in English,) in that year, Pedro de Avila sent a man named Martin Estete, at the head of a party of soldiers and Indians, to make an exploration both of Lake Nicaragua and Managua. They went into a province called Voto, which must have been to the northward of Lake Managua, but got involved with the natives, were attacked and driven back. They however saw, from the top of a mountain, a body of water, which they supposed to be a third lake. It was probably the great Gulf of Fonseca, which is nearly surrounded by land, and would, at a distance, be taken for an inland lake. Nothing of value resulted from this expedition. Subsequently, however, a private expedition was undertaken by Captain Diego Machuca, a friend of the historian Oviedo, which was more successful, and terminated in the discovery of the outlet of the lakes, down which the adventurers passed to the ocean. I shall let the old writer tell his own story. He says:

"Last year, (1540,) I met in the city of Santo Domingo the pilot Pedro Cora, who was one of those who had accompanied Estete in his trip to Voto, and had seen both the country and the dubious lake. He told me that he had come from New Castile, under the government of Francisco Pizarro, and that he had met at the port of Nombre de Dios some old friends whom he had known in the province of Nicaragua, and who had built a felouque and brigantine on the shores of the great lake of Nicaragua, called *Cocibolca* in the language of the country. With them was a man named Diego Machuca, with whom I have been well acquainted, and who had been commandant of the country of the Cazique Tenderi, and of the country around the lake of Masaya. After having spent some thousands of dollars in building and arming these vessels at their own expense, they embarked with the intention of exploring these lakes thoroughly, or of perishing in the attempt. Captain Diego Machuca advanced by land, at the head of two hundred men, taking the same course with the boats, which were accompanied by some canoes. They, in course of time, arrived at the spot where the waters of these lakes appeared to flow into the North Sea. As they knew not where they were, they followed the sea coast in an eastern direction, and finally arrived at the port of Nombre de Dios, where this pilot met them. He conversed, ate, and drank often with those who had thus passed out of these lakes into the sea. He also told me that Doctor Robles held these men as prisoners, because he himself wished to found a colony at the outlet of these lakes, and thus profit by the labor of another, as is the custom with these men of letters, for the use that they make of their wisdom is rather to rob than to render justice; and this was true of this man more than of others, for he was not only a *licenciado*, or *bachelor*, but a *doctor*, the highest grade of science, and has therefore shown himself the greatest tyrant! For this reason, his employment has been taken away from him. Besides, if he had undertaken to found a colony at this outlet, he would have met there Captain Machuca, who would not have consented to have thus lost his time, money, and trouble; the old soldier would have proved himself too sharp for the wise lawyer. I asked the pilot, at what point on the coast these lakes emptied into the ocean, but he replied that he was not at liberty to tell. I believe that he wished to conceal it from me himself, and that it was on this business he was going to Spain, on behalf of those who made the discovery. I believe this place to be about one hundred leagues west of Nombre de Dios,[1] and if I obtain any new information on this matter, I will put it in the concluding chapters of this book.

"I do not regard what are called the two lakes of Nicaragua as separate lakes, because they connect the one with the other. They are separated from the South Sea by a very narrow strip of land; and I should say that the distance from their upper extremity to the outlet in the North Sea, is two hundred and fifty leagues.[2] The measures given by Pedro Arias and others are not true, since they did not know their extent. They have made a separate lake on the side where is Leon de Nagrando, on the lands of a cazique named Tipitapa, which communicates with a narrow channel with that of Granada (Nicaragua.) In summer there is but little water in this channel, so little that a man may traverse it; the water coming up no higher than his breast. This lake is filled with excellent fish. But what proves that they are both one lake is the fact that they equally abound in sea-fish and turtles. Another proof is that in 1529, there was found in the province of Nicaragua, upon the bank of this lake, a fish never seen except in the sea, and called the sword-fish, (*pexe biguela*,) on account of a bone armed on both sides with sharp points, placed in the extremity of its jaw. I have seen some of these fish of so great size, that two oxen attached to a cart could hardly draw them. A description of these may be found in Cap. iii. lib. 13, Part first of this work. The one found on the shores of this lake was small, being only about twelve

[1] This estimate was very accurate; the actual distance is but about two hundred and fifty miles in a right line.

[2] Oviedo overshoots the mark here; read miles for leagues, and the distance is very near the truth.

feet in length, and must have entered at the outlet of the lake. Its sword only of a hand's breadth, and of the width of two fingers.

"The water of the lakes is very good and healthful, and a large number of small rivers and brooks empty into them. In some places the great lake is fifteen or twenty fathoms deep: in other places it is scarcely a foot in depth; so that it is not navigable in all parts, but only in the middle, and with barks constructed expressly for the purpose.

"It has a large number of islands, of some extent, covered with flocks and precious woods. The largest is eight leagues in circumference, and is inhabited by Indians. It is very fertile, filled with deer and rabbits, and named *Ometepec*, which signifies *two mountains*. It formerly contained a population much more numerous than now, divided into eight or ten villages. The mountain on this island towards the east is lowest; the other is so high that its summit is seldom seen. When I passed by this island the atmosphere was very clear, and I could easily see the summit. I passed the night at a farm belonging to a gentleman named Diego Mora, situated on the main land near the island. The keeper told me that during the two years he had been in that place he had seen the summit but once, because it was always covered with clouds.

"On the south side of the great lake is a smaller one, called *Songozana*, which is separated from it by a flat shore, but one hundred and fifty paces wide. It is formed by rains, which fill it up in the rainy season; and as it is higher than the great lake, its waters bear away the sand, and empty into it. This laguna then becomes filled with alligators and all kinds of fish. But during the summer it nearly dries up. The Indians then kill with clubs great numbers of alligators and fish. It is about a league and a half in length, and three-fourths of a league in breadth. I visited it in the latter part of July, 1529, and there was but little water in it. The farmer whom I have mentioned had many hogs, which fed on the fish which they caught here, and were so large that they looked frightful, the more so, because they had the smell and taste of fish. For this reason they are now kept away from the laguna, and only allowed to approach to drink.

"In this vicinity there are numerous black tigers, which made great havoc in this farmer's flocks. He had some excellent dogs, which had killed many of these tigers; he showed me one in particular, that had killed two or three. The skin of one of these animals, which he showed me, was black, like velvet. This kind is more ferocious than the spotted variety. He said he would not take a thousand dollars for his dogs, for his pork was worth a thousand, and without the dogs the tigers would have destroyed them all."

A laguna, something like that of *Songozana*, described by Oviedo, occurs about six miles above the city of Granada, near the place called "Los Cocos," but I am not aware that it is ever dry. The statement that sword-fish have reached the lake seems somewhat apochryphal, although it should be observed that Oviedo is usually very accurate in matters of this kind. It is, however, a fact that sharks abound in the lake. They are called "tigrones" from their rapacity. Instances are known of their having attacked and killed bathers within a stone's throw of the beach at Granada; and I have myself repeatedly seen them from the walls of the old castle, dashing about, with their fins projecting above the water. Great varieties of fish are found in Lakes Nicaragua and Managua, which are extensively caught and used by the people residing on their shores. The lake of Nicaragua was supposed, at one time, to have tides like the ocean, and the fact that it has an ebb and flow led to the early be-belief that it was only an estuary, or bay of the sea. The phenomenon is, however, of easy explanation. As I have said, the prevailing wind in Nicaragua is the north-east trade, which here sweeps entirely across the continent. This is strongest in the noon and evening, when it drives the water upon the western shores of the lakes; it subsides towards morning, when the equilibrium is restored, and an ebb follows. The regularity with which the winds blow, give a corresponding regularity to the ebb and flow of the lake. Sometimes, when the wind blows continuously, and with greater force than usual, from the direction I have named, the low lands on the opposite shore of the lakes are flooded to a great extent. Such occurrences, however, are rare.

CHAPTER VII.

NARRATIVE CONTINUED—ARRIVAL OF THE GENERAL IN CHIEF—THE ARMY—FIREWORKS BY DAYLIGHT—PRISONERS—INTERVIEW WITH GEN. MUNOZ—ARRIVAL OF THE CALIFORNIAN ESCORT—"PIEDRAS ANTIGUAS"—THE STONE OF THE BIG MOUTH—"EL CHIFLADOR"—OTHER ANTIQUITIES—PREPARATIONS FOR DEPARTURE—CARTS AND "CARRETEROS"—VEXATIOUS DELAYS—DEPARTURE—HOW I GOT A GOOD HORSE FOR A BAD MULE, ON THE ROAD—DISTANT VIEW OF THE LAKES—THE FREEDOM OF THE FOREST—ARRIVAL AT MASAYA—GRAND ENTREE—DESERTED PLAZA—A MILITARY EXECUTION—A "POSADA"—"HIJOS DE WASHINGTON"—DISAPPOINTED MUNICIPALITY—WE ESCAPE AN OVATION—ROAD TO NINDIRI—APOSTROPHE TO NINDIRI!—OVERTAKE THE CARTS—"ALGO FRESCO"—APPROACH THE VOLCANO OF MASAYA—THE "MAL PAIS"—LAVA FIELDS—VIEW OF THE VOLCANO—ITS ERUPTIONS—"EL INFIERNO DE MASAYA," THE HELL OF MASAYA—OVIEDO'S ACCOUNT OF HIS VISIT TO IT IN 1529—ACTIVITY AT THAT PERIOD—THE ASCENT—THE CRATER—SUPERSTITIONS OF THE INDIANS—THE OLD WOMAN OF THE MOUNTAIN—THE DESCENT OF THE FRAY BLAS CASTILLO INTO THE CRATER.

SUNDAY, the day after the events recited in a previous chapter, was ushered in by a general ringing of the church bells, and a miscellaneous firing of bombas, on the part of the boys. High mass was said in "La Parroquia," for the safe arrival of the General and his army. I now discovered the efficacy of the "banda." Red and yellow cloth was suspended in front of all the balconies; gay curtains shaded every window; festoons of flowers hung above every door, and little flags and boughs of trees were strung in all convenient places. The decorations in the plaza were particularly profuse and fanciful. Altogether the streets looked much like those of some of our own cities, tricked out on the occasion of a political festival, or some similar occasion, when impunity is conceded to absurdity of every kind. Men, women, and children were all dressed in their best attire, and seemed to be in high spirits. There was a general reaction from the despondency which had so long afflicted the popular mind; and, as I strolled through the Jalteva, I observed that already many of the fugitive inhabitants had returned, and that the municipality began to have some semblance of life again. At about eleven o'clock messengers arrived, announcing that the General was at a "hatto," a league from the city, waiting for the coming up of the main body of his troops. Directly I heard the roll of drums in the plaza, and shortly after saw a large cavalcade, embracing the municipal and departmental officers, and a body of several hundred of the leading inhabitants, defile past to meet and welcome the General. When they had departed, there was a lull in the city; the quiet of expectation had succeeded the bustle of preparation; and, there being nothing more to see, I went back to my quarters, and lying down in my hammock, suspended beneath the corridor of the house, where the fresh breeze circulated freely, rustling the orange leaves, took up Layard's Nineveh, which had been published a day or two before I left the States. I read of winged bulls, priestly processions, and Arab bands, and in a state of half-consciousness was trying hard to make out something about the Yezidis, who would, nevertheless mix themselves up with the marineros of the lake, and the Naïdes of San Migueleto, when the discharge of a cannon, and the simultaneous clang of every bell in the city, startled me to my feet, and announced the approach of the long-expected, and long-wished-for General.

I took my place in the outer corridor, to see whatever there might be to see. The streets were lined with people, mostly women, their heads protected by gaudy rebosos; while every door, window, and balcony was occupied by the better portion of the population, dressed to the limit of their finery.

The discharge of cannon continued at regular intervals, becoming more and more distinct as the guns approached, while the bells kept up an incessant and almost deafening clangor. The General, I thought, was slow in his movements, and a long time in coming; for it was full an hour before the head of the procession appeared, turning sharp around a corner near my quarters. A mass of horsemen, filling the entire street, passed along in utter confusion; but these, I soon saw, were the citizens who had gone out to act as an escort. Following these was a small detachment of lancers, who moved in entire order, and made a good appearance. After them came a party of officers, brilliantly dressed, preceded by the flag of the republic, around which the people pressed in a dense body, shouting "Viva el esclarecido General!" "Viva el Gobierno Supremo!" "Viva la Republica!" "Muerte à los enemigos del orden!" Death to the enemies of order! I had no difficulty in distinguishing amongst the fine body of men composing his staff, the erect and commanding figure of Gen. Muñoz himself. He was splendidly mounted, and wore a neat undress uniform of blue, turned up with red, and a Panama hat, covered with black oiled silk. He bowed in an easy and graceful manner, in acknowledgment of the "vivas" directed to him, and of the salutations of the señoras and señoritas in the balconies. I observed his face closely when he approached; it was animated but firm,—expressive of his true character, which is that of a humane, chivalrous, high-minded, and brave man. I then thought, and still think him the finest looking officer I ever saw.

Behind the General and his staff, was another detachment of lancers, followed by a band of music; then came the soldiers in divisions. First were the "veteranos," or soldiers of the line, in a uniform of white pantaloons and jacket, a little black cap with a red ball perched in front, a species of network knapsack, a blanket thrown, toga-like, over one shoulder, and a musket resting on the other. This is their whole equipment; they require no tents, baggage, or provision wagons. If it rains, they throw their blankets over their shoulders and the locks of their muskets, turn their pantaloons up to their thighs, and march on. At night they roll themselves in their blankets, and lie down anywhere. A plantain and a bit of cheese, or tortilla, or a cup of *tiste*, constitute their simple rations, and on such fare they will march forty and fifty miles a day, through a country where an equal European or American force would not average ten. This body of "veteranos," marched with great precision and in good order, and was followed by the new recruits, who were rather a hard looking set, dressed in every variety of costume, and not particular about keeping in line or marking step. Some wore only pantaloons and hat, the latter not always of the most classical model; some had long legs to their breeches, some short, and some none at all; but they all seemed to be in good spirits, and ready for almost any thing which might turn up. They bowed frequently, beckoned, and sometimes spoke to acquaintances amongst the spectators,—improprieties of which the "veteranos" were never guilty. In fact, the latter, who were almost entirely Indians, seemed as impassible as men of bronze. Amongst the officers in the General's staff I observed a full-blooded negro; but his features were as regular as those of any European. He afterwards distinguished himself by his bravery and fidelity, and was promoted in consequence.

Upon the entrance of the procession into the plaza, although it was broad daylight, a series of fireworks and rockets were let off, which produced a great noise and smoke, but none of those brilliant results for which they are got up amongst us, and of which the people here seem to have no idea. The primary object appeared to be to make a great noise, and in this they were perfectly successful.

That afternoon, a division of troops, which had been sent

out the previous day, to break up a party of insurgents, who had concentrated at the Indian pueblo of Diriomo, came in, having effected their object, and bringing a number of prisoners. Among them was one of Somoza's lieutenants, who was pinioned, and marched in at the point of the bayonet. A litter followed, bearing a wounded soldier, half of whose face had been shot away in the encounter, presenting a shocking spectacle.

Before night, it became evident that a decided hand had now the control of affairs; men were despatched to bring down the boats sent for safety to "Los Cocos;" scouts detached to gather information; a new regiment of enrolled men ordered to report themselves under arms next morning; and a proclamation issued, guarantying the safety of all those arrayed against the government who should come in and surrender their arms. The patrols were doubled, and that night we were treated to an extra number of "alertas," from watchful sentinels. In the evening a council was held, to which all the leading citizens, whatever their previous differences, were invited, and where the General himself set the example of patriotic forbearance and fraternization, by proffering his hand to men from whom he had been estranged for years. The result was auspicious, and the council resolved upon the most prompt and decided action.

Next morning, before sunrise, as I rode to take my daily bath in the lake, I saw the General in the Plaza, wrapped in his military cloak, drilling his troops in person. At eleven o'clock he paid me a formal visit, accompanied by his staff. My previous favorable impressions were more than confirmed by the interview. He spoke of the troubles in the country with the regret of a patriot, but the determination of a general, and sketched their origin, and the popular demoralization, boldly and impartially. Upon general topics he was familiar, and conversed with force and freedom. He had once been in New Orleans, where he had seen Mr. Clay, who appeared to have left a characteristic impression on his mind. I found him perfectly well acquainted with the origin and progress of the Mexican war, and with the relative parts sustained in it by the American officers. Upon the subject of British aggressions, he spoke with great bitterness, and in a manner which showed how deep and ineffaceable were the feelings of hatred which they had engendered. These aggressions, he said, made at a time when the country had begun to recover from its distractions, and when its more patriotic and intelligent citizens, before expatriating themselves in despair, were making a last effort in its behalf, and for the restoration of quiet and good government, were crimes against humanity not less than against the State. Just as the government had succeeded in reforming the army and restoring public confidence, when all its resources were wanted to carry out its new and enlightened policy, it found itself involved in a foreign controversy, shorn, on the shallowest pretexts, of half its territories, its revenues cut off, and all its energies crippled by a nation professing to be the most enlightened and philanthropic in the world! He had often felt dispirited, but had struggled on in the vague hope that the condition of the country might attract the sympathy and secure the good offices of other nations in its behalf,—as he now believed it had done those of the United States. The present disturbances, he added, had been directly charged upon the English, but however that might be, that people was directly responsible for its consequences; for the insurgents would never have dared to commit overt acts, whatever their disposition, had they not thought that the controversy with England had weakened the hands of the government, and rendered it almost powerless; and that in attacking it, they would receive some kind of countenance and support from British agents, if not from the British Government.

I am thus particular in giving the exact tenor of this conversation, as it was afterwards grossly misrepresented, and made the subject of not over-polite, but very characteristic official correspondence, on the part of the British agents.

In the afternoon of this day, the first division of our Californian escort, in a uniform of red shirts, and armed like brigands, made their appearance. They reported that the remainder had stopped for the night at the town of Masaya, in order to visit the extraordinary lake at that place, and would come on in the morning. The march of the General had cleared the roads, and as our arrival at the capital was anxiously expected, I determined to leave Granada at the earliest possible moment, and made my arrangements accordingly.

In the evening I visited a singular relic of antiquity, called the "piedra de la boca," the *stone of the mouth.* It is planted

"PIEDRA DE LA BOCA."

on the corner of one of the streets leading to the Jalteva, and consists of a large and singularly carved stone, which had been brought here by a curious "marinero," from an island in the lake. The accompanying engraving will convey a better idea of it than any description, and will explain why it bears its present name. It now projects about three feet above the ground, and is two feet broad by one and a half in thickness. I had made diligent inquiry for "*piedras antiguas*," ancient stones, but got very little information concerning any,—no information, in fact, except from an old priest and some boatmen, who represented that many were to be found on the island of Ometepec, and on the large uninhabited island of Zapatero. I had, however, no time to visit them now, but made a note of them for a future occasion. At the "esquina," or corner of the old Convent of San Francisco, was another "piedra antigua," called "*El Chiflador*," the whistler. It had been much broken, and the head and upper part of the body were entirely destroyed. The fragments which remained showed that it had been well and elaborately carved. Tradition says that, when it was perfect, its mouth was open, into which the blowing of the wind made a mournful, whistling noise, exciting suspicions that it was the incarnation of one of the ancient "demonios" of the Indians. The pious padres demolished it in consequence; but probably less on that account than because they often found offerings before it, which the superstitious Indians had deposited during the night time. Another figure stood, and probably still remains at the south-eastern corner of the great Plaza, carved in black basalt. It represents a human figure, with jaws widely distended, and protruding tongue. Upon the head is crouched the representation of some kind of wild animal, of the cat kind. It is comparatively small, but well carved, and bold and striking in its outlines. This, and "el chiflador" were brought from the island of Zapatero.

During the day, the remainder of the American division arrived at Granada. Including my own party, we mustered twenty-five strong, each man withal a walking arsenal. Two days were devoted to rest and visiting, and the morning of the third of July fixed for our departure. The evening previous, our baggage was packed in carts, and sent ahead, under the escort of a detachment of lancers.

In the inhabited parts of Nicaragua, where the country is entirely level, or but slightly undulating, carts are almost universally used for the transportation of goods and the natural products of the country. They are exceedingly rude contrivances, but seemed to meet every requisition. The body consists of a stout frame-work of wood, and the wheels, as I have already said, are solid sections, cut from some large tree of hard wood, usually the mahogany. These are not sawed, but chopped into shape, and with an eye rather to use than to symmetry or beauty. The oxen, which are compact, active, and hardy animals, are not fastened in a yoke, as with us, but to a bar passing across their foreheads, and firmly lashed to their horns. Two pairs are the usual complement of a cart, but sometimes three pairs are used. When the "carreteros" have far to go with heavy loads, an extra yoke or two is either led or driven along, to be used in case of accident, and to relieve the others when tired. Two men are attached to each *carreta*; one armed with his *machete*, or a gun, goes ahead, to clear away obstacles, and to indicate the path, for the oxen are trained to follow him; while another either walks behind or rides in the cart, and has a long pole pointed with an iron spike, with which he "touches up" the animals if they are inclined to loiter or be lazy. This kind of admonition is accompanied by shouts to them collectively or individually, for each one has a name, and with epithets more forcible than elegant. So the approach of a cart is often known while it is half a mile or more distant; not solely by the shouts and maledictions of the "carreteros," but by the awful squeaking and shrieking of the wheels, which never fail to set the strongest nerves in a quiver. The roads in Nicaragua are lined with fragments of broken carts, here a wheel split in pieces, and there an axle broken in two. The axles are the first to fail, and therefore every cart carries two or three extra axles, in reserve for emergencies. If, however, the carretero should be unprovided, he selects the first hard wood tree of the proper size which he can find, makes a new axle, and in half an hour is on his way again. The loads which are carried in these rude vehicles are almost incredible. Twenty-five hundred pounds is the standard freight, and is carried from twenty-five to

HIDE-COVERED CART IN NICARAGUA.

forty miles a day, depending somewhat upon the season. The morning, from three and four o'clock until eight or ten, and again in the evening from four until nine, are the usual hours for moving, for then the air is comparatively fresh and cool. Each cart carries a certain amount of "sacate" and corn for its animals, and their masters bivouac by the roadside wherever night overtakes them. The oxen are fastened to trees, the men light a fire and cook their coffee, and afterwards wrap up their heads in handkerchiefs, and if it is the dry season, swing their hammocks between two trees and go to sleep. It usually happens that two or more carts go in company, for mutual aid in case of accident, and then their encampments, upon which the traveller often comes suddenly at night, are highly picturesque. On such occasions, some swing carelessly in hammocks, others recline on the ground, and others busy themselves around the fire, while all smoke with unbroken energy. Half the night is sometimes spent in card playing, by fire light; and bursts of laughter and snatches of song startle the sleepy traveller jogging through the forests, and are answered by the growls of the wild beasts or the howls of the "mono colorado." They are stalwart, jolly fellows, these "carreteros," and like the "arrieros," or muleteers of Mexico, invincibly honest. Merchants never hesitate in entrusting the most valuable goods to their care, and I believe no instance is known of their proving faithless to the trust reposed in them. On the contrary, the poor fellows, when attacked by robbers, as they sometimes are, will fight to the death in defence of their carts. Like the "marineros" on the lake, they constitute an almost distinct class of citizens, and in the city of Leon live in a certain "barrio," or ward, that of San Juan. Some of them have a large number of oxen and carts, which they sub-let to the poorer members of the fraternity of "carreteros," among whom exists an *esprit de corps* which will permit no underbidding or other irregular practices.

The morning of our departure came, and agreeably to instructions, Ben roused us at early dawn. We were individually ready to move at sunrise; for, although we only proposed to go to the city of Managua, a distance of fifty miles, the first day, we wished to take the journey leisurely, as became travellers in a new and strange country. Don Frederico, as our old friend, Monsieur Sigaud, at San Juan, had done before, smiled incredulously when we talked of an early departure; but, as the horses and mules were positively engaged to be at our door at sun-rise, and as the man who let them was a person of mark, and an old Spaniard to boot, we felt a good deal of faith in our plans. The sun rose, and after walking up and down the corridor, in heavy boots, with clanking spurs, for half an hour, with a growing conviction that we were somewhat verdant, we were called to breakfast. Don Frederico looked provokingly good-natured, and when Ben, who had been despatched to stir up the laggard "*em-prestador*," returned, with the news that the men had only just gone to hunt up the animals in the fields, he laughed outright, and so did we, notwithstanding our vexation. We shortly found that our escort was no better off; their horses had not yet come in. So we all went to the plaza, and sat until past nine o'clock, witnessing the drilling of the new recruits. All things must have an end, and so did our suspense. The horses finally came; and, after a world of tryings on and takings off, pulling here and padding there, the beasts were saddled, and we marched to the plaza, where, according to previous understanding, we were met by the General and his staff, and a crowd of citizens on horseback, who had gathered to escort us "with all the honors" out of the city. My young medical friend from New Haven had won the privilege of carrying the flag at the head of the cavalcade, and after him, under the marshalling of a stalwart Buckeye, who had served amongst the dragoons in the Mexican war, the "Californian division" was arranged in column with military precision. The troops were all drawn up, and presented arms as we defiled by, under a discharge from the cannon in front of the "Cuartel General." The people lined the streets, and shouted as earnestly for "los Estados Unidos del Norte," and its representative, as they did for the "esclarecido General," upon his arrival a few days before.

I could not help thinking of the figure which our singular cavalcade must have cut in the eyes of an uninterested spectator, nor resist smiling at my own part in the affair. It, however, was a bona fide ceremonial, and so received and valued. As we approached the arsenal, we found its garrison on the *qui vive;* a little wreath of smoke shot up, and boom went the cannon there. Altogether this was more imposing than our departure from San Carlos, and not a whit less entertaining.

I was mounted on a large white mule, which the *emprestador* had specially recommended to me as "muy manso y comodo" very gentle and easy; but which I soon found was an old broken-winded beast, and a villanously hard traveller. The General observed that I had been taken in, and glancing round, fixed his eyes on the dashing horse of a young fellow, deputed by the government to accompany us on our march as commissary and provider. Directly he stopped short, and ordered him to dismount and change animals with me. The order was promptly obeyed,—for there was no parleying with the General; and although I thought the proceeding rather summary, I was too glad to get rid of the mule to offer the slightest objection to the arrangement. Besides, the deposed horseman should have provided us with better animals—of course he should!

Our escort accompanied us about two miles, to a point where the short cut, or mule path, to Masaya diverged from the *camino real;* and here, after a profusion of bows, an interminable shaking of hands, and "buenas viajes," and "Dios guardes," in every tone and emphasis, we separated from the crowd, and went on our way alone. The path was narrow, and led through bush and brier, under gigantic trees, draped all over with vines, down into dark ravines, where the sun's rays never reached, over ridges covered with grass, with here and there clusters of luxuriant trees, gemmed all over with fragrant flowers, where we could catch views of the glittering lake, with its distant shores, and several islands. Thus we went, in Indian file, the red shirts and gleaming arms of the men giving life and relief to the scene, and making the noisy parrots, which fluttered beside the path, still more noisy; while brightly colored birds glanced in and out of the thick green coverts, or a startled deer bounded hurriedly before us! Altogether, the novelty, excitement, and beauty filled me with that wild delight which only the Arab feels, or the free Indian on his prairie ocean, and one hour's enjoyment of which were "worth ten years of quiet life!" My chest expands, and every nerve becomes tense, even now, while I write, at the recollection of that glorious morning, and that march to Masaya. Occasionally we came upon a cane house, nestled in some quiet glen, or upon some beautiful slope, surrounded by palms and plantains, and fields of tobacco and maize, in the doors of which stood women and knots of frightened children, who gazed wonderingly upon our strange party. They all seemed reassured when we cried out "adios amigas!" and responded with "Dios guarde à Ustedes, caballeros!" "God preserve you, Sirs!" At about six miles from Granada, we reached the highest point of ground between that city and Masaya; one of those ridges of land which seem to radiate like the legs of a lobster from the great volcano of Momobacho, and which are, for the most part, destitute of trees. From this point we obtained our finest view of Lake Nicaragua, the river, or estuary of Tipitapa connecting it with Lake Managua, and of that lake itself, hemmed in, upon the east, by the high irregular mountains of Matagalpa and New Segovia. Between us and the lakes was a magnificent slope, leagues on leagues in extent, a sea of dense tree-tops, unrelieved, so far as the eye could discover, by a single acre of cleared or cultivated ground. Yet there were many haciendas and estates, the positions of which were indicated by wreaths of smoke rising in thin curls here and there above the trees. We dismounted, and sat for half an hour beneath a spreading tree, to enjoy the prospect, and pay our respects to the canteens of water, (diluted with *ardiente*,) with which each man was supplied.

The path by which we journeyed had been used, from time immemorial, for mules and horses, and in many places, particularly on the declivities of the swells of land, where water had contributed its aid, it was worn deep in the soft rock and compacted earth, and so narrow as utterly to preclude all turning around after it had once been entered. Upon approaching such places, if their whole extent cannot be discovered, it is usual to halloo loudly, in order to ascertain if any one is approaching; for if horsemen meet in these places, one or the other must back out,—a process sufficiently difficult.

At about one o'clock the more frequent occurrence of cultivated grounds, of little "hattos" and cane cabins, showed that we were approaching the large Indian pueblo of Masaya. The path became broader, and showed constant use; and numerous little paths diverged in every direction. Where they joined the main road, crosses were in some cases erected, on which hung wreaths of faded flowers, perishing tokens of pious zeal. We now met and overtook numbers of Indians, singly and in groups, carrying netted sacks, filled with ears of maize, with vegetables, or meats: some had braided mats, hats of woven palm leaves, hammocks, and other articles for sale or use. They all silently gave us the road on our approach. They seldom spoke unless first addressed; but then always replied politely, sometimes adding, interrogatively, "California?" They were small, but well-formed, with features much more regular than our Indians, and of singularly mild, and expressive features, and docile manners.

The entrance to Masaya was by a long and broad street, lined on both sides by a forest of fruit-trees, beneath which were clustered the thatched cane houses of the inhabitants. We had previously waited until the rear of our party had come up, and now spurred through the streets in a solid column. As we went on, the houses became more numerous, and occasionally one of adobes, with a tiled roof, appeared amongst the frailer structures which I have described. After going nearly half a mile, we turned short to the right, and riding for a number of blocks in streets precisely resembling those of Granada, passing an abandoned convent or two, we galloped into the principal plaza. In the centre of this stood the great church, a long, heavy building, with a very fair façade and tower, and much exceeding in size any of the churches of Granada. On the sides of the plaza were several rows of fine shops, with their doors and shutters covered with tin; for more foreign goods are retailed in Masaya than in any other town in the State. Its people are regarded as the most industrious, and are celebrated throughout all Central America for the extent and variety of their manufactures. Cordage, hammocks, saddles, cotton cloth "petates" or mats, hats, shoes, in short, all the articles of common use in the country, are produced here, besides large quantities of *dulces* (sweetmeats and jellies,) which were, at one time, extensively exported to Peru and South America. But the shops, in consequence of the existing troubles, were shut, and the plaza was almost entirely deserted. Near the dead wall of the church a rude chair was standing; it was the fatal "*banqueto*," upon which, a few days before, one of the leading "facciosos" of the city, after having been tried and condemned by a court-martial, had been shot. Near by the sod was turned up, marking the spot where the body of the executed man was buried. He had been tried at one o'clock, condemned at two, shot at three, and buried at four. Short shrift, indeed; but such is the summary process of martial law in Nicaragua, when, as in this instance, the guilt of the criminal admits neither of doubt nor extenuation. Some of our party had witnessed the execution, which they described as very impressive. It was done in sight of the entire army, from which a corporal's guard was detached for the service. The prisoner was first taken within the church, where he confessed and received the sacrament. He was conducted to his seat by two priests, a little cross put in his hands, and a blessing invoked on his soul. Guns, in half of which only were balls, were placed in the hands of the guard, who fired at the distance of ten paces. The man fell dead at the first discharge. The example was deemed necessary, and it no doubt was so in this instance. It should, however, be observed, that no officer has established a higher character for humanity than General Muñoz, who has never stained his reputation by any of those butcheries and wanton cruelties which have been the rule, rather than the exception, in the civil wars of Spanish America.

We rode to a *posada* kept by an exceedingly fat and cheerful lady, who was so happy that her "pobre casa" should be honored by the "hijos de Washington," the sons of Washington! In a few minutes, several of the alcaldes of the town came in, out of breath, and in great tribulation because they had not been apprised of our approach. They proposed even now to ring all the bells, and were urgent that we should stop the rest of the day, so as to give them an opportunity of making a demonstration commensurate to the importance of the occasion. But we pleaded haste, and promised to return soon, and thus escaped being lionized in Masaya. We had proposed to stop here several hours, and visit the remarkable volcanic lake, from which the town is supplied with water, but the delay of the morning compelled us to cut short our stay, if we would reach Managua, twelve leagues distant, that night. So we only allowed the horses to breathe awhile, and then mounted again and resumed our march. We went quite two miles from the plaza before we got fairly out of the city, which has some fifteen or eighteen thousand inhabitants, and covers full a square league.

Beyond Masaya is a broad and beautiful avenue, lined on either hand by luxuriant fields: in this respect far surpassing the country around Granada. This avenue leads to the pueblo of Nindiri, and people mounted or on foot passing to and fro, gave it an appearance of animation beyond what we had hitherto seen out of the towns. About midway between Masaya and Nindiri, the road passes over a bubble-shaped hill, raised by volcanic forces from below, the uplifted strata curving with all the regularity of the rainbow. Although it would have been easy to have passed around it, yet as the Indians before the conquest had probably gone directly over, the same path has been continued, for no better reason, ever since. It however had been much improved, and a deep notch had been cut or worn in the soft sand rock, to the depth of forty or fifty feet, resembling very much the deep cuts on the lines of some of our railroads. Upon one side, in a little nitch, stood a small cross, covered with wilted flowers. Beyond this defile, the road resumed its broad and level course, and we rode rapidly over its gravelled bed into the town of Nindiri.

Nindiri! How shall I describe thee, beautiful Nindiri, nestling beneath thy fragrant, evergreen roof of tropical trees, entwining their branches above thy smooth avenues, and weaving green domes over the simple dwellings of thy peaceful inhabitants! Thy musical name, given thee long ages ago, perhaps when Rome was young, has lost nothing of its melody; *Neenda*, water, and *Diria*, mountain, it still tells us, in an ancient and almost forgotten tongue, that thou slumberest now, as of yore, between the lake and the mountain! Amongst all the fairy scenes of quiet beauty which the eye of the traveller hath lingered upon, or the fancy has limned with her rosy-hued pencil, none can compare with thee, beautiful Nindiri, chosen alike of the mountain Fairies and forest Dryads, of the Sylphs of the lake, and the Naiads of the fountain! Nindiri!

This little Indian village far surpassed, in point of picturesque beauty, anything we had yet seen. Oranges, plantains, marañons, jocotes, nisperos, mamays, and tall palms, with their variously-colored fruits blushing brown or golden among the leaves, and here and there a low calabash tree, with its green globes strung on every limb, all clustering together, literally embowered the cane huts of the simple-minded and industrious inhabitants. Indian women, naked to the waist, sat beneath the trees spinning snow-white cotton or the fibre of the *pita*, (*agave*,) while their noisy, naked little ones tumbled joyously about on the smoothly-beaten ground, where the sunlight fell in flickering, shifting mazes, as the wind bent the branches of the trees with its unseen fingers. Quiet primitive Nindiri! seat of the ancient caziques and their barbaric courts,—even now, amidst the din of the crowded city, and the crush and conflict of struggling thousands, amidst grasping avarice and importunate penury, bold-fronted hypocrisy and heartless fashion, where virtue is modest and vice is brazen, where fire and water, and the very lightnings of heaven, are the slaves of human will, how turns the memory to thee, as to some sweet vision of the night, some dreamy Arcadia, fancy-born, and half unreal!

We rode through the arched and hedge-lined streets into a broad open plaza, in the centre of which stood a quaint old church. A few sleek cows were lying in its shade, chewing their cuds in a meditative way, and hardly opening their sleepy eyes as we trotted by. Beneath some large trees upon one side of the plaza, we descried our carts and their escort, taking what at home would be called "a nooning." The lances of the men were stacked together, and their horses fastened with *lariats* to the carts, forming, with their gay trappings, a striking group, abundantly set off by the reclining figures of their riders, who had disposed themselves in attitudes expressive of the fullest abandonment to individual ease. We were not long in joining the party. The officer in command, in anticipation of our arrival, had prepared two or three jars of "algo fresco," something fresh, delightfully compounded of water, the juice of the cocoa-nut, and of the acidulous marañon,—a delicious and refreshing beverage, to which we paid our respects in protracted draughts, not forgetting "*mil gracias*," and sundry *medios* to a plump, laughing Indian girl who dispensed it, in snowy calabashes, to the thirsty strangers.

The only part of the road which was supposed to be frequented by the *ladrones* was now passed, and although the commander of the escort was very willing to proceed with the carts, I did not think it necessary, and so it was agreed that he should return. This arranged, we all mounted again, and the last we saw of our military friend was the gleaming lances of his men, and the fluttering of their little red streamers, as they galloped back through the streets of Nindiri.

Beyond the town we struck into the forest, and began to ascend one of the slopes or spurs of the volcano of Masaya. Occasional openings among the trees enabled us to catch glimpses of lake, plain, and mountain, more extended even, and more beautiful than those which we had witnessed in the morning, from the heights beyond Masaya. The road passed over fields of disintegrating pumice and lava-beds ages old, and now covered with accumulated soil and a thick forest. At the distance of about a league, however, we came to what is called the "*mal pais*," literally, the *bad country*. It was an immense field of lava, which at the last eruption of Masaya had flowed down from the volcano, for a distance of fifteen or twenty miles, in the direction of the lakes. The road crossed it on the summit of a ridge running transversely to the lava current, where the field was narrow, but spreading out on both sides to a great distance. It looked like a vast plain of cast iron, newly cooled, black and forbidding. In places it was rolled up in frowning masses, elsewhere piled one flake on the other, like the ice in the spring time, upon the shores and low islands, or in the narrow channels of our rivers. An ocean of ink, suddenly congealed during a storm, if the imagination of the reader can picture it, would better illustrate its appearance than anything else which occurs to me at this moment. Here and there great, ragged masses, fifty or a hundred feet square, had been turned completely over by the current as it flowed beneath, exhibiting upon the exposed surface a regularly striated appearance, like the curling fibre of the oak or maple. I dismounted and scrambled out amongst the *crinkling* fragments, but did not go far, as the sharp edges and points cut through my boots like knives. At one place I observed where the half-cooled lava had wrapped itself, layer on layer, around a large tree, which, subsequently burning out or decaying, had left a perfect cast of its trunk and principal branches, so accurate that the very roughness of the bark could still be traced. But what struck me with most surprise was the circumstance that the flood of lava had flowed over the narrow ridge where I was standing, and that a depression existed between me and the volcano whence the molten matter had come. It was clear enough that the popular adage and axiom about the indisposition of water to flow up hill, does not always apply to lava. The explanation of the phenomenon may perhaps be found in the fact that the surface of the lava cooling, is thrown off in fragments, building walls on either side, between which the lava current continues to flow, until rising high, and the vertical pressure becoming great, it breaks through the barrier, and discharges itself laterally. Or, the intermediate valley being filled by the melted substance with a rapidity which would not admit of its finding its level at once, it is easy to understand that it might discharge itself over the ridge; and the supply subsequently ceasing, the accumulated matter in the valley, spread out laterally and subside, in the manner here exhibited.

Not a tree intervened between me and the volcano, only the broad, black and rugged waste of lava. I could therefore distinctly see the mountain, and trace the ragged outlines of its ancient and principal crater. This latest discharge of lava, however, does not seem to have been made from this mouth, but from a lower elevation, upon the slope of the volcano. This elevation had a reddish, scoriaceous appearance, and its crater, one side of which had been broken down by the lava, was comparatively small. In fact there were a number of orifices, or craters, at other points, which had been the vents in previous eruptions. It was evident enough that there had been hot work here in past times, although everything looked quiet enough now.

The early chroniclers have a great deal to say about this volcano, which was called "*El Infierno de Masaya*," the Hell of Masaya. Its last eruption, when the lava field which I have described was formed, occurred within the historical period, in 1670. No detailed account of it has ever been published, although there is little doubt that it was duly recorded by some of the ecclesiastics of the country, whose relations still exist amongst the archives of the Church in Spain or Italy.

Since this final eruption, the volcano has been in a dormant state. It was visited in 1840 by Mr. Stephens, who discovered no signs of activity. Yet, at the time of the Discovery, it was regarded as one of the greatest wonders of the New World. The chronicler Oviedo visited it in 1529, and has left us a very complete account of its appearance and condition at that period. He says:

"There is another mountain in this province, called Masaya, of which I can speak as an eye-witness, having visited it in person, after having heard many fables related by those who pretended to have ascended to the crater. I once went up Vesuvius, and beheld a crater of twenty-five or thirty fathoms in diameter, from which smoke rose perpetually, which smoke people say changes to a very bright flame at night. I remained there a whole night, with the Queen of Naples, whose chief of the wardrobe (guarda ropa) I was, whither I accompanied her in 1501. From thence we went to Palermo, in Sicily, near which is Mount Etna." Oviedo here makes a long enumeration of the volcanoes known at the time he wrote, and continues: "But it seems to me that none of these volcanoes are to be compared with that of Masaya, which, as I have said, I have seen and examined myself. Of this the reader shall be the judge, after he has read the description of that mountain, whose name signifies 'the burning mountain,' in the language of the Chorotegans, in whose territory it is situated. In the language of Nicaragua it is called '*Popogatepec*,' which means 'boiling stream.'[1]

"I will now relate what I saw. I left the village of Managua, July 25, 1529, and spent the night at the house of Diego Machuca [who, we have seen, was the first explorer of Lake Nicaragua], being half a league from the foot of the mountain, on the shores of Lake Nindiri. I descended the same day to examine the lake; and the next, which was St. James' day, I started before the rising of the sun to ascend the mountain, and behold the flame, and the other extraordinary things worthy of mention. This mountain is very steep, and is surrounded by Indians of the Chorotegan nation. Tigers, lions [pumas], and many other ferocious animals abound here. Beyond this mountain stretches an uncultivated plain, which the Spaniards have named *el mal pais*. It is covered with rocks, resembling scoriæ. In this an isolated mountain rises up to the height of a league from foot to summit. The mountain may be three or four leagues in circumference at its base, and is entirely different from those in its neighborhood. I know that many Spaniards have sent descriptions of this mountain to the emperor; and that others, on their return to Spain, have given out what they have seen, whose relations I do not doubt. On the contrary, I rejoice that I am to speak of a matter so well known, and that there is no lack of witnesses who can attest the truth of my recital. Many of those who pretend to have visited this mountain have only seen it from a distance; and but few have ascended it. Some assert that the light of the flame is sufficiently strong to read by, at the distance of three leagues, which I cannot confirm.

"I left the house of Machuca in the middle of the night, as I have before mentioned, and I had nearly reached the summit at sunrise. It was not, however, light enough for me to read my prayers (breviary), which I had brought with me, when I was within a quarter of a league of the summit. Yet the night was very dark, in consequence of which the flame appeared more brilliant. I have heard persons worthy of credit say that when the night is very dark and rainy, the light from the crater is so vivid that one can see to read at the distance of half a league; this I will neither affirm nor deny, for at Granada or Salteba, when there is no moon, the whole country is illuminated by the flame of the volcano;

[1] This is a mistake of the chronicler. *Popo* or *poco* is the Mexican for smoke, and *tepec* mountain, i. e. "Smoking Mountain." *Ca* or *ga* is a word used to impersonate, embody, or individualize. It will shortly be seen that a Mexican colony existed in Nicaragua.

and it is a fact that it can be seen at the distance of sixteen or twenty leagues; for I have seen it at that distance myself. However, we cannot call that which proceeds from the crater precisely a flame, but rather a smoke as bright as a flame; it cannot be seen at that distance by day, but only at night, as I have said.

"But to return to my journey; I was accompanied by a cazique whose baptismal name was Don Francisco; in the Chorotegan language he was called Natatime; also by a negro and two faithful Indians. Although the negro was a safe man, I acknowledge that I was wrong to put myself in such company; but I made up my mind to do so from the desire I had to succeed in this enterprise. I had found Machuca sick; those who were to accompany me had broken their word, and returned to Granada; yet I was not willing to suspend my journey, so great was my desire to learn what truth there might be in the relations of those who pretended to have been there. When it was no longer possible to go on horseback, I dismounted, and put sandals of wood on my feet, for shoes would not answer for such a road. I left one of the Indians to take charge of my horse, and went forward with the cazique, who served us for a guide, and who, with the negro and the other Indian, I made to go before me. When the cazique arrived near the crater, he sat down, fifteen or twenty paces off, and pointed out to me with his finger the frightful spectacle. The summit of the mountain forms a *plateau*, covered with red, yellow, and black rocks, spotted with divers colors. Except on the eastern side, where I stood, the whole plateau is occupied by a crater, whose orifice is so large, that in my opinion a musket ball could not traverse it. There proceeds from it a continual smoke, but not so thick as to prevent one from examining it both internally and externally; for, as the east wind blows continually here, it bears the smoke away to the opposite side from the spectator. This crater is, to the best of my judgment, and of those whom I have heard speak of it, about one hundred and thirty fathoms in depth; the width continually diminishing as it descends. This mountain is not as high on its southern and eastern sides as on the others, and looks like human workmanship, so regular are its outlines; excepting, however, the side where I was, which, as I have before mentioned, is covered with rocks. There were also some caverns, but one could see little or nothing but their entrances; and the sides of the crater could scarcely be seen; for no one durst advance sufficiently near.

"At the bottom of the crater could be seen a place perfectly round, and large enough to contain a hundred cavaliers, who could play at fencing and have more than a thousand spectators; it would hold even more than that, were it not for another crater in the middle of it, inclining a little to the south, which can be very distinctly seen. It appeared to me to be from forty to sixty fathoms in depth and fourteen or fifteen paces in circumference. It might be much more; for I viewed the opening from a very high point, and the depth from a still higher point. On the north side, the crater is three times as far from the interior wall of the volcano as on the south side.

"Happening to be at Valladolid in 1548, at the court of the prince N. S. Don Rodrigo de Contreras, who was once governor of this province, he told me that the depth of the volcano had been measured in his presence, and found to be one hundred and thirty fathoms; and from the bottom to the burning fluid, forty fathoms more; but a circumstance, mentioned to me by the commander, Fr. Francis de Bobadilla, still more astonished me, viz.: that when he ascended to the crater of Masaya, with some other persons, the holes were in the middle of the place, and the burning matter had risen to within four fathoms of the top; and yet six months had not elapsed since my journey. I am of the opinion, however, that he told the truth; for besides his being a man worthy of belief, I have heard Machuca say that he had seen the burning matter rise even with the top.

"I said that I beheld at the bottom of the second crater a fire, which was as liquid as water, and of the color of brass. This fire appeared to me more violent than any I had ever seen before, and entirely covered the bottom of the crater. From time to time this matter rose into the air with great force, hurling large masses to a height of many feet, as it appeared to me. Sometimes these masses were arrested on the sides of the crater, and remained there, before becoming extinguished, time enough to repeat the *credo* six times, and then looked like the scoriæ of a forge. I cannot believe that a Christian could behold this spectacle unmindful of hell, and unrepentant of his sins; particularly whilst comparing this vein of sulphur with the eternal grandeur of everlasting fire which awaits those who are ungrateful to God!

"Towards the middle of the first crater, a large number of parroquets might be seen, circling around, of that species having the long tails, and called *jijaves*. I could only see their backs, for I was much higher than they. They make their nests among the rocks, below the spectator. I threw some stones into the abyss, and made the negro do likewise, but could never distinguish where they fell; which proves clearly how high was the place where I stood. Some persons have asserted that when the parroquets are fluttering among these places, and one looks fixedly, he seems not to see fire but sulphur. I am not far removed from this opinion, but leave the decision to those knowing more of the matter than myself.

"On the top of the volcano, on the eastern part, an elevation rises up, in which is an opening like to the crater, but deeper. A smoke ascends through it, which cannot be seen during the daytime, but which projects into the darkness a great light, uniting itself to that proceeding from the larger opening. This opening does not terminate in a broad bottom, but is a funnel-shaped orifice, apparently filled with coals. The cazique told me that, in the times of his ancestors, the main crater was here, but that subsequently it changed its location to the spot it now occupies. These two craters are separated from each other only by some rocks. The ground is covered with barren trees, yielding no fruit, except one alone, which produces yellow berries, about the size of a musket ball, named *nanzi;* they are good to eat, and the Indians say that they are good for bowel complaints. No birds are seen on this mountain, except crows, and the parroquets I have spoken of.

"A remarkable circumstance, told me by Machuca and Fr. Francis de Bobadilla is, that the melted matter sometimes mounts to the top of the crater, whilst I could see it only at a great depth. Having made due inquiry in regard to this, I have learnt that when much rain falls, the fire does, in fact, ascend as far as the top; for the cavity becomes filled with water, which flows in from all parts of the mountain, and remains full until it has been overcome and destroyed by the heat of the opposing element. This view of the matter is confirmed by what Olaus Magnus says of the volcanoes of Iceland, which do not consume the combustibles around them, but the water which they contain. It must be so at Masaya; for when the flame is seen at the distance of a league and a half, it does not look like flame, but burning smoke which covers the whole mountain. If it were fire, it would leave neither tree, leaf, nor verdure; on the contrary, the whole mountain is covered with trees and herbage, almost to the borders of the crater.

"I spent two hours here, gazing and drawing, till ten o'clock; it was the day of St. Anne; I then resumed my route to Granada, or Salteba, which is three leagues from Masaya. Not only in this city, but even at the distance of two leagues beyond it, the volcano gave as much light as the moon some days before she fulls.

"I have heard the cazique of Tenderi [Nindiri] say that he has often gone, in company with other caziques, to the edge of the crater; and that an old woman, entirely naked, has come forth from it, with whom they held a *monexico*, or secret council. They consulted her in order to know if they should make war, or decline or grant a truce with their enemies. They did nothing without first consulting her; for she told them whether they were to conquer or to be conquered: she told them also, if it were about to rain; if the harvest of maize would be abundant; and, in fine, all future events. And every thing always came to pass just as she had predicted it would. On such occasions, a man or two, some women, and children of both sexes, were sacrificed to her; the victims offering themselves voluntarily. He added that since the Christians came into the country, the old woman had appeared only at long intervals; that she had told them the Christians were wicked; and that she did not wish to have any communication with the Indians until they had driven the Christians from their country. I asked him how they got below. He answered that formerly there was a road; but that the cavity had been enlarged by the caving in of the land around it, and thus the path had been destroyed. I asked him what they did after their council with the old woman, and what was her appearance. He replied that she was old and wrinkled; that her breasts hung down over her belly; that her hair was thin and erect; that her teeth were long and sharp as a dog's; her skin of a darker color than Indians ordinarily have; eyes fiery and sunken; in short, he described her as like the devil, which she must have been. If this cazique told the truth, it cannot be a matter of doubt that the Indians were in connection with him. When the council was over, the old woman entered within the crater, and never came out except to a new council. The Indians often converse about this superstition, and many others; and in their books they represent the devil with as much leanness and with as many *queues* as we are in the habit of painting him at the feet of the archangel Michael, or the apostle St. Barthelemy. I am of the opinion, therefore, that they have seen him, and that he has shown himself to them; since they place his image in their temples, where they perform their diabolical idolatries. On the side of the crater of Masaya there is a large heap of cups, plates, and basins, of excellent crockery, made in the country. Some had been broken, others were entire. The Indians had brought them there filled with all kinds of meat, and left them, saying they were for the old woman to eat, in order to please or appease her when an earthquake or violent tempest takes place; for they attribute to her all the good or evil that happens to them. As to the substance, in which, according to the cazique, this *old one* made her retreat, it appeared to me to resemble glass, or the metal of bells in a state of fusion. The interior walls of the crater are of hard stone in some places, but brittle almost everywhere. The smoke goes from the crater on the eastern side, but it is driven towards the west by the breeze. A small quantity of smoke comes out on the northern side of the crater.

"The mountain of Masaya is six or seven leagues from the South Sea, and about twelve and a half degrees from the Equator. I have now completed all I promised to say in this fifth chapter."

Oviedo also gives us a long and entertaining account, at second hand, of the descent of the Fray Blas del Castillo into the crater of Masaya, and what befel him there. This will be found translated in another place.

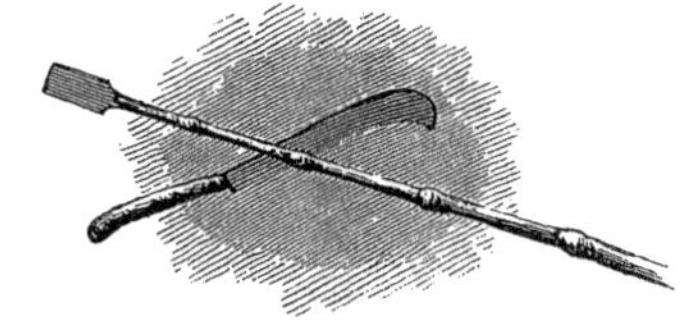

MACHETE-CALABOZO. MACANA.

CHAPTER VIII.

MAGNIFICENT VIEWS OF SCENERY—"RELOX DEL SOL"—JOHN JONES AND ANTIQUITIES—AN "ALARM;" REVOLVERS, AND A RESCUE—DISTANT BELLS—DON PEDRO BLANCO—MANAGUA—ANOTHER GRAND ENTREE—OUR QUARTERS—SUPPER SERVICE—ENACTING THE LION—VIRTUES OF AGUARDIENTE—AN "OBSEQUIO" OR TORCH-LIGHT PROCESSION IN HONOR OF THE UNITED STATES—A NATIONAL ANTHEM—NIGHT WITH THE FLEAS—FOURTH OF JULY AND A PATRIOTIC BREAKFAST—SAINT JONATHAN—LEAVE MANAGUA—MATEARES—PRIVILEGES OF A "COMPADRE"—LAKE OF MANAGUA—A MAGNIFICENT VIEW—THE VOLCANO OF MOMOTOMBO—A SOLITARY RIDE—GEOLOGICAL PUZZLE—NAGAROTE—THE POSADA—MULES ABANDONED—A SICK CALIFORNIAN—DINNER AT A PADRE'S—THE SANTA ANITA—VIRTUES OF A PIECE OF STAMPED PAPER—A STORM IN THE FOREST—PUEBLO NUEVO—FIVE DAUGHTERS IN SATIN SHOES—UNBROKEN SLUMBERS—ADVANCE ON LEON—AXUSCO—A FAIRY GLEN—THE GREAT PLAIN OF LEON—A "TOUCH" OF POETRY—MEET THE AMERICAN CONSUL—A PREDICAMENT—CAVALCADE OF RECEPTION—NEW ILLUSTRATION OF REPUBLICAN SIMPLICITY—EL CONVENTO—A METAMORPHOSIS—THE BISHOP OF NICARAGUA—FORREST, MISS CLIFTON, MR. CLAY—CRITICISM ON ORATORY—NINE VOLCANOES IN A ROW—DISTANT VIEW OF THE GREAT CATHEDRAL—THE CITY—IMPOSING DEMONSTRATIONS—THE GRAND PLAZA—A PANTOMIMIC SPEECH AND REPLY—THE LADIES, "GOD BLESS THEM!"—HOUSE OF THE AMERICAN CONSUL—END OF THE CEREMONIES—SELF-CONGRATULATIONS THEREON—A SERENADE—MARTIAL ASPECT OF THE CITY—TROUBLE ANTICIPATED—PRECAUTIONS OF THE GOVERNMENT.

BEYOND the "mal pais" the road passed over a beautiful undulating country, with occasional open, grassy spaces, dotted here and there with little clumps of bushes and trees, from whence the eye caught glimpses of the distant lakes and mountains. For many miles, scoria and disentegrating lava showed the extent of volcanic action in ancient times; in fact, for the whole distance to Managua, volcanic traces and products were to be seen on every hand. Half way between Masaya and Managua we came suddenly upon a large, erect stone, which, at first glance, I supposed was one of the "piedras antiguas" of the country ; a veritable monolith, like those discovered by Mr. Stephens at Copan. It however proved to be "un relox del sol," an ancient sun dial, erected by the early Spaniards for the double purpose of marking the distance and the hours. There had been an inscription upon it, but it was obliterated now, and a rude cross had been deeply graven in its place. I dismounted to examine it more closely, and found "John Jones" scratched upon one of its sides. Ubiquitous "John Jones!" He had been convicted of bigamy, and sent to the State prison but two days before I left New York! W. inquired if "Jones" was an Aztec name, and I felt cheap enough about "monuments," and was mounting again in great disgust, when we were all startled by the sudden discharge of a pistol, in a dark ravine which we had just passed, followed by a confused shout, and another discharge, and then a volley in quick succession. An attack, in the present unsettled state of the country, was by no means an impossibility; and the firing continuing, we turned our horses' heads and galloped back, weapons in hand, to the rescue. A moment brought us within view of half a dozen of our party, their horses plunging in dire confusion, while their riders fired their revolvers with the greatest rapidity into the forest. Glancing amongst the trees, we discovered the enemy, a troop perhaps thirty or forty strong, crashing amongst the bushes, in full retreat. It was a squadron of large, yellow monkeys upon which the party had fired, in frolicksome mood, with a design rather to alarm their comrades than injure the monkeys, who escaped with no further damage than a prodigious fright, sufficient to last them for the remainder of their natural lives. The cacchinatory exercises following upon such a feat over, we all moved on together. The road was deeply shaded, but broad and smooth; and, as the sun went down, conversation gradually ceased, and the horses, invigorated by the cool atmosphere, all fell into a rapid pace, the clatter of their hoofs alone disturbing the silence of the evening.

Hark, a bell! the sound vibrating even into the depths of the leafy forest! It is the *oracion*, and we are near Managua. But it was nearly an hour before we emerged into the open fields surrounding the city, and then it was so dark that we could discern nothing except the lights of the houses, and the occasional gleaming of the lake beyond.

Here we were met by Don Pedro Blanco, to whom I was specially recommended by Don Frederico. He had come to put his "pobre casa" at my disposition. Don Pedro was for doing things in a grand way, and accordingly desired us to wait for all the stragglers to come up, so as to make an imposing entrée, which we did, at a round pace, to the great alarm of the infantile, and the utter indignation of the canine portion of the population. It was too dark to see much of the town, and I only remember interminable streets lined with huts and low houses, a big church with a spectral white archway in front, and a great plaza flanked by two or three two-story buildings, with another large church in its centre. All this was out of our way, for Pedro was determined to impress us with the magnitude of the town, and I began to think that it had no end, when suddenly Pedro turned short, ducked his head, and dashed beneath the "Porteria" into the *patio* or court yard of his own house, whilst our escort filed off, at a tearing rate, for the public posada. Fortunate escort!

Don Pedro's house was not the most aristocratic in the place, nor yet the cleanest, although his wife was amongst the fattest and fairest. It had but two rooms, and one of these was a *tienda*, or store, where our hostess dispensed candles and candy, dry goods and dulces, toys and tobacco, vegetables and medicines, in quantities to suit purchasers.

Here a couple of new hammocks were forthwith swung, into which we rolled without ceremony, and with all the satisfaction of tired men. Pedro's grand *entrée* had almost finished us; but he had considerately ordered supper before leaving home, and I almost forgave him the awful trot he had given us, when I saw the cloth spread and the savory dishes make their appearance one by one. M., who had never before ridden two consecutive miles on horseback, and who, thoroughly "used up," had lain like a log in his hammock, began now to show some signs of life, and even sat up and looked voraciously at the table. I asked for a basin of water before sitting down, which Don Pedro produced at once, but protested against our washing ourselves then, as it was "muy malo," and would bring on the *calentura*, or fever. This superstition, I afterwards found, was not only general amongst the natives, but also amongst foreigners resident in the country. I however never regarded it, and yet escaped the calentura.

Pedro's supper was well enough served, only there were neither knives nor forks. Ben supplied these from his *alforjas*, and we got on very well, or rather might have done so; but before we had fairly taken the edge off our appetites we heard a great uproar in the direction of the plaza, succeeded by the firing of guns and the whizzing discharge of bombas. I glanced round at our host, who so far from exhibiting any alarm seemed to be mightily exultant. I had made up my mind to be surprised at nothing, and so asked no questions. Meantime the tumult increased, and the squeaking of violins was to be heard in the pauses of the shouting and firing. By-and-by we distinguished "*Vivan los Estados Unidos!*" "*Vivan los Americanos del Norte!*" and the appalling consciousness was forced upon us that we were to be lionized forthwith, and supper but half finished! I appealed to Pedro to shut the door and say we were ill, and would see the people in the morning; but he either did not understand, or affected not to do so, and before I could explain, the crowd was at the entrance, and pouring into our apartment. The alcaldes came first, and a dozen fiddlers followed. Then came the people in solid column, while the outsiders kept up a perfect storm of vivas,—their upturned, swarthy faces looking singularly wild and forbidding under the light of their torches. Not a tithe was able to enter, yet every one seemed determined to find a place inside, and crowded one upon the other to such a degree that we should have been suffocated outright, had not the alcaldes formed a cordon around us, and kept off the crowd with their canes. The principal or first alcalde, made a speech, full of welcome, and well spiced with patriotism, in which he called us, and all the people of the United States, collectively and individually, friends and brothers, and a great many other endearing names, which I have forgotten; and then everybody wanted to shake hands, and thrust them forward over the heads and under the arms of the front rank, a hundred at a time. But as our visitors generally did not seem to have any clear conception as to which of the party was the illustrious object of their homage, I instructed my companions to shake all the hands within their reach, and pass the owners on. In this wise, and by causing Pedro to invite the entire crowd to drink my health, at my expense, at the next *pulperia*, I finally succeeded in clearing the house,—but our chocolate was cold, and some of our worthy visitors had availed themselves of the "noise and confusion" to pocket all the baked meats. And as we sat disconsolately waiting for more to be cooked, we voted the system of lionizing a bore, and M. quoted Shakspeare:

> "Uneasy lies the head that wears a crown,"

with variations suited to our present condition.

The idea of getting the crowd off to the pulperia we all

thought was a particularly happy one; but the sequel proved otherwise. In half an hour our admiring friends, greatly augmented in numbers, all returned; and if they were fervent and enthusiastic before, what were they now? I appeared on the steps of the house and bowed low, and retired. But bows wouldn't answer. Nothing short of a grand procession would furnish an adequate vent to the overflowing feelings of the citizens. Pedro begged for my flag, while messengers were despatched to the Californians at the posada, to solicit their participation in the grand "obsequio." Pending the completion of the arrangements, the crowd continued to increase, completely choking up the street for an entire block. The confusion was dire; the violinists played as if working for their lives, while bombas were let off as fast as they could be collected. Finally, the Californians, refreshed by an ample supper, made their appearance, and at once fell into the spirit of the affair. The flag was unfurled at the head of the column, surrounded by an armed guard of honor; next came the officers and the *musicos*, and then, as the programmes at home say, "the citizens generally." The procession marched through all the principal streets, hurrahing at every corner for "El Norte," the "bello sexo," "Gen. Taylor," the "Supreme Government," in fact for nearly everything, but particularly for the "glorious flag of the North." The national anthem was sung in the plaza, the multitude joining in the chorus with almost frantic fervor, and then the Californians were called upon to sing the national air of the United States, but being unable to give it to their own satisfaction, they sang "Dearest May" instead, with great applause, and as Pedro afterwards told us, "con mucho espiritu," with great spirit!

It was full midnight when the "obsequio" was brought to a close, and our dispositions made for the night. And such a night! I had now my first introduction to the kind of bed in common use in the country, and which I verily believe was instituted as a punishment for the sins of the people. It consists of an ox-hide drawn, while green, tightly over a stout framework of wood, and afterwards elaborately polished, so as to look like the head of a drum When dry, a slab of marble is a soft and downy thing in comparison with it. It was on such a bed as this, with a smooth and gaudily colored "petate," or mat, and a single sheet spread over the hide, that I was invited to repose. I examined this new instrument of torture narrowly, and finally turned in, with heavy misgivings, particularly as I found that Pedro's mansion was full of fleas, which had already set my nerves on a gallop. I was weary enough, but it was impossible to sleep—the fleas came in hungry squadrons, and the hide bed grew momentarily more rigid and obdurate. I felt my own pulse; it was up to the fever rate, and I began to wish Don Pedro and Don Frederico to regions unmentionable for getting me into such a scrape. A bed on the ground, with my saddle for a pillow and the sky for a roof, would have been luxury itself, compared with this. I got up, unbarred the door, and went out on the corridor. The cool evening air was most welcome, and I vowed audibly not to go inside again. So I roused Ben, who strung me a hammock between the columns of the corridor, in which I succeeded in getting an hour or two of slumber.

When morning came, I told Don Pedro that it was the anniversary of American Independence, and that it was meet and becoming to breakfast with the rest of the Americans at the posada. And leaving Ben to bring round the animals and baggage, I got away as fast as possible from Don Pedro's hospitable but awfully flea-infested dwelling. I found the posada a very nice place indeed, and had the satisfaction of learning that each one of the Californians had had a comfortable *cot* or camp bed, with only a reasonable amount of fleas.

We all breakfasted together, and drank patriotic toasts,

and sang Yankee Doodle, and were altogether appropriately patriotic, to the great delectation of the quidnuncs of Managua, who gathered in crowds around the open doors and windows. They were properly instructed as to the nature of "the day we celebrated," that it was the great feast of St. Jonathan; whereupon they hurrahed for the saint, and even proposed to ring the church bells in his honor. But fearful of another "obsequio," we discouraged this idea, and made all haste to get off as quietly as possible.

At eight o'clock we were in the saddle. It was a gorgeous morning, and the lake of Managua flashed brightly in our eyes as we rode through the grand plaza. The opposite shore was dim and distant, but high and rough in outline, while nearer, a volcanic ridge, or succession of volcanic peaks, projected boldly into the lake, forming a sort of bay, at the head of which Managua was situated. A broad, well-beaten, and level avenue led out from the city, lined on both sides by forests, into which paths diverged in every direction. The road was filled with men and women going to their day's labor in the fields; and from their cheerful, frank air and manner, it was easy to see that we were beyond "war's alarms." At the distance of two leagues we came to the foot of the ridge which I have already mentioned, rising abruptly before us. Here, under a gigantic cebia, girths were tightened, and preparations made for the ascent, which is by a broad path, partly cut in the hill and built up with masonry. This road was constructed by Gen. Muñoz, to avoid the circuit of the camino real, or cart road, and is creditable to its originator. The ascent was laborious, but the toil was repaid by the views which we caught of the lake and its shores, from places where the precipices allowed no foothold for trees, and whence the eye roamed freely over league upon league of forest and undulating hills, terminating in the blue belt of Chontales and New Segovia. It was a singular position to be thus perched on the face of a cliff, with high, black, and frowning volcanic rocks on one hand, and a precipice, sheer and yawning, upon the other.

After winding about for half an hour, we reached the summit, from which, upon the other side, the land fell off in a gentle slope. This is the only hill or mountain to be encountered in the whole length of Nicaragua, between the lakes and the Pacific; and this may be avoided by taking the circuit of the cart road. From the summit, two hours and a half of hard riding, over a beautiful country, brought us to the little village of Mateares, distinguished as being utterly destitute of a single object of interest. It is a sort of half-way house in the journey from Granada to Leon, and has a miserable posada or two, where coffee and tortillas may be obtained cheaply, and fleas gratis. We divided our party between the two rival establishments, and ordered water and sacate for the animals, preliminary to undertaking the hot and unprotected ride of three leagues upon the sandy shore of the lake, which came within the next stage of our journey. Don Enrique Pallais, a Frenchman, domesticated in the country, a man of large experience and a kind heart, who was of our party, had his "comadre" in the posada where we stopped, who embraced him affectionately as we entered. She was exceedingly pretty, with a mild, sweet face, and as she was apparently the mistress of the mansion, I felt a little scandalized to find Don Enrique on such familiar terms with her; but he explained this extraordinary relation of "comadre" and "compadre," to my entire satisfaction. He had been sponsor at the baptism of her child, a little yellow chap just tottering about the house, and had thereby assumed the relation of compadre—a kind of second husband, without, however, any marital rights beyond the privilege of an embrace at meeting, after the manner I had witnessed. I afterwards observed that the fervor of the embrace bore a pretty exact ratio to the good looks of the señora. The fact is, I am a "compadre" myself now, and the relation brings to mind a girlish little creature, singing softly to her baby, at this very hour I dare say, somewhere amongst the hills of San Salvador!

At Mateares the traveller turns suddenly to the right, and descending a steep bank comes at once upon the shore of the lake. For two or three miles a belt of trees intervenes between the water and the cliff, beneath which passes the broad, gravelly road. I had gone ahead of my companions, who were deeply engaged in the concoction of lemonades at the posada, and had this part of the ride alone. I took off my hat, and throwing the rein upon my horse's neck, gave myself up to the silence and the scene. The air was literally loaded with fragrant odors from a hundred varieties of flowers, which blushed amongst the green thickets on every hand, while the waters of the lake flashed here and there between the trees like silver bars; and brilliant birds, noisy parrots, and dignified macaws in fiery plumage, looked down upon me in a familiar way, as if I were an old acquaintance. Several portly iguanas, who were enjoying themselves amongst the loose gravel of the road, seemed to be doubtful whether they should turn out, or force me to do so; and when they did leave the path, it was in a very leisurely manner, and with an expression equivalent to "what a *gringo*, to be riding at noonday, and disturbing respectable iguanas!"

After riding about a league, the belt of forest terminated in a a few gigantic cebias, and beyond was a broad beach, the bare cliff rising abruptly on one side, and the lake spreading out on the other, without as much as a shrub to break the fervor of the tropical sun. Here a party of muleteers, returning from Leon, were taking their noonday siesta, while the mules straggled about at will, nibbling the green bushes. Here too, for the first time, came fully in sight the great volcano of Momotombo, with the conical island of Momotombita in front, and the broken cones of the volcano of Las Pilas upon its flank. The foreground of rocks and trees, the strolling mules and reclining figures, completed a picture unsurpassed, in point of novelty and beauty by any which I had seen before, or have witnessed since. Its predominant features are very imperfectly conveyed in the accompanying drawing, subsequently taken from the same point of view.

The muleteers sat up as I rode by, answering my "adios Señores" with "buen viaje, Caballero," and then fell back in the sand again, and drew their sombreros over their faces. The sand of the beach was fetlock deep, and covered all over with white and rose-colored pebbles of pumice-stone. I spurred my horse up to the water, and dismounting led him along its edge, amusing myself by tossing the light pebbles out upon the tiny waves, and watching them come tipping back again, buoyant as corks. Hundreds of wild fowl, cranes, herons, and water-hens lined the shores, or stood soliloquizing on the rocks and sand-spits which projected into the water. They had the courtesy to give me the road as I walked along, but hardly anything more; and only ejaculated "cluck!" when I shouted at them, which I suppose meant "don't be kicking up a row here, at noonday." In fact I began to think that all nature, animate and inanimate, had entered into a grand compact to take a quiet snooze at this precise hour every day. The lake itself seemed dreaming, and the smoke from Momotombo rose in such a sleepy way, that I almost felt drowsy in watching it, and should certainly have lain down in the sand and taken a nap, had there been a tree or bush to protect me from the hot sun. My only alternative was therefore to jog on, which I did until I came to a place where the cliff projected forward almost to the water's edge. Here I paused, and looked back for my companions, but they were not to be seen.

Beyond this point the lake formed a little bay, and rocks worn into fantastic shapes by the water supplanted the sandy beach. These rocks seemed to be composed of a kind of volcanic breccia, for fragments of pumice-stone, bits of primitive rock, and an occasional large piece of trachyte were visible in the white and slightly porous masses. Yet, at a little distance, stratified sand rock appeared, overlying the breccia, and anon a vein of basaltic or trachytic rock, or a frowning heap of rough, black, and blistered masses of these materials, superimposed on the sand rock or conglomerate, would completely confound my uneducated notions of geological propriety. I presume all this apparent confusion is of easy explanation amongst those versed in the natural sciences; and if (as is more than likely) these can make nothing out of my description, they had better go there and examine for themselves. Geologically, as well as geographically and topographically, there is no more interesting region than that of Nicaragua, nor one which can better repay the investigations of the student of nature.

I continued beneath the broiling sun for nearly a league further, passing through patches of chapparal, or thorny bushes, resembling the willow in the shape and color of their leaves, which found a precarious hold amongst the rocks and in the barren sands. Beyond these the track divided, one branch running up a ravine into the woods, and the other keeping along the lake. I was at a dead loss as to which to take, and did not much relish the idea of sitting there solus until the party came up. While in this perplexity I heard the crowing of cocks in the direction of the ravine, and riding in, soon found myself in a broad path which led to a cluster of huts, situated so as to command a full view of the lake, without being seen from the shore. I despatched one of the niños, under promise of the magnificent reward of one medio, to watch for my companions, and tossing the bridle to a mozo, walked into the best hut and took possession of the best hammock, which a motherly old lady undertook to swing backward and forth for me, while I should endeavor to compensate myself for my broken slumbers of the preceding night. Sleep came without coaxing, and I had a grand siesta there amongst those kind Indians. I was roused by our *comisario*, who was hurrying on to order dinner for us at Nagarote, and I determined to push on with him. He had seduced one of the party to take his old mule, and had now got the best horse in the company, my own excepted. It was a sharp proceeding, as will be seen in the sequel.

The ride to Nagarote was a fine one; in places the road came down to the lake, and then wound back again amongst the hills, affording a most agreeable diversity to the traveller. At one place we reached a small valley, at the bottom of which flowed a limpid, rippling little stream—the only one we had encountered since we left Granada. The ground was beaten hard, and the underbrush removed over a wide space, for this was a famous resting place with the carreteros and arrieros. Two or three little groups of travellers were now waiting there, mixing their cups of *tiste* from the stream, while their animals were left to roam at discretion. They invited us to join them, but with the prospect of a good dinner only one league ahead, we declined, and galloped on, and on, until I began to think that our going to Nagarote was a grand flam, or that the town itself had walked off. That famous league we ever aftewards distinguished as the "five mile league." We nevertheless finally came to Nagarote, a little scurvy looking town, redeemed by but one really good looking house, which I was glad to learn was the posada. The landlady was "fat and forty," and welcomed us right cordially; she liked the Americans, she said; they had "mucho dinero," much money, and paid double what other folks did, without grumbling. I ordered the best dinner she could afford for the entire party, and then took to the hammock again, to catch another installment of sleep. It was full an hour before the remainder of the party came dropping in, one by one, for the order of march had been completely broken up, after leaving Matearas. Dinner was almost ready, but yet three or four were missing. Finally these arrived, two of them on foot, and holding one of their companions in his saddle. He was the verdant young gentleman who had exchanged his horse for the mule of the comisario, which had completely broken down some two or three leagues back, and had been abandoned in the woods. He had attempted to walk the rest of the way, but the exercise brought on chills and fever. He was put to bed, bathed with brandy, and wrapped in blankets, and having perspired freely, came on next morning, all the better apparently for the attack.

I dined with Don Enrique, at the cane-built house of a poor priest, with whom he was acquainted. The padre was absent, but his housekeeper, a tall, pale woman, with large, expressive black eyes, welcomed us very cordially. She had about her some fifteen or twenty little children, collected from the poorest families, to whom she taught reading and writing. Her humble dwelling was destitute of a single article of luxury or embellishment, unless a finely painted face of the Virgin, suspended over a little altar in an inner room, can be called such. I asked her if she was paid for her pains? She shook her head, and her eyes kindled and her brow expanded, as she slowly raised her face to heaven: her reward was there. How little do the sectaries and bigots of our own country know of the devotion, and fervent, unselfish piety of many of those whom they so unsparingly denounce as the impure ministers of a debased religion! When I last passed through Nagarote, I called to see the gentle teacher, but the hut was deserted, and rank weeds were growing around it. I inquired for her at the posada; the old lady did not answer me, but her eyes filled with moisture. The Santa Anita was dead; she had gone to the reward for which she had striven; the reward of the meek and the lowly in spirit! Shall I confess it? The heretic stranger dropped a tear to the memory of the Santa Anita.

We experienced great tribulation in Nagarote in getting animals to replace two or three of the scurvy mules which had been imposed upon us in Granada, and which were here unanimously condemned. We told the man whom the emprestador had sent with them, that he must supply their places; but he couldn't. All the horses and mules in the place had been sent to the fields, to prevent their being seized for the use of the army. "No hay, Señor!" there are none, was the invariable response to our inquiries. But we were bound to get on; so I instructed our *comisario* to produce the government order, which he carried in his pocket, and take it to the first alcalde, with my compliments, and the intimation that horses must be forthcoming, or his name should be faithfully reported to the "Gobierno Supremo." The effect was magical; horses, and good ones, appeared incontinently; whereupon I conceived a high respect for the dingy bit of paper which had wrought the miracle, and copied it for the benefit of future travellers. Here it is:—

Sebastian Salinas, Ministro de Relaciones del Supmo. Gobno. del Estado de Nicaragua.

De orden del mismo, hago saber á todas las autoridades de los pueblos del transito de esta Ciudad á la de Granada, q. el Sr. Oficial Don Jose Dolores Bermudez, á la cabeza de nueve o diez Norte-Americanos, va á conducir á esta dicha Ciudad al Exmo. Sr. Jorge Squier Mntro. Pleinpotenciario del Gobno. Supmo. de los Estados Unidos del Norte cerca del de Nicaragua residente en Granada. Ordeno y mando á las espresadas autoridades del transito q. no les pongan embarazo á dichos Sres, y ademas en su regreso con el Sr. Squier le guarden á este los respetos y consideraciones q. exije su alto caracter.

Dado en Leon, Sellado con el Sello del Estado, en la Casa de Gobno. a los 28 dia del mes de Junio, de 1849.

Les prestaran los recursos que necesiten previa indennizacion. [L.S.] S. SALINAS.

It was late in the afternoon, and dark thunder clouds were gathering in the east, clustering around the bald, burned peak of Momotombo, when we started from Nagarote for Pueblo Nuevo, where we were to pass the night. The winds were fitful, but cool and refreshing, and I unstrapped my poncho and threw it over the saddle bow, preparatory to encountering the storm that was closing around us. It came, fierce and black, before we had accomplished a single league of the five which intervened between the two villages. In an instant we were enveloped in the thick darkness, and the rain poured down in torrents. We could distinguish each other only when the lightnings blazed lividly around us. We left the horses to their own guidance, only taking care not to be dragged from our seats by the projecting limbs and overhanging branches, which constitute the chief source of danger in travelling in these countries in the night-time. The road became one pool of water, and the unshod horses slipped constantly, in a way not at all calculated to quiet one's nerves. By-and-by the storm passed, rushing forth upon the expanse of the Pacific, and the full moon glanced through the rifts of the passing clouds, in a strange, fitful way, momentarily revealing tall spectral trunks and skeleton branches, and then leaving us in utter darkness. It was a wierd looking forest through which we passed, and the entire party seemed to catch its gloomy influences, and rode on, for more than hour, slowly and in silence. Suddenly, however, the spell was broken by one of the number striking up "Hail Columbia;" the others joined spontaneously in the chorus; and when it was done, a great shout was given, and every horse was spurred into a gallop, spite of mud and water, nor was a rein drawn until, emerging from the forest, we found ourselves saluted by a myriad dogs in the streets of Pueblo Nuevo. Here we were met by two or three Americans who had started with the escort, but had been left here in charge of one of their number who had been injured by a fall. Anticipating our arrival, they had secured places for us in the village, quartering one detachment here and another there, in true military style. The house assigned to me and my personal companions was the most imposing and aristocratic mansion in the place, inasmuch as it was twice as large as any other, plastered with mud, and whitewashed withal. It was occupied by a well-dressed Señora and her five daughters, all attired in their finest array, with satin slippers, and their dark hair newly braided, and tipped out with a bunch of variegated ribbons. Upon one side of the principal apartment was an immense hollowed log, which was the granary; and upon the other a wax figure of Christ on the cross, surrounded by weeping Marys and bearded Romans, superabundantly tinselled; the whole enclosed in a large glass case, hung round with chaplets of fresh flowers. The five daughters were evidently putting their best feet foremost, but seemed to be greatly perplexed as to which was "El Ministro." Bespattered with mud, wayworn and weary, none of the party looked particularly imposing, and I thought I could discover symptoms of disappointment amongst the señoritas. They nevertheless were attentive, and gave us cigaritas all round, and brought coals in a silver cup for us to light them by; and what was better, they gave us a capital supper, with knives for three, and forks and spoons for four of the eight who sat down at the table, which was rather more than the usual allowance. Before we had finished, however, the alcalde came, but we declined talking until supper was over; and meantime the municipal dignitaries perched themselves on the big log, and looked at us in silence. We were getting very indifferent to official attentions; and so dismissed our visitors with all practicable expedition, but with a great profusion of compliments, which they seemed to relish mightily.

I got a bed with a canvass bottom, and slept dreamlessly the entire night, and until eight o'clock the next morning. The atmosphere was all the clearer for the storm of the preceding evening, and the village looked particularly bright and cheerful under the morning sun. Differing from the other towns which we had passed, each house was here surrounded by a hedge, or rather fence, of the columnar cactus, which in some places was low and even, but in others shot up to the height

31

of fifteen or twenty feet, resembling palisades, above which just appeared the thatched roofs of the dwellings. "A great country, this," said W——, "where they plant their fences!"

We were now within eight leagues of Leon, and, with the whole day before us, were not so expeditious in our movements as we might have been under other circumstances. We breakfasted leisurely, and departed with becoming deliberation. Beyond Pueblo Nuevo, the road, as usual, was through a forest, with here and there open spaces called "*jicarales*," from the *jicara*, or calabash trees, that were scattered over them, and which in size, and the appearance of the leaves and fruit, resembled the apple trees at home.

The broad and well beaten road, hard and smooth from the rain of the preceding night, was lined with palms and trees covered with blossoms, which loaded the air with their rich perfumes, and from which the white and rose-tinted petals fell like snow, beneath the touch of the cool morning breeze. Here a group of monkeys looked down upon us with queer grimaces—there a flock of parroquets, nestling *perdu* amongst the leaves, dashed wildly away upon our approach, while pigeons, and red-legged partridges graciously condescended to step out of the way and allow us to pass, without, however, exhibiting the slightest degree of alarm. Hundreds of lizards, bright green and gold, darted like rays of light before us; and large ants, each bearing a fragment of a green leaf above its back, marched across the path in solid columns, like fairy armies with their tiny banners. Their nests, built in the forks of the trees, resembled large bee-hives, and their paths, from which all obstacles were removed, for the width of several inches, could be traced by the eye in every direction amongst the bushes.

We rode briskly along, and in less than two hours came to a ravine, shut in by high banks, and descended by a series of steep steps which would have been deemed utterly impractica-

INDIAN HUT, WITH CACTUS HEDGE.

ble at home, but which seemed to be quite a matter of course to the horses here. This place was called Axusco ; and the ravine once entered, it was picturesque beyond description. The soil seemed moister than on the higher ground, and the verdure was correspondingly rich and dense. Masses of vines, leaves, and flowers were piled one on the other in the utmost luxuriance, and the shadows fell with a breadth and depth seen nowhere except under the tropics, and rarely equalled even there. It was a suspicious place nevertheless; and one or two dilapidated crosses, hardly visible amongst the undergrowth, showed that it had been the scene of tragic events, of robbery and murder. I afterwards often passed it in the night, but never without my hand on my sword-hilt.

We rested awhile at Axusco, then spurring up the opposite bank, resumed our march. The same forest shut us in, but paths, diverging here and there to distant estates and haciendas, gave evidence that we were approaching the city of Leon. Finally we arrived where the trees became more scattered, and through occasional openings we caught confused glimpses of broad fields, green hills, and towering volcanoes. These glimpses revealed a section of country surpassing in its capabilities any we had yet seen. I hurried on impatiently, and in a few moments, emerging from the forest, the great plain of Leon opened grandly before me!

I had left my companions behind, and stood alone on the borders of this ocean of verdure. Stretching away, chequered with hedge-rows and studded with tree clumps and tall palms, the eye traversed leagues on leagues of green fields, belted with forests, and bounded on the right by high mountains, their regular cones rising like spires to heaven, while low hills of emerald circled round on the left, like the seats of an amphitheatre. In front the view was uninterrupted, and the wearied eye sought in vain to discover its limit. A purple haze rested in the distance, and beneath it the waves of the great Pacific rolled in, unbrokenly, from China and the Indies!

It was the beginning of the rainy season, and vegetation had shot up in renewed youth and vigor; no dust had yet dimmed the almost transparent green of the leaves, nor had the heat withered the delicate blades of grass and spires of maize which carpeted the level fields, nor the young tendrils which twined delicately around the branches of the trees, or hung, blushing with buds and flowers, from the parent stem. Above all shone down the glorious sun, and the whole broad expanse seemed pulsating with life beneath its genial rays.

Never before had I gazed upon a scene so grand and magnificent as this. Well and truly has the ancient chronicler described it as "a country plain and beautiful, full of pleasantness, so that he who fared therein deemed that he journeyed in the ways of Paradise." The impression produced upon my companions, who had in the meantime joined me, was not less striking than on myself. We had heard much of the great plain of Leon, but the reality far surpassed the anticipations which we had formed of its extent and beauty. As we rode on, however, we were surprised to find that, although a great quantity of land was cleared, not more than half of it was really under cultivation; a remark which we had subsequently frequent occasion to make, for agriculture, since the independence, owing to the unfortunate condition of the country, has very much declined.

We had anticipated some kind of demonstration upon our arrival in Leon, and remembering our plight at San Carlos, had fixed upon "El Convento," about four miles from the city, as the place where we should make the necessary changes in our garb, preparatory to encountering the dignitaries and citizens of the capital. The convent was yet a league in advance, and meantime we wore the soiled and mud-bespattered garments with which we had passed through the storm of the preceding night. We had not gone far, however, into the open plain, before we discovered a party of horsemen galloping rapidly towards us. As they approached, we perceived that some wore military uniforms, while the others were dressed as simple citizens. They came near, and one of the party, who was evidently an American, looked hard at us, and for a moment seemed in doubt. We bowed, and would have passed on, but turning short, our supposed countryman inquired, in English, if we had passed a party of Americans, and the American minister, on the road. The question was an awkward one; I laughed outright, and matters were taking a very ridiculous turn, when one of our escort opportunely coming up, introduced us to Dr. Livingston, American Consul in Leon, by whom we were duly presented to the accompanying officers. The scene was sufficiently ludicrous all round, and I thought the seriousness of our new friends was strongly tried. I might have enjoyed the affair very much, had I not been at once informed that a large company of gentlemen from the city, a hundred or two in number, with the principal officers of State, and the Bishop of the church, in person, at their head, were coming out to meet us. But when it was added that they had already passed the convent, and were not half a mile distant, I was horrified. I entreated the doctor to ride back, and say that we would join them beyond the convent, but before the movement could be made, the whole cavalcade came in sight, and descrying our group, approached us at a gallop. There was no retreat, and we moved on in despair. First came the Bishop in his purple robes, splendidly mounted, flanked by a group of priests, and followed by a train of officers, in uniforms absolutely dazzling in the noonday sun! * * * * * *

Suffice it to say, we met, and there were congratulations, and welcomes, and many fine things said,—and if we did not leave a sufficiently distinct idea of republican simplicity on the minds of our new friends, it will be useless for any one to undertake it hereafter. They were, however, all well-bred caballeros, and with true Spanish *politesse*, kept their gravity, which, W. remarked, displayed "extraordinary self-control!" I nevertheless observed that some of the younger officers had occasion to wipe their faces with their handkerchiefs very often, and were long about it. But then it was a hot day, and they had ridden fast.

I was, however, determined not to enter the city in my present plight, and when we reached the convent, excused myself, and left the cavalcade to proceed, promising to rejoin it in a few minutes. The "convento" was only an Indian hut, of which I incontinently, and not in the best of humors, took possession, politely turning the family, old ones, babies, pigs, and chickens, all out of doors. Ben produced the diplomatic suit, which I had not seen since it left the tailor's, and displayed extraordinary address in adjusting it. Ten minutes sufficed to complete the transformation, but I discarded the *chapeau*, and stuck to the broad-brimmed Panama which I had purchased in Granada, much to Ben's dissatisfaction, who was bent on retrieving the credit of the legation.

We overtook the cavalcade a few hundred yards from where we had left them. They had halted beneath some large trees, and our escort, which had meantime come up, we also found on the spot, marshalled in the same order as when we left Granada. A dashing young officer rode up to me, as I approached, and begged to be permitted "to carry the glorious flag of El Norte," which request was, of course, graciously acceded to. Matters now began to take a more promising turn, and as per *programme* of arrangements, I found myself, with Dr. Livingston and the bishop, placed at the head of the procession, which formed in column, three deep. The Bishop, Don George de Viteri y Ungo, impressed me, from the first, as a man far above the ordinary mark, well informed, courteous, and affable, with manners which would have graced the proudest courts of Europe. I soon found that he had been in the United States, had travelled extensively in the Old World, and altogether knew more of men and things than could have been surmised of an ecclesiastic, however high in station, in this secluded part of the world. I was nevertheless taken a little aback, I must confess, when he inquired of me about Forrest and Miss Clifton, and whether they were yet on the stage. He had seen them both at the Park Theatre, and had been delighted, he said, with their acting, although he had not understood a word which they said. I told him that the Park had been burned, and that it probably would never be rebuilt, and concurred with him in regarding it as a "great pity." Mr. Clay, too, he had heard speak, and had *felt* all he said, without understanding his language. "Ah!" exclaimed the Bishop, "after all, there is more in the feeling of the speaker himself, and in his manner, than in his words;—to arouse the sympathy of the hearer is the true secret of oratory!" Not bad criticism, I thought, for Nicaragua.

As we advanced over the plain, the cultivated fields became more numerous, and the evidences of industry more abundant. It was with something, I thought, of the spirit of prophecy, that the Bishop swept his hand around the horizon and said, "We want only an infusion of your people, to make this broad land an Eden of beauty, and the garden of the world." He pointed out to me the nine volcanoes which skirted the plain; the gigantic Viejo; the regular Telica; the riven Orota, and lofty Momotombo, which now rose clear and distinct before our eyes; these, said he, are the works of the Great Architect, and *that*, the puny achievement of man! I looked in the direction which he pointed, and there rose the towers of the great Cathedral, white and massive above a wilderness of tiled roofs, foliage, and fruit trees. Notwithstanding his philosophical depreciation, I thought there was an expression of pride in the face of the Bishop, as his eyes rested upon this architectural wonder of Nicaragua; nor was his complacency unwarranted, for the Cathedral of Leon is a structure not unworthy a place beside the most imposing sacred edifices of either continent.

We now rapidly approached the city, and entered the suburbs, which corresponded entirely with those of Granada and Masaya. Here was drawn up the carriage of the Bishop, in readiness for use, in case I should prefer it. I however, chose to continue on horseback, and the polite Bishop commended my choice. Passing the Indian barrio, or suburb of Guadelupe, the people falling on their knees as the Bishop approached, we descended abruptly into a deep ravine, at the bottom of which flowed a clear and beautiful stream, and ascended upon the other side by a broad, graded way, paved with stones, into the city proper. I had merely time to observe that the streets were in gala dress, when the thunder of cannon, and the sudden pealing of the bells of the churches, above which those of the cathedral rose full and distinct, proclaimed our arrival. "Vivan los Estados Unidos del Norte!" exclaimed the officer who bore my flag, as he dashed at full speed to the head of the column. The whole party caught the spirit, and echoed the "viva," and the Bishop himself waved his hand and cried "Adelantamos!" On! I remember but little more, except a confused sound of trampling horses, shouting people, the ringing of bells, the thunder of cannon, and a cloud of dust, until we rode into the great plaza. Here the entire garrison was drawn up, who presented arms and cheered for the United States as we entered. The band struck up a martial air, and the ladies of the metropolis waved their handkerchiefs to us from the balconies of the House of the Government. We halted for a moment, and the alcalde mayor made a speech, which was delightfully short, but of which, amidst the clangor of the bells and the shouts of the multitude, I heard not a word. I responded in three sentences, which I presume were equally unintelligible; and then we moved on, amidst a dense throng, to the house of the American Consul, above which the stripes and stars floated proudly to the breeze. It was with unmingled feelings of satisfaction that, shaking hands with the Bishop, and bowing to the rest of the cavalcade, I spurred through the archway into the court of the Dr.'s residence, and away from the noise and the dust of the crowded streets. But the public curiosity was not yet satisfied, and the people thronged into the courtyard to stare at the apparition from El Norte. Nor was it until the gateway was closed and barred that we succeeded in escaping from the multitude, and even then the iron gratings of the windows were festooned with inquisitive boys, who seemed to hang one to another like swarming bees. Some considerate alcaldes, however, by a judicious application of their canes, finally cleared these away, and then we got an hour for privacy and dinner.

High mass had been said the day before in the church of La Mercedes for our safe arrival, and now a Te Deum was chaunted in the cathedral in acknowledgement of the protection which Heaven had vouchsafed to us. In the evening fireworks were let off in the plaza, and we were serenaded by the band attached to the garrison, which, to our surprise, we found almost as effective as any that we had ever heard.

We found that the city was not free from the alarm which had existed at Granada; and although no outbreak had occurred in this part of the state, the government, acting on the principle that "precaution is the parent of safety," had taken the most complete measures to guard against surprise, and to check promptly the first indications of disorder. The roof and towers of the cathedral, an impregnable fortress in itself, were occupied by troops; so too was the church of La Mercedes; and the evacuated convent attached to it had been converted into a cuartel of cavalry. It was immediately opposite the house of Dr. Livingston, and I observed that the horses of the lancers were kept constantly saddled, in readiness for action at a moment's warning. Advanced posts of troops were also established in every principal street, and after the eight o'clock bell had struck, there was no cessation of the fierce "*Quien vivas?*" and wakeful "*Alertes!*" of the sentinels.

The day subsequent to our arrival was devoted to receiving visits from the functionaries and leading citizens of Leon. Amongst them all, none impressed me more favorably than the Presbitero Dr. Disiderio de la Quadra, then Vicar of the bishopric, a man of great dignity of manners, and of a character above the remotest taint of suspicion. He was accompanied by a number of the dignitaries of the church, and spoke of his country, its wants, and prospects, with a force and freedom which I had little expected to hear. Indeed, I soon discovered that the better portion of the population fully comprehended the evils under which they suffered, and only required that exterior influences should be exercised in their favor, instead of against them, as it had been hitherto, in order to effect their removal. The revolutionary spirit had exhausted itself, and the universal desire was now for peace and quiet, stability in public affairs, and moderation in their administration. All hoped much from the sympathy and co-operation of the United States, and took new energy from the circumstance that they had attracted the attention and awakened the interest of its government. No better evidence of the truth of these observations could be desired, than the feeling exhibited on the occasion of my official presentation, which took place a few days after my arrival, publicly, in the hall of the Government House, which was appropriately fitted up for the occasion. The proceedings were characterized by the greatest decorum, and a degree of enthusiasm which it would hardly be proper for me to attempt to describe. Indeed, in introducing my own address on the occasion, with the reply of Señor Ramirez, the Supreme Director of the State, I am conscious that I am incurring the risk of being misunderstood and misrepresented; but as I have set out with the purpose of vindicating the public sentiment of Nicaragua, not less than of making known the character and condition of its people, I conceive that I cannot do better than to introduce occasional documents of this kind, especially when they contribute to the completeness of my narrative, and to the understanding of the present posture of affairs in that country.

ADDRESS.

"Senor Director of the Republic of Nicaragua:

"I have to-day the honor of laying before you my credentials as the Representative of the United States of North America, near the Government of this Republic. The personal satisfaction which I feel upon this occasion is greatly enhanced by the many evidences which I have already had afforded to me, of the friendly sentiments which are entertained by the Government and people of Nicaragua towards those of the United States. I can assure you, upon behalf of my Government, that these sentiments are fully reciprocated, and that it is its earnest desire to cultivate, in every way, the most cordial relations with this Republic. Of this the official letters from the city of Washington, which I have now the honor to deliver to yourself and his Excellency the Minister of Foreign Relations, will give abundant evidence.

"It shall be my aim, Sir, in my official and personal intercourse with the Government and people of this State, not only to confirm the present harmony and good correspondence which exist between the two Republics, but to create new ties of friendship, and to promote a closer and more intimate relationship between them. They, Sir, possess common interests; they both stand before the world the avowed supporters of liberal principles, and the vindicators of Republican Institutions; the true policy of both is the preservation of order, and the encouragement of education and industry at home, and the maintenance of peace abroad. It is proper, therefore, that they should present an example of that fraternity which it is the desire of my Government, as I know it is of your Excellency, should exist between the two Republics.

"To this end, and to secure the permanent welfare of both, it is essential that they should pursue a system of policy exclusively American. In the language of an eminent statesman of my own country, (whose memory is reverently cherished, and whose words are treasured with care by every American citizen,) 'in order that the fabric of international connections between the Republics of this continent may rise, in the lapse of years, with a grandeur and harmony of proportions corresponding with the magnitude of the means placed by Providence in their power, its foundations must be laid in principles of politics and morals new and distasteful to the thrones and dominions of the elder world, but coextensive with the surface of the globe, and lasting as the changes of time.'

"A cardinal principle in this policy is a total exclusion of foreign influence from the domestic and international affairs of the American Republics; and while we would cultivate friendly intercourse, and promote trade and commerce with all the world, and invite to our shores and to the enjoyment of our institutions the people of all nations, we should proclaim, in language distinct and firm, that the American continent belongs to Americans, and is sacred to Republican Freedom. We should also let it be understood, that if foreign powers encroach upon the territories or invade the rights of any one of the American States, they inflict an injury upon all, which it is alike the duty and determination of all to see redressed.

"Señor Director! Providence has peculiarly favored the country of which you are the worthy Chief Executive. I have passed through your territories from the Atlantic ocean, through your rivers and magnificent lakes, along the bases of your lofty mountains, and over your broad and beautiful plains, until the wide expanse of the Pacific opens before me, and I can almost hear the sound of its waves as they break upon your western shores. At every step I have been deeply impressed with the capabilities of the country, and the vastness of its internal resources. I have seen, also, with pleasure, the many evidences of industry and civilization which exist within your borders, and I have been led to indulge the belief that the time is not far distant, when the commerce of two hemispheres shall find within your territories an easy passage from sea to sea. It is one of the objects of my mission to assist in an enterprise so important to the whole world—an enterprise, the successful prosecution of which must enable this country to attain a degree of prosperity second to that of no other on the globe. With your cordial co-operation, (of which I am well assured,) and of that of the citizens of this Republic, I hope soon to have it in my power to announce to my Government, that the initiatives to this grand and glorious enterprise have already been taken.

"And here, Sir, you will permit me to express the profound regret which I feel, that I find this Republic afflicted by civil commotions. Both the principles and policy of the United States make us desire that this and the other Republics of Central America should be prosperous and powerful. We feel a deep interest in their welfare, but this we know can only be promoted by enlightened and stable Governments. The enjoyment of liberty, and the maintenance of individual rights, cannot be secured without permanent order, and this can only spring from a sacred observance of law. I trust, Sir, that the patriotic citizens of Nicaragua, whatever their differences of opinion, will all unite in an earnest endeavor to restore peace to the State. Nothing, Sir, could give me personally greater satisfaction, and I am certain nothing could be more acceptable to the Government and people of the United States, and to the friends of Republican Institutions throughout the world.

"I will not, Sir, detain you further. I can only reiterate the friendly sentiments of my Government and countrymen, and assure your Excellency, and the distinguished officers of the State and army around you, as also the illustrious Bishop and reverend prelates and clergy, of my personal high consideration and regard. Allow me also, through you, to return my thanks for the many kind attentions which I have received from the magistrates and citizens of the Republic, and to express the high pleasure which I have experienced in learning from my countrymen, who have lately been detained by unforeseen circumstances in the country, the uniform kindness and courtesy with which they have been treated. I am proud to learn that the name of AMERICAN has been a passport to every Nicaraguan heart. That the new relations which are this day opened between this Republic and my own, may result in lasting benefit to both, is, Sir, my sincere prayer, and to this end I shall direct my most earnest endeavors."

To this address the Supreme Director, Señor Don NORBERTO RAMIREZ, replied as follows:

REPLY.

"SIR,—The satisfaction which I experience in having the honor of receiving, for the first time, a representative of the Republic of North America, is only equalled by the aspirations and high hopes which that event inspires. The gratitude with which your words have animated me, the extraordinary intervention of your Government under the circumstances with which Nicaragua is surrounded, impose on me the pleasing duty of returning thanks to Divine Providence for its benefits.

"Nicaragua has long felt the necessity of sheltering itself under the bright banner of the North American Confederacy; but the time which the Arbiter of nations had designated for such high happiness and consequent prosperity had not arrived. Before we despatched a Legation to the American Minister at Guatemala, and even before the treaty relative to a canal was entered into with Dr. Brown, (a citizen of your Republic,) we had made some advances to the American Government with a view to this happy consummation; but our hopes were scarcely sustained by their result. But I now see all the elements of a happy future brought before us; there is good faith in the Government with which I am connected; the friendliest feelings towards North America pervades every NICARAGUAN heart; and we have the assurances of the sympathy and support of the American Government. We have consequently all things which can be desired to make available the advantages with which Heaven has surrounded us. Our State, considering its geographical position, ought to be the most prosperous in Spanish America; but our inexperience at the time of our separation from Spain—our limited resources, and the civil commotions that have intervened, have retarded the happy day which is now dawning upon us. I am certain that the Government which you represent, can appreciate the difficulties which have surrounded this Republic. Your Excellency being able properly to estimate these circumstances, must already have formed a just idea of the condition of this part of Central America, and of the position of its Government. Believing therefore that the best intentions exist upon your part towards us, as I know there is the happiest disposition on ours, I entertain no doubts that we shall succeed in establishing the most intimate relations between the two Republics, and in opening the way to the consummation of that most glorious enterprise which it has been reserved for the successors of the immortal Washington to undertake and perfect. I shall have the greatest pleasure in being able to contribute my humble share towards this result, and to the consequent happiness of Nicaragua. I thank you, Sir, and through you, your Government, for its proffered coöperation in so glorious an enterprise.

"Let us begin, Sir, this great work under these bright auspices, and we shall be sure of obtaining the best results. The people of the two American Continents are contemplating us; it is possible that for what we shall do, future generations shall cherish our memory: at least we shall have the conscious satisfaction of having neglected no means, omitted no sacrifice, in securing the grand objects so ardently desired by two sister Republics, determined mutually to sustain their interests, their honor, their integrity, and the principles of continental freedom."

An incident occurred, at the close of this reply, which perhaps would have startled more rigid sticklers for form and etiquette than were assembled on that occasion; but which I mention, for the same reasons that have induced me to give place to the above quotations. The Director had just concluded his reply, and the entire assemblage was yet still and attentive, when a young officer, distinguished not less for his ardent patriotism than for his bravery in the field, and his usefulness as a citizen, Col. FRANCISCO DIAZ ZAPATA, advancing suddenly beyond the line of officers, commenced an impassioned apostrophe to the flag of the United States, which, entwined with that of Nicaragua, was suspended above the chair of the Executive. The effect was electrical, and the whole of the assemblage seemed to catch the spirit of the speaker, whose appearance, action, and language were those of the intensest emotion. They pressed eagerly forward, as if anxious to treasure every word which fell from his lips; and when he had concluded, forgetting all other considerations, their enthusiasm broke forth in loud and protracted "vivas," which were caught up and echoed by the people in the plaza, and the soldiers of the garrison. I subjoin a literal copy of the address:

SALUTACION A LA BANDERA DE LOS ESTADOS UNIDOS.

POR SENOR FRANCISCO DIAZ ZAPATA.

"¡Presajio de poder y de grandeza!
¡Enseña illustre de virtud y gloria!
Yo te contemplo en tu sublime alteza;
Y al contemplarte siento
Que de mi Patria ensalzaras la historia.
Esas franjas hermosas,
Y el emblema feliz de tus Estrellas,
Que ajitadas del viento
Ondean y relucen majestuosas

Como astros rutilantes, y mas bellas:
El hasta fuerte y noble,
Y ese cuadro, del sólido figura;
Que la herida cerviz ya, no mas doble
Nicàragua en su triste desventura;
Revélanme que harás con tu presencia,
Rodeada de esplendor y de potencia.
"Bajo tu sombra, libertad respira
El activo Varon americano,
Que la memoria deificar aspira
De Washington glorioso:
Bajo tu sombra, se alza soberano
El poder de las leyes;
Y el saber y la ventura crecen
Con vigor prodijioso,
Que pesa sobre el cetro de los Reyes.
Y los Heroes de America enaltecen
Su memoria sagrada,
Sus sepulcros, su sangre de guerreros,
Y el triunfo de tu espada,
Bajo el dulce brillar de tus luceros.
Todo bajo tu imperio tiene vida,
Portentosa Bandera esclarecida.
Yo te saludo de entusiasmo lleno;
Y henchido de placer y de esperanza,
Mi corazon palpita dentro el seno
Con tan fuerte latido,
Que el pecho ardiente á respirar no alcanza.
La suave y fresca brisa,
Del alto Sol los claros resplandores,
El aire enrarecido,
De los Cielos la placida sonrisa,
Y el balsamico aliento de las flores,
Saludante conmigo.
Celebrando del modo mas plausible
Tu advenimiento amigo
A mi Patria doliente y compasible,
Llenala de tu honor y tu grandeza,
Y abate á su adversario la cabeza."

CHAPTER IX.

THE CITY OF LEON—ORIGINALLY BUILT ON THE SHORES OF LAKE MANAGUA—CAUSE OF ITS REMOVAL—ITS PRESENT SITE—DWELLINGS OF ITS INHABITANTS—STYLE OF BUILDING—DEVASTATION OF THE CIVIL WARS—PUBLIC BUILDINGS—THE GREAT CATHEDRAL—ITS STYLE OF ARCHITECTURE; INTERIOR; MAGNIFICENT VIEW FROM THE ROOF—THE "CUARTO DE LOS OBISPOS," OR GALLERY OF THE BISHOPS—THE UNIVERSITY—THE BISHOP'S PALACE—"CASA DEL GOBIERNO"—"CUARTEL GENERAL"—THE CHURCHES OF LA MERCED, CALVARIO, RECOLECCION—HOSPITAL OF SAN JUAN DE DIOS—STONE BRIDGE—INDIAN MUNICIPALITY OF SUBTIABA—POPULATION OF LEON—PREDOMINANCE OF INDIAN POPULATION—DISTINCTION OF STOCKS—MIXED RACES—SOCIETY OF LEON—THE FEMALES; THEIR DRESS—SOCIAL GATHERINGS; THE "TERTULIA"—HOW TO "BREAK THE ICE" AND OPEN A BALL—NATIVE DANCES—PERSONAL CLEANLINESS OF THE PEOPLE—GENERAL TEMPERANCE—"AGUARDIENTE"—AND "ITALIA"—FOOD—THE TORTILLA—FRIJOLES—PLANTAINS—THE MARKETS—PRIMITIVE CURRENCY—MEALS—COFFEE, CHOCOLATE, AND "TISTE"—DULCES—TRADE OF LEON.

THE city of Leon is situated in latitude 12° 25′ north, and longitude 86° 57′ west. As I have elsewhere mentioned, it was founded in 1523, by Hernandez de Cordova, the conqueror of the country and the founder of Granada. Its original site was at the head of the western bay of Lake Managua, near the base of the great volcano of Momotombo, at a place now called Moabita, or, as it is spelled in the early chronicles, Ymbita, where its ruins still exist, overgrown by trees undistinguishable from those of the surrounding forests. This site was abandoned in the year 1610, for that now occupied by the city, which was then the seat of a large Indian town called Subtiaba. There is a tradition that a curse was pronounced upon the old town by the Pope, when he heard of the murder there, in 1549, by Hernando de Contreras, of Antonio de Valdivieso, third bishop of Nicaragua, who opposed the cruelty and oppression towards the Indians practised by Contreras, and who, for this reason, fell under his anger. In consequence of this curse, it is said, the city was visited by a succession of calamities, which became insupportable; and the inhabitants, driven to despair, finally, on the 2d of January, 1610, after a solemn fast, with the flag of Spain and the officers of the municipality at their head, marched to the site now occupied by the city, and there proceeded to lay out a new town. The cruel and sacrilegious deed of Contreras is, even yet, mentioned with horror; and many of the people believe that the stains of the blood of the bishop, who fled to the church, and died of his wounds at the foot of the altar, are yet visible upon its ruined walls, a lasting evidence of God's displeasure.

In common with Granada, Leon suffered from the attacks of the pirates, during their predominance in the South Sea. In 1685, a party of English freebooters, amongst them the celebrated Dampier, landed in the Estero Doña Paula, and advancing rapidly upon the city, surprised and captured it, notwithstanding the brave resistance of the little garrison of fifty men. They sacked the entire city, and burnt the cathedral, the convent of La Merced, the hospital, and many of the principal houses.

Leon is situated in the midst of the great plain of the same name, which I have described, about midway between the lake and ocean. The choice of position seems to have been determined by the same considerations which influenced the Indians in selecting it for one of their own towns, viz.: the proximity of water. Upon both sides of the city are deep ravines, in which are a multitude of springs of pure water, forming perennial streams of considerable size, which unite at the distance of half a mile from the city. From these the supply of water for the town is chiefly obtained. In later times many wells have been sunk, but they require to be of great depth—from one hundred and twenty to two hundred feet—and the water is not esteemed to be as good as that from the ravines.

Like all other cities under the tropics, Leon covers a large area of ground. It is regularly laid out, with squares or plazas, at intervals, in each ecclesiastical or municipal district. The houses, like those of Granada, are built of adobes, and are rarely of more than one story. Each one encloses a spacious *patio* or courtyard, filled with fruit or shade trees. Sometimes the building has an inner or back court for the domestic animals, while that immediately connected with the dwelling is ornamented with shrubbery and flowers, and surrounded on all sides by a broad corridor. This style of building, which is well adapted to the climate, and rendered necessary in a country where earthquakes are so frequent, admits of very little architectural display. The builder has no opportunity of exhibiting his taste or skill, except in the "*puerta*," or "*zaguan*"—portal, or principal entrance,—and in the elaboration of the balconied windows. These portals are often high and imposing, and profusely and tastefully ornamented. Some are copies of the Moresque arches so common in Spain, and are loaded with ornaments peculiar to that style of architecture. Others are of the severer Grecian styles, and others of orders utterly indescribable, and eminently original. Above these arches the old aristocracy often placed their arms; those of a military turn carved groups of armor, and those piously inclined a prayer or a passage from the Bible.

Formerly, very few of the buildings had more than two or three openings on the street, but of late years windows are becoming more numerous. These windows are broad and high, projecting two or three feet, and are guarded by iron balconies. Within the balconies are seats, which in the evening are occupied by the señoras, who here receive their visitors, and return the salutations of their passing friends. The gallant saunters from one to the other, and pays his devoirs without entering; an easy custom, which, in the early evening, gives the streets an air of great gayety and cheerfulness. He often carries his guitar with him, and sings a song when conversation flags. Sometimes the mounted cavalier reins in his steed before the balcony, to pay his compliments to the fair occupants,—stealthily pricking the animal with his spurs, to show off his skill in managing him, and to impress the señoras with admiration for his spirit. They are quite up to these little tricks in Nicaragua, as well as in other countries.

The interiors of the dwellings of the better classes convey an idea of great comfort, in a country where room and ventilation become necessary conditions of existence. The principal apartments, with rare exceptions, open upon the corridor, and are also connected by inner doors. In the main body of the building is the grand *sala*, or what we would call a parlor, used only for receptions, or as a sitting-room for the ladies. On either side are the private rooms of the families, while the wings are appropriated for sleeping apartments, to the servants, and for stores. Very few are ceiled, but are open to the roof, allowing a free circulation of air between the tiles. The floors are paved with large square tiles or bricks, occasionally with marble, and are usually kept well watered. And as the windows are never glazed, every passing breeze enters freely, and the ventilation is made perfect. Meals are taken in the corridor, on the side most shaded from the sun; and here hammocks are swung for those who choose to occupy them. The walls, both of the corridors and inner rooms, are sometimes painted, in imitation of marble or of hangings; but owing to the lack of skill on the part of the artists, the effect is not usually good. The accompanying ground-plan will convey an idea of the arrangement of the various parts of a Central American dwelling, from which the details may be discovered without further explanation. I need only repeat that, however at variance with established rules of architecture in other countries, they are probably better adapted to the climate and country than edifices of a more pretending character.

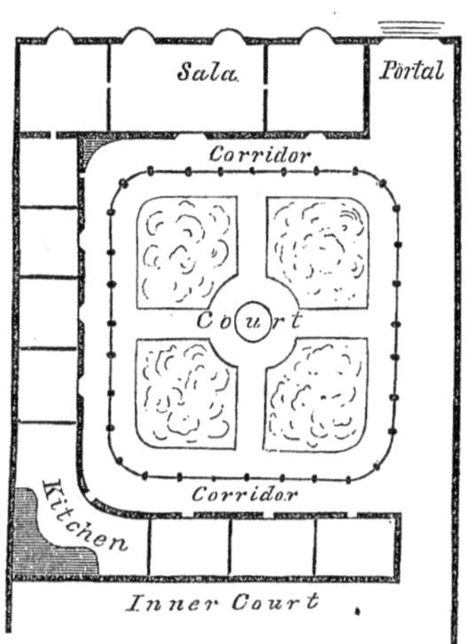

PLAN OF A DWELLING-HOUSE IN LEON.

In Leon, as in Granada, the dwellings on the outskirts of the city are simple cane structures, covered with thatch, but sometimes plastered with mud and roofed with tiles. And here, as in all the other towns, they are embowered in trees, and surrounded with cactus fences. The accompanying engraving of a hut in the barrio of Saragossa, may be taken as a type of all the others.

The streets in the central part of the city are paved. The object principally had in view is the prevention of dust, which, towards the close of the dry season, is almost unendurable in the unpaved parts of the town.

Perhaps no city in America has suffered more from war than Leon. During the contest between the aristocrats and liberals which followed the declaration of independence, a large part, embracing the richest and best built portions, was destroyed by fire. Over one thousand buildings were burned in a single night. The great cathedral is surrounded by entire squares of ruins of what were once palaces. The lofty and elaborate archways, by which they were entered, still indicate their original magnificence. Entire streets, now almost deserted, are lined with the remains of large and beautiful edifices, destroyed in the civil wars. Within their abandoned courts stand rude cane huts,—as if in mockery of their former state. Leon was formerly one of the best built cities in all Spanish America. "It is," says the old traveller, Gage, writing in 1665, "very curiously built; for the chief delight of the inhabitants consists in their houses, in the pleasure of the country adjoining, and in the abundance of all things for the life of man. They are content," he adds, "with fine gardens, with the variety of singing birds and parrots, with plenty of fish and flesh, with gay houses, and so lead a delicious, lazy, and idle life, not aspiring much to trade and traffic, although they have the lake and ocean near them. The gentlemen of Leon are almost as gay and fantastical as those of Chiapas; and it is especially from the pleasure of this city that the province of Nicaragua is called Mahomet's Paradise."[1]

The public buildings of Leon are among the finest in all

[1] The pirate, Dampier, in giving an account of the capture and burning of Leon by himself and his associates, says:

"Our countryman, Mr. Gage, who travelled in these parts, recommends Leon as the pleasantest place in all America, and calls it the Paradise of the Indies. Indeed, if we consider the advantages of its situation, we may find it surpassing most places for health and pleasure in America; for the country about it is of a sandy soil, which soon drinks up all the rain which falls. It is encompassed with savannas, so that they have the benefit of the breezes which come from any quarter; all of which makes it a very healthy place."—*Dampier's Voyage round the World*, vol. i. p. 218.

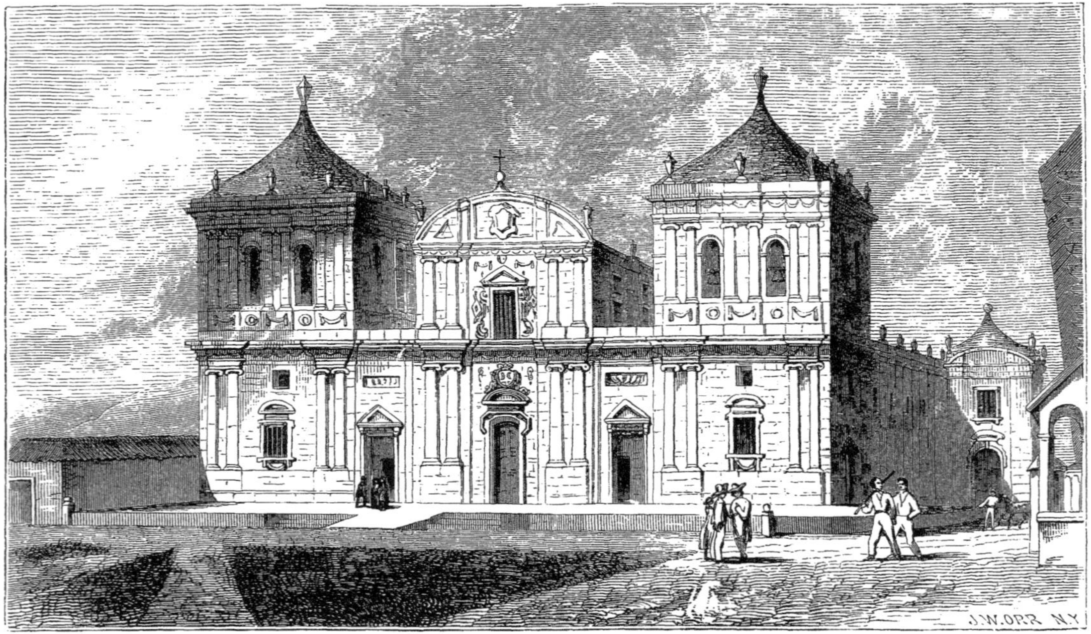

CATHEDRAL OF ST. PETER, LEON

Central America. Indeed, the great cathedral of St. Peter may perhaps be regarded as second to no similar structure in any of the Spanish American States. It was finished in 1743, having occupied thirty-seven years in building. The cost is said to have been five millions of dollars, but this seems to be an exaggeration. It covers an entire square, and its front extends the whole width of the grand plaza. It is constructed of cut stone, and is one firm mass of masonry. The roof is composed of massive arches, and has all the solidity of a rock. Nothing can better illustrate its strength, than the fact that it has withstood the storms and earthquakes of more than a century ; and, with the exception of one of the towers, which during my residence in the country was struck by lightning, and cracked from top to bottom, it is now nearly as perfect as it came from the hands of its builders. Yet it has often been converted into a fortress, and has sustained more than one cannonade and bombardment from besieging forces. In 1823, it is said, no less than thirty pieces of artillery were planted on its roof. On its most exposed side, towards the east, there is hardly a square inch of its walls which is not indented with shot.

Its ornaments are of stucco, and are simple and chaste. Viewed from an eminence, the entire structure is very imposing, but seen from the plaza, it appears low in proportion to its width. The interior is not unworthy of the exterior ; but is comparatively bare of ornament. At the head of the principal aisle, beneath a lofty, spacious dome, is the great altar, composed of silver, elaborately chased. The side chapels are not remarkable for their richness or beauty. For, in the civil commotions of the country the churches have not escaped the rapacity of the soldiery. The cathedral was once possessed of extraordinary wealth, and the costliness and variety of its ornaments were a proverb in Spain itself; but now it has little to boast beyond its massive proportions and architectural design.

I visited it shortly after my arrival, under the guidance of one of the canónigos, who was conscientious in pointing out to me everything worthy of notice. What most interested me, however, was a small room, in which were contained all the portraits of the bishops, commencing with Zuniga. They were forty-four in number, and displayed every variety of feature and complexion. The dark skins and black hair of some of the bishops showed that native or Indian blood had been no bar to ecclesiastical preferment, and contrasted strongly with the fair complexions of others of European birth. Most had an expression of great austerity; types of rigorous zealots, who looked as if every sentiment and feeling of humanity had been rudely rooted from their hearts; while others wore more cheerful faces, and a few, I am sure, had been right jolly old fellows in their day, not averse to the grape, nor wholly indifferent to the smiles of beauty.

Both the façade and rear of the cathedral were once ornamented with the royal arms of Spain, but these were removed in the first fervor of republican zeal, and their places yet remain blanks,—emblematic of a country which has got rid of one government, without having as yet fully succeeded in establishing another in its place.

One of the finest views in the world is commanded from the roof of the cathedral; and standing here, I saw for the first time the waters of the Pacific, a rim of silver on the edge of the western horizon. In the east bristled the nine volcanoes of the Marabios, which I have already mentioned, their outlines sharply defined against the sky, and in their regularity of outline emulating the symmetry of the pyramids. From this position alone is a good view to be obtained of the city, which, seen from one side, or from a distance, presents only a monotonous succession of tiled roofs, half-buried amongst the trees, and only relieved by the white walls of the churches.

To the left of the cathedral, and separated only by the

street, is the "Palacio del Obispo," the Episcopal Palace. It was described as follows, in 1751, by the then Bishop of Nicaragua, Señor Don Pedro Augustin Morel de Sta. Cruz, and has changed but little since.

"The Episcopal Palace is situated at the corner of the principal plaza, contiguous to the Sagrario; it is built of adobes and tiles, with two balconies, and is distinguished by a certain air of respectability. It is entered by a portico of good proportions, and has not less than fourteen apartments, furnished and ornamented with pictures, canopies, curtains, tables, silk beds, and many well-carved chairs. The principal sala and the oratorio are the largest; the others are proportioned to their purposes. They all open upon a broad piazza, running entirely around the court, within which is a garden, with many trees and flowers, and à fountain very beautiful and refreshing to the sight. Back of the building is another square for the servants, stables, etc. In short, nothing is wanted to make it a suitable habitation for the prelate, except a revenue sufficient to enable him to keep up a style oommensurate to the edifice."

Adjoining the palace of the Bishop, is the Tridentine College of St. Ramon, established in 1675. This institution was once very flourishing, and had numerous students, with professorships of law and medicine. It has, however, shared in the general decadence of the country, and has now but little more than a nominal existence. Efforts have lately been made to revive it upon a new foundation; and with an improvement in the country at large, there is no doubt it may regain something of its former position.

The government house, which occupies the northern side of the grand plaza, is distinguished for nothing except that it is somewhat more lofty than its neighbors, and has a raised corridor extending along its entire front. Opposite to this is the Cuartel General, or head-quarters of the regular forces of the government, with a guard of soldiers constantly on duty; for, in case of disturbance, this is the first place to be attacked, inasmuch as it is the general depository of the arms of the State.

The churches of La Merced, the Recoleccion, and Calvario, are remarkable for their size and their fine façades. The front of the latter is ornamented with panels containing Scriptural groups, admirably executed in bas-relief, and with niches containing statues of the saints. It has suffered much from shot, having been twice occupied by besieging forces, while the superior position of the cathedral was in possession of the other party. The Merced has also suffered from the same cause, but in a less degree. It contains some fine paintings, and its principal altar is an elaborate and very beautiful piece of composition. A convent was once attached to this church, as also to the church of the Recoleccion, and to that of San Juan de Dios. But these have been abolished; and the convent buildings of the Merced, at the time of my arrival, were used as cavalry barracks, while those of San Juan de Dios had been converted into a hospital. Besides the churches which I have named, there are ten or twelve others, but less in size, and of more moderate pretensions. And as each of these has a chime of bells, and nearly every day is dedicated to some saint, in whose honor it is essential to ring them all, a continual clangor is kept up, which, until the stranger becomes habituated to it, or is deafened outright, is excessively annoying.

When to this list I have added the stone bridge across the ravine to the south of the city, connecting with the barrio de Guadelupe, I have finished the architectural notabilities of Leon. This bridge was never fully completed, but was boldly projected, and the arches spanning the stream are models of symmetry and good workmanship.

The Indian pueblo of Subtiaba is really part of the city of Leon, although constituting a distinct municipality. It has also its grand plaza, and separate public buildings. Its great church is second in size to no other in Nicaragua, except the cathedral of Leon. The façade is quaint, with numerous niches filled with figures of grim old saints. It is substantially built, and has a very high antiquity. "The Parroquial of Subtiaba," said the old Bishop, Augustin Morel, writing of this church in the year 1751, "is the largest and most beautiful in the Bishopric. The principal and side chapels, and baptistery, are arched, and high and ample. The body of the church consists of three naves; the columns are of cedar, with gilt capitals. It has eight altars, four chapels, a neat sacristy, and is admirably decorated. Its towers are well proportioned, and its façade imposing and tasteful, and altogether the edifice is fit for a cathedral."

Subtiaba has suffered no less than Leon from intestine wars, and is but a shadow of what it once was, when it could muster two thousand fighting men in its plaza at a moment's warning.

It is difficult to form a correct estimate of the population of Leon. The city is spread over so wide a space, and so involved amongst trees that, even after a three months' residence, I found myself constantly discovering new and secluded portions, of the existence of which I was before ignorant. And although at first I thought twenty thousand an over estimate, I ultimately came to regard the number set down in the census attempted in 1847, viz: thirty thousand, as probably nearer the truth. In this calculation I include the Indian municipality of Subtiaba, which is generally, but erroneously supposed to be a town separate from Leon.

Here, as everywhere else in Nicaragua, the Indian and mixed population greatly predominates, and the pure whites constitute scarcely one-tenth of the whole number. The general complexion is however considerably lighter than at Granada, but not so clear as at Managua and some of the smaller towns. An infusion of Indian blood is easily to be detected in a large proportion of those who claim to be of pure Spanish descent. It displays itself less in the color of the skin than in a certain quickness of the eye, which is a much more expressive feature in those crossed with the

Indians than in either of the original stocks. In respect of *physique*, leaving color out of the question, there are probably no handsomer men in the world than some of the Sambos, or offspring of Indian and negro parents. They are of course darker than the Indian, but taller and better developed. It should however be observed that the negroes of Nicaragua differ very widely in appearance from those of the United States. They must have been derived from an entirely different portion of the African continent. They have, in general, aquiline noses, small mouths, and thin lips,—in fact, with the exception of the crisp hair and dark skin, they have few of the features which, with us, are regarded as peculiar and universal in the negro race.

The fusion between all portions of the population of Nicaragua has been so complete, that notwithstanding the diversity of races, distinctions of caste are hardly recognized. The whites, in their social intercourse, maintain a certain degree of exclusion, but in all other relations the completest equality prevails. This would not probably be the case if the white population was proportionably greater, and possessed the physical power to keep up the distinctions which naturally separate the superior and inferior families of men. With a full consciousness of their numerical inferiority, their policy is plainly that of concession; and however repugnant it may have been originally to their pride, it has now come to be regarded as a matter of course, and is submitted to with a good grace.

A few days in Leon sufficed to show me that, in the tone of its society, and the manners of its people, it had more of the metropolitan character than Granada. And although the proportion of its inhabitants who laid claim to what is called "position," was even here comparatively small, and not at all rigid in its adherence to the conventionalities of the larger cities of Mexico, South America, and our own country; yet, in the essential respects of hospitality, kindness, and courtesy, I found it entitled to a position second to no other community. The women are far from being highly educated, but are simple and unaffected in their manners, and possessed of great quickness of apprehension, and a readiness in good-natured repartee, which compensates, to a certain extent, for their deficiency in general information.

The condition of the country for many years has been such as to afford few opportunities for the cultivation of those accomplishments which are indispensable accessories of refined society; and we are therefore, not justified in subjecting the people of Leon, or of any other city of Central America, to the test of our standards. I can conceive of nothing more painful, or more calculated to awaken the interest of the visitor from abroad, than the spectacle of a people, with really high aspirations and capabilities, borne down by the force of opposing circumstances, conscious of its own condition, but almost despairing of improving it.

In dress the women of Leon have the same fashions with those of Granada, but the European styles are less common, owing to the circumstance that there are fewer foreign residents to infect the popular taste. They have an equal fondness for the cigarito; and in the street are not less proud of displaying a little foot and a satin slipper. As everywhere else in the world they are very attentive in their devotions, but beyond their daily visit to the churches, rarely go out of doors, except it is in the early evening, when visits are paid informally. If chance brings together a sufficient number, a "*tertulia*," or dance, is often improvised. Set parties or balls are of rare occurrence, and are generally given only on public occasions, and then with great state and ceremony.

We were witnesses of a tertulia at our own house, the second evening after our arrival. A dozen señoras casually found themselves together, a dance was proposed by the gallants loitering at the balconies, and the proposition meeting with favor, they at once dispersed to bring in recruits and the "musicos." In an hour the grand sala was filled. The females as they came in were all ranged on one side of the room, and the males on the other. This looked rather stiff, and I began to fear that a *tertulia* was no great matter after all. Directly, however, a single couple took the floor; the music struck up, and as they moved down the room, the measure brought the lady first on one side, and then on the other. As she passed she alternately tapped a señor and señora on the shoulder with her fan, thus arbitrarily determining the partners, who were obliged at once to join in the dance. In this manner the whole party was brought to its feet, *nolens volens*,—and such I found was a frequent mode of opening the tertulia. After the first set is over, the ice once broken, and the excitement up, the gallants are permitted to exercise a choice. I thought the practice a good one, obviating a great deal of awkward diplomacy at the outset, and putting every one very speedily at their ease. As the evening progressed the party augmented, and before ten o'clock we had got together the *élite* of Leon. All joined heartily in the spirit of the affair, and when the bell of the cathedral tolled eleven, I think I never saw a more animated assemblage. The polka and the waltz, as also the bolero, and other well known Spanish dances, were all danced gracefully and with spirit; and besides these, after much persuasion, we had an Indian dance, a singular affair, slow and complicated, and which left upon my mind a distinct impression that it was religious in its origin. After the dancing, we had music, but beyond the national air, which was given with force and spirit, I cannot say much for the singing.

During the whole evening, the windows were festooned with urchins, and the doors blockaded by spectators, who when they were particularly pleased, applauded tumultuously, as if the whole affair had been got up for their special entertainment. The police would have driven them off, but I won an enduring popularity by interceding in their behalf, and they were consequently permitted to remain. Upon the occasions of the more formal balls subsequently given, soldiers were stationed at every entrance, and the crowd kept at a distance.

Amongst the lower classes, fandangoes and other characteristic dances are frequent, and are sufficiently uproarious and promiscuous. For obvious reasons, I never witnessed any of these in the city, although I stumbled upon them occasionally in the villages, during my excursions in the country.

The people of Nicaragua are generally scrupulously clean in their persons, except when travelling or ill, and then the touch of water is prohibited. But beyond the grand sala, and the apartments appropriated to visitors, their houses are frequently very far from being patterns of neatness. I have seen sleeping apartments, occupied by families of the first respectability, which certainly had not been swept for weeks, not to say months. Yet the beds in these rooms were clean and neat—the more so perhaps from the contrast. These remarks are less applicable to Granada than Leon, for in the former city the example of the foreign residents has worked a partial reformation amongst the native housekeepers.

The Spanish people, in all parts of the world, are temperate in their habits. Those of Nicaragua in this respect do no discredit to their progenitors. Strong liquors are little used except amongst the lower orders of the population; and even here excess is less common than with us. The sale of brandy and the "aguardiente," or native rum, is a government monopoly, and is confined to the "estancos," or licensed establishments, where it pays a high duty to the State. I do not remember to have seen a single respectable citizen drunk during the whole of my residence in the country. Yet a bottle of "cogniac" is usually offered to the stranger, whenever he pays a visit. A considerable quantity of sweet or Spanish wines, are used in the principal towns, but the lighter French wines have the largest consumption. There is a delicious kind of *liqueur* made from the Muscatel grape, called "Italia," cr "Pisco," which is brought from Peru. It is, however, produced in small quantities, upon I believe a single estate, and is consequently introduced in Nicaragua to a very limited extent. Should it ever become generally known to the people of the United States, it would, no doubt, create for itself a large demand. But whether it can be produced in sufficient quantities to supply a considerable market, is a point upon which I am ignorant.

In their food, the Nicaraguans are also exceedingly simple. Tortillas and frijoles are the standard dishes. The first are composed of maize, and if well made are really palatable.

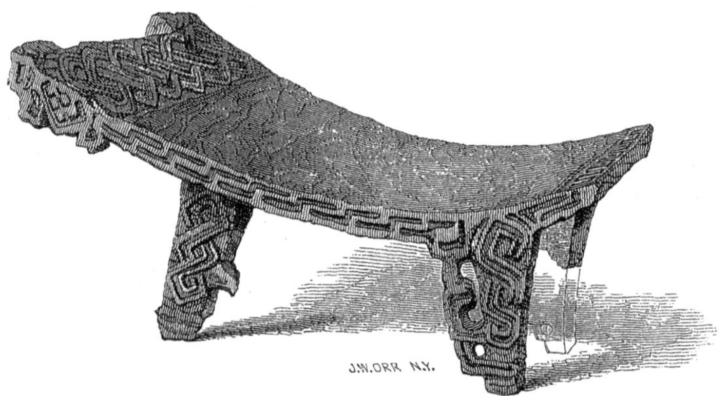

ANCIENT METLATL, OR GRINDING STONE.

Fresh and unblemished maize on the ear is always selected. It is shelled, soaked in alkali to remove the hull, and then carefully and repeatedly washed in cold water. It is afterwards placed on a *metlatl*, or grinding stone, and reduced to the extremest fineness. A very little cheese is ground with it, to give it consistency. A roll is then taken in the hands, beaten into a flat cake, and placed on an earthen pan, already heated upon the fire. When sufficiently done upon one side, it is adroitly turned on the other, and is finally served hot and crisp at the table. I "cottoned" to the tortilla from the start, and always preferred it to the native bread, which although light and fair to the eye, is invariably spoiled by sweetening. The tortilla is an aboriginal invention; and the foregoing engraving represents an ancient *metlatl* or grinding stone which was dug up during my residence in Leon. The form is unchanged to this day, although few are as elaborately ornamented as that here introduced, which is a favorable specimen of aboriginal carving.

It will be observed that this stone is curiously ornamented with *grecques*, which are shown more distinctly in the subjoined enlarged sketches of the upper and lower extremities of the *metlatl* (*a. b.*)

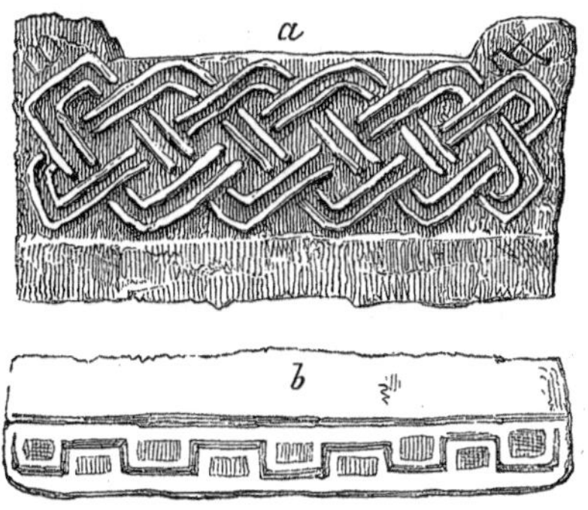

ORNAMENTS OF THE METLATL.

Frijoles, in plain English, are baked beans; but the beans are quite of a different flavor from those in use in more northern latitudes. They are small, white, black, or brown in color, and indigenous in the country. They are not usually relished at first, but a taste for them is gradually acquired, and a meal without *frijoles* finally comes to lack an essential ingredient. The man who cannot "go" the *frijoles* had better keep away from Central America. For the weary traveller, in soliciting the bill of fare at the Indian hut where, four times out of five, he is obliged to stop for the night, has generally this brief catalogue, "*hay tortillas, frijoles, frijolitos, frijolitos fritos, y huevos,*"—"tortillas, beans, little beans, little baked beans, and eggs!"

Excellent beef and pork are to be obtained, at cheap rates, in all the principal towns, and poultry is abundant. A pair of chickens costs from a *quartillo* to a *medio,*—i. e. from three to six cents. Next to the tortillas and frijoles, however, the chief articles of consumption are rice, plantains, and a kind of cheese, which is supplied in great quantities from the "haciendas de las vacas," or cattle estates. The plantains are cooked in many ways,—boiled, fried, and roasted,—and are singly capable of sustaining life. And when I add that, in many parts of the state, they may be had for the asking, and that everywhere six cents worth will sustain a small family for a week, it will be understood that the incentives to labor cannot be very strong, and that the poorest wretch need not go hungry.

The markets of Leon display the greatest profusion of fruits and vegetables, of which it would be almost impossible to give a complete list. Water and musk melons, papayas, pine apples, oranges, mamays, nisperos, pomegranates, marañons, jocotes, yucas, plantains, bananas, beans, maize, and occasionally small potatoes but little larger than bullets, brought in bales from the highlands of Costa Rica and Honduras, and sold by the pound. And as the smallest coin in the country is a *quartillo*, or three cents, which would purchase more of almost any of these articles than most families would require at one time, change is made in the aboriginal coin of the country, namely *cacao nuts*, of which four are about equivalent in value to one cent of our currency.

But two meals a-day are eaten by the inhabitants at large. A cup of coffee or chocolate is served at the bedside, or immediately upon rising in the morning. Breakfast follows at nine or ten o'clock in the forenoon, and dinner at three or four in the afternoon. Tea is only drunk by foreigners, and by them to a very limited extent. It is not to be found therefore in any of the shops. A cup of chocolate, or more frequently a cup of *tiste* (parched corn ground with chocolate and sugar and mixed with water), passed unceremoniously in the evening, supplies its place, and is not an unacceptable substitute. It should be mentioned, however, that large quantities of "dulces," literally "sweets" or sweetmeats are eaten between meals, especially by the women. The Spanish taste for "dulces" long ago passed into a proverb, but it rather surpasses itself in Nicaragua. The venders of "dulces," generally bright Indian girls, gaily dressed, and bearing a tray, covered with the purest white napkins, and temptingly spread, upon their heads, pass daily from house to house; and it is sometimes difficult, and always ungallant to refuse purchasing something, however trifling, from their stock. The "mil gracias Señor!" in the silverest of voices, is always worth the money, and so one gets the "dulces" gratis. They sometimes, however, trespassed a little upon my good nature, and carried off more of my loose change than was proper, considering that, having a reasonable regard for my stomach, I never ate any of their dyspeptic compounds.

Leon has little trade beyond the supply of its local wants. The principal import and export business for this portion of the state is done in the large and flourishing town of Chinandega, situated within two leagues of the port of Realejo. Its shops are nevertheless well supplied, and it has some wealthy merchants. Its principal inhabitants, however, are "propietarios," owners of large estates which are carried on through agents. Attempts have recently been made to augment the commercial importance of Leon by opening a shorter and direct communication with Realejo; but its interior position will always prove a bar to its progress in this respect. Chinandega has already a start, which it will doubtless keep, unless a town, more favorably situated nearer the port, should spring up under the requirements of commerce.

Since the above was written, a new town called "Corinth," has been laid out on the south shore of the harbor of Realejo, in the direction of Leon, which will greatly benefit the latter city.

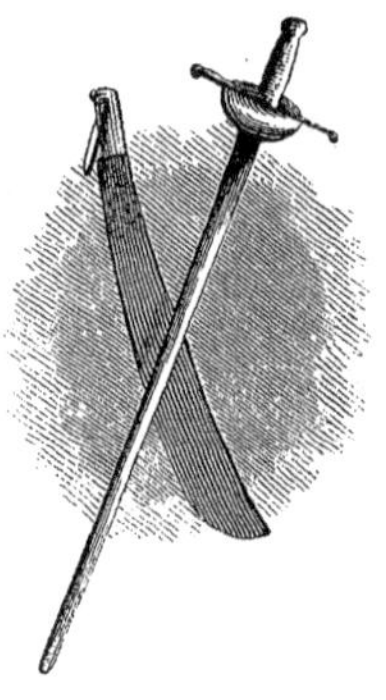

MACHETE AND TOLEDO.

INNER COURT OF "OUR HOUSE" AT LEON.

CHAPTER X.

THE VICINITY OF LEON—THE BISHOP'S BATHS—FUENTE DE AXUSCO—"CERRO DE LOS AMERICANOS"—A MILITARY BALL AND CIVIC DINNER—GEN. GUERRERO—OFFICIAL VISIT FROM THE INDIAN MUNICIPALITY OF SUBTIABA—SIMON ROQUE—A SECRET—ADDRESS AND REPLY—VISIT RETURNED—THE CABILDO—AN EMPTY TREASURY—"SUBTIABA, LEAL Y FIEL".—ROYAL CEDULAS—FORMING A VOCABULARY—"UNA DECIMA"—THE INDIANS OF NICARAGUA; STATURE; COMPLEXION; DISPOSITION; BRAVERY; INDUSTRY; SKILL IN THE ARTS—MANUFACTURE OF COTTON—PRIMITIVE MODE OF SPINNING—TYRIAN PURPLE—PETATES AND HAMMOCKS—POTTERY—"AGUACALES," AND "JICARAS,"—COSTUME—ORNAMENTS—ABORIGINAL INSTITUTIONS—THE CONQUEST OF NICARAGUA—ENORMITIES PRACTISED TOWARDS THE INDIANS—PRESENT CONDITION OF THE INDIANS—THE SEQUEL OF SOMOZA'S INSURRECTION—BATTLES OF THE OBRAJE AND SAN JORGE—CAPTURE AND EXECUTION OF SOMOZA—MODERATE POLICY OF THE GOVERNMENT—RETURN OF GEN. MUNOZ—MEDALS—FESTIVAL OF PEACE—NOVEL PROCESSION—A BLACK SAINT.

THE country adjacent to Leon is very fine, and the "paseos" or rides in the vicinity, although lacking an important element of beauty, the proximity of water, are not without variety and interest. My first expedition on horseback was to a place called the Bishop's Baths. We rode through the barrio de San Juan, where the *carreteros* most do congregate, to the edge of the northern ravine. Here we found a path literally shut in with cactuses and trees covered with vines, which led to the ruins of an ancient gateway, beyond which had once been the suburban seat of the Bishops of Nicaragua. It was a beautiful spot; the ground had been artificially smoothed, and beneath the large trees which shadowed over it, were the remains of stone seats, and of pedestals which had once sustained crosses and the statues of the saints. In front of where the house had stood, before its destruction during the troubles of the revolutionary period, there was an abrupt slope to the stream at the bottom of the ravine. This slope had formerly been terraced, and descended by a winding way. The baths were of stone, and although now in ruins, still gave evidences of the taste and luxury which had led to their construction. A couple of women, naked with the exception of a single cloth around their loins, were washing in the principal bath, but they vacated it temporarily at our request, and we took possession. The seclusion of the place, the limpid purity of the water, and the deep shade in which everything was shrouded, enchanted me with the spot, and I could not help thinking that it must have been selected by one of the rosiest and jolliest of the old bishops whose portraits had tipped me a friendly wink from the walls of the heavy room where they were imprisoned in the cathedral. But I afterwards found that this was but one only of a thousand equally beautiful spots in the neighborhood of the city. That, however, to which my memory reverts most frequently, is the "fuente de Axusco," distant about two miles to the southward of the town. It is a broad pool, at the bottom of a ravine, shut in by steep banks on every side, and reached by a single narrow path. The water is tepid, and bursts, pure as crystal, in a large volume from beneath the rocks. It is literally arched over with trees, and curtained in with vines. This place was my favorite resort during the whole of my residence in the country. I rose at early dawn, despatched a cup of coffee, and mounting my horse, generally reached the place just as the sun began to tinge the summit of the distant volcanoes. The path lay through fields covered with trees and bushes, spangled all over with flowers, and glittering with dew-drops. The cool, bracing morning air, the quick action of the horse, and the grateful plunge into the quiet pool,—I think I never enjoyed so much the mere pleasure of existence, as during my visits to the "fuente de Axusco." There stood a cross in a nook near the pool, and I often observed chaplets of fresh flowers suspended upon it. It puzzled me exceedingly, and one day, finding a little boy seated beside it, I asked him why it was there? It commemorated an awful murder, he said, and that was all he knew, except that the victim was a woman. Beyond the "fuenta," is the range of low hills which I have mentioned as bordering the plain of Leon on the side of the ocean. I had the trees cut down on the most commanding peak, and rode there so frequently that the rancheros in the vicinity christened it "el cerro de los Americanos," the hill of the Americans. From this point the eye traversed the whole vast plain, and took in every object of interest. Upon one hand the forests alone shut the lake of Managua from view, while upon the other the broad Pacific lay bright and beautiful on the edge of the horizon. With a glass the vessels in the harbor of Realejo, and the outlines of the volcano of Coseguina, distant more than a hundred miles, could easily be distinguished. A view from the "cerro de los Americanos" is an incident in a man's lifetime not likely to be forgotten. Its impression upon my own mind is too distinct ever to be effaced.

Our second week in Leon was signalized by a military ball and a government dinner, both on a scale far surpassing anything of the kind which had been witnessed in the city for many years. The ball was under the special patronage of Gen. Don Jose Guerrero, who had just finished a term as Director of the State, but who had accepted the command of the garrison in the absence of the General-in-chief. It was during his administration that the seizure of San Juan by the English had taken place, and it was his eloquent appeal, in a circular addressed to all civilized nations, which had arrested the attention and awakened the sympathy of General Taylor and his cabinet. My arrival in the country, it can readily be understood, was to him a source of the profoundest satisfaction; and during my official residence in Leon, I had no warmer friend than General Guerrero. May he live to witness the fruition of the policy which he marked out for his country, and the realization of those high and patriotic hopes which he has so long and so devotedly cherished!

Amongst the most pleasing incidents connected with my arrival was a formal visit from the municipal authorities of the Indian pueblo of Subtiaba, who, in their way, are amongst the sturdiest republicans in all Nicaragua. At their head was Simon Roque, with whom I afterwards established an intimate friendship. He presented me an address, written both in the Indian language and in Spanish, and accompanied it with a speech, which was far above the average, both in language and sentiment, and altogether a favorable specimen of Indian eloquence. Simon and his companions were dressed in spotless white, and each wore a red sash about his waist, and carried a gold-headed cane, an insignia of office, in his hands. They were curious to know about the Indian population of the United States, and I blush to say it, I was ashamed to tell them the truth. They had heard that I was a great friend of the Indians, and on the lookout for "piedras antiguas." They had something to tell me on that subject, but it could only be done when we were alone. So the sala was cleared, and Simon, after some circumlocution, informed me that they knew of certain ancient stones which their ancestors had buried a very long time ago, and which, if I wished, they would present to me, on the peremptory condition, however, that their locality should be kept a profound secret. I was too glad to have an opportunity to assent to any conditions, and it was finally agreed that, as it would be impossible for me to attend to the business now, some of the stones should be excavated at once, and sent to my residence. They were as good as their word; and a couple of mornings thereafter we were surprised at finding two statues at the threshold of the portal; and a few nights later a cart appeared with two more,—of all which a description will be given in another place. This little piece of confidence over, I treated the company to as much claret as they chose to drink, and we parted with the understanding that I should return the visit at an early day. The address and reply were as follows:

ADDRESS.

"SIR:—The municipality of the Pueblo of Subtiaba, of which we are members, entertain the highest enthusiasm in view of the relations which your arrival induces us to believe will speedily be established between Nicaragua and the United States, the greatest and most glorious republic beneath the sun. We rejoice in the depths of our hearts that a man like yourself has been chosen to convey to us the assurances of future prosperity, in the name of the sons of Washington; and we trust in the Almighty, that the flag of the United States may soon become the shield of Nicaragua on land and sea. Convey our sincerest thanks for their sympathy to the great people which you represent, and give to your generous government the assurances of that deep gratitude which we feel but cannot express. We beg of you, Sir, to accept this humble evidence of the cordial sentiments which we entertain both for you, your countrymen, and your Government, and which are equally shared by the people which we represent.

(Signed) JOSE DE LA CRUZ GARCIAS,
SIMON ROQUE,
FRANCISCO LUIS ANTAN.

REPLY.

"MY FRIENDS OF THE MUNICIPALITY OF SUBTIABA:

"I experience great pleasure in receiving from your hands this brief but earnest address; and I return you my thanks, both personally and in behalf of my Government, for the friendly sentiments which it contains. I sincerely hope that the high anticipations which you have formed from a more intimate relation between your country and the United States, may be fully realized."

The reader may be assured that I did not forget my promise to the municipality of Subtiaba. A day was shortly afterwards fixed for my visit, and I was received with great ceremony at the cabildo, or council chamber, where I found collected all the old men who could assist me in forming a vocabulary of the ancient language, which I had casually expressed a desire to procure. It was with difficulty that we could effect an entrance, for a half-holiday had been given to the boys of all the schools in honor of the occasion, and they literally swarmed around the building. We were finally ushered into an inner room, where the archives of the municipality were preserved. Upon one side was a large chest of heavy wood, with massive locks, which had anciently been

LA PARROQUIAL DE SUBTIABA.

the strong box or treasury. A shadow fell over Simon's face as he pointed it out to me, and said that he could remember the time when it was filled with "duros," hard dollars, and when, at a single stroke of the alarm bell, two thousand armed men could be gathered in the plaza of Subtiaba. But those days were passed, and the municipality now scarcely retained a shadow of its former greatness. Under the crown it had earned the title "leal y fiel," loyal and true; and in reward of its fidelity it had received a grant of all the lands intervening between it and the ocean, to hold in perpetuity for the benefit of its citizens. And Simon showed me the royal letters, signed "Yo, el Rey" (I, the King), which the emperors of Spain had thought it not derogatory to their dignity to address to his predecessors in office; and notwithstanding his ardent republicanism, I thought Simon looked at them with something of regret. I inquired for manuscripts which might throw some light upon the early history of the country, but found only musty records, of no interest or value.

My attempts to fill out the blank vocabulary with which I was provided created a great deal of merriment. I enjoyed it quite as much as any of them, for nothing could be more amusing than the discussions between the old men in respect to certain doubtful words and phrases. They sometimes quite forgot my presence, and rated each other soundly as ignoramuses; whereat Simon was greatly scandalized, and threatened to put them all in the stocks as "hombres sin verguenza," men destitute of shame. "Ah!" said he, "these old sinners give me more trouble than the young ones"—a remark which created great mirth amongst the outsiders, and especially amongst the young vagabonds who clung like monkeys to the window bars. The group of swarthy, earnest faces gathered round the little table, upon which was heaped a confused mass of ancient, time-stained papers, would have furnished a study for a painter. It was quite dark when I had concluded my inquiries, but I was not permitted to leave without listening to a little poem, "Una Decima," written by one of the schoolmasters, who read it to me by the light of a huge wax candle, borrowed, I am sure, from the church for the occasion. My modesty forbids my attempting a translation, and so I compromise matters by submitting the original:

DECIMA.

Nicaragua, ve hasta cuando
Cesara vuestro desvelo,
Ya levantara el vuelo
Hermoso, alegre, y triunfante;
Al mismo tiempo mirando
De este personage el porte,
Y mas sera cuando corte
Todos los agradecimientos:
Diremos todos contentos
Viva el Gobierno del Norte! D. S.

As I mounted my horse, Don Simon led off with three cheers for "El Ministro del Norte," and followed it with three more for "El Amigo de los Indios" (the friend of the Indians), all of which was afterwards paraded by a dingy little Anglo-servile paper published in Costa Rica, as evidence that I was tampering with the Indians, and exciting them to undertake the utter destruction of the white population!

The Indians of Nicaragua, who, as I have said, predominate in the country, are singularly docile and industrious, and constitute what would, in some countries, be called an excellent "rural population." They are a smaller race of men than the Indians of the United States, but have fine muscular developments, and a singularly mild and soft expression of countenance. In color also they are lighter, and their features less strongly marked. Some of the women are exceedingly pretty, and when young, have figures beautifully and classically moulded. They are entirely unobtrusive in their manners, seldom speaking unless first addressed, and are always kind and hospitable to strangers. They are not warlike but brave, and when reduced to the necessity, fight with the most desperate obstinacy. Leon has more than once owed its safety to the Indian battalion of Subtiaba, which, in the civil wars of 1838–39, marched triumphantly from one end of Central America to the other.

The agriculture of the State is almost entirely carried on by them; but they are not deficient in mechanical skill, and with the rudest tools often produce the most delicate and elaborate articles of workmanship. The women manufacture a large quantity of cotton for their own consumption and for sale. And in riding through Subtiaba in the afternoon, no spectacle is more common than to see a woman naked to the waist, sitting in the doorway of almost every hut, or beneath the shadow of an adjacent tree, busily engaged in spinning

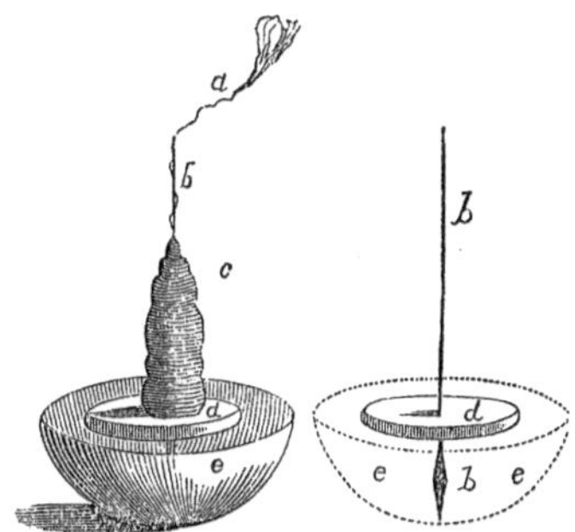

PRIMITIVE SPINNING APPARATUS.

cotton. A little foot-wheel, such as was formerly in use for spinning flax in our own country, is here commonly used for this purpose. But the aboriginal contrivance is not yet wholly displaced. It is exceedingly simple, consisting of a thin spindle of wood fifteen or sixteen inches in length, which is passed through a fly, or wheel of hard, heavy wood, six inches in diameter, resembling the wheel of a pulley, except that it is convex instead of concave on the edge. The spindle thus resembles a gigantic top. When used it is placed in a calabash, or hollowed piece of wood, to prevent it from toppling over, when not in motion. A thread is attached to it, just above the fly, and it is then twirled rapidly between the thumb and fore-finger. The momentum of the fly keeps it in motion for half a minute, and meantime the thread is drawn out by the hands of the operator, from the pile of prepared cotton which she holds in her lap. It is then wound on the spindle, and the process repeated, until the spindle is full of thread.

In the foregoing cut *a* represents the cotton; *b*, *b*, the spindle; *d*, the fly; *c*, the thread already spun and wound; and *e*, *e*, the outlines of the calabash. A precisely similar mode of spinning was practised by the ancient Mexicans, who, however, inserted the lower end of the spindle in a hole made in a block of wood, as shown in the accompanying engraving. The mode of weaving amongst the Indians of Nicaragua was anciently the same as that of the Mexicans, which is sufficiently well illustrated in the following engraving, copied from the Codex Mendoza, a Mexican manuscript or painting.

SPINNING, FROM A MEXICAN MANUSCRIPT.

Some of the cotton fabrics manufactured by the Indians are very durable, and woven in tasteful figures of various colors. The color most valued is the Tyrian purple, obtained from the murex shell-fish, which is found upon the Pacific coast of Nicaragua. This color is produced of any desirable depth and tone, and is permanent; unaffected alike by exposure to the sun and to the action of alkalies. The process of dying the thread illustrates the patient assiduity of the Indians. It is taken to the seaside, when a sufficient number of shells are collected, which being dried from the sea water, the work is commenced. Each shell is taken up singly, and a slight pressure upon the valve which closes its mouth forces out a few drops of the coloring fluid, which is then almost destitute of color. In this each thread is dipped singly, and after absorbing enough of the precious liquid, is carefully drawn out between the thumb and finger, and laid aside to dry. Whole days and nights are spent in this tedious process, until the work is completed. At first the thread is of a dull blue

PRIMITIVE WEAVING; FROM A MEXICAN MANUSCRIPT.

color, but upon exposure to the atmosphere acquires the desired tint. The fish is not destroyed by the operation, but is returned to the sea, when it lays in a new stock of coloring matter for a future occasion.[1]

The manufacture of "petates," or variegated mats, from the bark of the palm, and hammocks from the "pita," a species of agave, is exclusively in Indian hands. They are also skillful in the manufacture of pottery, which has remained unchanged from the period before the Conquest. The

[1] "The cotton-yarn thus dyed is known in the country by the name of '*hilo morado*,' and is highly prized by the Indian women of all the States, who are extremely partial to it for adorning the dresses used on festive occasions. Formerly, high prices were paid for it; being frequently sold in Guatemala and other principal towns, for from ten to fourteen dollars the pound. In recent times purple thread has been imported from Europe, and sold at a much cheaper rate; but the color is neither as good nor as durable, and notwithstanding its economy, does not supplant the native product. The Indians are not easily deceived by offering them the one for the other, as they can readily distinguish the foreign from the genuine by some peculiarity of smell in the latter, which, although the dearest, is always preferred."—*Baily*, p. 125.

"cantaros," water-jars, and other vessels in common use, amongst all classes, are made by them. They are formed by hand, without the aid of the potter's wheel, and are variously and often elaborately colored and ornamented, baked, and when intended for purposes requiring it, are partially glazed. The water-jars, however, are porous, so as to admit of enough water passing through to keep the outer surface covered with moisture, the evaporation of which rapidly and effectually cools the contents of the vessel. Oviedo commends highly the skill which the ancient inhabitants displayed in the manufacture of their pottery, and which is very well sustained both by the fragments which are found, and by the wares which the Indians still manufacture. "They make basins, plates, jars, and pitchers, of very fine pottery, black and smooth as velvet, and brilliant as jet. I have brought some specimens, which are so fine that they might be offered to a prince." Thus saith the chronicler.

Mr. W. H. Edwards, in his narrative of "A Voyage up the Amazon," p. 114, describes the preparation and painting of pottery by the Indians on that river. The brushes or pencils were the small species of palms, and the coloring matter the simplest kinds. The blue was indigo; black, the juice of the mandioca; green, the juice of some other plant; and the red and yellow, clays. The colors were applied in squares and circles, or if anything imitative was intended, in the rudest outlines. The *glazing* was produced by a resinous gum found in the forests, which was gently rubbed over the vessels, previously warmed over a bed of coals. This description applies equally to the modes practised in Nicaragua.

They also make drinking vessels from the calabash; the largest varieties are called "*guacals*," or "*aguacals*," and the smaller ones, made from the long or pear-shaped calabash, "*jicaras*." These last are often tastefully carved upon their exteriors, and are generally used instead of tumblers. It is indispensable that "*tiste*" should be served in "jicaras," and amongst the people at large they are also used for coffee and chocolate. But as their bottoms are round, little carved stands are made to receive them. The Indians near the city of Nicaragua make similar cups from a variety of cocoa-nut peculiar to that vicinity, which are celebrated throughout their country for their beauty of shape and ornament. They are black, and highly polished, and when mounted with silver, are greatly prized by foreigners.

JICARA. GUACAL. CANTARO. TINAJA.

The dress of the Indians is exceedingly simple. On ordinary occasions, the women wear only a white or flowered skirt, fastened around the waist, leaving the upper part of the person entirely exposed, or but partially covered by a handkerchief fastened around the neck. In Masaya and some other places, a square piece of cloth, of native manufacture, and of precisely the same style and pattern with that used for the same purpose before the Discovery, supplies the place of the skirt. It is fastened in some incomprehensible way, without the aid of strings or pins, and falls from the hips a little below the knees. The guipil and nagua are however adopted in nearly all the large towns, and are everywhere worn on festival days and Sundays. The men wear a kind of cotton drawers, fastened above the hips, but frequently reaching no lower than the knees. Sandals supply the place of shoes, but for the most part both sexes go with their feet bare. The taste for ornament is universal; and a rosary, to which is attached a little golden, silver, or ebony cross, is suspended from the necks of male and female, old and young. They are also fond of flowers, and the girls are seldom without some of them entwined amongst the luxuriant locks of their long, black hair, or braided in a chaplet and encircling their foreheads.

AN INDIAN GIRL OF SUBTIABA IN HOLIDAY COSTUME.

The municipality of Subtiaba, in common with the barrios of some of the towns, holds lands, as I have said, in virtue of royal grants, in its corporate capacity. These lands are inalienable, and are leased to the inhabitants at low and almost nominal rates. Every citizen is entitled to a sufficient quantity to enable him to support himself and his family; for which he pays from four rials (half a dollar,) to two dollars a year. This practice seems to have been of aboriginal institution; for under the ancient Indian organization, the *right to live* was recognized as a fundamental principle in the civil and social system. No man was supposed to be entitled to more land than was necessary to his support; nor was he permitted to hold more than that, to the exclusion or injury of others.

In fact, many of the institutions of the Indians in this country were recognized, and have been perpetuated by the Spaniards. Some of the ceremonies of the aboriginal ritual have also been incorporated amongst the rites of the Catholic Church. In many respects it is hard to say whether the conquerors have assimilated most to the Indians, or the Indians to the Spaniards. For, however rude and subverting the first shock of Spanish conquest in America, the subsequent policy of Spain, framed and directed by the famous Council of the Indies, was that of conciliation. In common with the church, it conceded much to the habits and feelings of the aborigines, and to a certain extent conformed to them.

The conquest of Nicaragua was effected with no less violence than that of Mexico and Peru; and if we may credit the account of Las Casas, the pious bishop of Chiapa, who visited the country in person, it was both attended and followed by extraordinary cruelties. He charges the enormity chiefly upon Pedro Arias de Avila, Governor of Darien, who sent Cordova to subdue the country, and who himself afterwards became its governor.

"The Indians of this province," he says, "were naturally of a mild and peacable temper; yet notwithstanding this, the Governor, or rather Tyrant, with the ministers of his cruelty, treated them in the same manner as they did those of the other kingdoms. They committed murders and robberies, more than it is possible for pen to relate. Upon the slightest pretexts, the soldiers massacred the inhabitants without regard to age, sex, or condition. They exacted from them certain measures of corn, and certain numbers of slaves, and if these were not rendered, hesitated not to kill the delinquents. And the country being plain, the people were unable to escape to the mountains as they did elsewhere, and were consequently at the mercy of the Spanish horse. They carried off many thousands as slaves, slaying those who fainted or wearied on the march.

"The Governor once arbitrarily changed the distribution of the Indians, conveying most of them to his favorites, to the exclusion of those with whom he was displeased. The result of this was a great scarcity of food; and the Spaniards seizing upon the provisions of the Indians, caused a great distress, and induced a disorder which destroyed upwards of thirty thousand of the people.

"All the cities, and fields around them, were like pleasant gardens, which the Spaniards cultivated according to the share which each one had assigned him by lot; and to save their own revenues, supported themselves from the stores of the Indians, thus consuming, in a short time, what these poor people had got together with great care and toil. Nobles, women, and children were all compelled to work day and and night; many died under the burthens which were imposed upon them. For they obliged them to carry on their shoulders to the ports, which were in some cases distant thirty leagues, the plank and timbers used in building vessels."

Las Casas, however, regards the practice of exacting slaves from the caziques, for transportation and sale elsewhere, as one of the chief causes of the depopulation of the country. Five or six ship-loads were annually taken to Peru and Panama, and sold there. He calculates that half a million of Indians were thus drawn out of Nicaragua alone; but this number appears incredible. The statement that from fifty to sixty thousand perished in the wars of the Conquest is perhaps, nearer the truth; for, as he observes, "this was one of the best peopled countries in all America."

When the Council of the Indies began to repress the cruelties of the conquerors, the governors of Nicaragua proved themselves refractory; indeed, Rodrigo de Contreras openly disobeyed his instructions in this respect, which was the proximate cause of the insurrection headed by his son, to which I have elsewhere alluded.

The following incident, related by Oviedo, will illustrate the severe and repulsive measures which were practised towards the Indians at this early period. "In 1528, the treasurer, Alonzo de Peralta, and a man named Zurita, and the brothers Ballas, left the city of Leon, each to visit the villages and Indians belonging to him. They never returned, having been destroyed by their own vassals. Hereupon Pedro Arias de Avila sent out soldiers to bring in some of the malefactors. They arrested seventeen or eighteen *caziques* whom Pedro Arias caused to be strangled by dogs. The execution took place in the following manner, on Tuesday, the 16th of June of the same year, in the public square of Leon. Each cazique was armed with a stick, and told to defend himself against the dogs, and to kill them if he could. Five or six young dogs were first set upon them, which their masters wished to train, as they were yet without experience. They ran baying around the Indian, who easily kept them off with his stick; but the moment he thought himself conqueror, a couple of mastiffs, or well-trained hounds, were sent against him, who threw him in a moment. The other dogs then fell upon him, biting and choking him, tearing out his entrails, and devouring him, as it were. In this manner the eighteen were soon disposed of. They were from the valley of Olocoton, and its vicinity. When the dogs were satiated, the dead bodies remained in the same place, it being forbidden to carry them off, under penalty of being served in like manner; otherwise the Indians would have taken them away. They were thus left in order to frighten the natives; but on the second day the stench of the dead bodies became insupportable. And on the fourth, it was so horrible that, being compelled to pass there in going to the house of the governor, I begged him to give permission to have them carried away;

which he did the more readily, since his house was situated near the square."

But whatever their former condition, the Indians of Nicaragua no longer labor under any disabilities. They enjoy equal privileges with the whites, and may aspire to any position, however high, both in the Church and State. The system of *peonage* (slavery under a less repugnant name) is here unknown. Yet the Indian retains his traditionary deference for the white man, and tacitly admits his superiority. In some of the States of Central America, a jealousy of caste has been artfully excited by unscrupulous partisans, for unworthy purposes, which has led to most deplorable results; but in Nicaragua, if this feeling exists at all, it is only in a latent form. At any rate, it has never displayed itself in any of those frightful demonstrations which have almost desolated Guatemala and portions of Peru, and which threaten the entire extinction of the white race in Yucatan. This quiet, however, may be that of the slumbering volcano; and its continuance may depend very much upon the judicious encouragement of white emigration from the United States and from Europe.

The original inhabitants of Nicaragua, and of Central America generally, seem to have been of the true Toltecan stock. So too were the nations of Anahuac, the Aztecs or Mexicans, but modified and deteriorated by association and intermixture with the barbarous Chichemecas. From this source they derived the fiercer and more savage traits in their characters; and even now, notwithstanding that they have to a great extent adopted new customs, and been subjected to the influences of Spanish association for more than three hundred years, the distinguishing traits of the two families are easily to be recognized. The mild, brave but not warlike, industrious, intelligent, and law-abiding Indians about Leon, of the purer Toltecan blood, furnish in their smaller and more rounded forms, their regular features, clear eyes, and cheerful expression, a decided contrast to the restless, treacherous, and cruel Indians round the ancient city of Nicaragua. The latter are taller, more bony, with sharper and often irregular features, and with an always reserved if not sullen expression. The contrast is hardly greater than between the French and the Dutch. Yet none of these Indians could ever be confounded with the roving tribes of our latitude. They have certain generic or radical identities, but in most physical and mental features, are widely different. Those of Central America are capable of high improvement, and have a facility of assimilation or adaptation. They constitute, when favorably situated, the best class of citizens, and would anywhere make what in Europe is called a good rural or working population. I have found some really comprehensive minds amongst them,—men of quick and acute apprehension, and great decision and energy of character.

In brief, the better I become acquainted with the various aboriginal families of the continent, the higher position I am disposed to award them, and the less I am disposed to assent to the relative rank assigned them by the systematic writers.

I have already mentioned the interview between our American friend in Granada, and the rebel chief, Somoza. Soon after our arrival in Leon, positive information was received that he had been successful in his descent upon San Carlos, and had got possession of the arms and ammunition which had been deposited there. He, however, did not attempt to retain possession of the place, but returned immediately with his spoils to the city of Nicaragua. Meantime, nevertheless, as I have already intimated, the support which he had received from the party opposed to the government, had been entirely withdrawn, in consequence of the excesses which he had committed, and he came back to find his adherents dispirited and rapidly diminishing. The decision and energy of the government further contributed to weaken his power; and when the General-in-chief arrived in his neighborhood, he was left with less than half his original forces. His spirit, however, never failed him, and he boldly advanced to meet the troops of the government. The first battle was at a place called the "Obraje." Here he was worsted, and compelled to fall back upon his original position, at the town of San George, about a league distant from the city of Rivas, or Nicaragua. General Muñoz, having effected a junction with the volunteers from Granada, who had proceeded by water, attacked him here the next day, (July 14th,) completely routed his forces, and took him and his principal followers prisoners. It is hardly necessary to add that they were tried by court-martial, and shot.

The information of these events was received in Leon with extravagant demonstrations of joy, and for a whole day we were stunned by the firing of guns and the ringing of bells. In the evening the following Bulletin was issued:

"Bernabé Somoza, the author of misfortunes and the cause of evils which can never be repaired, was captured in San Jorge on the evening of the 14th inst., after the defeat of his forces by the army of the Government. Subsequently to the action he was taken to the city of Rivas, tried according to martial law, sentenced to death, and shot (fué pasado por las armas), on the morning of the 17th, in the presence of the entire army. The General in Chief then harangued the troops in the following impressive terms:

"'SOLDIERS! We have, in a very few days, completed a glorious campaign. This happy result is due to your valor, constancy, subordination, and endurance. The monster, Somoza, the terror of the innocent inhabitants of this department, has suffered the just punishment of his crimes. The robber, the incendiary, the desecrator of temples, the violator of female innocence, the murderer, has passed from beneath the sword of human justice to the awful presence of an offended God! Soldiers, you have saved the honor and preserved the integrity of the State, vindicated humanity, and avenged the violated laws. For this I thank you; you have merited and will receive the gratitude of your country. Should the occasion arise, (which God forbid!) I shall be proud to lead you again to victory. Long live the Government! God save the Republic!'

"Thus has triumphed the cause of order, of progress, and of reason! Thanks to the illustrious General Muñoz and his brave soldiers, the bulwark and safeguard of the State! Their deeds speak for themselves; they need no encomiums. They teach us an impressive lesson of patriotism and virtue."

These events put an end to the internal disturbances of the State. The followers of Somoza at once disbanded, and returned to their homes. A few arrests were made; but with a moderation which reflected honor upon the government, and commended it to the people at large, a general amnesty was conceded to all who had participated in the insurrection, upon the condition of the surrender of their arms, and the restitution of the property and valuables which they had taken, and which commissioners were appointed to receive, and to restore to their rightful owners.

Upon the 16th of August following, having completely reëstablished order, and taken proper precautions against further disturbances, Gen. Muñoz returned with his forces to Leon. He was met by a deputation from the city at the "Convento," where speeches were made, and congratulations exchanged, and whence the troops marched in triumph to the city. They were received with great enthusiasm, and proceeded in a body to the Cathedral, where the "Te Deum" was sung in acknowledgment of their safe return. The extraordinary battalion was at once disbanded, and the regulars only retained in the service. It was some months, however, before the vigilance of the government was at all diminished, and not until every revolutionary symptom seemed to have died out. Subsequently a medal was voted to the General, "for the excellent services which, under God," he had rendered the State. It was ordered to be of gold, and to contain upon one side a laurel wreath, with the words, "To the Defender of Liberty and Order in Nica-

RAGUA;" and upon the reverse a naked sword, with the inscription, "FOR HIS TRIUMPH OF JULY 14, 1849." Medals were also voted to the subordinate officers who had particularly distinguished themselves on the same occasion; and the "soldiers and patriots" who had fought in the ranks, were decorated upon the left shoulder with a shield, bordered with gold, containing a palm tree in the centre, with two swords crossed below, and the words "RIVAS, JULY 14, 1849." The State also voted a pension "to the wounded, and to the *fathers*, widows, and children of those who had fallen in the service." And at the same time decreed "that in profound recognition of his visible protection, the corporations and authorities of the State, civil and military, would unite in a public and solemn manifestation of thanks to God, in the holy Cathedral, on the 2d of September."

And while upon this subject, I may anticipate events a little, and describe the ceremonial, for which great preparations were made, and which was conducted with great solemnity. Upon the morning of the day high mass was said in the Cathedral, in presence of all the officers of State, and the army. The soldiers occupied the grand aisle, and the citizens filled the outer ones. After this was concluded, a procession was formed, preceded by a large silver cross, beneath which drooped the flag of the State. Then came the military band, next the host, borne by the Bishop in person, beneath a heavy crimson canopy of velvet. He was surrounded by the higher dignitaries of the church, and followed by the officers of the State and army, bare-headed, and all moving in a hollow square of soldiers, also with heads uncovered and guns reversed. Then came the chanters of the Cathedral, the soldiers, and the citizens. But the most singular features of the procession were the statues of the saints, which, borne on men's shoulders, were distributed at intervals throughout the line. Many of these were of the size of life, and in their golden, tinselled, and fantastic robes, produced a very singular effect. Amongst them was San Benito, a little black fellow, canonized, doubtless, by a far-seeing and politic church to conciliate the colored population. He is, by the way, the most popular saint in Nicaragua, and has a grand annual festival at Masaya, to which devotees flock from all parts of Central America. Men, women, and children alike joined in the " Procession of Peace," which moved slowly through the principal streets, stopping in front of each of the churches to chant a prayer of thanks. It finally returned to the Cathedral, where the " Te Deum" was sung, and the assemblage dismissed under a benediction from the Bishop. No sooner was this more sober part of the ceremony over, than the everlasting ringing of bells and the firing of guns commenced again, and was kept up until dark, when there was an exhibition of fireworks in the plaza.

Thus ended the insurrection of Somoza, and thenceforward Leon wore a more cheerful aspect. The conduct of the government, from its commencement to its close, was marked with great justice and moderation, and afforded, in these respects, a striking and most favorable contrast to that which has for many years distinguished military operations in Central America.

CHAPTER XI.

ANTIQUITIES—ANCIENT STATUE IN THE GRAND PLAZA—MONUMENTS ON THE ISLAND OF MOMOTOMBITA IN LAKE MANAGUA—DETERMINE TO VISIT THEM—THE PADRE PAUL—PUEBLO NUEVO AND OUR OLD HOSTESS—A NIGHT RIDE—"HACIENDA DE LAS VACAS"—A NIGHT AMONGST THE "VAQUEROS"—THE LAKE—OUR BONGO—VISIT THE HOT SPRINGS OF MOMOTOMBO—ATTEMPT TO REACH ONE OF THE "INFERNALES" OF THE VOLCANO—TERRIBLE HEAT—GIVE UP THE ATTEMPT—OVIEDO'S ACCOUNT OF THE VOLCANO—"PUNTA DE LOS PAJAROS"—MOMOTOMBITA—DREAD OF RATTLESNAKES—THE MONUMENTS—RESOLVE TO REMOVE THE LARGEST—A NEST OF SCORPIONS—TRIBULATION OF OUR CREW—HARD WORK—HOW TO SHIP AN IDOL—VIRTUES OF AGUARDIENTE—"PURCHASING AN ELEPHANT"—MORE "PIEDRAS ANTIGUAS"—THE ISLAND ONCE INHABITED—SUPPOSED CAUSEWAY TO THE MAIN LAND—A PERILOUS NIGHT VOYAGE—DIFFICULT LANDING—ALACRAN OR SCORPION DANCE—A FOOT MARCH IN THE FOREST—THE "HACIENDA DE LAS VACAS" AGAIN—SCANT SUPPER—RETURN TO LEON—THE IDOL SENT, VIA CAPE HORN, TO WASHINGTON—A SATISFIED PADRE—IDOLS FROM SUBTIABA—MONSTROUS HEADS—VISIT TO AN ANCIENT TEMPLE—FRAGMENTS—MORE IDOLS—INDIAN SUPERSTITIONS—"EL TORO"—LIGHTING ON TWO LEGS—A CHASE AFTER HORSES—SWEET REVENGE—"CAPILLA DE LA PIEDRA"—PLACE OF THE IDOL—THE FRAY FRANCISCO DE BOBADILLA—HOW HE CONVERTED THE INDIANS—PROBABLE HISTORY OF MY IDOLS—THE ANCIENT CHURCH "LA MERCEDES DE SUBTIABA"—ITS RUINS—GARRAPATAS—TROPICAL INSECTS—SNAKES AND SCORPIONS *versus* FLEAS AND WOOD-TICKS—A CHOICE OF EVILS.

AMONGST the objects of interest which early attracted my attention in Leon, was an ancient figure or statue of stone, planted at one of the corners of the principal plaza. It was of basalt, boldly sculptured, and represented a man with his hands clasped on his breast, and apparently seated upon some kind of pedestal. The lower part of the figure, however, had been broken, and the fragment which remained was little more than one-third of the original length. A fillet was represented bound around the brow, and the head was surmounted by a head-dress somewhat resembling those which are to be observed in some of the ancient Egyptian sculptures. The face was perfect, with the exception of a part of the mouth, which had been broken, and the eyes were apparently closed. The whole expression was grave

IDOL FROM MOMOTOMBITA. NO I.

and serene, and yet so characteristic, that I could not resist the impression that it was copied after a living model. The accompanying engraving will convey a very correct idea of the original, which I procured and presented to the Smithsonian Institution at Washington, where it is now deposited.

The back of the figure is square, grooved on the edge, and notched entirely across, so as to resemble overlapping plates. It will be observed that the shoulders appear to be unnaturally elevated; but upon closer examination it will be seen that the original design seems to have been to represent the figure in the act of supporting some heavy body; suggesting the probability that this, in conjunction with others of similar design, once supported an altar, or another and still larger statue. The flat top favors this supposition.

I found, upon inquiry, that this figure, together with many others, had been obtained from the island of Momotombita, in Lake Managua, where there were still a number of interesting monuments. I at once proposed an expedition to the island, and availing myself of the time pending the commencement of my negotiations with the government, set out on the 26th of July, in company with Dr. Livingston, and Padre Paul, editor of "El Correo del Istmo," the government paper, who was curious in matters of this kind. The Padre was a native of Spain, where he had received a liberal education, but by some mistake had become a priest. I say mistake, not because the Padre was not a good priest, but because nature had intended him for a licenciado, or a politician, if not for a traveller. The government, some days previous to our departure, had sent orders to Managua for boats to be in readiness at a point on the lake, nearest the island, called "Piedras Gordas," and there to await our arrival. It was late in the afternoon when we left the city for Pueblo Nuevo, where we proposed to pass the night. The road was the same over which we had travelled in our journey to Leon; but the season was now further advanced, and the great plain was shrouded with a vegetation three-fold more luxuriant than before. The maize, which a few weeks previously hardly covered the ground, was now breast high; the cactus fences too were relieved by yellow flowers, and the inner leaves surrounding the stalk, bending outward, displayed their delicate pink linings to the sun.

The Padre was mounted on a splendid mule, gaily caparisoned, and with his cassock tucked up, heavy riding boots, and massive silver spurs, followed by his servant, with an "alforjas," full of edibles, made a dashing figure at the head of our little cavalcade. He rode like a trooper, and seemed to enjoy the freedom of the forest quite as much as any sinner. A stranger might have taken him for a soldier in disguise, or an eager lover speeding to a distant mistress. It was a tearing ride, that twenty-four miles to Pueblo Nuevo, and in less than three hours we dismounted at the door of the house where I had slept on my previous journey. The old lady and her five daughters had had no warning of our coming, and were evidently mortified to be found *sans* satin slippers, and with hair dishevelled. But before supper was ready they all made their appearance in full costume, as before, and we ventured upon a compliment or two by way of compensating for the *contretemps* of our sudden arrival.

We found that it was yet upwards of three leagues to the "Piedras Gordas" where our boat was waiting, and as we were anxious to be there by sunrise, we resolved to proceed to a cattle estate, near the place, that night. The Padre did not relish the idea of leaving comfortable quarters for the doubtful accommodations of the "hacienda de las vacas" and was eloquent in describing the difficulties and dangers of riding through unfrequented forest paths in the night time; but the Padre was in a minority, and had to submit. We accordingly procured a guide, and started. For a couple of miles we kept the main road, and got along smoothly; we then turned off at right angles into the forest. The night was exceedingly dark, and the path narrow, and even in the daytime obscure. But our guide seemed entirely at home, and we followed as well as we were able. Occasionally he shouted "cuidado!" "take care," which was the signal to fall flat on our horses, in order to escape the limbs and branches of the trees. But notwithstanding all our caution, we got some most ungentle thumps and scratches, and were several times nearly dragged from our saddles. Once we became entangled for a quarter of an hour, in the top of a fallen tree, and had literally to cut our way through it with our swords and machetes. The Padre considerately kept in the rear, and got the benefit of all our experiences. Our progress was necessarily very slow, and I began to fear that we had lost our way, and almost to repent that we had not taken the Padre's advice, when we heard the lowing of cattle and the barking of dogs in the distance. Thus encouraged, we pressed on, and soon came into a broader path. We pursued this for some distance, the barking of the dogs becoming every moment more distinct, until finally emerging from the woods, we galloped towards a little eminence, where a number of fires proclaimed the existence of the cattle rancho. It was surrounded by a kind of stockade, or fence of upright posts, and, as we approached, we were saluted with a ferocious "*Quien vive?*" who are you? Night descents by robbers, on the haciendas, during civil disturbances in the country, are by no means uncommon occurrences; and as the estates have usually a considerable number of men attached to them, they sometimes result in severe fights. Our approach had therefore alarmed the establishment, and had not our guide been known, we might have been turned back with a volley, instead of having the gate opened to us with an invitation to enter. In the centre of the square was a mud house, surrounded by a thatched shed, beneath which a dozen hammocks were suspended. Three or four fires were smouldering just outside of this shed, and around them were reclining some calves which had been bitten by bats, or injured by wild animals. A dozen surly dogs stalked amongst the swarthy "vaqueros," or herdsmen, whose half naked figures were just visible by the faint red light of the fires. A couple of women, alarmed by the sound of voices, hurried, scantily dressed, from the house, but were at once reassured by the Padre. Altogether, with the champing horses, and the gleaming of arms, shut in as it was by the darkness as with a pall, the scene was singularly wild and picturesque.

The animals attended to, the next thing was to dispose ourselves for the night. The women offered us the house, in which were two naked hide beds. My bones were agonized at the sight of them, and I chose a hammock beneath the shed, and wrapping myself in my blanket, tumbled in. The men gave up their places without grumbling, and stretched themselves on the bare earth. Soon all was still, except the melancholy howl of the "mono colorado," and the low, distant murmur of the lake. I slept soundly until roused by Ben's morning gun at the earliest dawn. He had already prepared a cup of chocolate, which, with a cracker and a *jícara* of fresh milk, constituted our breakfast. The horses were saddled, and giving the princely sum of a rial each to the men whom we had so summarily dislodged, we started for the lake. The road was through a beautiful forest of large trees, which the cattle kept comparatively free from underbrush, and which had occasional open places, where the ground was covered with long fresh grass. Half an hour brought us to the shore. The sun had not yet risen, but a brilliant coronet of rays shot up above the sharply defined and fantastic outlines of the distant mountains of Segovia, and was reflected in the tremulous waters of the lake. Immediately in front, towered the volcano of Momotombo; its lower half purple in the shade, and its upper of the richest amber. A thin column of smoke rose almost perpendicularly from its summit, which first caught the crimson rays of the sun, and then changed to gold. Upon the right, a perfect cone, was the island for which we were bound, and in the foreground our boat, half drawn up on the shore, and near by, at the root of a great tree, clustering around their breakfast fire, was its crew. They had been encamped here for two days, awaiting our arrival; and would have waited a month for that matter—for what was time to them, so long as the lake furnished fish, and plantains were plenty?

Our horses were fastened to a long rope, one behind the other, and sent back in charge of our guide to the hacienda, with express instructions to have them on the shore again at nightfall, in case we should return. Our boat, like some of the bongos on Lake Nicaragua, was hollowed from the single trunk of a cebia tree. It was upwards of forty feet long, and full six feet broad, permitting a tall man to lie across its bottom. There was no wind, and the men were obliged to take to their oars. And as it was not greatly out of our way, we determined before going to the island to pass to the foot of the great volcano, and visit the hot springs at its base. The intervening bay is upwards of ten miles broad, but we crossed it before nine o'clock. While on the lake, we had an excellent opportunity to view the volcano. It is about six thousand feet, or one mile and a fourth, in perpendicular height, and very steep,—so steep, indeed, that even if there were no danger in the ascent, it would probably be impossible to reach its summit. Its lower half is covered with trees, which in the ravines that seam its sides run up still higher, gradually narrowing like the points of a ruff. The upper half seems made up of scoria, which, near the summit, gives place to ashes of a white color. The crater appears small and regular in outline; and there are some openings on the sides, towards its base, which emit steam and smoke, and around which sulphur is deposited on the rocks. These are called "infernales," and we observed one on the side towards us, at a comparatively small elevation, which greatly excited our curiosity, and which we resolved to visit.

At the point where we landed, the ground was composed of a kind of ochery earth, of a dark red color, varied with yellow, which the boatmen told us was used for paint. A fourth of a mile to the right, and immediately at the edge of the lake, were the "fuentes calientes," or hot springs. They are hundreds in number; in fact, for a considerable extent, the ground was covered with white incrustations, resembling a field of snow; and as we walked over it, the sound of the water beneath was like that of a violently boiling cauldron. There were numerous openings, from which rose columns of steam, and where the water boiled up to the height of from six inches to two feet. Around some of these places the deposites had gradually built up little cones, with openings in the centre, where the clear water bubbled as in a kettle. I sent specimens of the deposites to the United States for analysis, but they unfortunately miscarried, and I am consequently unable to give the constituents of which they are made up. They will no doubt be duly announced when the "Grand Volcano Hotel, and North American Natural Hot Spring Bath Establishment," shall be opened for invalids, on the shores of Lake Managua.

Between the shore and the true base of the volcano is a gentle slope, ridged with beds of lava, which run down into the lake, but which have become disintegrated on the surface, and are now covered with coarse grass, bushes, and clumps of trees. Here cattle from distant haciendas are allowed to roam from one year's end to the other, until they become almost as wild as the deer themselves. The vaqueros occasionally visit them, to mark the young ones, or to select the best ones for sale, but beyond this they receive no care or attention. We started over this slope, in the direction of the smoking orifice which we had observed from the lake. But we were under the lee of the mountains, where not a breath of wind reached us, and exposed to the full glow of the sun; and before we had gone a mile, we almost repented of our undertaking. The doctor, the padre, and myself alone persisted in proceeding. The surface became rougher as we advanced, and scrubby trees and thorny bushes impeded our progress, and shut out from view the place which we were struggling to reach. We next came to ridges of treacherous, scoriaceous sand, which yielded beneath our feet, and which we only ascended by clinging to the clumps of grass which grew here and there, and by driving our swords to their hilts in the ground, as supports. But our progress was slow and painful, and we were compelled to pause every second minute to recover our strength. Finally, the sun was no longer hot, it was withering, and the dry scoriæ became blistering to the touch. I looked up towards the top of the volcano, and shall never forget its utterly bald and desolate appearance. The atmosphere on its sides seemed to undulate with heat, and the reflected rays burned my eyeballs. I turned to my companions, and found that they suffered equally with myself. The padre had wisely bound his handkerchief over his head and eyes. It was folly, he said, to attempt to go further, and we concurred with him, and retraced our steps. The descent was of course comparatively easy, but when I reached the boat, I was completely exhausted, and adequately convinced of the folly of attempting to climb volcanoes under a tropical sun, at mid-day.

Oviedo speaks of this volcano as one very high, "its summit pierced by a multitude of separate orifices, whence smoke is always rising, which can be seen at the distance of twenty leagues. No flame," he continues, "is visible by day or night. An abundance of sulphur may be found here, according to the report of those who have used it in the manufacture of powder, and also of those who have used it for other purposes. On the sides and parts adjacent to this volcano, for a distance of five or six leagues, there is an abundance of springs of boiling water like the Sufretarari, (Solfatara,) that may be seen at Pouzzole, two or three leagues from Naples. I should think that all these mountains formed but one mine of sulphur. There are also orifices through which proceeds a stream of air, so warm as to be unendurable. If we approach it, we seem to hear the uproar of a vast number of forges in full blast, sometimes ceasing, and in a few moments recommencing again; but the time the noise can be heard is at least four times as long as the pauses. Near the village of Totoa is a thermal spring, so warm that the Indians use it for cooking their meat, fish, and bread. These articles of food are cooked in less time than it would take to repeat the *Credo* twice; and as for eggs, they would be *done* sooner than an *Ave*."

We found our men quietly smoking their cigars under the shade of a tree, perfectly careless as to whether they stayed there all day or proceeded. Such an imperturbable set I verily believe were never before got together. We told them to push off for the island, which they did in the most leisurely manner. The wind had begun to blow, and as it was against us, they towed the boat along under the lee of the shore, walking by its side in the water, which, at the distance of a quarter of a mile out, was hardly breast-deep. We saw many deer, and a number of lazy alligators on the shore, but beyond the reach of our rifles. We finally came to the "Punta del Pajaro," a high ledge of naked basaltic rocks projecting out into the lake, and covered with myriads of water-fowls. Here our men took to their oars, and paddled direct for the island. The afternoon wind was now blowing strongly, and the lake was rough. It required two hours' hard rowing to bring us to the island, where we pulled ashore in a little cove, protected from the swell of the lake.

This island is volcanic, and rises in a regular cone from the water's edge, to the height of two thousand eight hundred feet. It is about eight miles in circumference, and is covered with a dense forest. The shore where we landed was stony, but a short distance back the stones gave place to sand and a rich loam. Victorino, our patron, knew the locality of the monuments, and putting on his sandals, took his machete, and led the way, peering suspiciously to the right and the left. We inquired the cause of his caution, and received the comforting assurance "hay muchos cascabeles," "there are many rattlesnakes!" The Dr. whipped out his sword, stepped high, and constantly startled us by mistaking vines, coiling on the ground, for "cascabeles." After proceeding for about half an hour, we came to a spot where the underbrush and bushes gave place to high grass. Here was a kind of natural amphitheatre, within which the ground was smooth, sloping gently towards the lake, and shadowed over with high trees. This, Victorino informed us, was the site of the monuments, but they had all fallen, and the tall grass hid them from our view. We were compelled to beat it down with our machetes, and thus discover the figures one by one. As I have said, many had been carried away, and most of those which remained were broken, or so defaced as to be of little value for my purposes. Victorino said that he could remember when there were as many as fifty statues here, and when some of them stood erect. According to his account and that of others, they had been arranged in the form of a square, their faces looking inwards; and the position of those which remained, and of the fragments, confirmed the story. Amongst the few still entire, was one of large size, and which a party, sent by the English Consul, had a few years before endeavored to carry away for the British Museum, but after getting it part of the way to the lake, had abandoned it in despair. It was ruder than some of the others, but perfect, and I at once resolved to remove it, with a view of sending it to the United States. I accordingly sent Victorino to bring his boat and men to the nearest point possible, and with Dr. Livingston, the Padre, and Ben, began to cut down small trees of the proper size for skids or pries, and to open a path to the lake. When Victorino came with his lazy crew, we set them to work also, but they did not accomplish much, and we soon found that we had to bear the burthen of the labor ourselves. With great difficulty we cleared a road, and laying down large skids rolled the figure upon them. Beneath it a colony of "alacrans del monte," or black scorpions, had established themselves; and in an instant they swarmed around our legs. The half naked Indians retreated precipitately, but, protected by our high, thick boots we stood our ground, and stamped the little stinging monsters to death with our heels. It was not, however, until we had succeeded in moving the statue some distance from the spot, that we could persuade the Indians to rejoin us. After two hours' of hard work, we rolled it to the shore; but now the question was to get it in the boat. Victorino protested, in the first place, against trying to carry it at all, as it would surely crush the boat and drown us; and in the second place against putting it in the bottom, which he said it would inevitably break through. In fact we were a good deal staggered ourselves; we had not thought of this, but nevertheless determined not to lose our

IDOL FROM MOMOTOMBITA, NO. 2.

labor. If it was put at the bottom, even though it might not break through, it was clear that we never could muster force enough to get it out. So we decided that it should be carried by placing it lengthwise on the rowers' seats, which, in order to support the weight, were to be strengthened by crossbars. The men stood aghast at our proposition, and at first utterly refused to assist us. They took the padre aside and told him that "these Americans were certainly crazy." We however promised them each a half dollar extra, administered a dose of

FRONT VIEW OF HEAD OF NO. 2.

brandy and water, and finally got them to take hold again An inclined plane of timbers was built up against the boat, which was half filled with stones, to sink her as low as possible, and to fix her firmly in the sand. The statue was then gradually rolled on board. More than once I thought our fabric would break down; had it done so there would have been more crushed legs than whole ones in the company. After it was secured, part of the stones were thrown out, and we soon had the satisfaction of seeing the bongo afloat, and perfectly balanced. A profile view of this figure is given in the foregoing engraving. It is regularly cut in black ba-

40

salt, or trachyte, of intense hardness. The features of the face are singularly bold and severe in outline; the brow is broad, the nose aquiline, the cheeks high, the mouth open, and containing what we may infer (for reasons which will be given elsewhere) was intended to represent a human heart. The arms and legs are rudely indicated, but the distinctive sexual features are broadly marked. And here it may be observed that, while most of these statues represent males,

COLOSSAL HEAD FROM MOMOTOMBITA.

some of them represent females; and there are but few in which the sex is not distinguishable. The reason for these distinctions may be found in the fact that the doctrine of the Reciprocal Principles of Nature, or Nature Active and Passive Male and Female, was recognized in nearly all the primitive religious systems of the New as well as of the Old World, and in none more clearly than in those of Central America. Besides this figure, we carried off the colossal head represented in the above drawing; but found nothing more which would repay the trouble of removal. There may have been other figures of interest hidden in the long grass and bushes; and Victorino informed us that upon the opposite side of the island there was still another place, where there were formerly many "piedras antiguas;" but that also was overgrown with grass. It was now late, and unless we spent the night on the island, it was clear we could make no further examinations. And as I proposed to return in the dry season, when the grass might be removed by burning, we concluded to relinquish our explorations for the present.

The island of Momotombita was anciently inhabited, and called Cocobolo. I observed fragments of pottery, and of vessels of stone, strewed all over the shore; and in the little cove where we landed there were evidences that the rocks had been rolled away to facilitate the approach of boats to the land. At a point on the shore of the main land, nearly opposite the island, is a line of large stones, extending for the distance of one or two hundred yards into the water, and projecting above it. The Indians have a vague tradition that this was a causeway built by "los antiguos habitantes," extending from the shore to the island; and Capt. Belcher, of the British navy, who travelled here in 1838, seems to think the story not improbable. The supposed causeway is nothing more than a narrow vein of rock injected at some remote period through a fissure in the superior strata or crust of the earth; and being harder than the materials surrounding it, has retained its elevation, while they have been worn away by the action of the water.

It was quite sunset when we pushed off from the island; and when we got out from under its lee, we found the wind blowing a gale, and the sea high. Ours was a ticklish load; and, as the bongo had no keel, the necessity of keeping her directly before the wind was obvious; for had she rolled a foot on either side, the stone would have overset us in a twinkling. Victorino was anxious but cool, and his men were too much alarmed not to obey orders, and we put up the sail and got under way without accident. Fortunately the winds here blow with great steadiness, or our voyage might have been rendered more perilous than it was, and that would have been quite unnecessary. The night fell, dark and cloudy; the Padre and M—— soon became seasick, and the crew, consoling themselves that we had a priest on board, gathered around the foot of the mast, and silently told their beads. Ben stationed himself, knife in hand, at the halyards, and I clung to a stick of light wood which I found in the boat, and calculated the chances of getting ashore by its aid, in case our stone god should upset us. Altogether we had a serious time, and the three hours which we occupied in passing to the land seemed quite as long as six under ordinary circumstances. It was so dark that we could not distinguish the shore, but fortunately the fire, left by the men in the morning, fanned by the wind, had caught in the trunk of the tree at the foot of which it was built, and answered the purpose of a lighthouse in guiding us to our destination. Here we succeeded in landing under the lee of some large rocks, against which the surf broke with the force and noise of the ocean. I now quite comprehended why Capt. Belcher, old salt as he was, declined venturing upon this lake, even after having brought a boat for the purpose all the way from Realejo. I felt no ordinary degree of satisfaction when I found myself on terra firma once more. In removing the loose articles of our equipment from the boat, Ben was twice stung in the hand by a scorpion, and danced about the shore in an agony of pain. I however wrapped his hand in a cloth soaked in brandy, and gave him copious internal doses of the same,—the best, and usually the most accessible, remedy.

Our horses were not to be found; either our guide had not brought them down, or else had returned with them to the rancheria. We held a council as to whether it was best to camp on the shore or push through the forest to our quarters of the preceding night. The uncomfortable wind and a few heavy drops of rain decided us; and, with Victorino, bearing some brands of fire at our head, we set out. It was as dark as Erebus in the woods, and quite impossible to discern the person next in advance. We however followed the fire, and after a weary march came to the hacienda. We were tired and hungry, but there was nothing to eat except *tiste* and curds. We made the most of these, but went to our hammocks unsatisfied, consoling ourselves, however, with the prospect of an illimitable breakfast at the house of our hostess of the five slippered daughters, in Pueblo Nuevo.

Before leaving next morning, I distributed the promised favors amongst our crew, and engaged the entire force of the estate to assist our guide, who was to return with a cart for the statue. A few days after, it reached Leon, having broken down three carts on the road. I subsequently sent it to Realejo, whence it was shipped, via Cape Horn, for the United States. It is now deposited in the Museum of the Smithsonian Institution, at Washington. And thus terminated my first antiquarian episode in Nicaragua. The Padre expressed himself satisfied; one such ride, he said, was enough for a lifetime.

I have elsewhere said that the Indians of Subtiaba brought me two idols, shortly after my arrival in Leon. A reduced back view of the first of these is presented in the subjoined engraving. It had been broken, and a portion, perhaps comprising one-third of the entire figure, had been lost. The part which remains is something less than six feet in height by eighteen inches in diameter, or upwards of four feet in circumference. The face has been battered with heavy sledges, and its features obliterated. The ornaments upon the back and elsewhere are, however, very well preserved, and are quite elaborate; more resembling those of Copan than any others discovered in the country. The face seems to project through the widely distended jaws of some animal, the head of which serves as a head dress. The ancient Mexican soldiers had a common practice of wearing the heads of animals, or helmets in imitation of them, on their heads in battle, to render themselves horrible, and frighten their enemies. Upon its breast the figure sustains a kind of plate, or some piece of armor, and upon its right arm wears

IDOL FROM SUBTIABA. NO. 1.

a shield. The carving seems to have been very good; but the zeal of the early Christians, and the corroding tooth of time, have greatly injured the entire statue, which is now in the Museum of the Smithsonian Institution.

IDOL FROM SUBTIABA, NO. 2.—This figure closely resembles that just described, and, like that, has suffered greatly from the same cause. The features of the face are entirely obliterated; the design of the head dress is, however, more apparent, and is palpably what I have already indicated, the

Side. Back.

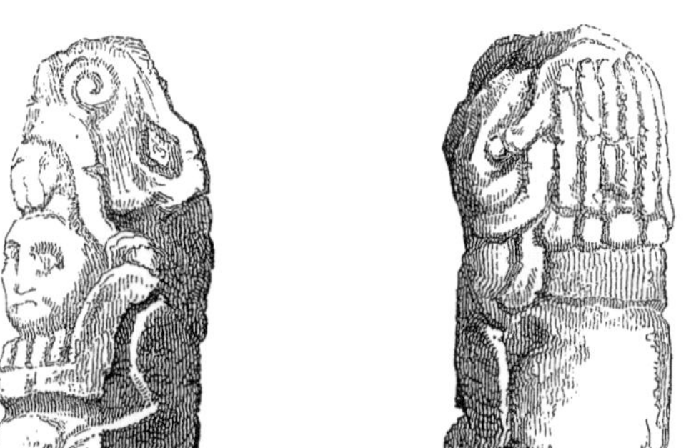

IDOL FROM SUBTIABA, NO. 2.

jaws of some monstrous animal, between which the face of the figure projects. It is less elaborately sculptured than No. 1, but of the same material, and corresponding in size. One hand rests upon the breast, the other hangs loosely at the side. This idol also is deposited in the museum of the Smithsonian Institution.

Idols from Subtiaba, No. 3.—Subsequent to the presentation of the two figures above described, I had a fragment brought to me, of which a front view is given in the annexed engraving. It is of sand-stone, two feet six inches high, by ten or twelve inches in diameter, much frayed and worn by exposure, and greatly injured by violence. It bears evidences of having been elaborately ornamented, and seems to have been designed to represent a female. Its most singular feature, however, is a mask of the human face, which is held upon the abdomen by both hands. Perhaps, however, the Indians were right in suggesting that it represents an opening in the abdomen, held apart by the hands, and exposing some mythological figure therein concealed. There are some reasons in support of this suggestion, which it would hardly be proper to submit in a work of this popular character. This figure has also been broken, and less than half of it now remains.

IDOL FROM SUBTIABA, NO. 3.

The idols above described, as I have already said, were brought to my house by the Indians; and I know nothing concerning them, except that they were exhumed near the base of the Cerro Santiago, to the south-west of Leon, where they had been buried for several generations. I subsequently learned of the existence of others in the same direction, and went, in company with a guide, kindly obtained for me by Gen. Guerrero, to examine them. Our route lay through Subtiaba, in the direction of the ocean. We passed over a beautiful undulating country, full of abandoned plantations, and watered by several fine streams, skirting the hills to the south-west of Leon. At the distance of about three or four leagues from the city, we came to a series of "jicarales," in the midst of which was a cattle estate. Cows and deer were herding together, the latter appearing quite as tame as the first. Beyond the hacienda was a high, bare hill, steep as the pyramids, called Mount St. Michael, the base of which is studded round with large loose stones, causing our horses to stumble fearfully, and over which we passed with great difficulty. We then came to the finest "jicaral" I had yet seen. It resembled a well-kept New England orchard; the trees had fewer parasites to rob them of their vitality, and the ground was covered with a smooth carpet of grass. Intermixed with these were numbers of the wild "jocote" or plum-trees, heavily laden with yellow and red fruit, which was not unpleasant to the taste, but which poisoned my lips, and made them sore for a week. The same fruit, when cultivated, is fine, and is used in a great variety of ways. The forest in which the idols were concealed commenced abruptly upon one side of the "jicaral," and was an almost impenetrable mass of vines, underbrush, and broad-leaved tropical plants. A thousand monuments might have been buried here for years without being discovered, except by the merest accident; and as we had to cut our path with our swords, I began to have serious misgivings as to the success of our expedition. Our guide, however, peering from side to side, seemed confident as to his whereabouts, as well as to that of the "piedras," and in half an hour we came to the spot where they had existed. I say had existed, for although the ground was strewn with fragments, but a single figure, "IDOL FROM SUBTIABA, NO. 4," remained entire. It stood as shown in the accompanying plate, partially buried in the earth. Its height above the ground was six feet four inches; the material, sand-stone. As in the other instances, the face had been mutilated, but the remainder of the figure was nearly perfect. The hair seemed to be thrown back from the forehead in rolls; or perhaps what I have supposed to be the hair is a modified example of that kind of ornamental featherwork so common in the ancient monuments of Mexico, Yucatan, and Central America. A broad collar passes around the neck, and a circular plate, or shield, with an attempt at a representation of a human face in the centre, is suspended from it, in front of the figure. A kind of belt passes around the body, above the hips, from which depends a flap, like that frequently worn by the Indians of the frontiers, even to this day. At the lower extremity of this is a round, cup-shaped hole, capable of containing about a quart, the purposes of which are not apparent.

In cutting paths around this figure, I came upon an oblong elevation of stones, which seemed to have been the base of some edifice, or one of the ancient teocallis or altars of the aborigines. It was about two hundred feet long, sixty broad, and ten high. Around the edges the stones still retained some degree of regularity, but the whole was nevertheless a ruin, and large trees were growing on its summit. The numerous fragments of sculpture scattered around this spot showed conclusively that it had been visited by systematic violence, not only anciently, at the period of the Conquest, but subsequently, and within a very few years. My guide told me that he could remember the time when the Indians came here secretly by night, and performed strange dances around these idols, and poured out libations before them. The ground around the single erect figure above described was comparatively free from undergrowth, showing that even now it is secretly visited, by the descendants of the people who first erected it, for the performance of traditionary, sacred ceremonies. The priests are vigilant in detecting and putting down these remnants of idolatry; and only a few months before my arrival had broken up a remarkable figure of an animal called "El Toro," the bull, which existed about a league distant from this very spot, and to which the Indians, for a long time, openly resorted, to make offerings of *tiste*, and to perform dances preparatory to putting their crops in the ground. The destruction of the idol was effected secretly, and afterwards proclaimed to have been done by the lightnings of indignant heaven; but one of my Indian friends told me privately that the Indians understood the trick, and knew that this lightning went on two legs, and wore a cassock! I would have gone to the spot, and endeavored to have restored the fragments for a sketch, but my guide told me that the natives had carried them off and buried them.

While engaged with the stones, we had carelessly, and as usual, let our horses go loose. For the first time, they now took it into their heads to abuse this indulgence, and trotted off. The more we endeavored to coax them back the more vicious they were, and finally dashed off at full speed into the "jicaral," where they kicked up their heels in great glee. The prospect of a walk back to Leon, with the loss of saddles, pistols, swords, and other et ceteras, if not of the brutes themselves, was little calculated to excite our admiration of these antics. The chase continued half an hour, when we succeeded in securing the horse of our guide; but unfortunately he was the poorest of the whole, and not able to come near the others in a race. Luckily our guide had a lasso, and after another half hour of manœuvring, in which we all got heated and angry, my own horse was secured. He was duly "lathered" for his pains, and was handed over to the guide to pursue the others; being the fleetest, the business was soon done. We took precious good care that they should not get the upper hand of us again that day, and rode them home with a malignant pressure on the terrible Mexican bit, and with no stinted application of the equally terrible Spanish-American spur.

Upon our return, the guide conducted us out of our way into a kind of amphitheatre amongst the hills, to what he called the "Capilla de la Piedra," the Stone Chapel. It was a large rock of conical shape, placed high on the slope facing the entrance to this natural circus, and upon that side had a niche, or hollow, capable of containing four or five persons, and which seemed to have been cut in the rock. I failed to satisfy myself whether it was natural or artificial; but finally concluded, from its position and regularity, that it was a natural opening in the rock, enlarged and modified by art. There were traces of fire, and fragments of broken pottery around it, and immediately in front a large flat stone, which might have been used for an altar. As I looked at it, surrounded by rough, frowning rocks, and shrouded with vines, I fancied it an appropriate niche for an idol, and imagined this natural amphitheatre filled with a superstitious multitude, in blind adoration before it, while the blood of human sacrifices flowed perhaps on the very spot where I now stood.

I have said that I knew not whence the Indians obtained the idols which they brought to me, beyond that they were exhumed at the base of the Cerro de Santiago, near Subtiaba. Now the Fray Francisco de Bobadilla, of the Order of Mercy, was especially active in the conversion of the Indians of Nicaragua, which process, according to the chronicler Oviedo y Valdez, consisted in baptizing them, giving them a Christian name, and exacting forty grains of cacao! Bobadilla converted forty thousand in three months in the dominions of the cazique of Nagrando, whose principal town was where the city of Leon now stands. He also prevailed upon the cazique to allow him to throw down the idols which stood in "the spacious and sumptuous temple which the Indians, under the special direction of the devil, had erected there," and to set up the cross in their stead. After he had battered the faces of these idols with a mace, Bobadilla threw them down from their high places, intending to burn them with fire, in order to show the Indians the impotence of their *teots;* but, "during the night some did take them away and buried them, so that they could not be found." And it is

RUINS OF THE ANCIENT CHURCH OF LA MERCED DE SUBTIABA

not unlikely that those are the very idols exhumed for me by the Indians of Subtiaba, two of which, after doubling the Horn, now frown down upon the "hijos de Washington," from the west corridor of the Smithsonian Institution!

Upon the site of this temple was afterwards built the Christian church "La Mercedes de Subtiaba," which for more than two hundred years has been in ruins. Its adobe walls have subsided into brambly mounds, and all is formless save the piers on which its wooden pillars stood, and its low, Moorish archway, flanked by two slender columns, which rise white and spectral above a tangled mass of verdure. The town, of which it was once the centre, has shrunk in the lapse of time, and is now a mile distant; and the aboriginal city of which Bobadilla speaks, which covered three square leagues, and had more than one hundred thousand inhabitants, has dwindled to less than one fourth of that number. We visited this church on our return. Ben cut away the bushes with his *machete*, and we rode over the outline mounds, and stood where the simple Indians had knelt, centuries ago, in silent awe before the symbols of a new and imposing religion. A few rude wooden crosses marked the deep pits within which were heaped the victims of the cholera, when in 1837, five years after it had devastated our country, it more than decimated the population of Leon. Two or three Indians, returning from their daily toil in the fields, hearing our voices, pushed their way through the bushes, and reverently took off their hats, when they entered the sacred area. We asked them if they knew aught of the ancient church, or who built it? "*Quien sabe?*" was the sole reply, and they moved the forefinger of the right hand slowly back and forth, in token of ignorance. It was very ancient, they said—"muy, muy antigua!" Upon the smooth stucco beneath the arch, rudely scratched in the lime, I read, "JUAN PERALTA, *Estranjero*, 1732."

This church was built before Hudson floated on the waters of the magnificent river bearing his name; before the Pilgrims knelt on the wintry shores of New England, and before Smith spread the terrors of his arm among the Indians of Virginia. And unless some sacrilegious hand shall level the ancient archway, it will yet stand for centuries to mark the site of aboriginal superstition, and attest the zeal of the Fray Bobadilla, who baptized forty thousand Indians, receiving therefor, if they all "paid up," one million six hundred thousand grains of cacao. Pious Bobadilla!

There are several other ruined and abandoned Christian churches now buried in the forests in the suburbs of Subtiaba, the dwelling-places of the bats and birds, over whose crumbling walls, and around whose falling columns, creep the wild vines, blooming with flowers, and shedding their fragrance above the silent and deserted altars of the Most High. Ruins upon ruins—Christian church and heathen shrine, they have all sunk down together.

We returned to Leon to find ourselves covered with "agarrapatas" or wood ticks, with which the forest fairly swarms during the dry season, and which are brushed off upon travellers by the thousand. They penetrate straight to the skin, and bury their heads in the flesh, causing an irritation which drives many people to distraction. When once fastened it is impossible to detach them by force, without leaving the head in the flesh, where it gets along on its own account, apparently a great deal better than when encumbered by the body. The only mode of removing them is with a ball of soft wax, which is rubbed over the body, and to which they adhere. Some are small, hardly visible to the naked eye, others are of the size of flax, and even of melon seeds; but "the smaller the worser." Next to the fleas they rank as the predominant annoyance of the country. Musquitoes (sancudos), in Leon, the principal towns, and the open parts of the country generally, there are none; but compared with fleas and "agarrapatas," the snakes, scorpions, "chinches," "sancudos," and all the other abominations of tropical climates are mere bagatelle, and scarcely worth the mentioning.

SIDE VIEW OF IDOL FROM SUBTIABA, NO 1.

CHAPTER XII.

AMUSEMENTS IN LEON—COCK FIGHTING—"PATIO DE LOS GALLOS"—DECLINE OF THE COCK PIT—GAMING—BULL BAITING—NOVEL RIDING—"UNA SAGRADA FUNCION," OR MYSTERY—A POEM, AND A DRAMA—"UNA COMPANIA DE FUNAMBULOS," OR ROPE DANCERS—GREAT ANTICIPATIONS—A NOVEL THEATRE—THE PERFORMANCE—"LA JOVENA CATALINA," AND THE "ECCENTRIC CLOWN, SIMON,"—"TOBILLOS GRUESOS," OR "BIG ANKLES."—"FIESTAS," AND SAINTS' DAYS—THE "FIESTA" OF ST. ANDREW—DANCE OF THE DEVILS—UNEARTHLY MUSIC—ALL-SAINTS' DAY—A CARNIVAL IN SUBTIABA—AN ABRUPT CONCLUSION.

THE novelty of a first visit once worn off, there is little to interest the stranger in Leon. There are no "stated" amusements, except at the cock-pit, which is open every Sunday afternoon. This is always crowded, but not often visited by the better portion of the population. It is a smooth spot of ground in the court-yard of the proprietor's house, fenced in by canes to the height of about four feet, surrounded by high benches, and covered with a thatched roof. In the corridors of the house are little stalls, in which the cocks are kept, and here the wife and daughters of the proprietor sell chocolate and dulces to the visitors. No liquors are allowed upon the premises; and the Government, with a wise prevision, has always an alcalde and a file of soldiers present to preserve order. Visitors are admitted at a medio a head, and each one is at liberty to bring his "bird" with him. If a match cannot be made otherwise, the proprietor is obliged to accept the challenge of any of his visitors. A certain sum is paid to him on each cock entered, one-fourth of which goes into the city treasury. I visited the place but once, and suppose that the manner of fighting the cocks can afford but little, of what, I believe, is called "sport." After a match was made up, the cocks had long, sword-shaped gaffs, double-edged, sharp as needles, and in some cases three or four inches long, bound on their legs, with which they almost invariably crippled themselves in their preliminary manœuvers. The contests were consequently very brief; one or two passes generally finished them. The bets were never high, but the excitement none the less in consequence. In former times, the proprietor told me, he numbered all the "caballeros" of the city amongst his visitors, and then golden ounces were wagered instead of dirty rials,—and he drew a handful of the latter from his pocket with a contemptuous sneer, and then violently thrust them back again. He longed for a change; any change would be acceptable to him which should bring back the caballeros and the golden ounces!

But because the more respectable people of Leon do not frequent the cock-pit, it is not to be inferred that they are wholly averse to the species of amusement practised there. On the contrary, in the back corridors of the houses,—and in none more frequently than in those of the padres,—a dozen fine cocks may almost always be found, or at all events heard, if not seen. Quiet little parties are got up of afternoons, cocks fought, and not unfrequently, on such occasions, if report speaks true, golden ounces find themselves suddenly transferred from one "bolsa" to another.

Gaming is a passion amongst the people of all Spanish America. But in Nicaragua it is conducted with less publicity and perhaps to a less extent than in most of the Spanish States. Nevertheless, I heard of instances during my residence in the country, in which thousands of dollars had changed hands in a single evening. The game is, I believe, universally, the well-known "*monte.*" There are several billiard-rooms in Leon, which seemed to be always full; but they were not very elegant nor even clean. And in the

Calle Real there was a licensed gaming-house, "Casa de Juego," the only one, I believe, in the city. It was crowded every night by the lower classes of the population. The gambling, as might be inferred from the character of its frequenters, was of a petty kind,—of the "dirty rial" order of our friend of the "patio de los gallos."

Central America commenced its Republican career with very sweeping reforms, taking the United States for its model. Amongst the earliest acts of its government was the prohibition of bull-fighting. The old taste for that amusement has not, however, died out, but has assumed a somewhat different form. It was a festival week in the barrio of the Calvario,—*what* festival I do not remember, for there was no end to the fiestas and saint's days,—and we were told that it was to end with "uno juego de los toros," or bull baiting, (as near as I could understand it,) in the plaza of the church of that district. In fact the cura waited upon us in person, and invited us to attend. We went in the afternoon, and found a high, strong fence built around the square, with a supplementary enclosure outside, leading into the larger one by a narrow passage closed with heavy bars. The roof and towers of the church were covered with people, mostly women, and amongst them was a band of music. All around the square, and clinging to the fence was a swarm of naked muchachos, and outside of these a great number of horsemen, who, seated on their steeds, could distinctly witness the whole performance. Amongst these we took up our position, the crowd giving us the most commanding place, while an officious alcalde whipped the boys off the fence in front, so as to allow an uninterrupted view. The music kept up a great noise, but the crowd had waited a long time, and were impatient, and assuming the universal prerogatives of crowds, cried out to the musicos "to stop their noise," and to the managers "to bring in the bulls." Directly the bars of the smaller enclosure were raised, and a horseman dashed in with a lasso attached to his saddle, dragging after him a large black bull, by the horns. He drove at full gallop around the square, and then adroitly pulled the bull, which was now furious, to a stout post in the centre, where by a few dexterous evolutions he fastened him securely, with his head motionless against the post. Three or four men now approached, and cautiously, and with much difficulty, fastened an "albardo" or common saddle of the country on the back of the bull, securing it firmly by bands around the body of the animal. Fireworks were then fastened to its horns and tail, and an invitation extended to whoever might choose *á manejar el toro.* Two or three stalwart fellows, ambitious of distinction, volunteered, one of whom was chosen. He mounted very adroitly, and securing himself in his seat, the fireworks were lighted, and the rope cut. The bull bounded away amidst the explosion of bombas, the beating of drums, and the shouts of the multitude, foaming with rage, making awkward but prodigious leaps, and driving at every object which came in view. There were three or four horsemen in the ring with staves having a little red flag at one end, and a sharp spike at the other. These they alternately dashed before the eyes of the bull, or drove into his flanks. When the fireworks commenced to explode, the toro no longer made at any particular object, but dashed blindly from side to side, throwing the rider from his seat into the dust, where, for a moment, I thought he would be trampled to death, but he scrambled up and made a rapid retreat, evidently more frightened than hurt, over the barricade, amidst the jeers of the crowd, who would have been better satisfied if he had come off with a broken limb or two, or had been killed outright. The exertion was too much for the bull himself, and after chasing the horsemen around for awhile, he marched off, with his tongue hanging from his mouth, and covered with foam, into a corner of the enclosure. There was no more sport to be got out of him, and the crowd vociferated "take him away! take him away!" So one of the horsemen threw a lasso over his horns and dragged him out.

Another bull was then introduced, and the same process repeated. But this time the rider kept his seat to the end, and for his skill or good luck, got a plentiful supply of vivas from the boys, and of waving of scarfs from the women. It is impossible to describe the excitement of the multitude during the active parts of the exhibition; some stamped and leaped about, and all shouted at the top of their lungs. When the bull lacked spirit, they cried "away with the old cow! take away the heifer!" and stoned him from the enclosure. I soon got enough of the exhibition, and would have gone off, but the cura prevailed on me to stay for the final act, which he said would be "muy glorioso," very glorious. Four bulls were then let loose together, but this time the officer in command of the file of soldiers which was present, permitted no riders. The precaution was a wise one, for only a few months before two men had been killed by way of a "grand finale." The bulls, maddened by the noise and fireworks flashing in their eyes and whizzing in their ears, attacked each other with the greatest fury, and one was dragged out dead from the encounter. His flesh was claimed for the poor of the barrio, and according to usage he was surrendered to them. This kind of amusement I found was a favorite one throughout the State.

I subsequently witnessed an exhibition of a different kind, in the same place. It was announced as "*Una Sagrada Funcion*," sometimes called "*Sainete*," a solemnity or mystery. It fell on a clear moonlight night, and was one of the most singular spectacles which can be imagined. A kind of stage was erected upon one side of the plaza, raised some six feet from the ground, with a place behind, concealed by variously colored cloths, for the participants. In front was a framework of wood, supporting a great number of flaring tallow candles. When we reached the plaza it was crowded with spectators. Many had brought their chairs with them, and were seated in a semi-circle, in front of the stage, but most were standing in groups and engaged in earnest conversation. All the gallants were out, and nearly all carried long naked Toledos under their arms,—a common practice on the occasion of night gatherings. The law, however, forbids pistols, as well as swords or knives under a certain length. It was a famous opportunity for all kinds of intrigue, and I soon began to suspect that there would be more love-making than anything else during the "funcion." But what I saw and heard bearing upon this point, is neither here nor there. Enough for me to say, I got a comfortable seat in the midst of a bevy of the fairest señoritas, and enjoyed the "funcion" as much as the best of them.

In front of the stage was a kind of orchestra, made up of an infinitude of fiddles and cracked clarionets, which discoursed most melancholy music, for half an hour after we came upon the ground. At the end of that time, it was announced that Señor Z., a young man who wrote poetry and wore his hair long, after the manner of bardlings the world over, would recite an appropriate poem. The Señor came forward, bowed low, and after telling us what he proposed to say in plain prose, commenced his poem. It related to Christ, dealt largely in superlatives, and complimented our Saviour much after the manner a love-sick youth might be supposed to address his mistress. The only redeeming point was the manner, and the clear, distinct enunciation with which it was given. It was listened to with attention, and vehemently applauded at its close. While the speaker was in the midst of his heroics, and the entire assemblage silent, I heard a heavy regular tramp, and turning, saw a detachment of troops, marching slowly through the crowd, their arms glancing in the moonlight. They defiled into the shade, close to the wall of the church, and at the word of command, their muskets came down with a startling clang upon the pavement. There they stood, like bronze statues during the whole evening. This incident will illustrate the condition of the country better than an essay.

After the poem, the music struck up again, and we were treated to a lugubrious song by two men and three women, but I could not make out what it was about. Vocal music is certainly at a low ebb in Nicaragua; *nasal* music, however, is flourishing. Fortunately the people make no pretensions to musical accomplishments, and thus criticism is disarmed.

A kind of drama, in two acts, borrowed from the Bible, followed the vocal entertainments, in which a shallow, rattling character or clown was introduced, with other comic accessories. This was by far the best part; the clown was a rare fellow, and acquitted himself well; but the serious part was very serious. The characters talked in a kind of monotonous recitative, like automatons, and without a particle of action. An hour's endurance of this was enough for a Christian, and throwing some silver in the box of a man who went round for the purpose of making a collection for the benefit of the church, I left, in company with the señoritas, who inquired if similar "funcions" were common in the United States? I told them yes, but that our padres consigned all those who frequented them to the demonio, whereupon the señoritas opened their big, black eyes, and ejaculated "Mira!" do tell!

But all these "funcions" paled before an exhibition by "Una Compañia Española de Funámbulos," under the direction of Sr. D. Pedro Serrate, which came to Leon shortly after our arrival. It made a great sensation amongst the people, whose curiosity was raised to the highest degree by flaming handbills, reciting the wonderful feats to be performed by "la hermosissima Jovena Catalina," "by the the most beautiful young Kitty," and the equally astonishing extravagances of the "eccentric clown Simon," all of which "the enlightened and *dignified* public of Leon" (thus ran the invitation) were solicited to felicitate themselves by witnessing,—admittance two rials, niños (little ones) one rial, and niñitas (*very* little ones) a medio only. The following Sunday, at three o'clock, was the time fixed for the performance. We were all specially invited to attend by Señor Serrate in person, and of course accpted the invitation. Meantime the excitement became universal; it was as good as a revolution, and not half as dangerous. As the time approached, men marched through the streets, beating the rappel at the corners, which was the signal for gathering. The next thing to be seen was a swarm of servants, carrying chairs for their masters and mistresses; and then came the masters and mistresses themselves, in gala dress. I had not yet seen such an exhibition of satin slippers! We fell into the movement, and duly brought up at the house where the "Funambulos" or rope-dancers, had established themselves. It belonged to one of the most respectable citizens of Leon, who had patriotically permitted it to be used for this interesting occasion. Soldiers were stationed at the door to keep out the rabble, which blockaded the street, and devised all sorts of ingenious methods to get a glimpse of the mysteries within. Here the wife of Señor Serrate received the rials with a courtesy and "mil gracias" for each. The building had a large square court, shaded by high trees, and surrounded by a broad corridor, raised a foot or two above the ground. Upon one side of the courtyard was erected a temporary, carpeted stage, which extended out into the area. Behind this was a gaudily painted curtain, concealing the penetralia within which the performers were to retire after their respective efforts. Altogether it was not a bad substitute for a theatre. The corridor corresponded to the dress circle, the courtyard to the pit, and the roof to the gallery. But I am at a loss where to class the occupants of the trees! The place was already crowded when we arrived; the Chief of the State, the General, in fact all the principal inhabitants, comprising the "beauty and fashion of Leon, and full two-thirds of all the padres, were present. All seemed at their ease, and, including the the ladies, smoked cigaritos. A seat was cleared for me by the side of the General, and the rest of our party took up their positions near by. The orchestra played with terrible energy, and some hens, perched amongst a lot of boys, in the trees, frightened at this unusual scene, cackled with equal vigor. The ground within the court was covered with muchachos, and nurses with children, who were wrought up to an alarming state of impatience, and only kept within the bounds of propriety by the canes of the vigilant alcaldes.

After an interval, a messenger approached the Director, and inquired if it was his pleasure the performance should begin; to which an affirmative response was given. The manager of the "Funambulos" then came forward and announced the "hermosissima Jovena Catalina," who would exhibit her dexterity on the tight rope. The next moment the Jovena advanced, and was, as the newspapers say, "rapturously received." She was dressed quite after the fashion of similar performers at home, in skirts equally brief, and seemed to me quite as dexterous. But she had monstrous ankles, and a foot none of the smallest, and was unmercifully criticised, particularly by the female spectators. "Mira!" exclaimed a belle by my side, who lifted her tiny hands in astonishment, "*Valgame Dios! es una pateza Inglesa!*" "See! Good Heavens! it is an English paw!" I glanced cautiously down at the little slippered feet at my side--they were really very small. My fair friend saw the movement, but nothing abashed, thrust them out the further, and rogueishly inquired, "How do you like them?" I professed to be looking for a fallen cigarito, but the dodge wouldn't answer. The Jovena, in a country where hardly any one who has his peculiarity escapes a nick-name, went afterwards by the unpoetical designation of "Tobillos gruesos"—"Big ankles!"

The Jovena had a sister, who was beautiful, and while she remained in the city, the reigning toast of the young officers and of the gallants generally. She however did not possess the skill of "Tobillos gruesos," but danced passably, and was very well in pantomime. The "eccentric clown, Simon," seemed to be the most popular feature of the exhibition; and although he was not always over-delicate, seldom failed to "bring down the house" by his hits. I was not long in discovering that the entire people had a keen appreciation of drollery, and what would perhaps be called "serious joking;" and have often witnessed impromptu scenes amongst the *mozos* by the roadside, or in the little villages, which were irresistibly comic, and saving time and place, might have been the originals from which Cervantes drew his immortal pictures.

After the performances on the rope, we had tumbling, in which two smart little boys, sons of the "director" of the Funambules, the clown, and a *woman* took part. But the Leonesas were shocked that one of the "bello sexo" should descend to that, and expressed their disapprobation in such a manner, that she never made her appearance again in the character of a "volteadora." Then came a pantomime, in which a fussy, gouty Englishman, travelling in Spain, and ignorant of the language, was the principal character. His mishaps created great merriment, and the raggedest boy in the *patio* seemed glad to have an opportunity of laughing at John Bull; who, as I have before said, is nowhere in the world more cordially hated than in Nicaragua.

It was quite sundown when Señor Serrate came forward and thanked his auditors for the honor of their attendance; and then the Jovena Catalina invited them all, in the choicest Castilian, to come again on the Sunday following. The "Funambulos," I may add, had a brilliant and profitable season of a month; and when they left, received a testimonial from the citizens, who "thought it worthy of remark, that in this exhibition the public had not, as on other occasions, been driven to the hard necessity of listening to indecent dialogues, to the prejudice of morals and good taste, or of abstaining from visiting the exhibition." The "Correo del

STREET VIEW IN LEON—CALLE DE SAN JUAN

Istmo" also complimented them as having "performed with skill and excellence," and with these recommendations they departed on a tour of the State.

I have said, at the commencement of this chapter, that there were no stated amusements in Leon; perhaps, however, the various fiestas and saints' days should come under that denomination. At any rate they were celebrated in anything but a serious manner; they were general holidays, in which everybody dressed in his best, and the more bombas fired and bells rung, the more "alegre" the occasion, and the greater the honor to the saints. As a consequence, being situated in the vicinity of the principal churches, we were treated to a "Fourth of July" as often as twice a week. Sometimes lines of bombas were arranged, not only around the churches, but on their roofs, and over their towers, with large ones at intervals, which, when they exploded, made a noise like a cannon. These were set off almost invariably in the daytime, and produced a deafening sound, like the rolling discharge of musketry under a cannonade, for nearly half an hour, creating a dense smoke, and filling the air with sulphurous odors. The bells were rung the while, and everybody seemed delighted, and none more so than the muchachos, who, like the *gamins de Paris*, swarmed everywhere, and were the foremost in all public demonstrations.

The fiesta of St. Andrew was celebrated with some novel features, and particularly commended itself to the muchachos. It was signalized by "un baile de los demonios," a dance of the devils. The devils were dressed in the most fantastic manner, wore masks, and sported barbed tails. One shrouded in black displayed a grinning death's head beneath his half-parted veil, and kept time to the music with a pair of veritable thigh bones. The dance, I should think, had been borrowed from the Indians; the music certainly was. It was almost unearthly, such as Cortez describes on the night of his retreat from Mexico, "which carried terror to the very souls of the Christians." It is impossible to describe the strange instruments. One consisted of a large calabash, over which was stretched the skin of some animal; this, when pressed in, recoiled with a dull, sullen noise, like the suppressed bellow of a wild beast, and the wail of some of the long reeds was like that of a man in the agonies of a violent death. The devils went whisking through the principal streets, followed by a gaping crowd, and entered all the principal houses, where, after a dance in the courtyard, they expected either to receive a rial or two, or to be treated to a dram of agua ardiente. They favored me with an extra display of their demoniacal abilities,—but were high-spirited devils, and declined to receive money from a stranger.

Another class of dancers, dressed in a profusion of tinsel, but not aspiring to the distinction of devils, parade the streets on certain saints' days, visiting all the houses where the heads of the family bear the name of the saint, where they expect a gratuity or a treat, in return for an exhibition of their skill. As I soon lost all track of the saints, I do not remember which were supposed to be propitious to this kind of diversion.

All-Saints' day was distinguished by a grand procession of all the saints, not excepting the little ebony San Benito, who, after airing themselves through the principal streets, visited the various churches in succession, including the Cathedral of Subtiaba, where there were some very curious and complicated ceremonies. The afternoon of this day was celebrated as a kind of carnival amongst the Indians of that municipality. It is their prerogative, on that occasion, to pelt all visitors with oranges, and to form rings of dancers around them, from which exit can only be procured by the payment of a certain sum to the church. Almost every one in the city went down, including the officers of State, whose position gave them no immunity,—on the contrary, they got more than their just share of the pelting. But as the visitors are usually mounted, a rapid retreat is always made, when the storm of the golden missiles grows too severe. I made it a point of duty to see everything, and accordingly rode to Subtiaba just before sunset, where the first object I saw was a venerable Doctor of Medicine, bareheaded, spurring at full speed, and dodging from side to side under a shower of oranges discharged upon him from an ambuscade. For it is considered a capital joke with the muchachos, to lie in wait under a ruin, or amongst the bushes, and let off a volley upon the unsuspecting horseman. When I entered the plaza it was occupied by groups of people, moving from side to side, shouting and laughing, in a furor of excitement and frolic, while the air was full of missiles. A few were discharged at me, but as soon as I was recognized, I was exempted from the usual ordeal. Suddenly I saw a movement in the direction of the cabildo, and the next moment was saluted with "Vivan los Estados Unidos!" "Vivan los amigos de Nicaragua!" These were given with the greatest enthusiasm.[1]

Posts were planted around the plaza, to which a double line of bombas was attached. These were to be let off (for a wonder) after dark, and my friend Simon Roque was urgent that I should stay to witness the explosion, and even offered to anticipate the hour fixed for lighting them; but I had had enough of bombas for a lifetime, and rode home in the twilight. The streets were full of life, and the band stationed upon the steps of the grand Cathedral played

[1] On the day set apart for the festival of All Saints, the shops are closed and business suspended. About ten o'clock the procession commences from the Cathedral. A troop of military, marching to a slow tune, lead the way, and are followed by six of the finest Indian girls that can be procured, bearing large wax candles, and dressed in the ancient costumes of their tribes, accompanied by the great drum, carried on the back of an Indian, and beaten by two others. These are succeeded by men bearing on their shoulders wooden platforms, on which are placed images of saints. Other representations of beatified cardinals and bishops follow, escorted by angels with spreading wings. Then succeeds an immense statue of St. Peter, bearing the keys, and supported by angels on each side. Other images pass forward in succession, and immediately precede the Host, which is carried under a splendid canopy, and accompanied by the archbishop and the dignified clergy. The various orders of friars, the priests, and the collegiate students, in their robes, follow; and fresh images of saints and angels, with a new troop of military, bring up the rear. . . The setting out and return to the Cathedral are notified by frequent discharges of sky-rockets."—*Dunn's Guatemala*, p. 114.

the national anthem, while the soldiers grouped around the various "cuartels" joined in the chorus. For once, thanks to the darkness, I escaped the eternal presentation of arms and beat of drum, with which I was always received in the plaza, and which induced me to avoid entering it, except in cases of necessity. I sat on my horse for a quarter of an hour, listening to the music and the merriment, and speculated whether, after all, spite of unstable governments, and destitute of all those accessories which, according to our utilitarian ideas, are necessary to the popular welfare,—whether the people of Leon were not on the whole happier and more contented than those of any city of equal size in our own country? Here were no crowded workshops, where youth and age toil on, on, during the long day and by the pale gas light, amidst foul vapors, or in a corrupted atmosphere, that trade may thrive, and arrogant commerce strut in the Exchange! No thundering machines to disturb the calm of evening, to drown the murmurs of the night winds and the gentle melody of the falling dews, with their hoarse, unearthly clangor!

NICARAGUAN PLOUGH.

CHAPTER XIII.

A SORTIE FROM LEON—QUESALGUAQUE—EL ESTERO DE DONA PAULA—THE "MONTE DE SAN JUAN"—SUMMARY WAY OF DISPOSING OF "LADRONES"—"EL TIGRE," JAGUAR, OR OUNCE; ITS HABITS; HOW HUNTED—THE "LEON," OR PUMA—THE "COYOTE".—POSULTEGA—A SPECIMEN PADRE—SOBRINAS—CHICHIGALPA—POISED THUNDER-STORM—THE ORACION—HACIENDA OF SAN ANTONIO—CHINANDEGA—A CHALLENGE—EL VIEJO—FAMILIAR FIXTURES—AN ENTERPRISING CITIZEN AND HIS TRAGIC FATE—A DECAYING TOWN—MULES *vs.* HORSES—VISIT TO THE HACIENDAS—AN INDIGO ESTATE, AND A MAYOR-DOMO—FINE VIEW—THE SUGAR ESTATE OF SAN GERONIMO—BACHELOR QUARTERS AND HACIENDA LIFE—A FRUIT GARDEN—THE BREAD FRUIT—SUGAR-MILLS, AND THE MANUFACTURE OF AGUARDIENTE—A SINFUL SIESTA—VISIT FROM THE MUNICIPALITY—"UNA CANCION"—CHINANDEGA BY DAYLIGHT—REALEJO—PORT AND HARBOR—THE PROGRESS OF ENTERPRISE—THE PROJECTED NEW TOWN OF CORINTH—RETURN TO LEON.

EARLY after our arrival in Leon, amongst many others of like character, we had received an invitation from the wealthy and influential family of Venerio, to spend a week at their establishment in Viejo Chinandega; which, as it was coupled with a promise to give us an initiation into the mysteries of hacienda life, we had at once accepted. Up to this time, however (Sept. 3, 1849), I had been unable to leave the capital. But now my official negotiations were happily terminated, and pending the action of the Legislative Chambers, which were called to meet on the 22d of the same month, I had an opportunity of seeing something more of the magnificent plain, in the centre of which we were residing.

I have already said that, for obvious reasons, most of the travelling in Central America is done in the morning or evening. It was four o'clock in the afternoon, therefore, when we started for El Viejo, twelve leagues, or thirty-six miles distant. This, with us, would be considered quite a day's journey in itself, but here it is what is called an evening "paseo," or ride. Our course led through Subtiaba, crossing the stream which flows past that pueblo at a place where art had cut down the steep banks, and nature woven an evergreen roof above—one of those dark, cool nooks in which the water birds love to gather, and where the Indian girls come to bathe—beyond which spread out the luxuriant maize fields, traversed by hedge rows like the lines on a chess board. The road, bordered with trees, to protect the traveller from the sun, wound amongst these fields for five or six miles, when it entered the forest again, and soon came to a deep ravine, with abrupt banks, seventy or eighty feet high, at the bottom of which flows a large clear stream, called, at this point, Quesalguaque. It rises near the volcano of Telica, and for some distance from its source it bears the name of Rio Telica. It flows into the harbor of Realejo, and for a number of leagues from its mouth, is a tide-water stream, and called "El Estero de Doña Paula."

This is the largest stream on the plain of Leon, and is probably that to which some map-makers have given the name of Rio Tosta. The cart-road descends the ravine circuitously, and ascends in like manner; traversing nearly a mile in passing from one bank to the other. The mule-road, however, is direct, but the descent and ascent are both abrupt and difficult. I hardly thought either possible, and was really amazed to find my horse attempt them without so much as the touch of the spur, and quite as a matter of course. Emerging from the ravine, we came to some cleared fields, (one of which was planted with pine-apples, now nearly ripe, and looking wonderfully tempting in the sun), in the midst of which was a small collection of huts, called the Pueblecita de Quesalguaque. We stopped for a moment to fill our pockets with delicious *nisperos* from a tree overhanging the road, its treasures free to all who chose "to come and eat," and then diverging from the camino real, struck into the narrow mule-path which leads through the Monte de San Juan. This portion of the road has a bad reputation throughout the whole country; and during the late troubles had been the scene of several tragic occurrences. The robbers or ladrones who infested it, however, had been hunted by volunteers from Leon and Chinendaga, and shot down like wild beasts; a summary, but most effectual way of preventing further depredations. At one point we passed a number of newly-erected crosses, marking the place where murder had been done. But all was still and peaceful now, and we saw nothing to startle us except a *Tigre*, which leaped across the path a few paces in advance, disappearing instantaneously in the forest.

What is here called the Tigre or Tiger, is the true *Jaguar*, or *Ounce;* and the animal which is called the *Lion* is the maneless Mexican Lion, or Puma. Ounces are abundant throughout the entire country, and often commit serious depredations upon the cattle of the haciendas. They are of a tawny color, the body beautifully variegated with irregular oblong black spots, breast and belly whitish. They grow to the length of four or five feet, are powerfully built, with massive jaws, and possess a strength and activity superior to any of the feline race of equal size. They unhesitatingly attack all animals, of whatever proportions, which are not fully capable of defending themselves; and in riding through the woods I have several times seen full grown heifers, which they had not only killed, but dragged to considerable distances,—in one instance not less than a hundred yards.

The Tigre, however, sometimes meets his match in a sturdy bull or spirited cow, and is compelled to retreat. The vaqueros of the haciendas, who are fluent on the subject of tigers, and often able to show ghastly scars in confirmation of their stories of adventures, relate instances in which the tiger has been killed outright in his encounters with the *toros*. A bull of venerable aspect, but exceedingly mild demeanor, was pointed out to me in Honduras, which was the hero of many battles, successful in all, and in three instances killing his adversary. I quite respected this protector of his herd, and thought he should at least receive the title of the "Great Defender." The herdsmen concur in saying that the tiger is generally too cunning to attack the cattle, except singly, when separated from each other, as they all make common cause against him when he ventures amongst the herd. The ounce seldom attacks man, unless pressed by hunger, or by the hunters. This is a fortunate circumstance; for otherwise travelling in Central America, where, in the secluded parts of the country, hardly a day passes without seeing one or two of them, would be attended with the greatest danger. In some localities, however, the ounce is represented to be more ferocious than in others, and so bold as to slip into the villages in broad daylight, in search of his prey. There are many men distinguished for success in hunting this animal, who arrogate to themselves the title of *tigreros*. They use no arms, except a long and stout spear or lance, and their machetes. Their first object, with the aid of dogs, is to drive the tiger into a tree, or bring him to bay. When this is done, the tigrero wraps his poncho around his left arm, and approaches the fierce and excited animal, with his lance so fixed as to be able to receive him on its point when he shall make his spring. This requires great coolness and firmness, for everything depends upon the hunter planting his spear full in the animal's breast. If this be not done, a terrible fight ensues, from which the strongest and bravest man is fortunate if he escapes with life. The genuine tigrero scorns to use firearms,—"no tiene valor, nada," they are of no use, none! Some of these men number their victories by scores, and are considered invincible.

The *tigre negro*, or black ounce, is erroneously regarded by the natives as a distinct species; and, perhaps from his more forbidding appearance, is supposed to be stronger and fiercer. They are undoubtedly a little larger in size than the other variety. In Nicaragua they are rarely seen, but are quite abundant, it is said, in the mountainous districts of Honduras.

The Lion, or Puma, notwithstanding his name, has fewer of the traditional magnanimous traits of the lion proper than the tigre. He is altogether a sneaking fellow, and attacks cattle only when he finds them wounded, entangled in thickets, or embarrassed in swamps, where he has everything to his own advantage. He flies from man, but will prowl stealthily after him in the evening, like the wolf. He is consequently approached with difficulty, and rarely killed. His color is a pale, brownish red, inclining to black on the back, but light under the belly. In shape he is slenderer than the ounce, his legs and tail longer, and his claws and head slighter. "A full grown tiger," said an old hunter to me, "is a match for half a dozen of the cowards." The weary traveller, sleeping in the forest, has more to dread from the puma than any other wild animal. Besides the ounce and the puma, there are several varieties of tiger, or mountain cats, which commit depredations on the fowls and smaller domestic animals of the ranchos, but from whom man has nothing to fear.

The "coyote," wild dog, or as he is sometimes called, wolf, is common in some parts of Central America. I never saw any of them, but they are said to differ as widely from the true wolf as from the common dog. Some have conjectured that they are descended from the bloodhounds which were used by the early Spaniards in hunting down the natives. But all attempts to reclaim them, although carried on during two or three generations, have failed. Like wolves, they generally hunt in packs, making no noise beyond a low howl, and follow their prey with a perseverance which is almost always successful in the end. It is said that, although individually arrant cowards, they will collectively attack the tiger himself, drive him into a tree, and besiege him for many days, until exhausted, in attempting to escape, he falls a victim to the number of his assailants. The natives have a singular notion, however, that the coyotes never beleaguer the tigre unless he has committed some outrage on the fraternity, robbed them of their prey, or made a meal of some straggler.

To return from this digression. Two leagues beyond Quesalguaque, the intervening country level and magnificently wooded, and the road broad and smooth, is the Pueblo of Posultega, an unpretending town of some five or six hundred inhabitants, and distinguished for nothing except an ancient church, more remarkable for its dilapidation than its architecture. The cura, who had called on me in Leon a few days before, was swinging in his hammock, between a couple of orange trees in front of his house; he leaped up as we approached, stopped me in the open street, and gave me an embrace "as was an embrace," and from my elevated position on my horse, quite too near the belt to be comfortable. He insisted on our stopping for the rest of the afternoon and for the night at his poor house, (every house in Central America is called "*mi pobre casa*" by its owner), which I declined doing with a prodigious affectation of regret, that became real a moment after, when I discovered the padre's *sobrina* or niece, a fair, full-breasted girl, peeping slyly out between the bars of the window. Of course it is not reputable for padres to have females in their establishments, except near relatives,—aunts for housekeepers, and nieces for——companions! The aunts, I observed, were always old, but the nieces almost invariably young and pretty, as nieces are bound to be.

The country, from Posultega to Chichigalpa, a considerable town, two leagues further on, preserves its flat surface, the monotony but slightly relieved by the occasional narrow and shallow channels which carry off the superabundant water of the rainy season. Chichigalpa, formerly a very large Indian town, still numbers from three to five thousand inhabitants; it is regularly laid out, and has a neat and attractive appearance. It was just sunset when we entered its streets. A heavy thunder-storm was piling up its black volumes behind the volcanoes in the east, and the calm and silence which precede the tempest rested upon the plain; the winds were still, and the leaves hung motionless on the trees. The adult inhabitants seemed to sympathize with the scene, and sat silently in the open doorways; but the children were as playful and noisy as ever, their voices rendered doubly distinct, and almost unnatural in the pervading quiet. Suddenly the bell of the oracion struck; the careless voices of the children were instantaneously hushed, and we mechanically stopped our horses, and uncovered our heads. A low murmur of prayer floated forth on the undulating waves of sound which seemed to subside in circles around us;—again the bell struck, again, and then, when the pulses had almost ceased to beat, that the straining ear might catch the expiring vibrations, rolled in the muffled sound of the distant thunder. It came down from the mountains with the majesty of an ocean poured along their trembling sides!

The oracion, which never fails to impress the most careless traveller with a feeling of reverential awe, was but one element in this grand combination of the solemn and the sublime.

We rode through Chichigalpa without stopping, and pressed rapidly forward, with the design of reaching the estate of San Antonio, belonging to the family of my companion, before the storm should overtake us. Darkness, however, closed speedily around our path, and in ten minutes we were unable to discover our position, except as it was revealed to us by the lightning, which occasionally poured in lurid, blinding sheets, from the summits of the volcanoes, where the storm seemed to pause as if to concentrate its gloomy squadrons, before moving down upon the silent plain, and forth upon the dark Pacific. Fortunately the road was wide, and permitted us to ride rapidly, without any great danger from the projecting branches. We reached San Antonio, eight miles from Chichigalpa, in an hour.

The resident on the estate was an uncle of my companion, an amiable and gentlemanly person, who apologized for not coming to the door to receive us. His apology was a valid one. He had led the hunt after the ladrones who had infested the road to Leon, and had received a ball in his hip, in the final encounter with them. We were at once offered a cup of chocolate, which we accepted, in deference not less to our own tastes than to a sensible practice of the country, which is always to take whatever is tendered to you. Thus a caballero is offered a cigar; he at once accepts it with a bow, or "mil gracias," a thousand thanks, and if he does not care to smoke, puts it in his pocket. This will occur during the same sitting as often as the cigars are passed. With chocolate the case is a little different; it is not easily put in one's pocket, and is therefore otherwise disposed of. The house at San Antonio, I observed as soon as I entered it, was superior to any of the hacienda residences which had yet fallen under my notice. It was not only well constructed, but conveniently arranged, and painted in the interior. It had been built by a Mr. Bridge, an Englishman, who had established here one of the finest sugar plantations in the country. In common with most of the English residents, he had married a woman of the country, and what with trade, his hacienda, and an English vessel-of-war, always conveniently at hand to enforce any claim which he and his English brethren might find it profitable to set up against the government, had contrived to amass a considerable fortune.

Upon his death, however, the estate had been sold to its present proprietors, and although it had fallen somewhat out of repair, it still showed what might be accomplished in this favored land, with a very moderate share of enterprise and industry.

The wind had sprung up, and carried the impending storm off to the southward; so, after waiting half an hour at San Antonio, we again mounted and pursued our course. By the dim, reviving light, I could make out that we were now in an open and highly cultivated country, sprinkled over with houses. Half an hour more brought us to the suburbs of Chinandega, probably the most flourishing town in the State, and the only one, I believe, which has increased in population since the independence. The commerce of Realejo is conducted through it; here nearly all the merchants reside; and the inhabitants, some fifteen or sixteen thousand in number, are conceded to be the most industrious and thriving of any in the Republic.

It was too dark to distinguish anything beyond long, broad avenues, bordered with gardens, each one having a hut in the centre. The streets really seemed endless, and we passed square on square, for full a mile and a half, before we reached the paved streets surrounding the plazas, where the adobe and tile-roofed houses are built, and where the wealth and trade is concentrated. The people were still sitting at their doors and windows, in luxurious enjoyment of the cool breeze which the passing storm had evoked somewhere beyond the mountains. We would have ridden directly through the plaza, but were stopped by the sudden ring of a musket on the pavement, and a fierce order to halt and give the countersign. We did so, and then supposed we might go on. But the sentinel demanded that we should advance singly, and called to the officer of the guard. Finding that we should probably be detained for an indefinite period, I whispered to my companion to fall back, and avoid the plaza by making a circuit around it. He did so, muttering something about the stupid military, which might have cost him dear had it been overheard. A long detour brought us to the other side of the town, which is bounded by a considerable stream, flowing through a deep hollow. The path to the water was broad, and artificially graded, so, notwithstanding the darkness, we passed without difficulty. We were now in the plain road to El Viejo, and a brisk ride through the intermediate fields and the silent suburbs, brought us to a large house, fronting on the plaza. We stopped before a high and imposing portal, the massive gates of which parted in answer to the well known voice of my companion. In another instant we were beneath the trees in the courtyard, in the full blaze of hospitable lights, streaming through the open doors of the grand sala, where our friends were awaiting our arrival.

Upon entering the house, I was surprised to find myself surrounded by nearly all the well-known furniture of a parlor in New York. Here were sofas and rocking-chairs, and mirrors and clocks, of familiar fashion, holding something more than their own against hammocks and hide-bottomed *sillas*. A portrait of Washington and a fac-simile of the Declaration of Independence were suspended against the walls, and a bust of Shakspeare filled a vacant place on a little shelf in a distant corner. A clear blue eye, a rosy cheek, and the pleasant sound of our native tongue were alone needed to complete an illusion, in which the full form, the classic profile, pale complexion, large and liquid eyes, the stately grace, and low but cordial welcome of the mistress of the mansion, did not permit me to indulge.

I have said that the family whose hospitable courtesies I was now enjoying, was one of the wealthiest, and socially one of the most influential in the country. Yet its history for the past fifteen or twenty years is unfortunately too truthful an illustration of what the condition of the country has been during that disastrous period. Don Gregorio Venerio, the late head of the family, was one of the few men which Central America has afforded, possessing enterprise, a liberal and enlightened spirit, and that sound philosophy which consists in a practical disposition to make the best of existing circumstances. Overcoming most of the narrow prejudices which had grown up under the rigorous colonial system of Spain, and which fettered the mass of the people for a long time after the independence, he introduced improvements in agriculture, new machinery in the manufacture of sugar, and the preparation of cotton and indigo for foreign markets, and with a true patriotism and public spirit sought to direct the general attention to useful occupations and the development of the natural resources of the country, as the best means of insuring civil order and stability in government. His labors were, for a time, eminently successful, and he gave an impulse to industry and trade in the section of the state in which he resided, which has since doubled its wealth and influence. But envious and evil disposed persons were not wanting to misrepresent his motives, and to awaken distrust of the objects which he aimed to accomplish. The hostility of the ignorant masses was excited against him and his family; his machinery, it was said, would depreciate wages, and his products destroy the market for the productions of smaller proprietors. The ultimate result may be anticipated. The robber chieftain, Somoza, whose violent end I have already recounted, at the head of a band of assassins and robbers, entered his house at night, dragged him from his bed, and butchered him in cold blood, in the presence of his entire family, in the very room where I was now seated. Yet, up to the time of my arrival, the murderer had escaped apprehension and defied justice.

El Viejo Chinandega, Old Chinandega, or as it is briefly called El Viejo, is one of the most ancient towns in Nicaragua. It is beautifully situated upon a stream which flows through its centre, and contains between five and six thousand inhabitants. Formerly it was the principal town, next to Leon, in this department, and was the seat of the trade carried on through the port of Realejo. But the new town is located more favorably for commerce, and as that has increased in importance, El Viejo has declined. During the supremacy of the bucaneers in the South Sea, El Viejo was several times attacked, and once or twice burned. It has a large church, of high antiquity, situated upon an artificial terrace in the midst of a plaza. A fantastic wall runs along the edge of the terrace, and above each flight of steps, by which it is ascended, are lofty arches of fine proportions, which lend a very singular effect to the whole structure. Architecturally, El Viejo affords no other object of interest.

After breakfast, on the morning following our arrival, we started on a visit to the haciendas, or plantations, belonging to the family. I had a strong prejudice against mules, but my host quietly insisted that I should ride his *macho*, a sleek-looking, clean-limbed animal, upon which my saddle had already been placed. I complied without, at the moment, fully comprehending the reason of the request. But no sooner had we struck into the main road, than I found that, in respect of speed and of ease to the rider, no horse was comparable to the splendid animal upon which I was mounted. Without an apparent effort, and quite as a matter of course, he distanced all the horses of the party, and at what appeared to be his ordinary pace, kept them at a sharp gallop. "That macho," said my host, "cost me three hundred dollars; and I have ridden him sixty miles in six consecutive hours!" When I add that ordinary mules here cost only about twenty dollars, and that this one was valued at three hundred and fifty, the difference between them is brought to some standard of calculation. The pace is artificial; and when what is called "a good education" is joined to good proportions, soundness of limb, and high spirit, (for they differ widely in this respect,) mules are esteemed infinitely higher than horses. Their endurance is incredible, and they have the ability to take care of themselves where a horse would starve.

At the distance of a league from the town, we turned into a beautiful shaded lane, or avenue, running through the broad estates which we had come to visit. The fields, with the exception of one or two which were planted with maize, were overgrown with weeds. I inquired the cause, and was told that these were indigo grounds, the cultivation of which had been suspended from the impossibility of securing permanent laborers; for the processes in manufacturing the indigo are so delicate, that any deficiency in attention ruins the entire crop. When affairs became fully settled, it was intended to resume the cultivation of this valuable product; but until then, the ground, dams, vats, and machinery were valueless property. In the centre of this portion of the estate, on an eminence near an artificial pond covered with water plants, and constructed for supplying the indigo works, was the house of the superintendent,—a large two-story edifice, with a double corridor on every side, and surrounded by a little forest of magnificent trees, relieved by towering palms and the green columns of the cactus. The mayordomo, a venerable old man with his head bound in a variegated handkerchief, white shirt and breeches, and red shoes, himself one of the fixtures of the estate, received each of us with a hearty embrace, and then led us up a flight of broad stone steps, to the upper corridor. Here were the old man's daughters, three pretty, blushing girls, who were introduced individually as Paula, Manuelita, and Concepcion. "Their mother is a saint," said he, as he gazed on them with an expression of pride; "but happier times are coming for our poor country, and they will live to see them, I am sure!" and he tottered off, to procure "alguna fresca."

From the corridor we enjoyed a magnificent view of field

and forest, stretching away in billows of verdure to the base of the volcano of El Viejo, lifting its purple summit to mid-heaven, beyond and over all. I ventured to imagine the intervening plain in the hands of an enterprising and vigorous people, dotted over with villages, and loaded down with the richest products of all-bountiful Nature, and queried if this generation might not witness the change. Let the babbler about impossibilities, in this first decade of the last half of the nineteenth century, turn his eyes to the shores of the Bay of San Francisco, be silent, and mark the reality!

From the indigo estate, bearing the name of some favorite saint, which I have forgotten, we rode a mile or two further, to the sugar plantation of San Geronimo. The ground which it occupies is perfectly level, and by means of ditches, designed particularly for purposes of irrigation, is laid out in squares, or manzanas. The cane on some of these squares had been newly planted, and on others lately cut, while upon others it was now in perfection, and ready for use. The mills are here kept running steadily the year round, and by the time the cutters have gone through all the fields, those which were first cleared are ready for the knife a second time. Under favorable circumstances, three crops can be taken yearly; and the ground does not require to be re-planted oftener than once in ten or fourteen years.

A two-story house, newer and better built than that which I have already described, stood upon one side of the cane-fields, on the banks of a stream, and in the vicinity of the mills. It was approached by a broad avenue, kept scrupulously clean, and its white walls and red roof stood out against a dense background of trees, now in the perfection of their foliage, and loaded with fruit. The lower story was occupied by the mayor-domo and his family, and the upper by a bachelor brother of our host, whom we found in his shirt sleeves, swinging in a hammock suspended in the corridor on the shaded side of the building, and engaged in reading a translation of Sue's Mysteries of Paris! He rose hastily, uttered some indistinct apologies, and led us into the body of the building, where in an instant we were surrounded by a playful troop of blooded dogs, which our friend, who was a good deal of a Nimrod, had expressly imported from England and the United States. In one corner of the room stood an elegant rifle, with a brace of pistols, a sword, and a variety of bits and spurs grouped around it. In another corner was a guitar and a saddle, and on the table, in that delightful confusion seen only in bachelor establishments, a flute, some music, and books, and an infinity of cigars. An engraved portrait of Lola Montez was the only decoration on the walls, unless the skin of a monstrous tigre, stretched at one end of the apartment, might be called a decoration.

From the corridor, the eye traversed broad fields of cane, framed in by a dense forest, the view opening only towards the east, where the perspective of fields terminated, in the distance, with the tiled roof of the house belonging to the indigo estate, but half seen amidst the surrounding trees. A creaking cart came up the broad avenue towards us, loaded with stalks of the *caña*, which were piled in heaps in front of the mills situated in the valley of the stream, and partially concealed by the vapors rising lazily from the boiling kettles in which the juice was evaporated. The mozos engaged in the various processes moved about with a slow and careless air, in perfect harmony with the general quiet of the scenery, and in unison with the monotonous clatter of the mill, which seemed to be half asleep, and just about to stop altogether. I sat down in a vacant hammock, and for the first time fully comprehended the charms of hacienda life,—that aimless, dreamy existence, undisturbed by ambition or envy, and separated from the struggle of conflicting interests. Our bachelor friend vegetated here month after month, without a wish ungratified, making the most of the present, and careless of the future. Occasionally, he said, his slumbering energies would be roused for a moment, but lacking legitimate objects to occupy them, soon subsided again, and the stream of life flowed on as before. A turn with his dogs in the morning, a stroll of supervision through the mills, chocolate, a book, the hammock, and the siesta,—these, with now and then a ride to the village, or on extraordinary occasions a rapid descent of a single day on Leon, made up the sum of life.

Connected with this estate was a "huerta de las fruitas," a fruit garden, upon which the late Don Gregorio had expended a great deal of money and care. It covered several acres of ground,—a wilderness of oranges and lemons, white and yellow pine apples, melons, mamays, marañons, jocotes, limes, citrons, guavas, tamarinds,—in short all the innumerable varieties of tropical fruits and flowers, traversed by broad walks, here a vista terminating in a bower, and there ending with a glimpse of the deep pools of the neighboring stream; the whole surrounded by an evergreen hedge of cactuses, in full bloom, and loading the air with fragrance. Here was the odorous sweet lemon, and in the centre of the garden a group of bread-fruit trees, remarkable for their broad, deep green leaves, amongst which might be discerned the nuts, looking for all the world like the heads of young darkies. These trees had been introduced by Don Gregorio from the Sandwich Islands, and flourished quite as luxuriantly as in their native soil. But the fruit did not "take" with the Nicaraguenses, who preferred the tortilla and the plantain; the tree is therefore propagated solely from motives of curiosity.

From the garden we went to the mills. The machinery in use had all been imported from England and the United States, via Cape Horn. There was first the crushing or grinding mill, from which a copper conductor carried the juice through a strainer into a vat, communicating by means of tubes with the coppers or cauldrons. From these, when the reduction and clarification were sufficiently far advanced, the liquid was drawn off into other coppers, whence the scum was constantly removed, and thrown into a large trough, to be used in the distillation of *aguardiente.* When reduced to a certain strength or thickness, the sugar was transferred to the coolers and strainers, where the graining took place, and the molasses was separated. A large portion of the sugar is not subjected to this process, but while in its crude state, is laded into moulds of a certain size, forming what is called *chancaca*, sold for ordinary consumption amongst the poorer classes, at a *quartillo* (three cents) the cake, equivalent to about one cent and a half the pound. The finer qualities of sugar produced on this estate are nearly as white and hard as the refined sugars of commerce. Connected with these works is a complete apparatus for distilling *aguardiente*, capable of an indefinite production of that article of consumption. But this is a government *estanco*, or monopoly, and it cannot be manufactured on private account. The fact that the late Don Gregorio had obtained the contract for supplying the government, was one of the causes of hostility to him amongst the smaller proprietors, whose rude but costly modes of distillation were entirely supplanted by the introduction of his improved machinery. This hostility had not yet died out, and the family meditated throwing up the contract, and discontinuing the manufacture altogether, as the easiest mode of relieving themselves from the popular odium which it excited. We can hardly understand how such prejudices should exist, but it is nevertheless a fact that, at the first, every improvement in the useful arts, all social progress, and every advance in government, philosophy, and religion, have the world over been met and opposed in precisely the same spirit, and from precisely the same motives.

Upon our return to the house, we found a table spread with the rarest collection of tropical fruits and luxuries which I had yet seen, and which might have excited the envy of a king. We had "frescas" compounded from the marañon, the orange, and the juice of the cocoanut, slightly dashed with aguardiente, the coolest and most refreshing imaginable; and melons—such melons! And when we came to lie down in our respective hammocks, beneath the shaded corridor, for the afternoon siesta, it was unanimously voted that, with our present limited information on the subject of Paradise, we should be quite willing to accept perpetual youth and hacienda life "*down*," rather than incur the risk of attaining the former! "Opinions may differ about the propriety of confessing it," said W., "but really," and he took a long and lazy pull at his cigar, "I think this is quite good enough for a miserable sinner like myself!"

The smoke wreathed slowly up from each hammock, the mill clattered drowsily, and we slept until the cool evening wind, gathering strength as the sun declined, began to rustle amongst the orange trees which grew beside the corridor, and the creaking carts, which had stood idle during the heat of the day, again began to move in the direction of the cane fields. A hacienda dinner, and a cheery ride townward, in the twilight, completed the day; and we went to bed that night, with a most satisfactory conception of hacienda life.

I had flattered myself that my visit to El Viejo was unknown beyond the family with which we were stopping; I had, in fact, stipulated with our host, that our incognito should be rigidly preserved. He was, therefore, a good deal embarrassed, and I was not a little annoyed, when he announced the next morning at breakfast, that the municipality of the town had been there, before I was up, to say that they should do themselves the honor to pay their respects to "El Ministro" in form, at the early hour of ten o'clock. There was now no alternative but to submit to the arrangement, and make the best of what we would gladly have prevented. Punctual to the moment, when the clock struck the appointed hour, a band of musicos, preceded by half a dozen fellows firing bombas, emerged from the cabildo, on the opposite side of the square, in the direction of our house. They were followed by the municipal and spiritual fathers of the town, the former with their red sashes and gold-headed canes, and the latter in their black robes and broad-brimmed hats, after whom came a mingled mass of men, women, and children. The musicos played with an energy befitting the occasion, and the men with the bombas managed to keep up an incessant discharge. The musicos, the municipality, and the priests, with a very select few of the prominent citizens, alone entered the sala. The populace had to content themselves with gazing in turns through the open windows and doors. Amongst the ecclesiastics was the Dean REMIJO SALAZAR, one of the most imposing men in appearance, and most accomplished in manner and in education, of any in the country, and withal an orator and a philanthropist, and the venerable Padre JOSE MARIA GUERRERO, distinguished throughout the State for his exemplary piety, and noted as a musician and a composer of music. I experienced a real satisfaction in taking these men by the hand, and my subsequent acquaintance with them only served to deepen my respect and esteem. After the exchange of salutations, and a very neat welcome from the first alcalde, we were told that the musicos were prepared with a "Cancion," composed expressly for this occasion, which they begged permission to sing. The permission, accompanied with a glass of ardiente by way of clearing their respective whistles, was graciously accorded. It was but seven stanzas in length, but each stanza was seven times repeated, with a constantly increasing nasal intonation, until the sweat rolled down the faces of singers and players,—for each musico both sang and played. The infliction was severe, and would have been unendurable, had it not been for the amusing contortions of features, and strong muscular exercises of the performers, which far surpassed the most extravagant pantomime ever brought on the stage. A copy of the "Cancion" was handed to me at the conclusion of the performance, of which the title and a couple of stanzas will suffice to satisfy any curiosity which the reader may entertain in respect to it. I could not learn who was the author; for, with the modesty of true genius, he carefully concealed his name.

"CANCION.

"CON QUE LA MUNICIPALIDAD DE LA VILLA DEL VIEJO, EN UNION DE LOS SENORES PRESBITERIOS DON REMIJIO SALAZAR, DEAN DE LA SANTA YGLECIA CATHEDRAL, Y DR. DON JOSE MARIA GUERRERO, Y LICENCIADO D. EVARISTO ROCHA, FELICITARON AL SENOR MINISTRO PLENOPOTENCARIO DE LOS ESTADOS UNIDOS DEL NORTE, EN SU LEGADA A ESTA VILLA, EL 5 A SETIEMBRE, DE 1849.

"Digno hijo de Washington,
Seais bien venido,
Illustre bien hechor
De nuestro Istmo,
No hay recompensa
Que eguale al beneficio,
De Vuestra Empresa!

"Fue la America libre,
Hoy in su Centro,
Con Vos. se regocije
Hasta el estremo,
Es un deber
Pues que por Vos. adquiere
Un nuevo ser.

"Dichoso aquel momento
Bello, y deseado,
En que Vuestra Excelencia
Fue proclamado,
Para operar
La obra grande que el mundo
Debe admirar."

We remained but two days at El Viejo, and on the morning of the third started on our return to Leon. Chinandega, by daylight, more than confirmed the favorable opinion which I had formed of it from descriptions and starlight glimpses. It covers a very large space of ground, and is regularly laid out in "cuadras" or squares, which are again subdivided into what can best be described as gardens, each

VIEW OF CHINANDEGA FROM THE WEST.

one embowering a dwelling of some kind, generally built of canes and thatched, but often of adobes and neatly roofed with tiles. The central, or what may be called the business part of the town, in the vicinity of the grand plaza, is compact, and as well built as any part of Leon or Granada. Yet it is scarcely twenty years since there was but a single tile-roofed house in the town. Altogether, Chinandega has an air of thrift and enterprise which I have seen nowhere else in Central America; and as the trade now springing up on the Pacific coast increases, its importance will continue to augment. The country around it is flat, yet the soil is dry, and although the heat during the day is considerable, yet here, as in El Viejo, the evenings and nights are cool and pleasant. This is perhaps due to its position in respect both to the sea and the great volcano of El Viejo, which stands guard at this extremity of the plain of Leon.

Realejo is about two leagues distant from Chinandega. It is a small town, situated upon a tide-water stream, full five miles from the harbor proper, and can only be reached by the ordinary bongos or lighters, at high water. The position is low, and is reputed unhealthy. The customs' establishment is located there, but the merchants who conduct their trade through the port have their stores in Chinandega and Leon. It is said that the town was originally built nearer the harbor, and that the present site was afterwards adopted in consequence of the frequent attacks of the pirates, who, as I have already observed, infested this coast. The population of Realejo is about twelve hundred, who find employment in loading and unloading vessels, and supplying them with fruits and provisions. Recently the place has derived a great impulse from the Californian trade; docks and warehouses have been built, depôts for coal established, and several of the American steamers now touch there regularly for supplies; the station, in this respect, being favorably situated intermediately between Panama and Acapulco. It seems likely, however, that the old town will be abandoned and a new one built up, immediately on the harbor, opposite the anchorage, where there is a fine position, adapted to all the wants of commerce. A road has, in fact, lately been opened to the mouth of the Estero Doña Paula, by a company of native merchants, and the site of the new town has already been laid out under direction of the government. It is to bear the classical name of "Corinth," and will not be distant more than eighteen or twenty miles from Leon, to which place it is supposed it will sustain the same relation that Realejo has hitherto done to Chinandega. The official paper, the "Correo del Istmo," of the 30th of January last, advertises four hundred and twenty of the lots in "Corinth," varying from 1000 to 1500 square yards, and the minimum prices at which they are to be sold, i. e. from $25 to $37. There seems to be little doubt that this enterprise will prove successful, and that the Port of Realejo will become second in importance to no other on the entire Pacific coast from Panama northward.[1]

[1] Sir Edward Belcher, R. N., who surveyed this harbor in 1838, says: "The island of Cardon, at the mouth of the harbor of Realejo, is situated in 12° 28′ N., and 87° 12′ W. It has two entrances, both of which are safe, under proper precautions, in all weathers. Good and safe anchorage extends for several miles. The rise and fall of the tide is eleven feet, full and change 3h. 6m. Docks or slips, therefore, may easily be constructed, and timber is readily to be procured of any dimensions; wood, water, and immediate necessaries are plentiful and cheap.—"*Voyage round the World*," vol. ii. p. 307.

"I may confidently say," observes Dunlap, "that Realejo is as good a port as any in the known world. I have seen Portsmouth, Rio Janeiro, Port Jackson, Talhujano, Callao and Guayaquil, and to all of these I consider it decidedly superior. It is a salt water creek, into which several small streams of water empty themselves. The entrance is protected by an island about two miles long, which leaves at each end a channel where ships can enter the harbor, but extending opposite the main land, forming the port in such a manner as to protect it entirely from any wind that can possibly blow, and also breaking the swell which enters the outer bay of of Conchagua from the ocean. The north entrance is about a quarter of a mile wide, and that at the south of the island rather wider—both being entirely free from rocks or hidden dangers, and having in no part less than five fathoms depth of water. At one of these openings vessels can at all times enter with a leading wind, from whatever quarter it may blow. The inside consists of a noble basin of water, nowhere less than four fathoms deep, with a bottom of mud, where two hundred ships of the line might lie at all times in most perfect security. Merchant vessels generally lie about a mile from the entrance, in the branch of the creek which runs up to Realejo, where there are about five fathoms of water over a

The opening of the port of San Juan del Sur, or San Juan de Concordia, for purposes of transit across the Continent via Lake Nicaragua and the Rio San Juan, it has been supposed will seriously affect the importance of Realejo. The port of San Juan del Sur, however, can never meet the requirements of a considerable commerce. As a point of embarkation and disembarkation for steamers, it is unobjectionable; but it is small, and it is almost impossible for sail vessels to approach this part of the Nicaraguan coast. The north-east trade winds, which blow the entire year, here sweep across the whole continent, and for a considerable distance, and almost constantly, off the shore; where, meeting with other currents, they form those peculiar, revolving, contradictory winds known as Papagayos, which give their name to the Gulf within which this port is situated. Realejo, from this circumstance, and that of position in respect to the back country, must therefore remain the chief port of Nicaragua. It is undoubtedly the best for harbor purposes.

mud bottom. Opposite this port there is a fine level beach, possessing deep water close to the edge, which would form an admirable site for a town, and where, at very little expense, a wharf might be constructed, capable of accommodating almost any number of vessels."—*Central America*, p. 26.

CHAPTER XIV.

THE PRIESTHOOD IN NICARAGUA—DECLINE IN THE INFLUENCE OF THE CHURCH—BANISHMENT OF THE ARCHBISHOP—SUPPRESSION OF THE CONVENTS—PROHIBITION OF PAPAL BULLS—LEGITIMIZATION OF THE CHILDREN OF PRIESTS—THE THREE ABANDONED CONVENTS OF LEON—PADRE CARTINE, THE LAST OF THE FRANCISCANS—RECEPTION, OR CLOCK ROOM—THE PADRE'S PETS; HIS ORATORY; PRIVATE APARTMENTS; WORKSHOP—A SKULL AND ITS HISTORY—THE EGLESIA DEL RECOLECCION—THE PADRE AS A LANDLORD; AS A PAINTER; AS AN UNCLE; AND AS NEGOTIATOR IN MARRIAGE—AN AUSPICIOUS OMEN—DEATH OF THE VICAR OF THE DIOCESS OF NICARAGUA—HIS OBSEQUIES—A FUNERAL ORATION—PRIESTLY ELOQUENCE—AN EPITAPH—GENERAL FUNERAL CEREMONIES—DEATH AS AN ANGEL OF MERCY—BURIAL PRACTICES—CAPELLANIAS; THEIR EFFECTS, AND THE POLICY OF THE GOVERNMENT IN RESPECT TO THEM—POPULAR BIGOTRY AND SUPERSTITION—AN ANCIENT INDULGENCE—THE POTENCY OF AN EJACULATION—REMISSION OF SINS—PENETENCIAS—RATIONALE OF THE PRACTICE—NOVEL PENANCES—TURNING SINS TO GOOD ACCOUNT—GOOD FROM EVIL—SYSTEM OF THE PADRE CARTINE—THE DIOCESS OF NICARAGUA, AND ITS BISHOP—GENERAL EDUCATION—PUBLIC SCHOOLS—THE UNIVERSITIES OF LEON AND GRANADA—A SAD PICTURE.

ALTHOUGH there is probably less religious bigotry in Nicaragua and San Salvador than in most of the Spanish American States, yet the priests still exercise considerable influence amongst the popular masses. To their credit, however, be it said, that many of them, although not highly educated, are not only men of liberal sentiments, but amongst the most active promoters of measures of general improvement. Previous to the Independence, the Church in Central America was well endowed, and quite as exacting as in any other part of the continent, or in Spain itself. For some time subsequent to that event, it retained much of its strength, and was active in the political affairs of the country. Unfortunately, its influence was seldom felt in behalf of liberal institutions, general or local.

It is not to be doubted that the men who were the promoters of the Independence, and most active in the establishment of the Republic, were very little under priestly influence; for one of the first acts of the National Constituent Assembly was to prohibit the sale of Papal indulgences, and to limit the exactions of the Church. This policy arrayed the priestly influence against the new order of things, and it was henceforth exercised in favor of the aristocratical, monarchical, or Servile faction, against the Liberals and the Republic,—thus becoming one of the causes of many of the disasters to which the country has since been subjected. Yet the zeal of the Priests did not fail to react upon themselves. They entered into the arena of politics, and were treated as partisans in the civil contests. They espoused the cause of an obnoxious faction, and came to share its odium as well as its misfortunes. The Liberals, emancipated from the machinery of the Church, soon began to look with incredulity on its doctrines, and with contempt on its forms; and although the people of Central America are still nominally Catholics, yet amongst those capable of reflection, or possessed of education, there are more who are destitute of any fixed creed, rationalists, or what are sometimes called free thinkers, than Catholics, or adherents of any form of religion. Many of the priests share in the general skepticism.

The first decided encounter between the Church and the Republic, was in 1825, when the people of San Salvador, the stronghold of Liberalism, dissatisfied with the political tendencies of the Bishop of Guatemala, under whose ecclesiastical jurisdiction they were, elected a Bishop of their own, in defiance of the Archbishop and the Pope. This example was soon after followed by Nicaragua. The ignorant priesthood, the friars of Quesaltenango, siding with the Archbishop and the Serviles, infuriated by this and other bold innovations, contrived to excite the Indians in Los Altos, who in their fury cruelly slaughtered the vice-president of the Republic; and for a time the Liberals were overwhelmed by the coalition. They, however, afterwards rallied under Gen. Morazan. During his enlightened and vigorous sway, in 1829, it was discovered that the Archbishop was intriguing against the government; and it was then the Church received a blow from which it can never recover. Morazan was not a man to be trifled with; he boldly seized the Archbishop, and sent him out of the country under a guard of soldiers, forbidding his return under penalty of death. The monks and friars belonging to the various convents and monasteries of Guatemala, who were deeply concerned with the Archbishop, were expelled in an equally summary manner. But the measures thus commenced did not stop here. The Legislature of Guatemala decreed the suppression of all the male convents, prohibited females from becoming nuns for the future, and appropriated the revenues of the suppressed monasteries. This act was ratified by the General Congress, which, catching the same spirit, within two months after the banishment of the Archbishop declared all religious orders at an end throughout the Republic. This decisive measure met with the almost unanimous sanction of the people, and was at once carried into effect in the several States. The Congress also decreed not only complete Religious Liberty, but that the appointment to church dignities pertained to the nation, and should be made by the President of the Republic; prohibited the promulgation of all papal bulls, unless they had received the previous sanction of the Federal Government, as also the sale or use of papal dispensations, of whatever character. The State of Honduras shortly afterwards passed a law, which, I believe, was also adopted by all the other States, legalizing the marriage of the priests, and legitimatizing their children, so as to permit of their succeeding to their fathers' property.[1]

Subsequently to the dissolution of the confederacy, and under the direction of the Serviles, the convents of Guatemala were re-established, but the other States have persisted in the prohibitory action of 1829, or rather no attempt has been made to revive the monasteries suppressed under it. There were formerly, as I have already said, three convents in Leon; that of San Juan de Dios has been converted into a hospital; that of La Merced is only used by the government in case of need as a cuartel, or barracks. The largest, the Franciscan, although in a state of hopeless decay, is still watched over faithfully by the Padre Cartine. He has thus far preserved its precincts sacred from profane intrusion, and lingers silently amongst its dilapidated corridors, and weed-infested courts, like the antiquary amongst the tombs, the last of the powerful fraternity of San Francisco in Leon.

The Padre Cartine is a learned man, in the continental acceptation of the term of two centuries ago. That is to say, he reads Latin and the Fathers, and is familiar with the Natural History of Pliny,—the latest book on the subject with which he is acquainted, and which is his sole authority.

[1] In their zeal to educate the people, and to weaken their religious prejudices, theatres were established, in which the arts and objects of priestcraft were exposed to ridicule, contempt, and reprobation. A play called "La Inquisicion por dentro," or "A Peep into the Inquisition," had a great run, and brought that institution into effectual and lasting odium.

"In Guatemala," says Mr. Crowe, "Papal bulls of indulgence, which used to be as much valued as paper currency in other countries, are now used by the shopkeepers as waste paper for wrapping their goods. In San Salvador, the Bishop, a few years since, offered first twenty and afterwards forty days of plenary indulgence, to be deducted from the period of purgatorial sufferings after death, to all who should aid in removing an unsightly mound of earth which disgraced one of the squares of the city, and injured the effect of the Cathedral; but the mound remained, although the Bishop again doubled the promised remission."

The Padre is withal a mathematician, has a Latin edition of Euclid, and reads it once a year by way of amusement, and to refresh his memory. He is an architect, and has made a plan for the restoration of the convent, on a scale of splendor which would beggar a prince to carry out, and feels as anxious about its accuracy as if the masons were to commence to-morrow, and any defect in the plan would ruin the architectural effect of the structure for ever.

I am not likely to forget my first visit to Padre Cartine. I found him seated in a broad arm-chair, in the principal room of his house. He had been a man of fine proportions, but was now a little corpulent, a defect only to be observed when he was standing. His head was of fine outline, large, and massive, and his face had an expression of intelligence, dignity, and equanimity, at once pleasing and impressive. He wore a dress of coarse, gray serge, bound at the waist by a rough pita cord, for he still kept up many of the austere practices of his order. The furniture of the house was plain and simple, and I believe all of the Padre's own manufacture. Upon a low bench extending around two sides of the room, was a most incongruous assortment of clocks, of every date, pattern, and country, from a tall cupboard contrivance of the last century, dingy with age, in the corner, through every intermediate variety, to a little German or French concern, which ticked spitefully from the opposite wall. There were cases without clocks, and clocks without cases; besides a wilderness of weights, cords, pulleys, wheels, and springs; for the Padre was so passionately fond of clocks, that he not only kept an extensive variety of his own to tinker, but borrowed all of his neighbors', and encouraged the distant villagers to bring him theirs for gratuitous cleansing and repair. No Jew's second-hand furniture-shop in Chatham street could afford more than a very faint counterpart of this curious collection. The Padre observed that they attracted my attention, and commenced a philosophical lecture on horology, which I hastily brought to a close by suggesting a walk through the old convent and the church which had been attached to it. In the first courtyard were half a dozen deer, tame as kittens, which came bounding up at the sound of the Padre's voice; they licked his extended hand, and held down their heads to have them rubbed, but failing to cajole the Padre out of a plantain or tortilla, butted him playfully, and struck at him with well-feigned malice. Upon one side of this court the Padre had fitted up a private chapel. It contained a marble altar, a wax figure of Christ, and a great variety of valuable ornaments saved from the wreck of the monastery, and with which no earthly consideration could prevail upon the Padre to part. An expression, half of sorrow, half of pride, passed over the Padre's face as he held the door open that we might see the precious contents of his oratory. From this he took us to a large room, his own private apartment, in which was the rough hide bed whereon he slept, and which contrasted strangely with a rich set of travelling wine and liqueur bottles, which he complacently displayed to us, (not badly filled, by the way), in a secure closet. In another room the Padre had his workshop. In one corner was a foot-lathe of his own construction, in which he turned beads from the arm-bones of defunct Señoras, to be strung on consecrated rosaries, and sold for the benefit of piety and the church—whose interests have always wonderfully accorded. Here were kettles containing purified sulphur from the volcanoes, nitre, and charcoal, to be compounded for the glorification of the saints, the service of the Lord, and the utter desperation of heretics, in the form of bombas. Here, too, was a machine, also of the Padre's invention and construction, for grinding and polishing the glasses of spectacles, for the Padre, amongst his multifarious accomplishments, was an optician, the only one, probably, in all Central America. He had, in fact, constructed a telescope for the University of Leon, and astounded the citizens by showing them the rings of Saturn! "You are a most accomplished man, Padre," said I, glancing at his mechanical achievements. "*Juguetes*," playthings, mere playthings, responded the Padre, with a complacent smile, which was intended to be depreciatory. In the third courtyard, next the church, grew a magnificent mango tree. At its foot a mozo had been digging, to extirpate some burrowing animal, and had thrown up a variety of human bones, and amongst them a skull. Its delicate proportions attracted my attention, and I stepped aside and picked it up.

"Ah, Padre, this is a woman's skull, a girl's skull, I am sure! Padre, how came it here?"

The Padre took it quickly from my hand, looked at it, and then gazed in an abstracted, reflecting manner upon the spot which it had occupied. After a few moments' silence, he spoke, deliberately removing the earth from the eye sockets with his fore-finger;

"Ah, Señor! she was very beautiful, this girl. She was the youngest daughter of Señora M——! Heaven rest her soul! She died of the cholera in the year '37. Five thousand of our people died in four short months, Señor! The Señorita Inez! She was only sixteen years old, Señor; but yet a woman, and beautiful, very beautiful!"

And the Padre held the delicate skull before him, as if it was clothed with flesh again, and he gazed upon the smiling face once more.

"Very beautiful," he soliloquized. "She was amongst the first; there are five hundred buried in this very court, Señor," said the Padre rapidly, turning towards me, and crossing himself. "Five thousand in four months! in four short months!"

The expression of the old man's face, as the memory of those four months came back upon him, showed how terrible and ineffaceable were the scenes which they had witnessed. "She was very beautiful!" and the Padre placed the skull gently in the earth again, laid the delicate bones carefully around it, and with his naked hand scraped the loose earth above them.

The interior of the Eglesia del Recoleccion, which has a most elaborate façade, covered with shields on which are exhibited all the prominent devices of the church, was dark and gloomy. The altar was a fine one, and the Padre kept a lamp burning constantly before an image of the Virgin, which looked spectral enough beneath its feeble rays. A number of pictures were suspended upon the walls, among which were a variety of saints frying complacently upon gridirons, smiling from stakes of impalement, or sailing smoothly away amongst a swarm of baby angels and bodiless cherubs, to a most substantial looking heaven, elevated only a few yards above the earth. We ascended into the tower by a series of rickety stairs, with gaps here and there ranging from one to four steps, up which the prudent Padre did not essay to go. From this tower we obtained a fine view, second only to that to be had from the top of the Cathedral. As we descended, a huge owl, which we had startled from his roost in some dark corner of the tower, nearly knocked us over in his flight. We returned through the Golgotha, to the grand reception or clock room, where the Padre showed us his plan for restoring the convent, in red and black ink, which required only a single thing to its realization, and that was precisely what the Padre did not know how to obtain, viz., money! We nevertheless made him happy before leaving, by promising to write to the United States, on his behalf, to obtain a grand clock for his church, which should exhibit three dials, and strike the hours. "Con tres frentes!" repeated the Padre, calling after us as we passed down the street, "with three dials!"

The Padre ultimately became my landlord. I hired a house of him, which he had himself designed and built, opposite the old convento. It had a grand sala and two rooms on the street, with quarters for the servants, and a kitchen, arranged after the usual plan,—altogether one of the most desirable buildings in Leon. It had before rented for six dollars per month, but as I was a particular friend of the Padre, I got it for nine. The Padre was really ashamed to ask that sum, but then he had written a religious pamphlet, which he wanted to publish, and I told him that I should be too happy to contribute to that laudable object, and that the house was worth twice the money,—which was pretty good, considering that the best house in Leon rented for but fourteen dollars per month. The Padre had achieved a great triumph in painting the interior of this house. It was done in fresco, in a style as novel as complicated, and with as many colors as could conveniently be compounded. But the Padre's *chef d'œuvre* was the *menagerie*, as we called it, upon the wall of the servants' corridor. His models had been the figures of animals and objects represented in the Child's First Primer, or illustrated alphabet, a copy of which he must have obtained from the United States or England, for there was the entire series commencing "A was an Ape that ran after his tail," down to "Z was a Zebra who came from the Cape," all depicted of large size, and in flaming colors. This fact will perhaps sufficiently illustrate the state of decorative art in Nicaragua.

The Padre had a niece (*de facto*, oh skeptic!) who, with her mother, occupied a detached part of his own house, and over whom, as she was exceedingly pretty, he kept most rigorous watch. He gave out, for the benefit of gallants, that he would shoot the first who should be seen around the premises, and really kept a loaded musket for the purpose. The Padre was a man of his word, and the threat was effectual in its object; the gallants kept away. The last time I heard from Leon, a young American, from Boston, was diplomatizing with the Padre for the hand of his sobrina; it went hard to resign her to a heretic, but the Padre's heart is soft, and even rocks yield to time. Boston and Leon; Massachusetts and Nicaragua; the omen is auspicious and significant!

I have elsewhere mentioned the name of the Vicario of the Bishopric, Don Desiderio de la Quadra, who was the first of the clergy to pay his respects to me, upon my arrival in Leon. He was then ill, and died on the 4th of October following. His funeral was conducted with great ceremony and solemnity. On the morning of the 5th, circulars, of which the following is a copy, were directed to all the principal inhabitants, and left by a messenger bearing a silver cross shrouded in crape, from the Cathedral.

"AL SENOR;——

"A las seis de la tarde de ayer ha muerto nuestro muy amado tio el Sr. Vicario Capitular y Apostòlico, Presbitero Beneficiado Dr. Don José Desiderio Quadra: su cadáver será sepultado en la Santa Catedral Yglesia de esta Ciudad, saliendo el entierro á las cuatro de la tarde de la casa de su morada. Si U. se dignase honrarle con su asistencia, le serán muy reconocidos sus mas atentos servidores Q. B. S. M.

TRINIDAD QUADRA. MATEO MAYORGA.
Leon, Octubre 5 *de* 1849.

At the appointed hour we proceeded to the house which the Vicar had occupied. It was a large building, furnished in the simplest manner, for the Vicar was a practical as well as professed follower of Christ, and was faithful to his vows of poverty. All of his income, except the small sum necessary to supply his frugal wants, was devoted to charity. The courtyard and the corridor were already filled with people; and the clergy occupied the grand sala in which the corpse was lying. The ceremonies of the funeral had already commenced, we could hear the chants and prayers, and see the wax lights, but the place was overcrowded, and we did not attempt to enter. After a while a passage was opened through the assemblage for the bearers of the dead, preceded and surrounded by priests, full robed and with uncovered heads. The people in the courtyard knelt, as the remains were carried by. In the street was a sort of car, covered with drapery, upon which the corpse, dressed in the vicarial robes, was placed. Here another prayer was chanted; and when it was concluded, the car, surrounded by the entire body of the clergy, and preceded by the empty ecclesiastical carriage, moved towards the Cathedral. All the officers of State, and a large number of the principal citizens, bearing wax candles, followed; and then came the mass of the people, without order, but silently and decently. The cortege stopped at each corner, where a prayer was repeated in low recitative by the priests, who walked slowly around the car, and sprinkled the ground with holy water. The troops were drawn up with arms reversed, in the plaza, which the procession entered amidst the tolling of the muffled bells of the Cathedral. The body was carried up the main aisle, and placed upon an elevated platform, immediately in front of the great altar, while the choir filled the vast building with the solemn tones of the chant for the dead. The light fell from the dome full upon the rigid face of the corpse, calm and cold as marble, surrounded by earnest groups, standing silently in the shadows of the lofty arches. An extempore funeral oration was pronounced by the SENOR PRESBITERO DEAN D. REMIJIO SALAZAR, of the town of El Viejo. It was founded on the passage in the eleventh chapter of Leviticus, "Sed santos, porque yo soy santo." "Be ye holy, for I am holy," and was given with good oratorical effect and much feeling, and was altogether impressive and appropriate. Its tenor was to show that the deceased, from his observance of the requisitions of God and the church, was entitled to be regarded as a saint. The analysis of what constitutes "the Israelite indeed," was made with great clearness and eloquence, and in more pretending countries than those of Nicaragua, would have stamped its author as a man of no ordinary abilities.

"The true saint," said the speaker, "walks apart from the glittering road trodden by the proud and selfish world. His is the path in the valley of humility. He pants not for the glory of the soldier, or the fame of the statesman, the splendor of wealth, or the dignity of social position. Has he talents? He consecrates them to our holy religion. Has he wealth? It is a free offering at the feet of Charity. Has he a lofty lineage, and illustrious name? He humbly surrenders them at the shrine of the Church. All this did the venerated dead! He was a man who feared God, and adhered steadfastly to his service; irreproachable in conduct, a faithful son, a true friend, an obedient citizen, a man disinterested in his views and actions, moderate in his desires, uncomplaining in adversity, humble, in prosperity; purified in the fire, weighed in the balance, by the loftiest standard of the Holy Law, he is proved a saint! And now, amidst the glorious array of saints and martyrs, beyond the clouded atmosphere of earth, in the eternal sunshine of Divinity, dwells that pure and immortal spirit whose rejected tenement, cold and motionless, we have assembled to consign to the silent house appointed for all living. Our tears fall on the earth, but our smiles are reflected in Heaven!"

Amongst the many epitaphs and fragmentary poetical tributes elicited by the death of this Vicar, the subjoined may be taken as a very fair example. With what has been presented elsewhere, it will no doubt satisfy the reader that the tropical muse seldom rises to lofty flights.

EPITAFIO

A la muerte del muy illustre y venerable Prelado, el Señor Presbitero Dr. Don Desiderio de la Quadra, Vicario Capitular de esta Diócesis.

Despues de tantos años de virtud,
El feudo pagas cual mortal viviente,

Para acercaros al trono Omnipotente
De aquel Dios de eterna beatitud:
Allí, allí la inmensa multitud
De santos que te adoran reverentes,
Abriendo campo à tu espirítu inocente,
Ponen en tus manos sonoro laúd.
Goza esa vida inmortal que te deseo
Al mismo tiempo que tu muerte llóro;
Y mientras entre los justos yo te veo,
Disfruta cantando en alto coro
Safírica corona por troféo
De Opalo una palma, una Silla de oro.

Leon, Octubre 5 de 1849.

The funeral of the Vicar was far more solemn than any other which I witnessed in the country. In most instances the funeral ceremony has few of those gloomy accessories which our customs prescribe as no more than decorous. Youth, innocence, and beauty, like ornaments on the brow of age, or on the withered limbs of deformity, serve only to heighten the terrors of our grim conception of death, the gloomy and remorseless tyrant who gloats, fiend-like, over the victims of his skeleton arm. Theirs is a happier conception. Death mercifully relieves the infant from the sorrows and the dangers of life; and withers the rose on the cheeks of youth, that it may retain its bloom and fragrance in the more genial atmosphere of Heaven. The tear of grief falls only for those whose long contact with the world has effaced the stamp of divinity, whose matured passions have cankered the heart, and whose misdirected ambitions have diverted the aspirations of the soul and the energies of the mind from heaven to earth, from the grandeurs of Eternity to the frivolities of Time.

The youngest daughter of the Licenciado D. died and was buried in the latter part of October. She was young, scarce sixteen, and the idolized child of her parents. Her funeral might have been her bridal, in its total freedom from outward manifestations of grief. The procession formed before my window. First were musicians playing a cheerful strain, and next the priests chaunting a song of triumph. After them, on the shoulders of young men, was borne a litter, covered with white satin and loaded with orange branches, amidst which, dressed in white as for a festival, her head wreathed with pure white flowers, and holding in her hands a silver cross, was the marble form of the dead girl. The bereaved parents, the sisters and relations of the deceased followed; their eyes were tearless, and though the traces of sorrow were visible on their faces, yet over all there was an expression of hope, and of faith in the teachings of Him who has declared "Blessed are the pure in heart, for they shall see God."

The funerals of infants are much the same. The body is invariably dressed in white, and covered with flowers. Men firing rockets, and musicians playing lively airs, precede the corpse, and the parents and relatives follow. The rationale of this apparent want of feeling is to be found in the Romish doctrine of baptismal regeneration, according to which the departed spirit being in heaven, there is more cause for happiness than grief.

When an adult is dangerously ill, or dying, a priest is called, who goes for the Viaticum. An altar is hastily erected in the sick chamber; a crucifix is placed upon it, surrounded with lighted candles and flowers, a place being left for the *Costodia*, a vessel generally of gold and richly jewelled, containing the consecrated wafer. This is brought by a priest in a litter or carriage, surrounded by soldiers and boys bearing lighted candles, and preceded by music,—sometimes consisting only of a single violin. The people kneel as the procession passes through the streets. Arrived at the sick chamber, the sacrament and the last rites of the church are administered to the dying one, whose friends, gathering close around the bed, whisper "Jesus te ampara," "Jesus te auxilie," "Maria te favoresca,"—Jesus protect thee, Jesus help thee, Maria favor thee,—and then, when they suppose the final struggle transpiring, they ejaculate, "Jesus, Jesus, Jesus!"

"Among the more refined inhabitants," says Mr. Crowe, in his interesting book on Guatemala, (and the same practice is followed throughout the country,) "after the coffin, covered with black velvet, has been removed from between the gigantic candles which cast a pale glare upon it in the sombre apartment, it is followed by a long train of friends on foot, bearing lighted candles, to the church, and then to the cemetery. When the corpse has been finally deposited, the friends return slowly and in groups to the house of mourning, where the chief mourner has remained, and is now waiting to receive them in a large room or hall, hung with black cloth, at one end of which he sits, supported on his left or right by two near kinsmen or special friends. The visitors sit silently before him for a few minutes, on seats which are placed for them on either side of the room, and having thus manifested their participation in the grief of the family, they rise, one after another, gently press the hand of the chief mourner, and, if they are intimate friends, perhaps add a word or two of condolence. They then retire, and are succeeded by others in the same manner." [1]

There is, however, much that is repugnant in the burials, particularly as practised in Leon. Near most of the towns is what is called the Campo Santo, an enclosed consecrated cemetery, in which the dead are buried upon the payment of a small sum, which is devoted to keeping the grounds in order. But in Leon the practice of burying in the churches has always prevailed, and is perpetuated through the influence of the priests, who derive a considerable fee from each burial. The consequence is, that the ground within and

[1] Gospel in Central America, p. 373.

around the churches has become (if the term is admissible) saturated with the dead. The burials are made according to the amount paid to the church, for from ten to twenty-five years, at the end of which time the bones, with the earth around them, are removed and sold to the manufacturers of nitre! The government has opposed the entire practice for many years, and during the period of the cholera prohibited it. But the instability of affairs in the country has been such, that the authorities have hesitated to provoke the hostility of the entire priesthood by putting a peremptory end to the practice. Coffins are rarely used. The corpse is placed at the bottom of the grave, the earth rudely thrown in, and beaten hard with heavy rammers, with a degree of indifference, not to say brutality, which is really shocking, and which I never permitted myself to witness a second time.

Amongst the sources of revenue to which the priesthood has adhered with greatest tenacity, and the gradual abolition of which is one of the leading measures of the Government policy of Nicaragua, is what is called the *capellania*, or lien on property, conveyed to the priests by proprietors at their death, to secure certain masses or other priestly interpositions on behalf of their souls, or conveyed to churches for the same laudable objects. Thus Don Fulano finding his end approaching, gives to his priest a lien of twenty dollars a year on his estate, in consideration of which a certain number of masses shall be said for him annually. Next year the Doña Fulano dies, and, not to be outdone in piety, she secures to her favorite church another annual sum to be invested in "villainous saltpetre" for the glorification of her protecting Santa, and the benefit of her own "alma." It will readily be seen that the continuance of this process through a series of years must, in the end, seriously embarrass the real estate of the country, and prove an effectual check to the improvement of that species of property. Thus the most desirable portions of Leon, once covered with squares of palaces, are now waste and unoccupied, in consequence of the accumulation of the capellanias, which exceed in amount the market value of the ground.

During my stay in Leon, and in spite of the opposition of those interested in maintaining them, the Legislative Chambers decreed the abolition of ten per cent. of the capellanias, excepting those dedicated to educational purposes. Previously, I believe, fifteen per cent. had been appropriated by the Government, and offered for commutation at a nominal sum. The entire extinction of the capellanias, and the release of the property which they have so long burthened and rendered valueless, will be the ultimate and happy result of these advances.

I have said that the masses of the people still cherish something of their original religious bigotry. It is, nevertheless, fast giving way to more liberal sentiments, and no objection is made to foreigners on the score of religion, so long as they preserve a decent respect for the ceremonies of the church, and do not outrage the prejudices which education and custom have created, and which are no more numerous nor stronger than with us, although they have a somewhat different direction. That there is much of ignorance and superstition amongst the people, is unfortunately true; nor is the fact at all surprising, in consideration of their antecedents, and the circumstances under which they have been placed.

It is somewhat difficult to ascertain how far the faith of the better classes in papal infallibility, and other matters to which an apparent entire deference is accorded, really extends. We can hardly conceive that the following antiquated

[1] An English Protestant Missionary, Mr. F. Crowe, who was established in Guatemala for some years, until driven out by the servile Government, has recently published a work entitled the "Gospel in Central America," in which he observes:

"Of the fact that infidelity has spread extensively in Central America, indulgence should be posted upon every door in the houses of the most intelligent familes, except in politic conformity to prejudices, not shared by those families themselves, but which they do not care to oppose. Yet it met my eye almost everywhere, in the houses alike of the rich and the poor, of the Indian and the Cabellero :—

ALABADO SEA EL

SANTISIMO

SACRAMENTO

DEL ALTAR!

Nuestro Santìsimo Padre Paulo V. de felìz memoria, en su Bula de 17. de Abril despachada en Roma del año del Señor de 1612, concediò indulgencia plenaria, y remision de la tercera parte de los pecados, á cualquiera persona que en su casa tuviere escrito donde su pueda lér ☞ LA ANTERIOR JACULATORIA; ☜ y la misma indulgencia plenaria, todas las veces que lo leyéren, y el que no supiere lér, veneráre el escrito.

Copiado del original de indulgencias.

---

and particularly so amongst the very classes upon which Romanism had formerly the strongest hold, there can be no doubt. It is proved by the almost total abandonment of the outward observances of Popery by the better educated amongst the Ladinos, and, in spite of their political tendencies, by the whites and pure Creoles also. With the exception of the more weak amongst the women and children, scarcely any of these classes are now to be seen attending mass or confession, and other requirements are generally neglected by them. Numbers of infidel books are to be found in the libraries, and in the hands of all classes and sexes. So strongly are the minds of these classes imbued with deistical and atheistical notions, that it becomes apparent, and is unblushingly avowed in

PRAISE BE TO THE

MOST HOLY SACRAMENT OF THE ALTAR!

"Our most holy Father Paul V. of happy memory, in his Bull from Rome, April 17, in the year of our Lord 1612, conceded plenary indulgence and remission of the third part of his sins to whoever should write in his house where it might be read ☞THE PRECEDING EJACULATION☜; and the same plenary indulgence every time he should read it, or if he should not be able to read, every time he should venerate the writing," i. e., look upon it with veneration.

"Bendito y alabado sea el Santo Sacramento del Altar," Blessed and praised be the holy Sacrament of the Altar, is the common ejaculation of the servant who in the evening, first brings lighted candles into the occupied rooms of the various houses. It is uttered mechanically, in a drawling, nasal tone, and was formerly always responded to by the members of the family; but like many other customs, the latter part of the practice has now become obsolete. The recipient of a favor acknowledges it by "Dios se lo pague," God repay you; if an engagement is made, it is with the qualification, "si Dios quiere," if God wills; and when a bond is entered into, it is always with the reservation, "Primero Dios," i. e., if my first duty to God will permit. The "higher law" is always recognized, in form if not in spirit.

general conversation. Nay, some of the more candid among the priests openly espouse these notions."—p. 257.

Some of the priests, this author adds, ridicule the pretended authority of the Pope, and rejoice at the emancipation of the people from the Church of Rome. Mr. Crowe rejoices also, at the success of infidelity over Romanism, as likely to result in good. "The change from Popery, or any other analogous system," he writes, "to the entire rejection of revealed religion, is one which believers in Divine Revelation may hail with satisfaction, if they be prepared to take advantage of it; for it breaks up prejudices of education, leads to thought and inquiry, and sometimes to a sincere and earnest search after truth!"

"Dios sobre todos," God over all, is the commonest of proverbs.

The public Penitencias, or Penances, afford striking illustrations of the strength of the popular superstitions, and of the priestly influence. I witnessed one of these, shortly after my arrival in Leon. It consisted of a long procession of men and boys, one or two hundred in number, barefooted and stripped to the waist, their heads and faces covered with veils so as to prevent recognition, who marched through the public streets, from one church to another, flagellating themselves with raw hide thongs. They were preceded by a life-size figure of Christ on the cross, a score of musicians, and a crowd of priests and women, (all of the latter barefooted and some bearing heavy crosses on their shoulders,) who chanted prayers, while the penitents beat time with the thongs over their own shoulders. Each one carried a little cross before him in his hand, with his head bent forward as if in earnest contemplation of the sacred symbol. It was a singular spectacle; for there were black bodies, and brown, and white bodies, and yellow, and the sharp strokes of the thongs in the pauses of the slow and mournful music, fairly made the flesh of the spectator creep. There was, however, no special occasion for sympathy, for each penitent had it in his power to graduate the force of his own blows to his own notions of the enormity of his moral offences. Some laid it on gently,—moderate sinners!—merely as a matter of form; but there were others who punished themselves lustily, and drew blood from their quivering flesh at every blow, which ran down to their very heels, and purpled the ground where they trod.

It seems almost incredible that these heathenish practices, only one remove from human sacrifices, should yet be perpetuated amongst nations claiming to be civilized. Still, when we reflect that fasts and other mortifications of the body are prescribed by the rituals of our own churches, and proclaimed from the executive chair of our own nation, we ought not to be surprised at any manifestation of human folly, or wonder that the popular conception of God is not yet purified from the horrible and detestable features with which it was invested in the darkest ages of the world, and in the most debased stages of the human mind. The belief that the all-good and ominipotent Ruler of the Universe can be pleased with the self-inflicted punishment of his creatures, whether it be through fasting or flagellation, differs in no respect from that which actuates the frantic Hindoo, who prostrates himself before the crushing wheels of Jaggenath, or that inflamed the poor Mexican, who offered his willing breast to the knife of the Aztec priest, that his palpitating heart might bathe the lips of the idol which was the visible representation of his sanguinary God!

There were other Penitencias, not public, but which were perhaps more severe. A hundred or more of the penitents are sometimes locked within a church, where they remain for nine days, sleeping but four hours out of the twenty-four, and eating but once in that period. The rest of the time is divided between the various ceremonies prescribed by the rigid rules of the penitencia, upon their knees, or prone on the rough floor of the dark church in which they are confined. While I resided near the Eglesia de la Merced, one of these penitencias took place, and I was several times awakened in the dead of night by the wailings of the penitents, mingling harshly with the low and cheerful melodies of that Nature which harmonizes with its great Author, and upon whose laws kingcraft and priestcraft, the world over, and in every age, have waged a constant and most unnatural and unholy war. The horrible doctrine of original sin, and the efficacy of austerities, penances, and immolations, parts of one system, find the best evidence of their truth in the fact of their existence amongst men! I saw the enthusiasts when they came out of the church, pale, haggard, and filthy;

some, in fact, so exhausted that they could not walk without assistance, and who tottered from the scenes of their debasement to beds of sickness and death.

Very novel penances are sometimes prescribed by the priests by way of atonement for individual iniquities. The Padre Cartine was particularly ingenious and happy in imposing them. Lazy fellows and *bon vivants*, to whom he thought exercise and fasting would prove beneficial, he sent bare-footed and alone to El Viejo, or some place at a distance, under the restriction to speak to no human being on the way, nor to eat, nor yet to sleep, until their return. A heavy stone, rough and angular, had sometimes to be carried on the naked shoulders of the penitent, or a cross of heavy wood, according to the more or less heinous nature of the poor devil's offences. Carpenters, masons, and all other valuable sinners, whose labor could be turned to good account, the Padre set to work in repairing or improving his church and the buildings attached to it, and never failed to put the good workmen "well in for it." Occasionally he got hold of a stupid fellow who failed to perform a profitable day's labor. In such cases the Padre had a whip, made of the skin of the *dante*, or tapir, which he scrupled not to apply to the delinquent's back, for the benefit of his soul, and the acceleration of the particular job in hand. And it is reported that these applications are sometimes accompanied with terms more forcible than complimentary; but I don't vouch for the truth of that.

For one or two months during my stay in Leon, the Padre had under his surveillance a priest, suspended for licentious conduct, with whom he was extremely rigorous. I was an accidental witness of his severity on one occasion, when the Host was passing. The suspended Padre, in common with all the people, came to the door, but instead of bending like the rest on the hard threshold, he knelt comfortably in a soft-bottomed chair. The indignant monk saw the dodge, and rising hastily, with a vigorous blow of his foot knocked the chair from underneath the delinquent, who came down with a force which must have jarred every bone in his sinful body. The course of fasting and prayer through which that priest was "put" by the Padre Cartine, if report speaks true,—midnight vigils, and noonday masses,—would have reformed Silenus, and made a saint of Bacchus.

Nicaragua and Costa Rica together constitute a Diocess of a very ancient date. It was organized as early as 1526. For the period intervening between 1832 and 1849, the Bishop's chair was vacant; but in the latter year Don GEORGE VITERI Y UNGO, once Secretary of State of Guatemala, and subsequently Bishop of San Salvador, received the appointment, and is now in discharge of its functions. I have already described him as a man of great intelligence, and polished manners. He has travelled much, and never fails to leave a favorable impression on the minds of foreigners. Yet in the country he is accounted an *intrigante*, and does not seem to enjoy the full confidence of the leading inhabitants, who nevertheless treat him with all respect and courtesy. While Bishop of San Salvador, he is said to have taken an undue interest in political affairs, and this was the cause of his deposition from that diocess; for the people of San Salvador are quite as liberal in religion as politics, and will tolerate no interference in public affairs by the clergy, as such. They nevertheless concede to them the utmost latitude as individuals, and while making no distinctions in their favor, make none against them.

In respect to Education, both amongst the clergy and the people of Nicaragua, little need be said, except that the standard is exceedingly low. I spare myself the painful necessity of writing upon the subject, by translating the following impartial passages from a private letter on this point, addressed to me by one of the best informed and patriotic citizens of Leon. A knowledge of their own deficiencies and wants, by any people, is indispensable to secure a remedy; and the fact that some of the best men in Nicaragua are looking the evils of ignorance full in the face, is one of the best signs in the horoscope of the country.

"Education in Nicaragua," says my correspondent, "is generally much neglected; particularly in the departments of Chontales and Segovia, where there are some towns without a single teacher of any grade. Here the elements of education are only taught, if taught at all, by the fathers of families to their children, in the evening before going to bed; but this instruction seldom reaches beyond learning them to repeat their catechism. In these places, as also in some others where there are teachers, it is a common thing for parents to send their children to the house of some poor neighbor, where they are taught the catechism, and to make certain pot-hooks, called writing. These apologies for teachers have no recompense beyond an occasional small present. The mode adopted by them is to repeat the lesson once or twice *viva voce*, with the children; and their principal occupation consists in permittting the latter to do what they please, and in assisting them in doing it!

"In the towns where there are teachers, there are seldom more than one or two public schools; in the larger places there are, perhaps, a few more, but unfortunately all of pretty nearly the same character with those above described. In these schools are taught only the fundamental doctrines of Christianity, reading and writing; nor is this done in accordance with any good system, but generally by a process which is little better than a burlesque. The lesson is repeated after the master, simultaneously by the whole school, and it is difficult to say which shouts loudest, the master or the scholars; but it is always easy to tell the proximity of a schoolhouse, from the noise. The localities of these schools are generally bad and filthy, as is also the clothing of the scholars, which often consists of nothing more than a shirt.

In some of the towns, as Masaya, Managua, and Chinandega, the public schools are filled to overflowing, and as each one has no more than a single teacher, he can only bestow a very superficial attention upon the individual scholars. In these towns there are also some higher schools, in which Latin is taught, after the old method, painful alike to teacher and student, and generally with no result except the knowledge that Señor Fulano has studied this language for so many years! There are also, in these towns, phantom classes in what is called Philosophy, the extent of whose acquirements consists in studying badly, and understanding worse, some paragraphs in Lugdunensis.

"Besides their public schools, both Granada and Leon have each a University. That of Leon is oldest, having been founded in the year 1675.

"In these Universities are taught the following branches: Latin and Spanish Grammar, Philosophy, Civil and Canonical Law, and Theology. Lately a class in English has been organized in that of Leon; and a class in both English and French in that of Granada. Of Mathematics and other cognate branches nothing is taught, nor scarcely anything known. The authority in Spanish is Alemany; in Latin, Nebrisa; in Philosophy, Lugdunensis; in Civil Law, Salas; in Canonical Law, Devoti; in Theology, Larraga. The time devoted to these studies is, to Spanish, Grammar, and Latin, two years and a half; to Philosophy, two years; Civil and Canonical Law, and Theology, three years. But many have not the patience to go through the prescribed time, and leaping over these various branches of study, succeed in securing their titles. There are priests, in orders, who have never so much as read the Padre Larraga!

"In order to obtain the degrees and secure the tassel, it is not necessary to know much; it is enough to have a general idea or two, to stand well with the professors, be able to pay the fees punctually, to spread a good table of refreshments, and to have a blazing display of fireworks. I have known instances in which the candidate did not answer well more than a single question, and yet obtained unanimously the degree which he sought. There are more Bachelors than men; Doctors swarm everywhere; and there are families of wealth and influence in which the tassel goes (practically) by descent!

"The professors of Languages and Civil Law in 1850, in Leon, were very good; but the professor in the latter department, occupied with other matters, has permitted his place to be very poorly filled by certain Bachelors. In fact, all the professors do but little; principally because their salaries are insignificant in amount, seldom exceeding $200 per annum. Their lectures are got through with very rapidly, rarely occupying more than an hour each, and are scarcely ever illustrated, or enforced by examples in point.

"Concerning the University of Granada, I am not well informed, but it is doubtless on about the same footing with that of Leon; or, if any comparison may be instituted, something worse.

"To the defects in the system of Education in Nicaragua is to be ascribed, in great part, the troubles with which the State has been afflicted. There is nothing practical in the lessons which are taught in the schools; the studies are all abstract, and the fixedness of character and liberality of views which follow from a knowledge of the present condition and relations of the world, an understanding of modern sciences, Geography, Chemistry, Mineralogy, Mathematics, Engineering, etc., etc., are never attained. The men of education, so called, are therefore mere creatures of circumstances and impulses, in common with the most ignorant portion of the population, and fully as vacillating in their ideas. Their education is just sufficient to give them power to do mischief, instead performing the legitimate office of truly comprehensive acquirements, that of a balance-wheel.

What may be called the moral effect of an education, that which contributes to form the character of the man and mould it upon a just model, is wanting in the system, or rather no-system, not only of Nicaragua, but of all the other Spanish American States.

"In Nicaragua, therefore, in the absence of teachers, methods, books, instruments, and of nearly all the elements of teaching, there is nothing which can properly be called education.[1] Not because there are no latent capacities or dispositions for learning amongst the people; nor do I mean to say that there is a total absence of really cultivated and well-educated men. On the contrary, there a number who have had opportunities of acquiring education through the assistance of private teachers, or who have perfected themselves abroad; but these are lost in the mass of ignorance and shallow acquirements which surround them.

"In Leon, I may add, there are ten or a dozen schools, in some of which there is an average daily attendance of two hundred scholars. The highest pay of teachers is ten dollars per month."

But notwithstanding the general deficiency in education, and the means of acquiring it, there exists a most laudable

[1] "The books employed," says Mr. Crowe, "besides the gloomy character of their contents, are in bulk sufficient to discourage the most enterprising child. They are four or five in number, consisting of heavy volumes, which make an antique collection, heavy and dry enough to discourage adults. First 'La Cartilla,' containing the alphabet, the forms of prayer, and the commandments of the Church, with no attempt at gradation. The second, 'El Canon,' the third, 'El Catecismo,' and fourth, 'El Ramillete.' All these, which are much larger than the first, contain theological definitions, digests of doctrines, creeds, holy legends, and devotional formulas, addressed to the Virgin and the Saints. Through every one of these the unhappy scholar is doomed to wade from beginning to end; and so deep is his aversion to the task, and so great is the triumph when a child has overcome one of these obstacles to his progress, that the event is actually celebrated in his family by feasting."—p. 287.

ambition to secure its benefits. The States of Nicaragua, San Salvador, and Costa Rica, offer the largest encouragement to the establishment of schools of every grade. Under the old Confederation, during the dominance of the Liberals, the most effective means were adopted to educate the people. The officers of the army and the subordinates of the Government, when not occupied with the immediate duties of their stations, opened free schools in the barracks of the soldiery, in the offices of customs, and the rooms of the general and local courts. The house of the National Government, at the close of office hours, became an academy. But the system of education, as all the other plans of improvement originating with the Liberals, were suspended during the disturbances created by the Serviles, and overthrown whenever and wherever the latter attained ascendancy. In the new career now opening before Central America, the subject of education claims and no doubt will receive the first attention of the respective States. But nothing beneficial can be done without a complete abandonment of the old systems of teaching—old authorities and books, and the substitution of others adapted to the age, and the state of general knowledge amongst civilized nations. If creeds and catechisms are still required, let them be assigned their proper time and place; they constitute no part of an education, and are chilling and oppressing in their influences on the youthful mind. The sooner this fact is not only understood, but acted upon, in Central America, the better for its people.

CHAPTER XV.

VISIT TO THE CAPITAL CITY, MANAGUA—LEGISLATIVE ASSEMBLY; HOW TO PROCURE A QUORUM—EXECUTIVE MESSAGE—RATIFICATION OF TREATY WITH THE UNITED STATES—ANTIQUITIES—LAKE OF NIHAPA—HUERTAS—DIVIDING RIDGE—TRACES OF VOLCANIC ACTION—HACIENDA DE GANADO—AN EXTENSIVE PROSPECT—EXTINCT CRATER—ANCIENT PAINTINGS ON THE CLIFFS—SYMBOLICAL FEATHERED SERPENT—A NATURAL TEMPLE—SUPERSTITIONS OF THE INDIANS—SALT LAKE—LAGUNA DE LAS LAVADORAS—A COURIER—THREE MONTHS LATER FROM HOME—THE SHORE OF LAKE MANAGUA—ABORIGINAL FISHERIES—ANCIENT CARVING—POPULATION OF MANAGUA—RESOURCES OF SURROUNDING COUNTRY—COFFEE—INHABITANTS—VISIT TIPITAPA—SUNRISE ON THE LAKE—HOT SPRINGS—OUTLET OF LAKE—MUD AND ALLIGATORS—DRY CHANNEL—VILLAGE OF TIPITAPA—SURLY HOST—SALTO DE TIPITAPA—HOT SPRINGS AGAIN—STONE BRIDGE—FACE OF THE COUNTRY—NICARAGUA OR BRAZIL WOOD—ESTATE OF PASQUIEL—PRACTICAL COMMUNISM—MATA-PALO OR KILL-TREE—LANDING AND ESTERO OF PASQUIEL OR PANALOYA—RETURN—DEPTH OF LAKE MANAGUA—COMMUNICATION BETWEEN THE TWO LAKES—POPULAR ERRORS.

ALTHOUH Leon is *de facto* the seat of the Nicaraguan Government, yet the framers of the existing constitution of the State, in view of the rivalry and jealousy which exist between the cities of Granada and Leon, and in order to relieve the Legislative Assembly from the overawing political influence of the latter, designated the city of Managua as the place of its meeting. The choice was in many respects a good one; Managua is not only central as regards position, but its inhabitants are distinguished for their attachment to "law and order," and their deference to constituted government.

The task of getting together the members of the Assembly, which is comprised of a House of Deputies and a Senate, is not an easy one. The attractions of the city of Managua are not great: the pay is only a dollar and a half per diem, and such is the precarious condition of the Treasury, that this small sum is not always secure. Nor are there any profitable contracts to be obtained for friends, with contingent reversions to incorruptible members; no mileage to speak of; in fact, few if any of those inducements to patriotic zeal which make our citizens so ambitious of seats in the National Congress. As a consequence, it is usually necessary, in order to secure a constitutional quorum for the transaction of business, to announce beforehand that a sufficient sum for the payment of members is actually in the Treasury, and will be reserved for that express purpose. But even this is not always sufficient, and the Government has several times come to a stand still for want of a quorum. An instance of this kind occurred during the administration of Gen. Guerrero, who found himself for a week in Managua, with his cabinet officers around him, but utterly unable to act. The Assembly lacked two of a quorum, and precisely that number of members, elected from the city of Leon, were absent. They were the Licenciado Z., and the Doctor of Medicine J., men of mark in the country, but for a variety of reasons not then desirous of committing themselves on the measures of public policy which were to be brought before the Chambers. The Director wrote to them, stating the condition of the Assembly, and soliciting their immediate attendance. The lawyer excused himself on the ground of illness, and the doctor, because he had no horse, nor money for his expenses. But they mistook their man; in a few minutes after their replies were received, the General had despatched two officers of the National Guard to Leon, and before daylight the next morning the Licenciado was politely waited upon by one of them, attended by a file of soldiers, and informed that there was an-ox cart at the door, with a good bed of straw, in which the soldiers would carefully lift him, and where he would find the army doctor, to administer to his necessities during his journey to Managua. The Licenciado expostulated, but the officer looked at his watch and coolly observed that the cart must start in precisely three minutes, and dead or alive the Licenciado must go. The doctor was waited upon in like manner, with the information that the Director had sent his own horse for his accommodation, and four rials (half a dollar) for his expenses, and that he had five minutes wherein to prepare himself for the excursion! It is needless to add that the lawyer was suddenly cured, and that both he and the delinquent doctor duly filled out the quorum at Managua. They each tell the story now as an exceedingly good joke, but the General avers that at the time of their appearance in their seats, their manners and temper were far from angelic.

The Legislative Assembly had been called to meet on the 15th of September, to act on the treaty just negotiated with the United States, and on the canal contract which had been conceded to certain American citizens, under the conditional guaranty of their government. The hopes of the people were much elevated, from the nature of the subjects to be brought before the Assembly, and it was thought that the constitutional quorum would be got together at the time appointed, without resort to any extraordinary measures for the purpose of securing it. It was not, however, until the 19th that we received official information of the organization of the Chambers, and we lost no time in proceeding to Managua, where Pedro Blanco had long before received orders to prepare a house for our reception, and to adopt efficient measures for the extirpation of "las pulgas." We left Leon on the afternoon of one day, and reached Managua during the forenoon of the next. Don Pedro had newly white-washed a house, occupying the "esquina," or corner opposite his own, and installed a couple of servants, in anticipation of our arrival. So we were at once comfortably provided for.

The address, or message, of the Director had been delivered in joint meeting of the two Houses on the morning of our arrival, and everything was going on smoothly and harmoniously in the Assembly. It was, according to custom, delivered in person, to the two Houses in convention, and responded to by the President of the Senate. The subjoined passages from both the address and reply, for reasons already given, will prove of interest. The Director, Señor RAMIREZ said:

"I experience the liveliest emotions of joy in witnessing once more the union of the representatives of the Nicaraguan people, after the terrible tempest which has passed over the country, and which at one time threatened not only to subvert its liberties, but to destroy its very existence as a civilized nation. Brighter days have succeeded to that period of confusion and fear, and we are now again enjoying the unspeakable blessings of peace. In view of this happy result, your satisfaction, Citizen Representatives, must equal my own; and I am sure that the desires for the future happiness and prosperity of Nicaragua which swell my own bosom, and to which words are too weak to give utterance, exist also in yours.

"We have undoubtedly arrived at a crisis in our national career. After unparalleled sufferings, heroically endured, our country has risen from the abasement to which many years of civil war and the ferocious passions of men had reduced it. But these evils have only passed away to give place to others scarcely less deplorable, resulting from foreign pretensions and aggressions. From these it is our obvious duty, not less than our only safety, to solicit the interposition of some powerful and friendly arm. Should this be generously extended in our favor, we may smile at the intrigues and harmless malice of the enemies of society and social order, which exist in our midst. We may then look forward with well-grounded anticipations of a glorious future. We may then devote our energies to the development of our almost limitless resources, to the promotion of commerce and industry, the revival of education, the improvement of our roads and our navigable lakes and rivers;—in fact, to all those grand and useful objects to which no government, unless at peace with the world, and free from foreign interference and annoyance, can successfully devote its energies.

"For this relief we need not despair. We may yet be called upon to make sacrifices to secure it; but it must come with the successful prosecution of that grand enterprise of connecting the two great oceans, which is now occupying the paramount attention of the commercial world:—an enterprise which is not only fraught with immense results to trade, but which must work a total change in the political and moral relations of all the countries of the globe; the greatest work, not of this cycle alone, but of all ages.

"As a direct and essential step toward the consummation of this grand enterprise, with its train of consequences so important to our independence and prosperity, I have the honor to submit a Treaty of Alliance, Friendship, Commerce, and Protection, negotiated with the Honorable Plenipotentiary of the great and enlightened Republic of the United States of North America, and a contract for opening a Ship Canal, concluded between the agent of an American Company and this Government,—upon both of which you will be called to act, in conformity with the constitution."

The President of the Senate, Don Toribo Teran, responded to this address at length. The tenor of his remarks will appear from the following passages:

"Sir, this Assembly is actuated by the earnest desire of coöperating with the Executive in whatever shall promote the interests or the glory of the State; and offers its prayers to Heaven for light and guidance in the discharge of its intricate duties. It desires me to felicitate you upon the wisdom and firmness with which you discharged the responsible duties of your position during the late troubles, and which saved the State from the terrors which at one time impended on the political horizon. It congratulates you also upon the dignity and skill with which you have conducted the foreign relations of the country, which have raised it in the estimation of other and more powerful nations, and secured for it their sympathy and confidence.

"The efforts and sacrifices of the State in support of civil and social order have been great, but most happily successful; the hydra of anarchy is crushed, and, so far as the internal relations of our country are concerned, we look forward to a peaceful future, and a rapid and constant progress. To foreign pretensions and the territorial aggressions with which we have been persecuted, and which are now the only sources of disquiet to the State, let us hope for the early interposition of that nation to which we have always been accustomed to look as a model for ourselves—a nation powerful, enlightened, and naturally called to defend our territory, in conformity with the great and glorious principle which it was the first to proclaim, and which finds a response in every American heart, viz.: that 'The American Continent belongs to Americans, and is sacred to Republican Institutions.' "

It will not be out of place to add here, that both treaty and contract were unanimously ratified, at the earliest moment, after passing through the forms prescribed by the constitution,—a proof of the confidence and friendship of the people and Government of Nicaragua, which we, as Americans, should never forget. The news of the event was everywhere received with extraordinary demonstrations of satisfaction and joy; and it is most earnestly to be desired that the hopes which it created may not, from the mistaken policy of Government, or the bad faith of companies, owing their very existence to Nicaraguan generosity, give place to despair, and respect be changed into contempt, and friendship into hate.

I had heard much in Leon of ancient monuments in the vicinity of Managua, and particularly of an ancient Indian temple cut in the solid rock, on the shore of a small lake, amongst the hills at the back of the city. I now learned that the lake was called Nihapa, and that upon the rocks which surrounded it were many figures, executed in red paint, concerning the origin of which nothing was known, but which were reported to be very ancient, "hechando antes la Conquista," made before the Conquest. The next morning, having meanwhile procured a guide, we started for this lake. The path, for a league, led through a beautiful level country, magnificently wooded, and relieved by open cultivated spaces, which were the hattos and huertas of the inhabitants of Managua. Nearly every one of these had a small cane hut, picturesquely situated amidst a group of palms or fruit trees, in its centre, reached by broad paths beneath archways of plantains. Here the owners reside when weary of the town. We overtook hundreds of Indian laborers, with a tortilla and a bit of cheese in a little net-work bag thrown over one shoulder, pantaloons tucked up to the thighs, and carrying in the right hand, or resting in the hollow of the left arm, the eternal *machete*, the constant companion of every mozo, which he uses as an axe to clear the forest, a spade to dig the earth, a knife wherewith to divide his meat, and a weapon in case of attack. Passing the level country adjacent to the city, we came to the base of the hills which intervene between the lake and the sea. Here, at every step, traces of volcanic action met our view, and the path became rough and crooked, winding amongst disrupted rocks, and over broad beds of lava. The latter extended down the side of the ridge, showing that anciently there had existed a crater somewhere above us, now concealed by the heavy forest. The eruptions, however, must have taken place many centuries ago, for the lava was disintegrated at the surface, and afforded a luxuriant foothold for vines, bushes, and trees. For this reason, although we knew that we had attained an elevated position, we found it impossible to see beyond the evergreen arches which bent above us, and which the rays of the sun failed to penetrate. The ascent was steep, and our progress slow,—so slow that a troop of indignant monkeys, swinging from branch to branch, grimacing, and threatening vehemently, was able to keep pace with us. We fired our pistols at them, and worked up their feelings to a pitch of excitement and rage, humiliatingly like the ebullitions of humanity. These amusing denizens of the forest, I frequently observed, seem annoyed by the presence of white men, and will fret and chatter at their approach, while the brown natives of the country may pass and repass, if not without attracting their notice, at least without provoking their anger.

At the distance of about two leagues and a half from

Managua, we reached what appeared to be a broad, broken table-land, the summit of the dividing range intervening between the Lake and Ocean. We had not proceeded far, before we discovered a high conical peak, made up of scoriæ and ashes, and bare of trees, which had evidently been formed by the matter thrown out from some neighboring volcanic vent. Here our guide turned aside at right angles to our path, and clearing the way with his machete, in a few minutes led us to the edge of the ancient crater. It was an immense orifice, fully half a mile across, with precipitous walls of black and riven rocks. At the bottom, motionless and yellow, like a plate of burnished brass, was the lake of Nihapa. The wall of the crater, upon the side where we stood, was higher than at any other point, and the brain almost reeled in looking over its ragged edge, down upon the Acheronian gulf below. Upon the other side, the guide assured us there was a path to the water, and there too were the rock temple, and "los piedras pintadas." So we fell back into our path again, and skirting along the base of the cone of scoriæ to which I have referred, after a brisk ride of twenty minutes, came suddenly, and to our surprise, upon a collection of huts pertaining to a cattle estate. Here burst upon our sight an almost boundless view of mountain, lake, and forest. Behind us towered the cone of scoriæ, covered with a soft green mantle of grass. Upon one side yawned the extinct crater with its waveless lake; upon the other were ridges of lava, and ragged piles of trachytic rock, like masses of iron; while in front, in the foreground, stood the picturesque cane huts of the vaqueros, clustered round with tall palms and the broad translucent leaves of the plantain. But beyond all,—beyond the mountain slopes and billowy hills, shrouded with never-fading forests, among which, like fleecy clouds of white and crimson reflected in a sea of green, rose the tops of flowering trees,—beyond these, flashing back the light of the morning sun from its bosom, spread out the Lake of Managua, with its fairy islets and distant, dreamy shores!

We left our horses at the huts, and followed a broad, well-beaten path which led to the point where the walls of the extinct crater were lowest. Here we found a narrow path between the rocks, barely wide enough to admit a horse to pass. It had in part been formed by man, probably before the Conquest, when, according to the early chroniclers, even these hills were thronged by a happy and industrious people. The descent for a few hundred feet was very steep, between high walls of rock. It then turned short, and ran along the face of the cliff, where fallen masses of stone afforded a foot-hold, and clinging trees curtained with vines concealed yawning depths and perilous steeps, which would otherwise have dizzied the head of the adventurous traveller. Near the bottom the path widened, and at the water's brink we reached a kind of platform, edged with rocks, where the cattle from the haciendas came down to drink, and whence the vaqueros of the huts obtained water for their own use. Here a few trees found root, affording a welcome shelter from the rays of the sun; for the breezes which fan the hill-sides never reach the surface of this almost buried lake.

The walls of the ancient crater are everywhere precipitous, and at the lowest point probably not less than five hundred feet in height. Except at the precise spot where we stood, the lake washed the cliffs, which went down, sheer down, to unknown depths. We looked up, and the clouds as they swept over seemed to touch the trees which crowned the lofty edges of the precipice, over which the vines hung in green festoons.

Upon the vertical face of the cliff were painted, in bright red, a great variety of figures. These were the "piedras pintadas" of which we had heard. Unfortunately, however, long exposure had obliterated nearly all of the paintings; but most conspicuous amongst those still retaining their outlines perfect, or nearly so, was one which, to me, had peculiar interest and significance. Upon the most prominent part of the cliff, some thirty or forty feet above our heads, was painted the figure of a coiled, plumed, or feathered ser-

LAKE NIHAPA—AN EXTINCT CRATER.

pent, called by the Indians "el Sol," the sun. Amongst the semi-civilized nations of America, from Mexico southward, as also amongst many nations of the old world, the serpent was a prominent religious symbol, beneath which was concealed the profoundest significance. Under many of its aspects it coincided with the sun, or was the symbol of the Supreme Divinity of the heathens, of which the sun was one of the most obvious emblems. In the instance of the painting before us, the plumed, sacred serpent of the aborigines was artfully depicted so as to combine both symbols in one. The figure was about three feet in diameter, and is accurately represented in the accompanying Plate 1, Fig. 1. Above it, and amongst some confused lines of partially obliterated paintings, not represented in the sketch, was the figure of a human hand,—the red hand which haunted Mr. Stephens during all of his explorations amongst the monuments of Yucatan, where it was the symbol of the divinity KAB-UL, the Author of Life, and God of the Working Hand.[1]

Upon some rocks a little to the right of the cliff upon which is this representation of the serpent, there were formerly large paintings of the sun and moon, together, as our guide said, "con muchos geroglificos," with many hieroglyphics. But the section upon which they were painted, was thrown down during the great earthquake of 1838. Parts of the figures can yet be traced upon some of the fallen fragments. Besides these figures, there were traces of hundreds of others, which, however, could not be satisfactorily made out. Some, we could discover, had been of regular outline, and from their relative proportions, I came to the conclusion that a certain degree of dependence had existed between them. One in particular attracted my attention, not less from its regularity than from the likeness which it sustains to certain figures in the painted historical and ritual MSS. of Mexico. It is designated by FIG. 2, in the same Plate with the figure of the serpent already described.

Upon various detached rocks, lying next to the water,

[1] Those who feel interested in the subject of symbolism as it existed amongst the American semi-civilized nations, or as connected with their religions systems, will find it illustrated to a certain extent, in my work entitled "THE SERPENT SYMBOL AND THE WORSHIP OF THE RECIPROCAL PRINCIPLES OF NATURE IN AMERICA," in which particular prominence has been given to the worship of the serpent, so extensively diffused, and yet so enigmatical. These are subjects which it is not my design to discuss in a popular work like the present.

beneath trailing vines, or but half revealed above fallen debris and vegetable accumulations, we discovered numerous other outline figures, some exceedingly rude, representing men and animals, together with many impressions of the human hand. Some of these are represented in Plate II.

By carefully poising myself on the very edge of the narrow shelf or shore, I could discover, beyond an advanced column of rock, the entrance to the so-called excavated temple of the ancient Indians. I saw at once that it was nothing more than a natural niche in the cliff; but yet to settle the matter conclusively, I stripped, and, not without some repugnance, swam out in the sulphurous looking lake, and around the intervening rocks, to the front of the opening. It was, as I had supposed, a natural arch, about thirty feet high, and ten or fifteen feet deep; and seen from the opposite cliff, no doubt appeared to the superstitious Indians like the portal of a temple. The paintings of which they had spoken, were only discolorations produced by the fires which had once flamed up from the abyss where now slumbered the opposing element. Our guide told us that there were many other paintings on the cliffs, which could only be reached by means of a raft or boat. The next day M. returned with a canoe from Managua; it was got down with great difficulty, and in it we coasted the entire lake, but without discovering anything new or interesting.

We were told that there were alligators in this lake, but we saw none, and still remain decidedly skeptical upon that point, notwithstanding the positive assertions of the vaqueros. That it abounded in fish, however, we could not fail to discover, for they swarmed along the edge of the water, and at the foot of the cliffs. This lake was no doubt anciently held in high veneration by the Indians; for it is still regarded with a degree of superstitious fear by their descendants. Our guide told us of evil demons who dwelt within its depths, and vengefully dragged down the swimmers who ventured out upon its gloomy waters. It was easy to imagine that here the aboriginal devotees had made sacrifices to their mountain gods, the divinities who presided over the internal fires of the earth, or who ruled the waters. This half buried lake, with no perceptible opening, situated amidst melted rocks, on the summit of a mountain, with all of its accessories of dread and mystery, was well calculated to rouse the superstitious fears and secure the awe of a people distinguished above all others for a gloomy fancy, which invested nearly all of its creations with features of terror and severity,—creations whose first attribute was vengeance, and whose most acceptable sacrifices were palpitating hearts, torn from the breasts of human victims.

It was past noon before we had finished our investigations at the lake, and we returned to the huts of the vaqueros weary, hot, and hungry. The women—blessed hearts the world over!—swung hammocks for us in the shade, and we lay down in luxurious enjoyment of the magnificent view, while they ground the parched corn for the always welcome cup of *tiste*. And although when we came to leave, they charged us fully ten times as much for it as they would have required of their own countrymen, yet they had displayed so much alacrity in attending to our wants, that we sealed the payment with as hearty a "mil gracias," as if it had been a free offering.

Our guide took us back by a new path, in order to show us what he called the Salt Lake. It was not an extinct crater, like that of Nihapa, but one of those singular, funnel-shaped depressions, so frequent in volcanic countries, and which seem to have been caused by the sinking of the earth. It was a gloomy looking place, with a greenish yellow pool at the bottom, the water of which, our guide said, was salt and bitter. The sides were steep, and covered with tangled vines and bushes, and we did not attempt to descend.

There are other lakes, with musical Indian names, in the

vicinity of Managua, which closely resemble that of Nihapa, and owe their origin to similar causes. One of these occurs within a mile of the town, and is a favorite resort for the "lavadoras," or wash-women. It is reached by numerous paths, some broad and bordered with cactus hedges, and others winding through green coverts, where the stranger often comes suddenly upon the startled Indian girl, whose unshod feet have worn the hard earth smooth, and whose hands have trained the vines into festooned arches above his head. There is but one descent to this lake; which in the course of ages has been made broad and comparatively easy. The shore is lined with large trees of magnificent foliage, beneath the shadows of which the "lavadoras" carry on their never ending operations. The water is cool and limpid; and the lake itself more resembles some immense fountain, where bright streams might have their birth, rather than a fathomless volcanic pool, so well has nature concealed beneath a robe of trees, and vines, and flowers, the evidences of ancient convulsions, rocks riven by earthquakes, or melted by fires from the incandescent depths of the earth.

It was late in the afternoon when we returned from Nihapa; but whatever might have been the pleasure or satisfaction of our visit, it went for nothing as compared with that which we experienced in finding a courier from Granada, bringing us letters and papers from the United States, three months later than any we had yet received. Dinner was forgotten in the eager haste to learn what the great world had been about, all the time we had been vegetating amongst orange and palm trees in this secluded corner of the world. The trivial items of news which the dweller in Gotham, sipping his coffee over the morning papers, would pass by with an idle glance, were to us momentous matters, and every paragraph of every column was religiously read, with a gusto which no one but the traveller similarly situated can appreciate. The newspaper is a luxury which the poorest day laborer in the United States may possess; and the American would sooner deny himself his tea and coffee, than the satisfaction of glancing over its columns, however dull, in the morning, or after the labors of the day are closed, in the evening. We missed many things, in Central America, which we had come to regard as essential to our comfort and happiness, but the newspaper most. Its place was very poorly supplied by the Padre Paul's little "Correo del Istmo," filled with government decrees, and published twice a month. It was in vain that we looked there for our daily home pabulum of "Late and Important by Telegraph"—"Terrible Catastrophe!" "Horrible Explosion, and Probable Loss of Life!" served up in delectable fat type, and profusely seasoned with exclamation points. For three months we had not had our souls harrowed by the awful details of murder, nor our hearts sickened by recitals of treachery, infamy, and crime; knew nothing of what had followed the Astor riot, whether the struggling Hungarians were free or fallen. In fact the great drama of life, with its shifting scenery, and startling denouements, so far as we were concerned, had been suspended,— the world had gone on, on, and it seemed as if we alone had been left behind,—though living, yet practically dead and forgotten. No romance, with its plots and highly colored incidents, in which fancy and invention had exhausted itself, could compare in point of interest with the columns of these newspapers, redolent with the damp mustiness of a sea voyage, and the tobacco of the courier's *maléta*, which we now perused in silence, by the aid of the tropical evening light, slowly swinging in our hammocks, beneath the corridor of Pedro Blanco's house, on the shores of the Lake of Managua!

Towards evening all the women of Managua go down to the lake shore, under the plausible pretext of filling their water jars. And when it became too dark to read, we fell into the movement, and followed by a train of youngsters, mostly naked, also went down to the shore, which was enlivened by hundreds of merry groups—mozos bathing their horses out in the surf, and girls filling their water jars in the clear water beyond the breakers. At one point bushes were planted in the lake, like fish wears, between which women were stationed with little scoop-nets, wherewith they laded out myriads of little silvery fishes, from the size of a large needle to that of a shrimp, which they threw into kettle-shaped holes, scooped in the sand, where in the evening light, leaping up in their dying throes, they looked like a simmering mass of molten silver. These little fishes are called *sardinas* by the natives, and are cooked in omelets, constituting a very excellent dish, and one which I never failed to order whenever I visited Managua. The first travellers in Nicaragua mention this novel fishery as then practised by the aborigines, and it has remained unchanged to the present hour.

In returning through a bye street to our own house, we observed, within the open door of a rude cane hut, what we first took to be a large painting, but which upon examination proved to be a carving in wood. It was cut in high relief, and represented, nearly of the size of life, a mounted cavalier, dressed and armed after the style of the fifteenth century, having in one hand a cross and in the other a sword. We were struck with the spirit and execution of the carving, which filled one entire side of the hut, and were told that it was a representation of Hernando Cortez, the conqueror of Mexico. The people in whose possession it then was knew nothing of its history, beyond that it had been in the hands of their family for more than seventy years. I subsequently inquired of the "sabios" or sages of Managua about the figure, but they could give me no information, except that it was very ancient, and, according to tradition, represented Cortez. Don Pedro Blanco and some others suggested that it might have been intended for Santiago, the patron saint of Managua, but gave no good reason for their conjecture. That it is very ancient appears from a variety of circumstances, and from none more clearly than the now half-obliterated paintings

ANCIENT CARVING IN WOOD; MANAGUA.

which fill the panel around the figure. These, in style of execution, correspond entirely with the paintings made by the Indians immediately subsequent to the Conquest, and after their first acquaintance with the whites. They represent disembarkations, and battles between mounted, bearded white men and naked Indians armed after their primitive fashion. Dogs too, are represented participating in these encounters,—mute witnesses to those atrocities which everywhere attended the Spanish arms in America, and to which all the brilliancy of the achievements of Cortez, Alvarado, Cordova, or Pizarro, can never blind the impartial historian. Notwithstanding the popular tradition, I am disposed to regard the figure as a representation not of Cortez, but of Cordova, the conqueror of Nicaragua, or its first Governor, Pedro Arias de Avila; perhaps of that daring Contreras who meditated the vast design of separating all America from the crown of Spain.

A number of idols, obtained from Momotombita and other places, have been brought to Managua, from time to time, by the Indians, and planted at the corners of the streets. Nearly all of them, however, are small, and have been so much defaced as to possess little interest. But one particularly arrested my attention. It is set at one of the corners of a house, fronting on the little plaza of San Juan, and is very well represented in the accompanying engraving. It projects about four feet above the ground, and probably extends

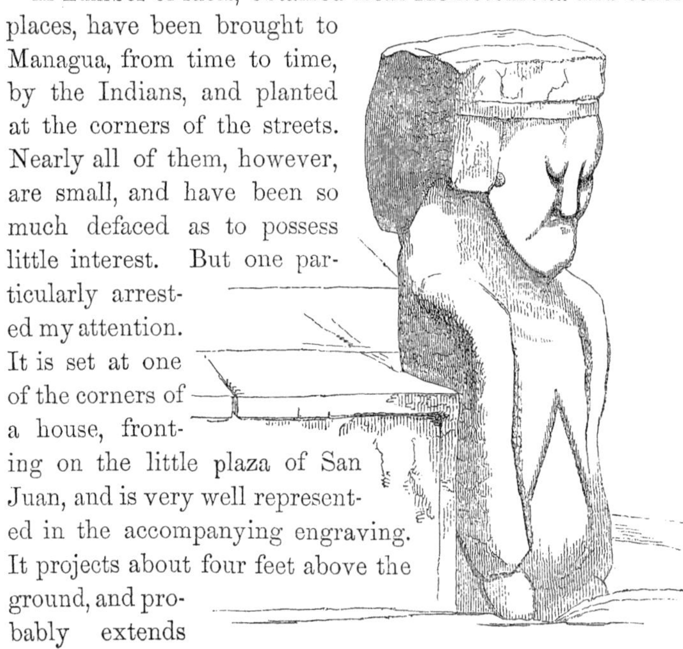

IDOL AT MANAGUA.

two or three feet below. In common with all others obtained from Momotombita, it is black basalt.

The town of Managua now contains about ten or twelve thousand inhabitants, who live in the simplest manner possible, manufacturing barely enough to supply their limited wants, and carrying on but little trade. The region around is very fertile, and capable of sustaining a large population. The hill-slopes, between the lake and the sea, are well adapted for the cultivation of coffee; and the quality of that which is produced from the few estates existing there, is regarded as superior to the coffee of Costa Rica, which ranks next only to the best Mocha. This valuable staple might be produced here to any extent, and at comparatively little cost; but the condition of the country, and the general lack of enterprise amongst the people, have prevented attention to this, as well as every other branch of industry or source of wealth. There is no part of Nicaragua which, from its position, beauty, salubrity, and capacity for production, surpasses the district around Managua;[1] and here, it seems to me, is the most favorable point for the commencement of any system of colonization from the United States or from Europe.

This portion of the country was densely populated in ancient times. After the expedition of Cordova, it was announced in Spain, that Managua was a city "nine miles long;" and this report of its extent and vast population, amongst other things, induced Oviedo to visit the country. He seems to have been disappointed in respect to its size,

[1] Capt. Belcher, who was here in 1838, says of Managua, that "it suffered severely in the late cholera visitation; losing six hundred out of the population of twelve thousand. Of this number it is rather remarkable that females between the ages of fifteen and twenty-five, and principally newly married, were the predominant victims. Generally this place is considered as peculiarly healthy, the average deaths seldom exceeding one per cent."—*Voyage round the World*, vol. i. p. 172.

and denounces the reports which had been made in Spain, as gross exaggerations. He nevertheless adds:

"It was inhabited by Chorotegans, and, to tell the truth, it was a beautiful and populous village, but so far from forming a city, was composed of isolated houses, at considerable distance from each other. Before it had been destroyed by war, it covered a great space, and resembled the villages to be seen in the valley of Alva, in Biscay, in Gallicia, among the mountains and valleys of Ibarra, where all the houses are in view of each other and occupy considerable room. This village of Managua extends in a line along the lake; but so far from having three leagues of extent, it scarcely has one. However, at the time of its prosperity, it was the finest place of the province, and contained 40,000 inhabitants, of which 10,000 were archers, or slingers. But when I visited it, six years after the Conquest, it was the most completely abandoned and desolate place of the government. It now contains 10,000 souls, of which 600 are archers. On the opposite side of the lake, is the domain of the Cazique, Tipitapa, which has an extent of six leagues, and 6,000 inhabitants, of which 800 are archers.

"In conclusion, from what I have heard from those who have visited this country from the times of Gil Gonzalez Davila to those of Captain Francisco Hernandez, the country was so populous that the inhabitants may be said to have fairly swarmed. But this is not the place to speak of the devastation of the country and the massacre of so many Indians."

From Managua we proposed to visit the Rio Tipitapa, or Panaloya, the stream which connects the lake of Managua with that of Nicaragua, and which, from the constant references made to it, in all speculations concerning the opening of a canal, has been invested with peculiar interest. We accordingly engaged Victorino, our patron in the expedition to Momotombita, to take us by water to the outlet of the lake, a distance of twenty or twenty-five miles. In order to have the entire day, or the greater part of it, to devote to our investigations at Tipitapa, we directed Victorino to be in readiness to start as early as two o'clock the next morning, thinking, from our past experience in native tardiness, that he would probably arrive at about four or five. But what was our horror, when he aroused us in the early stages of our first doze (for we had gone to bed late), with the information that all was ready! It was just half-past one; and although I suspected that this early call was one of Victorino's practical jokes, yet we had been too precise in our directions to have any good cause of complaint against him. So we dressed ourselves silently, and followed the patron to the shore of the lake. Here we found everything in readiness, and got off, for the first time, at the appointed hour.

As I passed through the corridor, I had caught up a blanket, with a vague idea of getting a nap in the boat, and after we pushed off, wrapped myself in it with a chuckle, and lay down to sleep. But the blanket was saturated with fleas; sleep departed, and I was exercised in a most lively manner, for the rest of the night. The men rowed in silence, and the water of the lake looked black and forbidding under the sable sky. It was with a feeling of relief, therefore, that I discerned the tintings of morning, in the east. First, a faint light revealed the outlines of the rugged mountains of Chontales and Segovia, followed by a yellow, then a rosy tinge, so faint that it might have been a mere fancy of the spectator; then it deepened, and the clouds, with their glowing edges, and purple folds, disclosed their rich, deep masses above the rim of the horizon, while the lake flung back tremulously from its quivering bosom the reflected radiance of the sky. Brighter and brighter, its rays shooting upwards to the empyrean, and glowing on the summits of the volcanoes, higher and higher, came up the monarch sun, until rising above the horizon, he shone forth on the queenly earth, its emerald robes sparkling with dew-drops, and gemmed with flowers.

Our men had improved the time, and at sunrise we found ourselves within six or eight miles of the outlet, moving along half a mile distant from a low and densely wooded shore. I thrust a pole over the side, and found that there was less than a fathom of water, with a soft muddy bottom. At various places I observed a slight bubbling on the surface of the lake, and a strong smell of sulphurous or mephitic gases; and in others rose little columns of vapor, indicating the presence of hot springs at the bottom.

We finally reached what appeared to be a narrow estuary of the lake, extending between two low bars, covered with reeds, and literally alive with cranes and other water fowls. The boat was directed into it, but it was so shallow that the mud rose to the surface with every stroke of the oars. I found, upon sounding, only two or three feet of water, with about an equal depth of soft gray mud—the dwelling-place of numerous alligators. We proceeded up this estuary for three or four hundred yards, the water every moment becoming shallower, until finally we stuck fast in the fetid mire. The crew leaped overboard and sunk at once to their armpits in the slime. They nevertheless pushed us some distance nearer the shore, and then, when the boat could be moved no further, we mounted on their shoulders and were carried to the land. We found the shore low, but gravelly, and covered with grass and bushes. A clear little stream of tepid water flowed at our feet, and at intervals all around us rose columns of vapor from thermal springs. We advanced a little further to what appeared to be a bank, covered with trees, and then discovered for the first time that the estero extended down a broad and rocky but shallow channel, which had anciently been the bed of the stream connecting the two lakes. No water flowed through it now, although there were pools here and there in the depressions of the rock, supplied with water from springs, or from the rains. Clumps of bushes were growing in the dry channel, and amongst them cattle and mules were grazing. I can readily believe that anciently, during the wet seasons, a small quan-

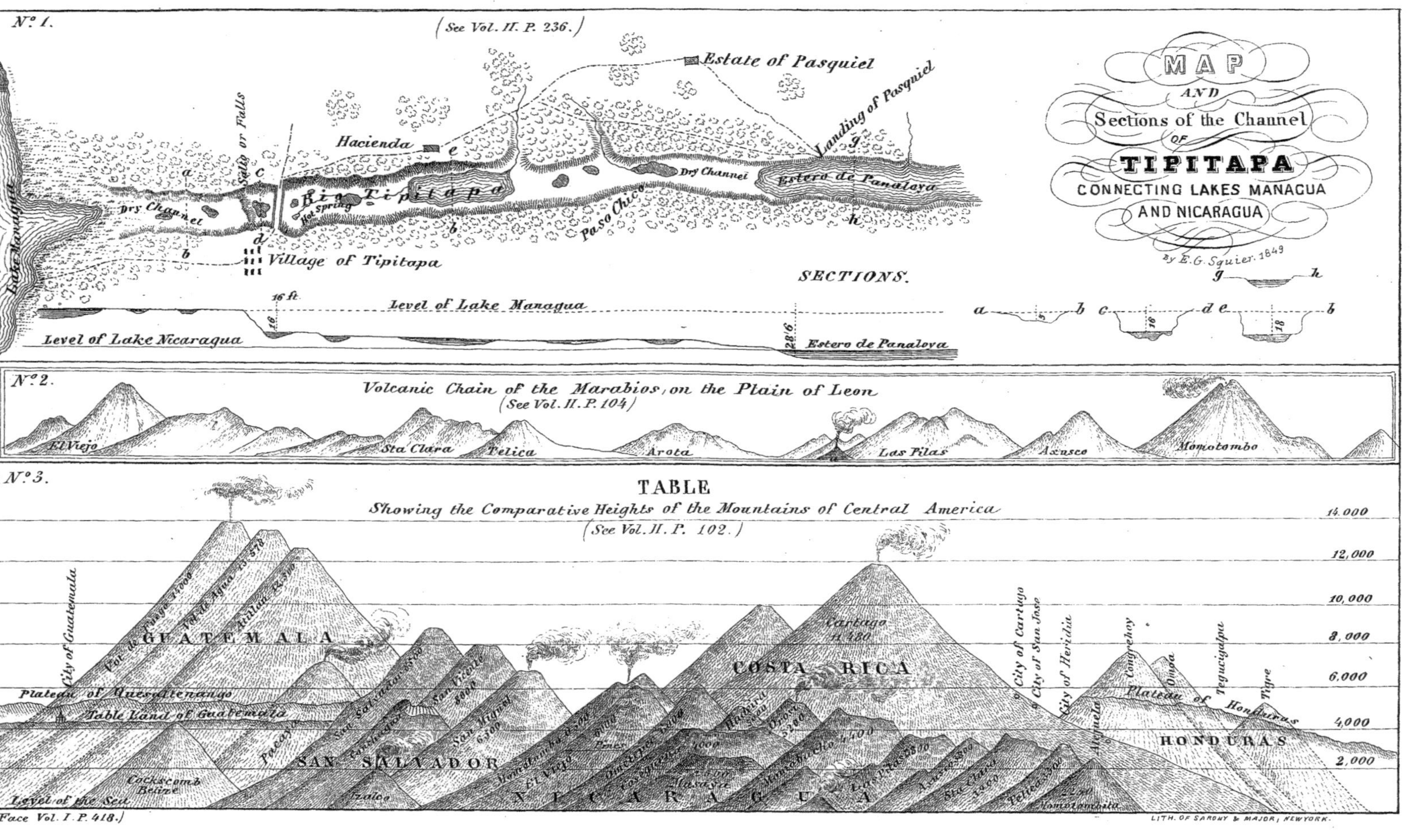

N° 1.
(See Vol. II. P. 236.)
MAP
AND
Sections of the Channel
OF
TIPITAPA
CONNECTING LAKES MANAGUA
AND NICARAGUA
By E. G. Squier. 1849
Estate of Pasquiel
Landing of Pasquiel
Hacienda
Salto or Falls
Rio Tipitapa
Hot Spring
Dry Channel
Paso Chico
Estero de Panaloya
Village of Tipitapa
Lake Managua
SECTIONS.
16 ft.
Level of Lake Managua
Level of Lake Nicaragua
28.6
Estero de Panaloya
N° 2.
Volcanic Chain of the Marabios, on the Plain of Leon
(See Vol. II. P. 104)
El Viejo
Sta Clara
Telica
Arota
Las Pilas
Axusco
Momotombo
N° 3.
TABLE
Showing the Comparative Heights of the Mountains of Central America
(See Vol. II. P. 102.)
14,000
12,000
10,000
8,000
6,000
4,000
2,000
GUATEMALA
City of Guatemala
Plateau of Quesaltenango
Table Land of Guatemala
Cockscomb
Level of the Sea
SAN SALVADOR
COSTA RICA
Cartago
11,480
NICARAGUA
City of Cartago
City of San Jose
City of Heridia
Congrehoy
Omoa
Teguciyalpa
Tigre
Plateau of Honduras
HONDURAS
(Face Vol. I. P. 418.)
LITH. OF SARONY & MAJOR, NEW YORK.

tity of water found its way through this channel, and over the falls, a mile below; but nothing is more evident than that no considerable body of water ever flowed here.

But if we were disappointed in the so-called outlet of the lake, our disappointment was more than compensated by the magnificent view which was afforded, from this point, of the great volcano of Momotombo, with its background of volcanic peaks, constituting the chain of the Maribios, and terminating with the tall Viejo, dim and blue in the distance. It seemed to rise from the bosom of the mirror-like lake, a giant guide to direct future navies across the continent from sea to sea. I could not help picturing the black hulls of great steamers trailing their smoky plumes at its base, and the white, cloud-like sails of majestic Indiamen, relieved against the purple of its arid sides.

After following along the bank of the vanished river for a short distance, we came to a path, by which the Brazil wood collected on the shores of the lake is carted to Pasquiel, the first and nearest landing point on lake Nicaragua. A rapid walk of a mile brought us to the village of Tipitapa, a miserable little place, of some two or three hundred inhabitants, with a tumble-down church or two, and a drove of cattle in quiet possession of the plaza. We found our way, with little trouble, to the house of the principal officer,—I have forgotten his rank,—a disagreeable fellow, who made himself unnecessarily offensive by one or two cross-grained attempts at being civil. He hadn't the decency to offer us breakfast; but that gave us little concern, for Ben had come supplied for contingencies, and had, moreover, a happy knack of pressing into his service many utensils and other articles of use which might come to hand. He despatched Victorino to the cura's for some milk, and helped himself to plantains from the garden. And after half an hour, which we had spent in drumming up horses, he announced a breakfast, if not fit for a prince, at any rate far from unacceptable to men who had started on an exploring expedition at two o'clock in the morning. Through the aid of the cura, who was a fine looking man, with rather a singular expression, nevertheless, for a padre, we got horses for our ride to Pasquiel; and the cura, accompanied by a young darkey who was qualifying himself for the church, volunteered to accompany us. We had brought no saddles, and were obliged to put up with "albardos" and wooden stirrups. Albardos were not in existence in Job's day; had they been, he would have wished his enemy to ride on an albardo, rather than write a book. A savage critique in the Jerusalem Quarterly could not have "used up" Job's enemies more effectually than an "albardo" and a hard trotter.

After riding for half a mile through deserted fields, now overgrown with tall, rank weeds, we came once more to the channel or river-bed, at a place called the *Salto* or falls. Here the rock, which appears to underlie the whole region, is entirely exposed, worn into basins and fantastic pot-holes by the water. It seems to be a calcareous or volcanic breccia, and though not hard, is solid. Through this the hot springs find their way to the surface. The Salto is a steep ledge of this rock, from twelve to fifteen feet in height, extending entirely across the ancient channel, which is here not less than two hundred yards broad. Although it was now the middle of the rainy season, not a drop of water flowed over it. A little distance below the Salto is a stone bridge, the second one which I had seen in the country, and the only one in actual use. At the foot of its western buttress, upon the lower side, I observed a column of vapor, and descending, found that it proceeded from a copious hot spring, from which flows a considerable stream of scalding water. It has formed a thick deposit upon the rocks and stones around it, the apparent constituents of which were carbonate of lime, sulphur, and sulphate of copper; the taste of the water is not unpleasant, and, as observed by Capt. Belcher, is esteemed a sovereign remedy, "if taken by the advice of the padre!"

From the bridge we rode along the eastern bank of the ancient channel, which below the falls becomes deeper and narrower, filled with detached and water-worn rocks, with here and there large pools of still water. We found the country level, with a soil of exceeding fertility, and dotted over with cattle estates. It is not densely wooded, but has many open glades, covered with grass, and affording rich pasturage. Here Nicaragua wood, or Brazil wood, is found in greatest abundance, and contributes materially to the value of the land. It is a tree which seems to require a rich, moist soil, and the absence of overshadowing trees of other varieties. Quantities of the wood, already cut and prepared for exportation, were scattered here and there over the savannahs. A ride of three miles brought us to the cattle estate of Pasquiel, one of the largest and most valuable in the country, belonging to our friend Don Frederico Derbyshire, of Granada. We were well received by his superintendent, who had seen us in Granada, upon our first arrival. The buildings on the estate consisted of two immense roofs, supported on posts, entirely open at the sides, and placed in the centre of a kind of stockade of posts. In a corner of one of these sheds, a number of poles set on end and withed together, fenced off a little space for the beds of the mayordomo and his spouse. Ailing calves, independent pigs, and multitudinous chickens shared the remainder of the accommodations, on terms of perfect equality and harmony with the children of the superintendent. Some large troughs, supported on posts, to receive the milk in manufacturing cheese, and a couple of rude presses for use in the same manufacture, also mounted on stilts, completed the furniture of the establishment. There was enough of novelty in all this, but nothing particularly attractive; and as I suspected there might be a "smart chance" of fleas in the sand under the roofs, I declined dismounting, but rode beneath the shade of a gigantic tree, called the *mata-palo*, or kill tree. It has great vigor, and preserves a dense green foliage during the dry season, when most other trees become seared. It starts as a kind of vine, and clasps itself around the first tree which it can reach; and as it grows with astonishing rapidity, in a few years it entirely destroys the tree which raised it from the ground, and occupies its place. It does not run up to any considerable height, but extends its branches laterally to a great distance, and like the banyan tree, sends down new trunks to the ground, which in their turn promote its vigor and its growth. These trunks come down with their roots ready formed, and look like a number of exceedingly bad brooms suspended from the principal limbs.

From the houses of the estate to the landing of Pasquiel there is a broad open road. The distance is little upwards of a mile. This landing is at the head of an estuary running up from the north-western extremity of Lake Nicaragua, in the direction of Lake Managua, and which is about fourteen miles in length. It is part of what is called the Rio Tipitapa, but is, in fact, the Estero de Pasquiel, or de Panaloya. The actual distance between the two lakes is therefore but little over four miles. The landing of Pasquiel is simply an open space on the bank of the Estero; there was neither house nor shed, nor sign of humanity, except several large piles of Brazil wood, and the ashes left by the sailors' fires. The Estero, at this point, is about one hundred yards broad, and six feet deep. This is, in fact, about its average depth; although in some places lower down, I was informed by the boatmen, it is as much as twelve and fourteen feet in depth.

There was very little to see; and so, after sitting on the shore for an hour, we started on our return, following a path which led along the bank of the Estero, with a view of determining how much higher it extended. We found that it came to an end a short distance above the landing, as did also our path. But we had started to go through, and persisted in our purpose. Between cutting, and stooping, dismounting and making a multitude of evolutions, we finally succeeded in clearing the forest, well scratched and smarting from rough contact with thorny bushes and prickly vines—for nearly every petty bush and contemptible vine in Central America is armed with thorns, great or small.

Stopping for a few moments at a cattle hacienda, where we left the cura making love to the daughter of the mayor domo, we returned to Tipitapa. Our gloomy host of the morning had mustered up a little good humor. The secret of his civility, however, came out before we left; he wanted a guitar, a guitar with four strings, a guitar withal worth seven dollars; and expected us to send him one of that description from the United States, which we, of course, promised to do, whereupon, in the fullness of his heart, he ordered his servant to assist Ben in preparing dinner.

At three o'clock, we had reëmbarked, and with a fair wind, were soon speeding our way to Managua, where we landed in the edge of the evening, well wearied with our day's excursion.

In returning, I had sounded the lake, and found the entire bay in front of Managua exceedingly shallow. For nearly a mile out it was only about a fathom in depth; and for full two miles further it preserved a uniform depth of about two fathoms. That part nearest the old outlet of Tipitapa was also shallow, and for a mile and upwards from the shore, nowhere exceeded a fathom and a half in depth. The middle portions of the lake, however, are represented to be very deep. The full statement of these facts and of a variety of others, bearing upon the question of a canal route, are reserved for another and more appropriate place, when I come to speak specifically of the canal project. It is only necessary to add here, that the grossest ignorance prevails as to the dependence between the two lakes of Nicaragua and Managua, and the nature of the communication one with the other. The publications of the British Society for the Diffusion of Useful Knowledge speak of Lake Nicaragua as *flowing* into Lake Managua; and nearly all geographical works refer to the river Tipitapa, or Panaloya, as a considerable stream, navigable were it not for the Salto or falls, which is almost uniformly represented to be nearer Lake Nicaragua than to Lake Managua. There is also an error prevalent amongst the natives of the country, which has been inconsiderately adopted by some recent observers, that the lake of Managua has formed a subterranean outlet, or has subsided, from some unexplained cause, within the past fifteen or twenty years. There is, however, little or no reason for supposing that any material or perceptible change has taken place in the level of the lake, or any diminution in its volume, since the period of the Conquest. The early explorers represented the two lakes as entirely disconnected; and Oviedo, although combatting this idea, nevertheless describes the communication to be very nearly what it now is. He says that in summer little water flows through the channel, and speaks of the "canal," by which is undoubtedly meant the Estero of Panaloya, as only breast deep. That the level of the lake changes somewhat with the different seasons, I can myself bear witness. The evaporation on the twelve hundred square miles of surface which this lake presents, beneath a tropical sun, is nevertheless quite sufficient to account for the absence of water at Tipitapa, without entertaining the hypothesis of a subterranean outlet.

A few days after, I was suddenly called to return to Leon, where I was detained by official business until the close of November. The events which transpired in the interval do not fall within the scope of my Narrative, and I shall consequently pass them by without remark.

END OF VOLUME I.

www.ingramcontent.com/pod-product-compliance
Lightning Source LLC
LaVergne TN
LVHW021122110826
845150LV00005B/921

* 9 7 8 1 4 2 5 5 5 0 9 0 5 *